3rd Workshop on Machine Reading for Question Answering 2021

Held online

Punta Cana, Dominican Republic
10 November 2021

ISBN: 978-1-7138-9179-6

Printed from e-media with permission by:

Curran Associates, Inc.
57 Morehouse Lane
Red Hook, NY 12571

Some format issues inherent in the e-media version may also appear in this print version.

Association for Computational Linguistics
209 N. Eighth Street
Stroudsburg, Pennsylvania 18360

Phone: 1-570-476-8006
Fax: 1-570-476-0860

acl@aclweb.org

Additional copies of this publication are available from:

Curran Associates, Inc.
57 Morehouse Lane
Red Hook, NY 12571 USA
Phone: 845-758-0400
Fax: 845-758-2633
Email: curran@proceedings.com
Web: www.proceedings.com

EMNLP 2021 Workshop

Proceedings of the 3rd Workshop on Machine Reading for Question Answering

November 10th, 2021

Message from the Organizers

Our workshop brings together researchers studying machine reading for question answering (MRQA). MRQA has emerged as an important testbed for evaluating how computer systems understand natural language, as well as a crucial technology for applications such as search engines and dialog systems. In recent years, MRQA systems have become much more accurate, and are even capable of retrieving evidence documents on the fly or answering without retrieved documents. Datasets and models have been developed to target many different aspects of the problem, including multi-hop reasoning, numerical reasoning, or commonsense reasoning.

Despite this progress, there are still many important desiderata that most MRQA systems do not adequately consider: multilinguality and interpretability. In the 3rd MRQA workshop, we therefore focus on these two emerging and crucial aspects of question answering models.

Systems today are predominantly evaluated by measuring accuracy on English benchmarks, yet an ideal question answering system would support a diverse range of languages. With recent developments of multilingual question answering datasets, it is timely to study how MRQA models can be designed to support typologically diverse languages.

Many systems produce correct answers for the wrong reason and are unable to explain their predictions. Given the opaque nature of modern large-scale pre-trained neural models, it is important to study how MRQA systems can offer users a way to trust (or not trust) an otherwise black-box model's predictions, as well as offer practitioners ways to diagnose critical modeling issues or dataset biases.

As in past years, we sought paper submissions of previously unpublished work. To reflect our focus on our two themes, we had separate tracks for multilinguality and interpretability-related papers, as well as a general research track. Across these three tracks, we received 21 total paper submissions after withdrawals – 14 for the general research track, 5 for the multilingual track, and 2 for the interpretability track. While the submission counts have decreased from last year, we found the average quality of submitted papers to be higher than previous years. After discussion among the organizers, we have accepted a total of 16 papers and awarded one best paper and two honorable mention papers. We also have accepted 23 non-archival submissions that were accepted at other related conferences (such as papers accepted at the main conference/findings of ACL, EMNLP, SIGIR) to be presented at our workshop. Our final program therefore includes 39 papers, of which 16 papers are included in these proceedings.

We are excited to host six stellar invited speakers. In the morning session, Reut Tsarfaty, Jon Clark, and Yiming Cui will give talks on multilinguality in question answering; in the afternoon session, Jonathan Berant, Marco Tulio Ribeiro, and Hannaneh Hajishirzi will give talks on interpretability in question answering. We thank these speakers, our program committee, the EMNLP workshop chairs, and our sponsors, Baidu and Facebook, for helping to make this workshop possible.

Organizing Committee

Adam Fisch, MIT
Alon Talmor, Tel Aviv University
Danqi Chen, Princeton University
Eunsol Choi, The University of Texas at Austin
Minjoon Seo, Naver & KAIST
Patrick Lewis, Facebook & University College London
Robin Jia, University of Southern California
Sewon Min, University of Washington

Program Committee

Akari Asai
Danish Contractor
Douwe Kiela
Eric Wallace
Gautier Izacard
Huan Sun
Jifan Chen
Jing Liu
Jinhyuk Lee
Jonathan Clark
Jonathan Herzig
Kai Sun
Kenton Lee
Kevin Lin
Matt Gardner
Matthew Lamm
Max Bartolo
Mor Geva
Nan Duan
Nitish Gupta
Panupong Pasupat
Pedro Rodriguez
Peng Qi
Rajarshi Das
Rodrigo Nogueira
Shayne Longpre
Shuohang Wang
Thomas Kwiatkowski
Tong Wang
Tushar Khot
Xiaodong Liu
Xinya Du
Yichen Jiang
Yizhong Wang
Yuxiang Wu

Invited Speaker

Reut Tsarfaty, Bar Illan University
Jon Clark, Google
Yiming Cui, Joint Laboratory of HIT and iFLYTEK Research (HFL)
Jonathan Berant, Tel Aviv University, Allen Institute for AI
Marco Tulio Ribeiro, Microsoft Research
Hannah Hajishirzi, University of Washington, Allen Institute for Artificial Intelligence

Table of Contents

Conference Program

Wednesday, November 10, 2021

9:00–9:15 ***Opening Remarks***

9:15–11:30 **Multilingual QA Invited Talk Session**

9:15–9:45 ***Invited Talk 1 - Reut Tsarfaty***

9:45–10:15 ***Invited Talk 2 - Jon Clark***

10:15–10:45 ***Invited Talk 3 - Yiming Cui***

10:45–11:30 ***Panel Discussion on Multilingual QA***

11:30–12:30 ***Lunch break***

12:30–13:10 **Best Paper Talk Session**

Wednesday, November 10, 2021 (continued)

13:10–14:10 Poster Session (archival track)

13:10–14:10 *GermanQuAD and GermanDPR: Improving Non-English Question Answering and Passage Retrieval*
Timo Möller, Julian Risch and Malte Pietsch

13:10–14:10 *Zero-Shot Clinical Questionnaire Filling From Hunan-Machine Interactions*
Farnaz Ghassemi Toudeshki, Philippe Jolivet, Alexandre Durand-Salmon and Anna Liednikova

13:10–14:10 *Can Question Generation Debias Question Answering Models? A Case Study on Question–Context Lexical Overlap*
Kazutoshi Shinoda, Saku Sugawara and Akiko Aizawa

13:10–14:10 *What Can a Generative Language Model Answer About a Passage?*
Douglas Summers-Stay, Claire Bonial and Clare Voss

13:10–14:10 *Multi-modal Retrieval of Tables and Texts Using Tri-encoder Models*
Bogdan Kostić, Julian Risch and Timo Möller

13:10–14:10 *Eliciting Bias in Question Answering Models through Ambiguity*
Andrew Mao, Naveen Raman, Matthew Shu, Eric Li, Franklin Yang and Jordan Boyd-Graber

13:10–14:10 *Bilingual Alignment Pre-Training for Zero-Shot Cross-Lingual Transfer*
Ziqing Yang, Wentao Ma, Yiming Cui, Jiani Ye, Wanxiang Che and Shijin Wang

13:10–14:10 *ParaShoot: A Hebrew Question Answering Dataset*
Omri Keren and Omer Levy

13:10–14:10 *Unsupervised Multiple Choices Question Answering: Start Learning from Basic Knowledge*
Chi-Liang Liu and Hung-yi Lee

13:10–14:10 *GANDALF: a General Character Name Description Dataset for Long Fiction*
Fredrik Carlsson, Magnus Sahlgren, Fredrik Olsson and Amaru Cuba Gyllensten

13:10–14:10 *Investigating Post-pretraining Representation Alignment for Cross-Lingual Question Answering*
Fahim Faisal and Antonios Anastasopoulos

Wednesday, November 10, 2021 (continued)

13:10–14:10 *Semantic Answer Similarity for Evaluating Question Answering Models*
Julian Risch, Timo Möller, Julian Gutsch and Malte Pietsch

13:10–14:10 *Simple and Efficient ways to Improve REALM*
Vidhisha Balachandran, Ashish Vaswani, Yulia Tsvetkov and Niki Parmar

13:10–14:10 Poster Session (non-archival track)

13:10–14:10 *Synthetic Target Domain Supervision for Open Retrieval QA*
Revanth Gangi Reddy, Bhavani Iyer, Md Arafat Sultan, Rong Zhang, Avirup Sil, Vittorio Castelli, Radu Florian, Salim Roukos

13:10–14:10 *Entity-based Knowledge Conflicts in Question Answering*
Shayne Longpre, Kartik Perisetla, Anthony Chen, Nikhil Ramesh, Chris Dubois, Sameer Singh

13:10–14:10 *Mitigating False-Negative Contexts in Multi-Document Question Answering with Retrieval Marginalization*
Ansong Ni, Matt Gardner, Pradeep Dasigi

13:10–14:10 *Generative Context Pair Selection for Multi-hop Question Answering*
Dheeru Dua,Cicero Nogueira dos Santos,Patrick Ng,Ben Athiwaratkun,Bing Xiang,Matt Gardner,Sameer Singh

13:10–14:10 *Learning with Instance Bundles for Reading Comprehension*
Dheeru Dua, Pradeep Dasigi,Sameer Singh,Matt Gardner

13:10–14:10 *Can NLI Models Verify QA Systems' Predictions?*
Jifan Chen, Eunsol Choi, Greg Durrett

13:10–14:10 *Knowing More About Questions Can Help: Improving Calibration in Question Answering*
Shujian Zhang, Chengyue Gong and Eunsol Choi

13:10–14:10 *RocketQA: An Optimized Training Approach to Dense Passage Retrieval for Open-Domain Question Answering*
Yingqi Qu, Yuchen Ding, Jing Liu, Kai Liu, Ruiyang Ren, Wayne Xin Zhao, Daxiang Dong, Hua Wu and Haifeng Wang

13:10–14:10 *Weakly Supervised Pre-Training for Multi-Hop Retriever*
Yeon Seonwoo, Sang-Woo Lee, Ji-Hoon Kim, Jung-Woo Ha and Alice Oh

13:10–14:10 *ReasonBert: Pre-trained to Reason with Distant Supervision*
Xiang Deng, Yu Su, Alyssa Lees, You Wu, Cong Yu and Huan Sun

Wednesday, November 10, 2021 (continued)

13:10–14:10 *Question Answering over Electronic Devices: A New Benchmark Dataset and a Multi-Task Learning based QA Framework*
Abhilash Nandy, Soumya Sharma, Shubham Maddhashiya, Kapil Sachdeva, Pawan Goyal and NIloy Ganguly

13:10–14:10 *Do We Know What We Don't Know? Studying Unanswerable Questions beyond SQuAD 2.0*
Elior Sulem, Jamaal Hay and Dan Roth

13:10–14:10 *Relation-Guided Pre-Training for Open-Domain Question Answering*
Ziniu Hu, Yizhou Sun and Kai-Wei Chang

13:10–14:10 *Beyond Reptile: Meta-Learned Dot-Product Maximization between Gradients for Improved Single-Task Regularization*
Akhil Kedia, Sai Chetan Chinthakindi and Wonho Ryu

13:10–14:10 *SD-QA: Spoken Dialectal Question Answering for the Real World*
Fahim Faisal, Sharlina Keshava, Md Mahfuz Ibn Alam and Antonios Anastasopoulos

13:10–14:10 *When Retriever-Reader Meets Scenario-Based Multiple-Choice Questions*
ZiXian Huang, Ao Wu, Yulin Shen, Gong Cheng and Yuzhong Qu

13:10–14:10 *Winnowing Knowledge for Multi-choice Question Answering*
Yeqiu Li, Bowei Zou, Zhifeng Li, Ai Ti Aw, Yu Hong and Qiaoming Zhu

13:10–14:10 *Extract, Integrate, Compete: Towards Verification Style Reading Comprehension*
Chen Zhang, Yuxuan Lai, Yansong Feng and Dongyan Zhao

13:10–14:10 *Reference-based Weak Supervision for Answer Sentence Selection using Web Data*
Vivek Krishnamurthy, Thuy Vu and Alessandro Moschitti

13:10–14:10 *NOAHQA: Numerical Reasoning with Interpretable Graph Question Answering Dataset*
Qiyuan Zhang, Lei Wang, SICHENG YU, Shuohang Wang, Yang Wang, Jing Jiang and Ee-Peng Lim

13:10–14:10 *Improving Numerical Reasoning Skills in the Modular Approach for Complex Question Answering on Text*
Xiao-Yu Guo, Yuan-Fang Li and Gholamreza Haffari

13:10–14:10 *R2-D2: A Modular Baseline for Open-Domain Question Answering*
Martin Fajcik, Martin Docekal, Karel Ondrej and Pavel Smrz

13:10–14:10 *AutoEQA: Auto-Encoding Questions for Extractive Question Answering*
Stalin Varanasi, Saadullah Amin and Guenter Neumann

14:10–14:30 ***Break***

Wednesday, November 10, 2021 (continued)

14:30–16:45 Interpretability in QA Invited Talk Session

14:30–15:00 *Invited Talk 4 - Jonathan Berant*

15:00–15:30 *Invited Talk 5 - Marco Tulio Ribeiro*

15:30–16:00 *Invited Talk 6 - Hannaneh Hajishirzi*

16:00–16:45 *Panel Discussion on Interpretability in QA*

16:45–17:00 *Closing Remarks*

MFAQ: a Multilingual FAQ Dataset

Maxime De Bruyn, Ehsan Lotfi, Jeska Buhmann, Walter Daelemans
CLiPS Research Center
University of Antwerp, Belgium
firstname.lastname@uantwerpen.be

Abstract

In this paper, we present the first multilingual FAQ dataset publicly available. We collected around 6M FAQ pairs from the web, in 21 different languages. Although this is significantly larger than existing FAQ retrieval datasets, it comes with its own challenges: duplication of content and uneven distribution of topics. We adopt a similar setup as Dense Passage Retrieval (DPR) (Karpukhin et al., 2020) and test various bi-encoders on this dataset. Our experiments reveal that a multilingual model based on XLM-RoBERTa (Conneau et al., 2019) achieves the best results, except for English. Lower resources languages seem to learn from one another as a multilingual model achieves a higher MRR than language-specific ones. Our qualitative analysis reveals the brittleness of the model on simple word changes. We publicly release our dataset[1], model[2] and training script[3].

1 Introduction

Organizations create *Frequently Asked Questions* (FAQ) pages on their website to provide a better service to their users. FAQs are also useful to automatically answer the most frequent questions on different communication channels: email, chatbot, or search bar.

FAQ retrieval is the task of locating the right answer within a collection of candidate question and answer pairs. It is closely related to the tasks of *non-factoid QA* and *community QA*, although it has its own specificities. The total number of possible answers is generally small (the average FAQ page on the web has 6 answers), and only one is correct. Retrieval systems cannot rely on named entities, as they are typically shared by many possible answers. For example, three out of four answers in Table 1 share the *COVID-19* entity. Lastly, new user queries are matched against pairs of questions and answers, as opposed to passages for non-factoid QA.

Example FAQs
Is it safe for my child to get a COVID-19 vaccine? Yes. Studies show that COVID-19 vaccines are safe and effective. [...]
If I am pregnant, can I get a COVID-19 vaccine? Yes, if you are pregnant, you can receive if COVID-19 vaccine.
What are the ingredients in COVID-19 vaccines? Vaccine ingredients can vary by manufacturer.
How long does protection from a COVID-19 vaccine last? We don't know how long protection lasts for those who are vaccinated. [...]

Table 1: Example FAQs about the COVID-19 vaccine from the CDC website.

Since FAQ-Finder (Hammond et al., 1995), researchers applied different methods to the task of FAQ retrieval (Sneiders, 1999; Jijkoun and de Rijke, 2005; Riezler et al., 2007; Karan and Šnajder, 2016; Sakata et al., 2019). However, since the advent of deep-learning and Transformers, the interest has somewhat faded compared to other areas of QA (Rogers et al., 2021). One possible explanation is the lack of a dedicated large-scale dataset. The ones available are mostly limited to English, and domain-specific.

On the other hand, the task of factoid question answering received the attention of many researchers. Recently, Transformers encoders such as Dense Passage Retrieval (DPR) (Karpukhin et al., 2020) have been successfully applied to the retrieval part of factoid QA, overcoming strong baselines such as TF-IDF and BM25. However, we show that DPR's performance on passage retrieval is not directly transferable to FAQ retrieval. Lewis et al. (2021) recently released PAQ, a dataset of 65M pairs of *Probably Asked Questions*. However, answers are

[1] https://huggingface.co/datasets/clips/mfaq
[2] https://huggingface.co/clips/mfaq
[3] https://github.com/clips/mfaq

Proceedings of the 3rd Workshop on Machine Reading for Question Answering , pages 1–13
Nov 10th, 2021

typically short in PAQ (a few words), which differs from FAQs where answers are longer than questions.

Another way to answer users' questions is to use *Knowledge Grounded Conversation* models as it does not require the pre-generation of all possible pairs of questions and answers (Komeili et al., 2021; De Bruyn et al., 2020). However, at the time of writing these models can hallucinate knowledge (Shuster et al., 2021), which limits their attractiveness in a corporate environment.

In this paper, we provide the first multilingual dataset of FAQs. We collected around 6M FAQ pairs from the web in 21 different languages. This is significantly larger than existing datasets. However, collecting data from the web brings its own challenges: duplication of content and uneven distribution of topics. We also provide the first multilingual FAQ retriever. We show that models trained on all languages at once outperform monolingual models (except for English).

The remainder of the paper is organized as follows. We first review the existing models and datasets available for the task of FAQ retrieval. We then present our own dataset and apply different models to it. We finally perform some analysis on the results and conclude. Our dataset and model are available on the HuggingFace Hub[4].

2 Related Work

In this section, we review the existing literature on FAQ retrieval. We first start by reviewing available models and then look at the available datasets.

2.1 Models

Since the release of FAQ-Finder (Hammond et al., 1995; Burke et al., 1997) and Auto-FAQ (Whitehead, 1995), several methods have been presented. We grouped them into three categories: lexical, unsupervised, and supervised.

Lexical FAQ-Finder (Hammond et al., 1995; Burke et al., 1997) matches user queries to FAQ questions of the Usenet dataset using Term Frequency-Inverse Document Frequency (TF-IDF). The system tries to bridge the lexical gap between users' queries and FAQ pairs by using the semantic network *WordNet* (Miller, 1995) to establish correlations between related terms. FAQ-Finder assumes that the question half of the QA pair is the most relevant for matching to a new query. Tomuro and Lytinen (2004) improved upon FAQ-Finder by including the other half of the QA pair (the answer). Xie et al. (2020) uses a knowledge graph-based QA framework that considers entities and triples in texts as knowledge anchors. This approach requires the customization of a knowledge graph, which is labor-intensive and domain-specific.

Sneiders (1999) used a rule-based technique called Prioritized Keyword Matching on top of a traditional TF-IDF approach. The use of shallow language understanding means that the matching is based on keyword comparison. Each FAQ entry must be manually annotated with a set of required and optional keywords. Sneiders (2002a,b, 2009, 2010) brings further developments on the idea. Moreo et al. (2013) proposes an approach based on semi-automatic generation of regular expression for matching queries with answers. Yang (2009) integrates a domain ontology, user modeling, and a template-based approach to tackle this problem.

Unsupervised Kim and Seo (2008, 2006) presented a clustering-based method of previous user queries to retrieve the right FAQ pair. The authors used a Latent Semantic Analysis (LSA) method to overcome the lexical mismatch between related queries. Jijkoun and de Rijke (2005) experimented with several combinations of TF-IDF retrievers based on the indexing of different fields (question, answer, with or without stop words, the full text of the page). Riezler et al. (2007) extended this method by incorporating a translation-based query expansion, as initially investigated in Berger et al. (2000).

Supervised Moschitti et al. (2007) proposed an approach based on tree kernels. Tree kernels can be defined as similarity metrics that compare a query to an FAQ pair by parsing both texts and calculating the similarity based on the resulting parse trees. Semantic word similarity can also be added to the computation. Filice et al. (2016) expanded on this method and achieved first place in the Community QA shared task at SemEval 2015 (Nakov et al., 2015).

Sakata et al. (2019) were the first to use BERT-based models (Devlin et al., 2018) for the specific task of FAQ retrieval. The relevance between the query and the answers is learned with a fine-tuned BERT model which outputs probability scores for

[4]dataset, model and training script

a pair of (query, answer). The scores are then combined using a specific method. Mass et al. (2020) also used a BERT model. Their method is based on an initial retrieval of FAQ candidates followed by three re-rankers. De Bruyn et al. (2021) used a ConveRT (Henderson et al., 2019) model to automatically answer FAQ questions in Dutch.

2.2 Datasets

In this section, we review the different datasets publicly available. FAQ retrieval datasets can be evaluated on four axes: source of data (community or organizational), the existence of user queries (paraphrases), domain, and language. See Table 2 for an overview.

Faq-Finder (Hammond et al., 1995; Burke et al., 1997) used a dataset collected from Usenet news groups. FAQs were created on several topics so that newcomers do not ask the same questions again and again. This dataset is multi-domain. More recently, Karan and Šnajder (2016) released the FAQIR dataset. It was collected from the "maintenance & repairs" section of the QA website *Yahoo! Answers*. The StackFAQ (Karan and Šnajder, 2018) dataset was collected from the "web apps" sections of *StackExchange*. Feng et al. (2015) collected a QA dataset from the insurancelibrary.com website where a community of insurance expert reply to users' questions. Several authors (for example Filice et al., 2016) also rely on Sem-Eval 2015 Task 3 (Nakov et al., 2015) on Answer Selection in Community Question Answering. It contains pairs of questions and answers in English and Arabic.

There exist few publicly available datasets for organizational FAQs. OrgFAQ (Lev et al., 2020) is a notable exception. At the time of writing, it is not yet publicly available.

3 Multilingual FAQ dataset

In this section, we introduce our new multilingual FAQ dataset.

3.1 Data collection

Instead of implementing our own web crawler, we used the Common Crawl: a non-profit organization which provides an open repository of the web.[5] Common Crawl's complete web archive consists of petabytes of data collected over 10 years of web crawling (Ortiz Suárez et al., 2020). The repository is organized in monthly bucket of crawled data. Web pages are saved in three different formats: WARC files for the raw HTML data, WAT files for the metadata, and WET files for the plain text extracts.

For our purposes, we used WARC files as we are interested in the raw HTML data. Similar to Lev et al. (2020), we looked for *JSON-LD*[6] tags containing an *FAQPage* item. Web developers use this tag to make it easy for search engines to parse FAQs from a web page.[7] The language of each FAQ pair is determined with fastText (Joulin et al., 2016). We also apply some filtering to remove unwanted noise.[8] Using this method, we collected 155M FAQ pairs from 24M different pages.

3.2 Deduplication

A common issue with datasets collected from the web is the redundancy of data (Lee et al., 2021). For example, hotel pages on *TripAdvisor* typically have an FAQ pair referring to shuttle services from the airport to the hotel.[9] The only changing term is the name of the hotel.

Algorithms such as SimHash (Charikar, 2002) and MinHash (Broder, 1997) can detect such duplicates. MinHash is an approximate matching algorithm widely used in large-scale deduplication tasks (Lee et al., 2021; Versley and Panchenko, 2012; Gabriel et al., 2018; Gyawali et al., 2020). The main idea of MinHash is to efficiently estimate the Jaccard similarity between two documents, represented by their set of n-grams. Because of the sparse nature of n-grams, computing the full Jaccard similarity between all documents is prohibitive. MinHash alleviates this issue by reducing each document to a fixed-length hash which can be used to efficiently approximate the Jaccard similarity between two documents. MinHash has the additional property that similar documents will have similar hashes, we can then use Locality Sensitive Hashing (LSH) (Leskovec et al., 2014) to efficiently retrieve similar documents.

In our experiments, we represented each page as a set of 3 consecutive tokens (n-grams). We worked with a document signature length of 100, and 20 bands with 5 rows as parameters for LSH.

[5] https://commoncrawl.org/about/

[6] JavaScript Object Notation for Linked Data

[7] More information on FAQPage markup

[8] Questions need to contain a question mark (including the Arabic question mark) to avoid keyword questions. Question and answer cannot start with a "<", "{", or "[" to remove "code like" data.

[9] Does Ritz Paris have an airport shuttle? Does Four Seasons Hotel George V have an airport shuttle?

Name	Size	Lang.	Domain	Source	Q>1	A>1
Usenet (Hammond et al., 1995)	-	En	Multi-domain	Usenet	No	No
FAQIR (Karan and Šnajder, 2016)	4,313	En	Maintenance	Yahoo! Answers	Yes	Yes
StackFAQ (Karan and Šnajder, 2018)	719	En	Web apps	StackExchange	Yes	Yes
InsuranceQA (Feng et al., 2015)	12,887	En	Insurance	Insurance Library	No	Yes
CQA-QL (Nakov et al., 2015)	2,600	En	Qatar	Qatar living forum	No	Yes
Fatwa corpus (Nakov et al., 2015)	1,300	Ar	Quran	Fatwa website	No	Yes
M-FAQ (ours)	6,134,533	Multi	Multi	Multi	No	No

Table 2: List of the common datasets used in FAQ retrieval. Size is the number of pairs available. Q>1 denotes if the dataset has multiple available questions for a single answer (i.e., does the dataset have paraphrases), while A>1 denotes if the dataset has multiple answers for a given question.

These parameters ensure a 99.6% probability that documents with a Jaccard similarity of 0.75 will be identified. We subsequently compute the true Jaccard similarity for all matches.

We follow the approach of *NearDup* (Lee et al., 2021) and subsequently create a graph of documents. Each node on the graph is an FAQ page, and they share an edge if their true Jaccard similarity is larger than 0.75. We then compute all the independent sub-graphs, each representing a graph of duplicated pages. We only keep one page per sub-graph.

Using this method, we trimmed the number of FAQ pages from 24M to 1M.

3.3 Description

After deduplication, our dataset contains around 6M FAQ pairs coming from 1M different web pages, spread on 26K root web domains.[10] This is significantly bigger than other FAQ datasets publicly available at the time of writing (see Table 2 for comparison).

Our dataset is composed of pairs of FAQs grouped by language and source page (URL). We collected data in 21 different languages.[11] The most common one is English, with 58% of the FAQ pairs, followed by German and Spanish with 13% and 8% respectively.

3.4 Training and validation sets

For a given language, the target size of the validation set is equal to 10% of the total number of pairs. However, two features of our dataset call for a more fine-grained approach.

3.4.1 Root domain distribution

Even though we deduplicated the dataset, FAQ pages tend to originate from the same root domain. As an example, kayak (*kayak.com*, *kayak.es*, etc.) is the largest contributor to the dataset. While this is not a problem for the training set (one can always restrict the number of pages per domain), it is an issue for the validation set, as we want to assess the quality of the model on a broad set of topics. Having several large root domain contributors skews the dataset to these topics. We make the simplifying assumption that different web domains have different topics of interest. Research on the true topic distribution is left for future work.

We artificially increased the topic breadth of the validation set by restricting the contribution of each root domain. In the validation set, a single root domain can only contribute up to 3 FAQ pages. This method reduces the contribution of the largest domain from 21% in the training set to 3% in the validation set. Furthermore, we make sure there is no overlap of root domain between the training and validation set.[12]

3.4.2 Pairs per page concentration

The distribution of the number of pairs per page is highly uneven (see Figure 1). Around 50% of the pages have 5 or fewer pairs per page. Intuitively, we prefer pages with a higher number of FAQs as it is harder to pick the right answers amongst 100 candidates than 5. We thus artificially increased the

[10] We define a root web domain as the last substring before the extension (e.g. TripAdvisor is the root web domain in fr.tripadvisor.com). In other words, we strip the extension and any subdomain.

[11] We did not target specific languages, however, we removed languages with fewer than 250 pairs. Common languages such as Chinese, Hindi, Arabic and Japanese are missing. Although we do not have an official reason why, we think it may be because of our initial filtering or the fact ldjson markup is not widely used in these languages.

[12] We use the root domain instead of the regular domain name to avoid having *help.domain.com* in the training set and *domain.co.uk* in the validation set

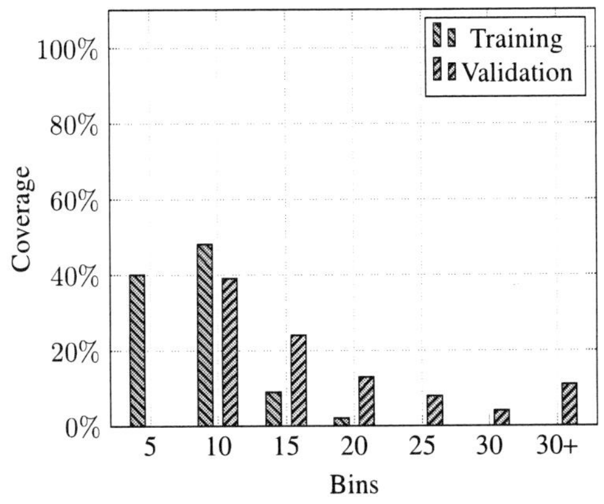

Figure 1: Bucketing of our dataset according to the number of FAQs per page. To make the validation set more challenging, we started by selecting pages with a higher number of pairs.

difficulty of the validation by first selecting pages with a higher number of FAQ pairs per page. See Figure 1 for a comparison between the training and validations set.

3.4.3 Cross-lingual leakage

The fact that our dataset is multilingual can lead to issues of cross-lingual leakage. Having pages from *expedia.fr* in the training set, and pages from *expedia.es* in the validation set can overstate the performance of the models. We avoid such problems by restricting root domains in the validation associated with only one language (e.g. *expedia* would be excluded from the validation set because it is associated with French and Spanish pages).

4 Models

In this section, we describe the FAQ retrieval models used in our experiments. Let P be the set of all user queries and $F = \{(q_1, a_1), ..., (q_n, a_n)\}$ be the set of all FAQ pairs for a given domain. An FAQ retrieval model takes as input a user's query $p_i \in P$ and an FAQ pair $f_j \in F$, and outputs a relevance score $h(p_i, f_j)$ for f_j with respect to p_i. However, our dataset does not contain live user queries (or paraphrases) P, we thus use questions q as queries $P = \{q_1, ..., q_n\}$ and restrict the FAQ set to the answers $F = \{a_1, ..., a_n\}$. The task becomes to rank the answers A according to the questions Q.

4.1 Baselines

We experimented with several baselines: two unsupervised and one supervised.

Language	Pairs	Pages	Domains
English	3,719,484	608,796	17,635
German	829,098	117,618	2,948
Spanish	482,818	75,489	1,610
French	351,458	56,317	1,795
Italian	155,296	24,562	685
Dutch	150,819	32,574	1,472
Portuguese	138,778	26,169	608
Turkish	102,373	19,002	580
Russian	91,771	22,643	953
Polish	65,182	10,695	445
Indonesian	45,839	7,910	309
Norwegian	37,711	5,143	198
Swedish	37,003	5,270	434
Danish	32,655	5,279	362
Vietnamese	27,157	5,261	469
Finnish	20,485	2,795	234
Romanian	17,066	3,554	152
Czech	16,675	2,568	182
Hebrew	11,212	1,921	205
Hungarian	8,598	1,264	150
Croatian	5,215	819	99
Total	6,346,693	1,035,649	31,525

Table 3: Summary statistics about our dataset.

4.1.1 TF-IDF

The traditional information retrieval method (Salton et al., 1975) uses a vector representation for q_i and a_i and computes a dot-product as similarity relevance score $h(q_i, a_i)$. We use n-grams of size (1, 3) and fit one model per FAQ page.

4.1.2 Universal Sentence Encoder

Encoding the semantics of a question q_i and an answer a_i can be achieved with the Universal Sentence Encoder (Cer et al., 2018). The model works on monolingual and multilingual data. We encode each question and answer independently, and then perform a dot-product of the questions' and answers' representations.

4.1.3 Dense Passage Retrieval (DPR)

Dense Passage Retrieval (DPR) (Karpukhin et al., 2020) is a state of the art method for passage retrieval. It uses a bi-encoder to encode questions and passages into a shared embedding space. We finetune DPR on our dataset using the same procedure described in Section 4.2.2.

4.2 XLM-Roberta as bi-encoders

Bi-encoders encode questions q_i and answers a_i independently and output a fixed d-dimensional representation for each query and answer. The encoder can be shared or independent to generate the representations.[13] At run-time, new queries are encoded using the encoder, and the top-k closest answers are returned. The representations for the answers can be computed once, and cached for later use. Similarity is typically computed using a dot product.

4.2.1 Multilingual

The state-of-the-art encoders such as RoBERTa (Liu et al., 2019) and BERT (Devlin et al., 2018) are trained for English only. As our dataset is multilingual we opted for XLM-RoBERTa (Conneau et al., 2019), it was trained using masked language modeling on one hundred languages, using more than 2TB of filtered CommonCrawl data. This choice allows us to leverage the size of the English data for less represented languages.

4.2.2 Training

Given pairs of questions and answers, along with a list of non-relevant answers, the bi-encoder model is trained to minimize the negative log-likelihood of picking the positive answer amongst the non-relevant answers. Non-relevant answers can be divided into *in-batch* negatives and *hard* negatives.

In-batch negatives In-batch negatives are the other answers from the batch, including them into the set of non-relevant answers is extremely efficient as their representations are already computed.

Hard negatives Hard negatives are close but incorrect answers to the questions. Including them improves the performance of retrieval models (Karpukhin et al., 2020; Xiong et al., 2020). Hard negatives can either come from a standard retrieval system such as BM25, or an earlier iteration of the dense model (Xiong et al., 2020; Oğuz et al., 2021). The structure of our dataset, pages of FAQs, facilitates the search for hard negatives. As an example in Table 1, three out of four answers share the term *COVID-19*. The model now has to understand the semantic of sentences instead of matching on shared named entities. By including all the pairs of the same page in the same training batch, we ensure that in-batch negatives act as hard negatives.[14]

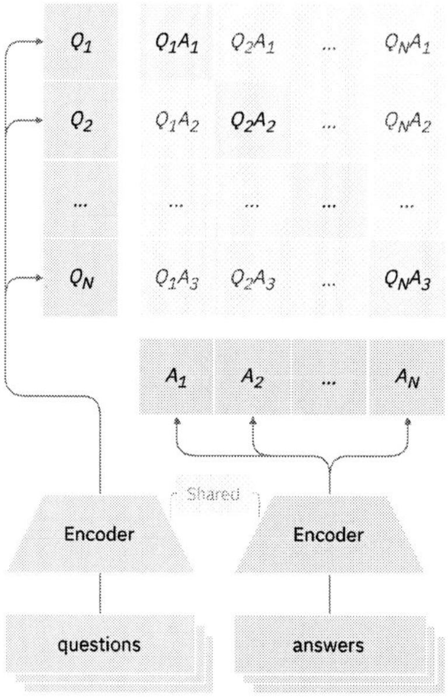

Figure 2: Diagram of our architecture. A shared encoder encodes the questions and the answers independently. Each question's representation (vector) is compared to each answer's representation from the same batch using a dot-product.

Multilingual Although XLM-Roberta is multilingual, we do not expect the model to perform cross-lingual retrieval (i.e. using one language for the query and another for the answer). We make sure that each batch is composed of pairs from the same language. This increases the difficulty of the task. Otherwise, the model could rely on the language of answers as a differentiating factor.

5 Experiments

In this section, we evaluate the retrieval performance of our model on MFAQ. In all our experiments, we use three metrics to evaluate the performance: precision-at-one (P@1), mean reciprocal rank (MRR), and recall-at-5 (R@5). For space reasons, we only report on MRR in the main text, the full results are available in the annex. We used the same parameters for all experiments unless mentioned otherwise.[15] We insert a special token <question> before questions to let the shared encoder know it is encoding a question. Answers are

[13]We use a shared encoder, which means we use the same network to compute the representation for questions and answers. DPR uses independent encoders.

[14]To create our batches of training data, we incrementally augment the batch with pairs of a given page. When the batch size reaches the desired size, we start over with the remaining pairs.

[15]We used a batch size of 800, sequences were limited to 128 tokens (capturing the entirety of 90% of the dataset), an Adam optimizer with a learning rate of 0,0001 (warmup of 1000 steps). Dropout of 25%.

Language	TF-IDF	USE	XLM-R
English	63.8	64.2	**82.5**
German	58.0	61.8	**81.3**
Spanish	60.5	61.6	**81.7**
French	60.6	62.4	**80.7**
Italian	58.6	55.7	**74.7**
Dutch	62.9	59.6	**81.2**
Portuguese	55.8	56.2	**77.4**
Turkish	59.2	55.7	**78.8**
Russian	59.2	63.1	**82.1**
Polish	59.2	59.9	**85.2**
Indonesia	71.3	62.1	**88.5**
Norwegian	58.9	36.9	**83.1**
Swedish	59.3	36.7	**83.3**
Danish	64.0	42.1	**82.7**
Vietnamese	73.3	43.2	**81.2**
Finnish	53.5	33.2	**82.6**
Romanian	57.8	40.7	**83.2**
Czech	48.2	26.9	**69.0**
Hebrew	61.5	26.5	**83.6**
Hungarian	38.1	28.6	**69.7**
Croatian	58.1	41.4	**83.6**

Table 4: MRR on MFAQ using various methods. XLM-RoBERTa is a single model trained on all languages at once.

respectively prepended with <answer>. All of our experiments use a subset of the training set: only one page per domain as this technique achieves higher results. Refer to Section 5.3 for more information.

We start by studying the performance of multilingual models, then compare it against monolingual models.

5.1 Multilingual

We present in Table 4 a summary of the results of our multilingual training. The model is trained concurrently on the 21 available languages. XLM-RoBERTa achieves a higher MRR on every language compared to the baselines. Low resource languages achieve a relatively high score which could indicate inter-language transfer learning.

5.2 Monolingual

Next, we attempt to study if a collection of monolingual models are better suited than a single monolingual model. We use language-specific BERT-like models for each language. The list of BERT models per language is available in the annex. We followed the same procedure as described in Section 4.2, except for the encoder which is language-specific.

Language	Monoligual	Multilingual
En. (DPR)	80.5	82.5
En. (RoBERTa)	**82.9**	82.5
German	81.1	**81.3**
Spanish	78.0	**81.7**
French	71.0	**80.7**
Italian	64.1	**74.7**
Dutch	70.4	**81.2**
Portuguese	68.4	**77.4**
Turkish	76.1	**78.8**
Russian	71.6	**82.1**
Polish	73.9	**85.2**

Table 5: MRR of monolingual models versus a single multilingual model. The multilingual model outperforms monolingual models in all languages, except for English.

We limited our study of monolingual models to the ten largest languages of MFAQ. We choose these languages as they have sufficient training examples, and pre-trained BERT-like models are readily available. To study the performance of monolingual models we train models using the same procedure as described in Section 4.2 except for the encoder.

The results in Table 5 indicates that a multilingual model outperforms monolingual models in all cases, except for English. These results indicate that leveraging additional languages is beneficial for the task of FAQ retrieval, especially for languages with fewer resources available. Interestingly, RoBERTa slightly beats DPR in English. This underperformance could be explained by the difference in batch size. Because of the dual encoder nature of DPR, we had to reduce the batch size to 320 compared to 800 for RoBERTa.

5.3 Cross-lingual

Our training procedure ensures that the model never has to use language as a cue to select the appropriate answer. Batches of training data all share the same language. We tested the cross-lingual retrieval capabilities of our multilingual model by translating the queries to English while keeping the answers in the original language. The French performance drops from 80.7 to 78.2, which is still better than the unsupervised baselines. The full results are presented in Table 6.

A subsectionSubset of training data We tested

Language	Cross-lingual	Multilingual
French	78.2	80.7
Hungarian	65.9	69.7
Croatian	71.2	83.6

Table 6: MRR results of our cross-lingual analysis. Questions were translated to English while answers remained in the original language.

the effect of limiting the number of FAQ pages per domain by limiting the training set to one page per web domain. Using this technique, we achieved an average MRR of 80.8 while using all the training data to reach an average MRR of 76.7. Filtering the training set flattens the topic distribution and better matches the validation set. Another possible approach is to randomly select a given page from a domain at each epoch. This technique would act as a natural regularization. This is left for future work.

6 Qualitative analysis

In this section, we dive into the model's predictions and try to understand why and where it goes wrong. We do so by focusing on a single FAQ page from the admission center of the *Tepper School of Business*.[16] The FAQs are displayed in Table 8 in the annex. The multilingual model is correct on 74.07% of the pairs, with an MRR of 85.49. Our qualitative analysis reveals that the model is bad at coreference resolution and depends on keywords for query-answer matching.

Coreference Resolution The model makes a wrong prediction in question 4 *Can the GMAT or GRE requirement be waived? No, these test scores are required.* The model is unable to guess that *test scores* refer to GMAT or GRE. By changing the answer to *No, the GMAT or GRE scores are required*, the model correctly picks the right answer.

Paraphrase To study if the model is robust to paraphrasing, we change question 1 from « *Are the hours flexible enough for full-time working adults?* » to « *Is it manageable if I already have a full-time job?* » In this case, the model correctly identifies the right answer. However, if we remove the *full-time* cue, the right answer only arrives in the fourth position. Next, we look at question 15, the model makes a wrong prediction as *opportunities* is not mentioned in the answer. Changing the question to « *It's a part-time online program, but are there any on-campus [experiences|activities] for students?* » leads to a correct prediction.[17]

Keyword search We replace some questions with a single keyword. We reduced questions 12, 14, 16 and 20 to *cohort, payment plan, soldier veteran* and *technical requirements*. In all cases, the model guessed correctly, showing the model can do a keyword-based search.

Although it can cope with some synonyms (activities - experiences), this qualitative analysis shows our model is overly reliant on keywords for matching questions and answers. Further research on adversarial training of FAQ retrieval is needed.

7 Future Work

Important non-Indo-European languages such as Chinese, Hindi, or Japanese are missing from this dataset. Future work is needed to improve data collection in these languages. Second, we did not evaluate the model on a real-life FAQ retrieval dataset (with user queries). Future work is needed to see if our model can perform question-to-question retrieval, or if it needs further training to do so. A linguistic study could analyze the model's strengths and weaknesses by studying the model's performance by type of questions, answers, and entities.

8 Conclusion

In this work, we presented the first multilingual dataset of FAQs publicly available. Its size and breadth of languages are significantly larger than other datasets available. While language-specific BERT-like models can be applied to the task of FAQ retrieval, we showed it is beneficial to use a multilingual model and train on all languages at once. This method of training outperforms all monolingual models, except for English. Our qualitative analysis reveals our model is overly reliant on keywords to match questions and answers.

9 Acknowledgements

This research received funding from the Flemish Government under the "Onderzoeksprogramma Artificiële Intelligentie (AI) Vlaanderen" programme.

[16] It was the first page with less than 25 pairs to end with a *.edu* extension.

[17] replacing *opportunities* with *events* does not work.

References

Adam Berger, Rich Caruana, David Cohn, Dayne Freitag, and Vibhu Mittal. 2000. Bridging the lexical chasm: statistical approaches to answer-finding. In *Proceedings of the 23rd annual international ACM SIGIR conference on Research and development in information retrieval*, pages 192–199.

A.Z. Broder. 1997. On the resemblance and containment of documents. In *Proceedings. Compression and Complexity of SEQUENCES 1997 (Cat. No.97TB100171)*, pages 21–29.

Robin D. Burke, Kristian J. Hammond, Vladimir Kulyukin, Steven L. Lytinen, Noriko Tomuro, and Scott Schoenberg. 1997. Question answering from frequently asked question files: Experiences with the faq finder system. 18(2):57–57.

Daniel Cer, Yinfei Yang, Sheng-yi Kong, Nan Hua, Nicole Limtiaco, Rhomni St. John, Noah Constant, Mario Guajardo-Cespedes, Steve Yuan, Chris Tar, Yun-Hsuan Sung, Brian Strope, and Ray Kurzweil. 2018. Universal sentence encoder. *CoRR*, abs/1803.11175.

Moses S. Charikar. 2002. Similarity estimation techniques from rounding algorithms. In *Proceedings of the Thiry-Fourth Annual ACM Symposium on Theory of Computing*, STOC '02, page 380–388, New York, NY, USA. Association for Computing Machinery.

Alexis Conneau, Kartikay Khandelwal, Naman Goyal, Vishrav Chaudhary, Guillaume Wenzek, Francisco Guzmán, Edouard Grave, Myle Ott, Luke Zettlemoyer, and Veselin Stoyanov. 2019. Unsupervised cross-lingual representation learning at scale. *CoRR*, abs/1911.02116.

Maxime De Bruyn, Ehsan Lotfi, Jeska Buhmann, and Walter Daelemans. 2020. Bart for knowledge grounded conversations. In *Converse@ KDD*.

Maxime De Bruyn, Ehsan Lotfi, Jeska Buhmann, and Walter Daelemans. 2021. Convert for faq answering.

Jacob Devlin, Ming-Wei Chang, Kenton Lee, and Kristina Toutanova. 2018. BERT: pre-training of deep bidirectional transformers for language understanding. *CoRR*, abs/1810.04805.

Minwei Feng, Bing Xiang, Michael R. Glass, Lidan Wang, and Bowen Zhou. 2015. Applying deep learning to answer selection: A study and an open task. In *2015 IEEE Workshop on Automatic Speech Recognition and Understanding (ASRU)*, pages 813–820. IEEE.

Simone Filice, Danilo Croce, Alessandro Moschitti, and Roberto Basili. 2016. KeLP at SemEval-2016 task 3: Learning semantic relations between questions and answers. In *Proceedings of the 10th International Workshop on Semantic Evaluation (SemEval-2016)*, pages 1116–1123. Association for Computational Linguistics.

Rodney A Gabriel, Tsung-Ting Kuo, Julian McAuley, and Chun-Nan Hsu. 2018. Identifying and characterizing highly similar notes in big clinical note datasets. *Journal of biomedical informatics*, 82:63–69.

Bikash Gyawali, Lucas Anastasiou, and Petr Knoth. 2020. Deduplication of scholarly documents using locality sensitive hashing and word embeddings.

Kristian Hammond, Robin Burke, Charles Martin, and Steven Lytinen. 1995. FAQ finder: a case-based approach to knowledge navigation. In *Proceedings the 11th Conference on Artificial Intelligence for Applications*, pages 80–86. IEEE.

Matthew Henderson, Iñigo Casanueva, Nikola Mrkšic, Pei-Hao Su, Tsung-Hsien Wen, and Ivan Vulic. 2019. Convert: Efficient and accurate conversational representations from transformers. *CoRR*, abs/1911.03688.

Valentin Jijkoun and Maarten de Rijke. 2005. Retrieving answers from frequently asked questions pages on the web. In *Proceedings of the 14th ACM international conference on Information and knowledge management*, pages 76–83.

Armand Joulin, Edouard Grave, Piotr Bojanowski, and Tomas Mikolov. 2016. Bag of tricks for efficient text classification. *arXiv preprint arXiv:1607.01759*.

Mladen Karan and Jan Šnajder. 2016. Faqir–a frequently asked questions retrieval test collection. In *International Conference on Text, Speech, and Dialogue*, pages 74–81. Springer.

Mladen Karan and Jan Šnajder. 2018. Paraphrase-focused learning to rank for domain-specific frequently asked questions retrieval. 91:418–433.

Vladimir Karpukhin, Barlas Oguz, Sewon Min, Patrick Lewis, Ledell Wu, Sergey Edunov, Danqi Chen, and Wen-tau Yih. 2020. Dense passage retrieval for open-domain question answering. In *Proceedings of the 2020 Conference on Empirical Methods in Natural Language Processing (EMNLP)*, pages 6769–6781, Online. Association for Computational Linguistics.

Harksoo Kim and Jungyun Seo. 2006. High-performance FAQ retrieval using an automatic clustering method of query logs. 42(3):650–661.

Harksoo Kim and Jungyun Seo. 2008. Cluster-based FAQ retrieval using latent term weights. 23(2):58–65. Conference Name: IEEE Intelligent Systems.

Mojtaba Komeili, Kurt Shuster, and Jason Weston. 2021. Internet-augmented dialogue generation. *CoRR*, abs/2107.07566.

Katherine Lee, Daphne Ippolito, Andrew Nystrom, Chiyuan Zhang, Douglas Eck, Chris Callison-Burch, and Nicholas Carlini. 2021. Deduplicating training data makes language models better.

Jure Leskovec, Anand Rajaraman, and Jeffrey David Ullman. 2014. *Mining of Massive Datasets*, 2nd edition. Cambridge University Press, USA.

Guy Lev, Michal Shmueli-Scheuer, Achiya Jerbi, and David Konopnicki. 2020. orgFAQ: A new dataset and analysis on organizational FAQs and user questions.

Patrick Lewis, Yuxiang Wu, Linqing Liu, Pasquale Minervini, Heinrich Küttler, Aleksandra Piktus, Pontus Stenetorp, and Sebastian Riedel. 2021. Paq: 65 million probably-asked questions and what you can do with them. *arXiv preprint arXiv:2102.07033*.

Yinhan Liu, Myle Ott, Naman Goyal, Jingfei Du, Mandar Joshi, Danqi Chen, Omer Levy, Mike Lewis, Luke Zettlemoyer, and Veselin Stoyanov. 2019. Roberta: A robustly optimized BERT pretraining approach. *CoRR*, abs/1907.11692.

Yosi Mass, Boaz Carmeli, Haggai Roitman, and David Konopnicki. 2020. Unsupervised FAQ retrieval with question generation and BERT. In *Proceedings of the 58th Annual Meeting of the Association for Computational Linguistics*, pages 807–812.

George A Miller. 1995. Wordnet: a lexical database for english. *Communications of the ACM*, 38(11):39–41.

A. Moreo, E. M. Eisman, J. L. Castro, and J. M. Zurita. 2013. Learning regular expressions to template-based FAQ retrieval systems. 53:108–128.

Alessandro Moschitti, Silvia Quarteroni, Roberto Basili, and Suresh Manandhar. 2007. Exploiting syntactic and shallow semantic kernels for question answer classification. In *Proceedings of the 45th Annual Meeting of the Association of Computational Linguistics*, pages 776–783. Association for Computational Linguistics.

Preslav Nakov, Lluís Màrquez, Walid Magdy, Alessandro Moschitti, Jim Glass, and Bilal Randeree. 2015. SemEval-2015 task 3: Answer selection in community question answering. In *Proceedings of the 9th International Workshop on Semantic Evaluation (SemEval 2015)*, pages 269–281, Denver, Colorado. Association for Computational Linguistics.

Pedro Javier Ortiz Suárez, Laurent Romary, and Benoît Sagot. 2020. A monolingual approach to contextualized word embeddings for mid-resource languages. In *Proceedings of the 58th Annual Meeting of the Association for Computational Linguistics*, pages 1703–1714, Online. Association for Computational Linguistics.

Barlas Oğuz, Kushal Lakhotia, Anchit Gupta, Patrick Lewis, Vladimir Karpukhin, Aleksandra Piktus, Xilun Chen, Sebastian Riedel, Wen tau Yih, Sonal Gupta, and Yashar Mehdad. 2021. Domain-matched pre-training tasks for dense retrieval.

Stefan Riezler, Alexander Vasserman, Ioannis Tsochantaridis, Vibhu O. Mittal, and Yi Liu. 2007. Statistical machine translation for query expansion in answer retrieval. In *Proceedings of the 45th Annual Meeting of the Association of Computational Linguistics*, pages 464–471.

Anna Rogers, Matt Gardner, and Isabelle Augenstein. 2021. QA dataset explosion: A taxonomy of NLP resources for question answering and reading comprehension. *CoRR*, abs/2107.12708.

Wataru Sakata, Tomohide Shibata, Ribeka Tanaka, and Sadao Kurohashi. 2019. FAQ retrieval using query-question similarity and BERT-based query-answer relevance. In *Proceedings of the 42nd International ACM SIGIR Conference on Research and Development in Information Retrieval*, pages 1113–1116.

Gerard Salton, Anita Wong, and Chung-Shu Yang. 1975. A vector space model for automatic indexing. *Communications of the ACM*, 18(11):613–620.

Kurt Shuster, Spencer Poff, Moya Chen, Douwe Kiela, and Jason Weston. 2021. Retrieval augmentation reduces hallucination in conversation. *arXiv preprint arXiv:2104.07567*.

Eriks Sneiders. 1999. Automated faq answering: Continued experience with shallow language understanding. In *Question Answering Systems. Papers from the 1999 AAAI Fall Symposium*, pages 97–107.

Eriks Sneiders. 2002a. Automated question answering: template-based approach.

Eriks Sneiders. 2002b. Automated question answering using question templates that cover the conceptual model of the database. In *International Conference on Application of Natural Language to Information Systems*, pages 235–239. Springer.

Eriks Sneiders. 2009. Automated FAQ answering with question-specific knowledge representation for web self-service. In *2009 2nd Conference on Human System Interactions*, pages 298–305. IEEE.

Eriks Sneiders. 2010. Automated email answering by text pattern matching. In *International Conference on Natural Language Processing*, pages 381–392. Springer.

Noriko Tomuro and Steven L. Lytinen. 2004. Retrieval models and q and a learning with FAQ files. In *New Directions in Question Answering*, pages 183–202.

Yannick Versley and Yana Panchenko. 2012. Not just bigger: Towards better-quality web corpora. In *Proceedings of the seventh Web as Corpus Workshop (WAC7)*, pages 44–52.

Steven D. Whitehead. 1995. Auto-FAQ: an experiment in cyberspace leveraging. 28(1):137–146.

Ruobing Xie, Yanan Lu, Fen Lin, and Leyu Lin. 2020. FAQ-based question answering via knowledge anchors. In *CCF International Conference on Natural Language Processing and Chinese Computing*, pages 3–15. Springer.

Lee Xiong, Chenyan Xiong, Ye Li, Kwok-Fung Tang, Jialin Liu, Paul N. Bennett, Junaid Ahmed, and Arnold Overwijk. 2020. Approximate nearest neighbor negative contrastive learning for dense text retrieval. *CoRR*, abs/2007.00808.

Sheng-Yuan Yang. 2009. Developing of an ontological interface agent with template-based linguistic processing technique for FAQ services. 36(2):4049–4060. Publisher: Elsevier.

Language	Random			TF-IDF			USE			XLM-Roberta (1 page per domain)			XLM-RoBERTa (full training set)			Monolingual		
	P@1	MRR	R@5	P@1	MRR	R@5	P@1	MRR	R@5	P@1	MRR	R@5	P@1	MRR	R@5	P@1	MRR	R@5
English	5.9	18.9	29.7	53.9	63.8	79.8	52.6	64.2	83.0	74.9	82.5	93.5	72.5	80.7	92.5	75.6	**82.9**	93.5
German	5.8	18.3	28.8	48.0	58.0	74.8	49.8	61.8	81.6	73.0	**81.3**	93.7	69.0	78.2	92.0	72.5	81.1	93.6
Spanish	7.3	22.3	36.7	49.2	60.5	78.9	49.3	61.6	82.0	72.8	**81.7**	94.5	68.9	78.6	93.2	68.6	78.0	92.3
French	6.1	19.4	30.3	49.9	60.6	78.0	50.2	62.4	82.5	72.2	**80.7**	93.3	68.9	78.0	91.8	60.5	71.0	87.4
Italian	5.2	16.8	26.2	49.0	58.6	74.4	44.1	55.7	75.2	65.9	**74.7**	88.6	60.2	70.2	85.6	53.3	64.1	81.6
Dutch	5.3	17.3	26.5	53.2	62.9	78.6	47.7	59.6	79.2	73.0	**81.2**	93.2	69.8	78.6	91.7	60.1	70.4	86.8
Portuguese	5.3	17.0	26.6	45.5	55.8	72.7	44.1	56.2	75.8	68.5	**77.4**	90.3	65.6	74.8	88.8	58.3	68.4	84.6
Turkish	6.2	19.0	31.0	49.3	59.2	75.2	43.5	55.7	76.4	70.2	**78.8**	91.6	64.5	74.5	89.6	65.7	76.1	91.4
Russian	7.1	21.7	35.7	48.5	59.2	76.7	49.8	63.1	83.8	73.5	**82.1**	94.4	68.9	78.7	93.1	61.0	71.6	88.3
Polish	6.1	19.4	30.4	49.9	59.2	74.9	47.4	59.9	81.2	77.6	**85.2**	96.0	73.2	81.6	94.6	64.0	73.9	89.8
Indonesian	8.0	23.8	40.1	61.8	71.3	86.4	49.3	62.1	83.5	82.2	**88.5**	97.2	76.6	84.3	95.4	-	-	-
Norwegian	5.5	17.8	27.5	48.8	58.9	75.9	25.3	36.9	57.4	76.5	**83.1**	93.7	70.6	79.4	93.3	-	-	-
Swedish	5.0	16.1	25.0	49.1	59.3	76.1	25.7	36.7	56.3	75.6	**83.3**	94.6	72.0	80.5	93.1	-	-	-
Danish	5.6	18.1	27.8	54.3	64.0	80.6	30.4	42.1	63.3	75.4	**82.7**	92.9	71.5	79.5	91.8	-	-	-
Vietnamese	11.3	30.6	56.6	62.7	73.3	90.6	28.4	43.2	70.7	73.9	**81.2**	92.5	69.8	78.3	91.6	-	-	-
Finnish	5.6	18.3	28.2	43.9	53.5	70.0	21.8	33.2	53.7	74.9	**82.6**	93.9	68.5	76.8	89.7	-	-	-
Romanian	6.4	20.3	32.1	48.6	57.8	73.0	29.3	40.7	62.0	76.9	**83.2**	91.5	66.6	75.4	88.2	-	-	-
Czech	3.8	12.9	19.0	38.3	48.2	64.0	18.3	26.9	42.4	59.6	**69.0**	83.5	50.1	60.2	77.2	-	-	-
Hebrew	8.6	25.1	42.8	49.3	61.5	81.3	14.5	26.5	50.7	75.3	**83.6**	95.5	68.8	78.7	93.7	-	-	-
Hungarian	4.1	13.3	20.4	30.3	38.1	52.1	21.0	28.6	41.4	60.6	**69.7**	83.7	54.1	64.1	80.5	-	-	-
Croatian	4.9	15.9	24.5	49.4	58.1	73.0	32.8	41.4	56.7	78.2	**83.6**	92.6	71.8	79.4	91.4	-	-	-

Table 7: Results of our experiments on MFAQ. XLM-RoBERTa (1 page per domain) is consistently better than the rest, except for English where a RoBERTa model achieves a higher MRR. P@1 = Precision-at-1 (accuracy), MRR = Mean Reciprocal Rank, R@5 = Recall-at-5, One page per domain = subset of the training set.

ID	Question	Answer
0	Are international students eligible for the MSBA program?	Yes, international students are eligible for the MSBA program. Please review the International Applicants page for specific requirements.
1	Are the hours flexible enough for full-time working adults?	Yes, the MSBA program accommodates students working full-time. Required weekly live sessions, lasting 75 minutes, are held in the evening, and the three residential components, two strongly recommended and one optional, take place over weekends. Students complete all other coursework on their own schedule, but must adhere to deadlines and be prepared to participate in weekly live sessions.
2	Can I take a course from a third-party provider, like Lynda or Coursera, to prepare for the programming requirements of this program?	Our goal is to make sure that everyone entering the program has the necessary background to be successful. We strongly recommend that applicants who feel they need additional preparation in programming languages take a for-credit course from an accredited two- or four-year institution.
3	Can I transfer credits into the program?	No, the Tepper School does not accept transfer credits.
4	Can the GMAT or GRE requirement be waived?	No, these test scores are required.
5	Do I have to maintain a certain GPA in the program to graduate?	Yes, MSBA degree candidates must maintain a minimum cumulative GPA of 3.0 to graduate.
6	Do you offer the opportunity to preview courses in your program to get a feel for what they are like?	Yes we do. To preview one of our courses, please visit our Virtual Class Visit page. You'll be able to register to virtually participate in a course of your choosing.
7	How do I learn more about the online learning environment?	To preview one of our courses, please visit our Virtual Class Visit page. You'll be able to view upcoming courses and register to virtually attend a course of your choosing.
8	How many hours per week should be dedicated to coursework?	Students take two classes at a time and should expect to spend at least 10 hours on each course, or 20 hours total for the week. Coursework includes live synchronous meetings, assignments, projects, readings, and quizzes.
9	If I need to withdraw from the program, will I get a refund?	If I need to withdraw from the program, will I get a refund?
10	If I'm already proficient in basic programming and probability/statistics, do I have to take these courses?	Yes, the 46-880 Introduction to Probability and Statistics and 46-881 Programming in R and Python courses are required for all MSBA students. These courses ensure that all students have the necessary skills and knowledge to succeed in courses that follow. For more information, visit the Curriculum page on our website.
11	Is the MSBA offered exclusively on campus?	No, the MSBA degree is offered only online, with three optional on-campus experiences. Though they all are optional, we strongly recommend that students attend the BaseCamp and Capstone Project experiences, which occur at the beginning and end of the degree program.
12	Is the MSBA program structured in cohorts?	Yes, the part-time, online MSBA is structured in cohorts to optimize student interaction and success in the program.
13	Is the Tepper School participating in the Yellow Ribbon Program?	Yes, the Tepper School is participating in the Yellow Ribbon Program. For more information, please visit the Tuition page or contact Mike Danko at uro-vaedbenefits@andrew.cmu.edu.
14	Is there a Tuition Payment Plan available?	Yes, for more information about a monthly payment plan and debt minimization services, please review our payment options.
15	It's a part-time online program, but are there any on-campus opportunities for students?	We have three on-campus experiences. The first is an orientation basecamp, where the students are introduced to the program, interact with faculty, and learn about their cohort. The second, an immersive analytics experience led by top CMU faculty, takes place mid-program. We end the program with a capstone experience where students can present their work to real-world clients and celebrate the end of the program. For more information, visit the On-Campus Experiences page on our website.
16	I'm an active duty soldier/veteran. Am I eligible for an application fee waiver?	Yes, as a GMAC military-friendly business school, we waive the $125 application fee for active duty U.S. military personnel, veterans and retirees. Please contact Mike Danko at uro-vaedbenefits@andrew.cmu.edu to discuss the fee waiver.
17	Must international students come to campus?	We recommend attendance at the on-campus experiences, but students who are unable to attend may participate remotely and still meet the requirements of the program. Please note that because the program is delivered online, enrollment in the MSBA will not qualify students for a student visa to enter the United States.
18	What are some examples of roles a graduate could pursue after the program?	Business analytics professionals hold a range of positions across sectors and industries. They have titles such as business intelligence analyst, operations research analyst, market research analyst and statistician. Other job titles for these professionals are available here.
19	What are the programming languages that I should have experience in before applying to the program?	Basic programming knowledge in a modern language is required for admission. You do not need to be familiar with any specific language or build advanced programming skills before applying to the MSBA program. Your courses in the program will introduce you to relevant languages and provide hands-on experience.
20	What are the technical requirements for the MSBA program?	All students must have access to the following technologies in order to participate in the program: Laptop with the following requirements: - Windows – Intel Core i5 processor or higher; 8GB RAM, 256+ hard drive capacity - Macintosh – 8GB RAM, 256+ hard drive capacity, Apple Boot Camp - Ability to run Microsoft Windows (run virtually for Macintosh computers) - Ability to install software locally (not cloud based) Full administrative rights for downloading software. - Camera and microphone for remote conferencing. Broadband internet connection (at least 5 MBPS) Ability to access the CMU Learning Management System, Canvas Ability to access the MSBA Web Conferencing Software, Vidyo Continual and unfettered use of the required IT environment, including uninterrupted access to a broadband internet connection, are integral to the program and to each student's ability to fully participate in, and complete, each aspect of the program and the program in its entirety. Students who do not have such access, and/or are not able to maintain such access, may be advised by a representative of the program to withdraw from the program, following the university's prescribed process for withdrawal, and subject to the tuition refund policy as outlined on the Student Financial Services website.
21	What career resources are available for MSBA students and alumni?	The Master's Career Center helps students develop strategies focused on their career needs through a variety of services. For example, the career center hosts workshops and webinars in job search fundamentals, such as resume writing, interviewing, and networking. One-on-one career coaching is offered for individualized career planning. Our coaches are steeped in experience in various industries and functions and can support a variety of student interests. Sessions are delivered virtually during times convenient to working professionals. Tepper leverages an extensive network of Fortune 500 companies to identify opportunities for MSBA candidates.
22	What happens if I need to defer starting or withdraw from the program?	Deferrals are granted only if an applicant must complete military service or has an extreme emergency. Deposits are refunded in these instances. Students are re-admitted the following year and must submit their deposit before the deadline for their start date. A withdrawal from the Tepper School or Carnegie Mellon University indicates that a student has no intention to return to the program. This process can be initiated by first meeting with an academic advisor to terminate a student's Campus ID and email account. A student who leaves the Tepper School or Carnegie Mellon with a sincere intention to return may petition for a leave of absence (LOA) for up to two calendar years. This process can be initiated by first meeting with an academic advisor to complete the required paperwork.
23	What is the average Quant and Verbal scores for the GRE and GMAT?	There is no average score expectation. The test scores are simply one component of the multifaceted admissions process that we consider when making an admissions decision.
24	What separates the Tepper School of Business' online MSBA program from other MSBA programs, either online or on-campus?	The Tepper School of Business is globally renowned for its analytical approach to business problem solving. It is an integral part of Carnegie Mellon University, a top-tier research university that has become the center for disciplines including data science, robotics, business intelligence and additive manufacturing. Several faculty members of the online MS in Business Analytics also hold appointments in other schools including Carnegie Mellon's top-ranked School of Computer Science. Our MSBA program provides students with exceptionally robust coursework in business analytics techniques, with a special focus on machine learning and optimization. All of the advanced analytics skills we teach are delivered in a business context, ensuring that students graduate knowing how to efficiently, effectively and creatively apply their analytics expertise to business problems. Furthermore, the Tepper School's Accelerate Leadership Center offers students the opportunity to improve their leadership, inter-personal and communication skills, through online assessments and one-on-one coaching. Additionally, the program's on-campus experiences provide opportunities for online students to interact closely with faculty, each other and industry professionals working at companies that look to Carnegie Mellon and the Tepper School for high-caliber talent.
25	What time(s) do the synchronous sessions take place?	The weekly live sessions are in the evening (U.S. Eastern Time) and typically last 75 minutes.
26	What types of financial aid or scholarships are available to online students?	Students may be eligible to take out federal and/or private education loans to cover tuition and other education-related costs. Please view our Tuition page for details. At this time, the Tepper School does not provide scholarships for the MSBA program.

Table 8: FAQ pairs from the Tepper School of Business

Rethinking the Objectives of Extractive Question Answering

Martin Fajcik, Josef Jon, Pavel Smrz
Brno University of Technology
{ifajcik,ijon,smrz}@fit.vutbr.cz

Abstract

This work demonstrates that using the objective with independence assumption for modelling the span probability $P(a_s, a_e) = P(a_s)P(a_e)$ of span starting at position a_s and ending at position a_e has adverse effects. Therefore we propose multiple approaches to modelling joint probability $P(a_s, a_e)$ directly. Among those, we propose a compound objective, composed from the joint probability while still keeping the objective with independence assumption as an auxiliary objective. We find that the compound objective is consistently superior or equal to other assumptions in exact match. Additionally, we identified common errors caused by the assumption of independence and manually checked the counterpart predictions, demonstrating the impact of the compound objective on the real examples. Our findings are supported via experiments with three extractive QA models (BIDAF, BERT, ALBERT) over six datasets and our code, individual results and manual analysis are available online[1].

1 Introduction

The goal of extractive question answering (EQA) is to find the span boundaries – the start and the end of the span from text evidence, which answers a given question. Therefore, a natural choice of the objective to this problem is to model the probabilities of the span boundaries. In the last years, there was a lot of effort put into building better neural models underlying the desired probability distributions. However, there has been a little progress seen towards the change of the objective itself. For instance, the "default" choice of objective for modelling the probability over spans in SQuADv1.1 (Rajpurkar et al., 2016) – maximization of independent span boundary probabilities $P(a_s)P(a_e)$ for answer at position $\langle a_s, a_e \rangle$ – has stayed the same over the course of years in many influential works (Xiong et al., 2017; Seo et al., 2017; Chen et al., 2017; Yu et al., 2018; Devlin et al., 2019; Cheng et al., 2020) since the earliest work on this dataset – the submission of Wang and Jiang (2017). Based on the myths of worse performance of different objectives, these works adopt the deeply rooted assumption of independence. However, this assumption may lead to obviously wrong predictions, as shown in Figure 1.

Question: What was the name of atom bomb dropped by USA on Hiroshima?

Passage: ...The Allies issued orders for atomic bombs to be used on four Japanese cities were issued on July 25. on August 6, one of its b - 29s dropped a little boy uranium gun-type bomb on Hiroshima. three days later, on August 9, a fat man plutonium implosion-type bomb was dropped by another b - 29 on Nagasaki...

Ground truth: little boy

P	Predictions from BERT-base
33.3	little boy uranium gun-type bomb on Hiroshima. three days later, on August 9, a fat man
32.15	little boy
23.51	fat man
3.60	a fat man
2.08	a little boy uranium gun - type bomb on hiroshima. three days later, on august 9, a fat man
1.03	a little boy

Figure 1: An example of an error which comes with an independence assumption. The model assigns high probability mass to boundaries around "little boy", and "fat man" answers. However, during decoding, the start of one and the end of another answer is picked up.

In addition, this assumption leads to degenerate distribution $P(a_s, a_e)$, as high probability mass is assigned to many trivially wrong[2] answers.

Some of the earlier work (Wang and Jiang, 2017; Weissenborn et al., 2017) and recent approaches including large language representation models

[1] https://github.com/KNOT-FIT-BUT/JointSpanExtraction.

[2] We define 'trivially wrong' as not resembling any string form human would answer, e.g., the first or the second last answer of Figure 1.

Proceedings of the 3rd Workshop on Machine Reading for Question Answering, pages 14–27
Nov 10th, 2021 ©2021 Association for Computational Linguistics

(LRMs) like XLNet (Yang et al., 2019), ALBERT (Lan et al., 2020) or ELECTRA (Clark et al., 2020) started modelling the span probability via conditional probability factorization $P(a_e|a_s)P(a_s)$. However, is it unknown whether this objective improves any performance at all, as almost none of the recent works reported results on its effect, not even described its existence (except ELECTRA paper). Additionally, this objective requires beam search which slows down inference in test time. Exceptionally, Lee et al. (2016) proposed one way for modelling $P(a_s, a_e)$ directly, but the approach was only sparsely adopted (Lee et al., 2019; Khattab et al., 2020). This may be caused by the belief, that enumerating all possible spans has a large complexity (Cheng et al., 2021). However, in practice we find the complexity to be often similar to assumption of independence, when implementing the objective efficiently. We continue the in-depth discussion on complexity in Appendix C.

In this work, we try to break the myths about the objectives that have been widely used previously. We experiment with joint objective and we also introduce a new *compound* objective, that deals with modelling joint probability $P(a_s, a_e)$ directly while keeping the traditional independent objective as an auxiliary objective. We experiment with 5 different joint probability function realisations and find that with current LRMs, simple dot product works the best. However, we show that this is not a rule, and for some models, other function realisations might be better. The conducted experiments demonstrate that using compound objective is superior to previously used objectives across the various choices of models or datasets.

In summary, our work contributions are:

- introduction of the compound objective and its comparison with the traditional objectives based on assumption of independence, conditional probability factorization, or direct joint probability,
- a thorough evaluation on the wide spectrum of models and datasets comparing different objectives supported by statistical tests,
- a manual analysis which provides closer look on the different impacts of independent and compound objectives.

2 Probabilistic Assumptions for the Answer Span

This section describes the common approach to the EQA, with its independent modelling of the answer span start and end positions. Secondly, it defines an assumption based on conditional factorization of span probability. Finally a function family for computing joint span probability and a combination of independent and joint assumption we call the *compound* objective are proposed.

The EQA can be defined as follows: Given a question q and a passage or a set of passages D, find a string a from D such that a answers the question q. This can be expressed by modelling a categorical probability mass function (PMF) that has its maximum in the answer start and end indices $a = \langle a_s, a_e \rangle$ from the passage D as $P(a_s, a_e|q, D)$ for each question-passage-answer triplet (q, D, a) from dataset $\mathcal{D}$. The parameters θ of such model can be estimated by minimizing maximum likelihood objective

$$- \sum_{(q,D,a)\in\mathcal{D}} \log P_\theta(a_s, a_e|q, D). \qquad (1)$$

During inference, the most probable answer span $\langle a_s, a_e \rangle$ is predicted. Although there are works that were able to model the joint probability explicitly (Lee et al., 2016), modelling it directly results in a number of categories quadratic to the passage's length. Optimizing such models may be seen challenging, as there are often more classes than the amount of data points within the current datasets. Therefore, state-of-the-art approaches resort to independence assumption $P(a_s, a_e|q, D) = P_\theta(a_s|q, D)P_\theta(a_e|q, D)$. The factorized PMFs are usually computed by the model with shared parameters θ, as introduced in Wang and Jiang (2017). For most of the systems modelling the *independent objective* with neural networks, the final endpoint probabilities[3] are derived from start/end position passage representations computed via shared model $\boldsymbol{H}_s$,$\boldsymbol{H}_e \in \mathbb{R}^{d\times L}$ as shown for $b \in \{s, e\}$.

$$P_\theta(a_b) = \text{softmax}(\boldsymbol{w}_b^\top \boldsymbol{H}_b + \boldsymbol{b}_b) \qquad (2)$$

The passage representations $\boldsymbol{H}_s$,$\boldsymbol{H}_e$ are often presoftmax layer representations from neural network with passage and question at the input. Symbols d and L denote the model-specific dimension and the passage length, respectively.

[3]For brevity, q, D dependencies are further omitted and bias terms are broadcasted along dimension L.

Occasionally, the conditional factorization $P(a_s, a_e|q, D) = P_\theta(a_s)P_\theta(a_e|a_s)$ is considered instead. The probabilities of span's start and end are computed the same way as in equation 2. The difference is in the end representations $\boldsymbol{H}_e = f(a_s)$, which now must be the a function of span's start a_s.

2.1 Joint Assumptions

However, one does not need to apply simplifying assumptions and instead compute joint probability directly. We define a family of *joint* probability functions $P_\theta(a_s, a_e)$ with an arbitrary vector-to-vector similarity function f_{sim} used for obtaining each span score (e. g., the dot product $\boldsymbol{H}_s^\top \boldsymbol{H}_e$)[4].

$$P_\theta(a_s, a_e) = \text{softmax}(\text{vec}(f_{sim}(\boldsymbol{H}_s, \boldsymbol{H}_e))) \tag{3}$$

Finally, we define a multi-task *compound* objective (4) composing the joint and independent probability formulations, computed via a shared model θ.

$$-\sum_{(q,D,a)\in\mathcal{D}} \log P_\theta(a_s, a_e)P_\theta(a_s)P_\theta(a_e) \tag{4}$$

Here $P(a_s)P(a_e)$ can be seen as a auxiliary objective for the more complex joint objective $P_\theta(a_s, a_e)$ used for decoding in test time. Empirically, we found the *compound* objective to be superior or equal to other assumptions.

3 Experimental Setup

We use Transformers (Wolf et al., 2019) for language representation model (LRM) implementation. Our experiments were done on 16GB GPUs using PyTorch (Paszke et al., 2019). For experiments with LRMs, we used Adam optimizer with a decoupled weight decay (Loshchilov and Hutter, 2017). The used hyperparameters were the same as the SQuADv1.1 default hyperparameters as proposed by specific LRM authors through all our datasets. For BIDAF, we tuned hyperparameters using Hyperopt (Bergstra et al., 2013) separately for independent and compound objectives[5]. See Appendix D for further details.

In all our experiments, we apply *length filtering* (LF). Therefore, probabilities $P(a_s = i, a_e = j)$ are set to 0 iff $j - i > \zeta$, where ζ is a length threshold. Following Devlin et al. (2019), we set $\zeta = 30$ in all of our experiments.

3.1 Similarity Functions

Here we sum up the definitions of similarity functions presented in the paper. We experimented with 5 similarity functions. For each start representation $\boldsymbol{h_s} \in \mathbb{R}^d$ and end representation $\boldsymbol{h_e} \in \mathbb{R}^d$, both column vectors from the matrix of boundary vectors $\boldsymbol{H}_s$, $\boldsymbol{H}_e \in \mathbb{R}^{d\times L}$ respectively. Note that d here is model specific dimension, L is passage length, $\circ$ denotes elementwise multiplication and ; denotes concatenation. The similarity functions above these representations are defined as:

- A dot product:

$$f_{dot}(\boldsymbol{h_s}, \boldsymbol{h_e}) = \boldsymbol{h_s}^\top \boldsymbol{h_e} \tag{5}$$

- A weighted dot product:

$$f_{wdot}(\boldsymbol{h_s}, \boldsymbol{h_e}) = \boldsymbol{w}^\top[\boldsymbol{h_s} \circ \boldsymbol{h_e}] \tag{6}$$

- An additive similarity:

$$f_{add}(\boldsymbol{h_s}, \boldsymbol{h_e}) = \boldsymbol{w}^\top[\boldsymbol{h_s}; \boldsymbol{h_e}] \tag{7}$$

- An additive similarity combined with weighted product:

$$f_{madd}(\boldsymbol{h_s}, \boldsymbol{h_e}) = \boldsymbol{w}^\top[\boldsymbol{h_s}; \boldsymbol{h_e}; \boldsymbol{h_s} \circ \boldsymbol{h_e}] \tag{8}$$

- A multi-layer perceptron (MLP) as proposed by Lee et al. (2019):

$$f_{MLP}(\boldsymbol{h_s}, \boldsymbol{h_e}) = \boldsymbol{w}^\top\sigma(\boldsymbol{W}[\boldsymbol{h_s}; \boldsymbol{h_e}] + \boldsymbol{b}) + \boldsymbol{b_2} \tag{9}$$

where $\sigma(x) = ln(relu(x))$ and ln denotes layer normalization (Ba et al., 2016).

3.2 Applied Models

Our experiments are based on three EQA models: **BERT**-base (Devlin et al., 2019) and **ALBERT**-xxlarge (Lan et al., 2020) are LRMs based on the self-supervised pretraining objective. During fine-tuning, each model receives the concatenation of question and passage are given as input. Outputs $\boldsymbol{H} \in \mathbb{R}^{d\times L}$ corresponding to the passage inputs of length L are then reduced to boundary probabilities by two vectors $\boldsymbol{w_s}$, $\boldsymbol{w_e}$ as $P(a_b) = \text{softmax}(\boldsymbol{w}_b^\top \boldsymbol{H} + \boldsymbol{b}_b)$ where $b \in \{s, e\}$.

[4]Here, we slightly abuse the notation for the sake of generality. See Subsection 3.2 for specific applications.

[5]We used f_{madd} similarity during parameter tuning.

To compute joint probability $P(a_s, a_e)$, start representations are computed using $\boldsymbol{W} \in \mathbb{R}^{d\times d}$ and $\boldsymbol{b} \in \mathbb{R}^d$ (broadcasted) as $\boldsymbol{H}_s = \boldsymbol{W}\boldsymbol{H} + \boldsymbol{b}$ and end representations as $\boldsymbol{H}_e = \boldsymbol{H}$. A dot product f_{dot} is used as the similarity measure.

$$P(a_s, a_e) = \mathrm{softmax}(\mathrm{vec}(\boldsymbol{H}_s^\top \boldsymbol{H}_e)) \quad (10)$$

For modelling conditional probability factorization objective, we follow the implementation from (Lan et al., 2020), and provide exact details in the Appendix B.

BIDAF (Seo et al., 2017) dominated the state-of-the-art systems in 2016 and motivated a lot of following research work (Clark and Gardner, 2018; Yu et al., 2018). Question and passage inputs are represented via the fusion of word-level embeddings from GloVe (Pennington et al., 2014) and character-level word embeddings obtained via a convolutional neural network. Next, a recurrent layer is applied to both. Independently represented questions and passages are then combined into a common representation via two directions of attention over their similarity matrix $\boldsymbol{S}$. The similarity matrix is computed via multiplicative-additive interaction (11) between each pair of question vector $\boldsymbol{q_i}$ and passage vector $\boldsymbol{p_j}$, where ; denotes concatenation and $\circ$ stands for the Hadamard product.

$$\boldsymbol{S_{ij}} = f_{madd}(\boldsymbol{q_i}, \boldsymbol{p_j}) = \boldsymbol{w}^\top[\boldsymbol{q_i}; \boldsymbol{p_j}; \boldsymbol{q_i} \circ \boldsymbol{p_j}] \quad (11)$$

Common representations are then concatenated together with document representations yielding $\boldsymbol{G}$ and passed towards two more recurrent layers producing $\boldsymbol{M}$ and $\boldsymbol{M}^2$ – first to obtain answer-start representations $\boldsymbol{H}_s = [\boldsymbol{G}; \boldsymbol{M}]$ and second to obtain answer-end representations[6] $\boldsymbol{H}_e = [\boldsymbol{G}; \boldsymbol{M}^2]$. The joint probability $P(a_s, a_e)$ is then computed over scores from vectorized similarity matrix of $\boldsymbol{H}_s$ and $\boldsymbol{H}_e$ using the 2-layer feed-forward network f_{MLP} as a similarity function.

3.3 Datasets

We evaluate our approaches on a wide spectrum of datasets. We do not split development datasets, as we use fixed hyperparameters with fixed amount of steps and use last checkpoint for our LRM experiments. This also makes our results directly comparable to other works (Devlin et al., 2019; Lan et al., 2020). The statistics to all datasets are shown in Table 1. To focus only on the extractive part of QA and to keep the format the same, we use curated versions of the last 3 datasets as released in MrQA shared task (Fisch et al., 2019).

[6]For details, see formulae 2 to 4 in Seo et al. (2017).

Dataset	Train	Test
SQuADv1.1	87,599	10,570
SQuADv2.0	130,319	11,873
Adversarial SQuAD	-	3,560
Natural Questions	104,071	12,836
NewsQA	74,160	4,212
TriviaQA	61,688	7,785

Table 1: Number of examples per each dataset used in this paper.

SQuADv1.1 (Rajpurkar et al., 2016) is a popular dataset composed from question, paragraphs and answer span annotation collected from the subset of Wikipedia passages.

SQuADv2.0 (Rajpurkar et al., 2018) is an extension of SQuADv1.1 with additional 50k questions and passages, which are topically similar to the question, but do not contain an answer.

Adversarial SQuAD (Jia and Liang, 2017) tests, whether the system can answer questions about paragraphs that contain adversarially inserted sentences, which are automatically generated to distract computer systems without changing the correct answer or misleading humans. In particular, our system is evaluated in ADDSENT adversary setting, which runs the model as a black box for each question on several paragraphs containing different adversarial sentences and picks the worst answer.

Natural Questions (Kwiatkowski et al., 2019) dataset consists of real users queries obtained from Google search engine. Each example is accompanied by a relevant Wikipedia article found by the search engine, and human annotation for long/short answer. The long answer is typically the most relevant paragraph from the article, while short answer consists of one or multiple entities or short text spans. We only consider short answers in this work.

NewsQA (Trischler et al., 2017) is a crowd-sourced dataset based on CNN news articles. Answers are short text spans and the questions are designed such that they require reasoning and inference besides simple text matching.

TriviaQA (Joshi et al., 2017) consists of question-answer pairs from 14 different trivia quiz websites and independent evidence passages collected using Bing search from various sources such as news, encyclopedias, blog posts and others. Additional evidence is obtained from Wikipedia through entity linker.

3.4 Statistical Testing

To improve the soundness of the presented results, we use several statistical tests. An exact match (EM) metric can be viewed as an average of samples from Bernoulli distribution. As stated via central limit theorem, a good assumption might be the EM comes from the normal distribution. We train 10 models for each presented LRM's result, obtaining 10 EMs for each sample. *Anderson-Darling* normality test (Stephens, 1974) is used to check this assumption – whether the sample truly comes from the normal distribution. Then we use the *one-tailed paired t-test* to check whether the case of improvement is significant. The improvement is significant iff p-value < 0.05. We use the reference implementation from Dror et al. (2018).

4 Results and Discussion

We now show the effectiveness of proposed approaches. Each of the presented results is averaged from 10 training runs.

	EM	F1	EM	F1
I	66.16	76.19	81.31	88.65
I+J	BIDAF		BERT	
f_{dot}	64.30	73.84	**81.83**	**88.52**
f_{add}	66.04	75.10	81.52	88.47
f_{wdot}	66.10	75.16	81.35	88.29
f_{madd}	66.11	75.23	81.45	88.44
f_{MLP}	**66.96**	**75.90**	81.61	88.44

Table 3: A comparison of similarity functions in the models trained via *compound* objective (I+J) and *independent* objective (I).

Similarity functions. We analyzed an effect of different similarity functions over all models in Table 3. We found different similarity functions to work better with different architectures. Namely, for BIDAF, most of similarity functions work equally or worse than independent objective. Exceptionally, f_{MLP} works significantly better. This is surprising especially because we tuned the hyperparameters with the f_{madd} function. For BERT, most of the similarity functions performed better than the independent objective and simple dot-product f_{dot} improved significantly better above all. We choose f_{MLP} for BIDAF and f_{dot} for our LRMs for the rest of experiments.

Comparison of objectives. Our main results – the performance of *independent* (I), *joint* (J), *joint-conditional* (JC) and *compound* (I+J) objectives – are shown in Table 2. We note the largest improvements can be seen for an exact match (EM) performance metric. In fact, in some cases objectives modelling joint PMF lead to degradation of F1, while improving EM (e.g., on SQuADv1.1 and NewsQA datasets for BERT). Upon manual analysis of BERT's predictions based on 200 differences between independent and compound models on SQuADv1.1, we found that in 10 cases (5%) the independent model chooses larger span encompassing multiple potential answers, thus obtaining non-zero F1 score. In 9 out of 10 of these cases, we found the compound model to pick just one of these potential answers[7], obtaining either full match or no F1 score at all. We found no cases of compound model encompassing multiple potential answers in analyzed sample.

Next, we remark that compound objective outperformed others in most of our experiments. In BERT case, the compound objective performed significantly better than independent objective on 5 out of 6 datasets. In ALBERT case, the compound objective performed significantly better than independent objective 5 from 6 times and it was on par in the last case. Comparing compound to joint objective in BERT case, the two behave almost equally, with compound objective significantly outperforming joint objective on the two SQuAD datasets and no significant differences for the other 4 datasets. However, in ALBERT case, the compound objective significantly improves results over joint objective in all but one case and is on par in this last case.

Conditional objective. Our implementation of the conditional objective performs even or worse than independent objective in most cases. Upon investigation we found the model tends to be overconfident about start predictions and underconfident about its end predictions, often assigning high probability to single answer-start. In Table 5, we analyze the top-5 most probable samples from BERT on each example of SQuADv1.1 dev data. We found that on average the conditional model kept it top-1 start prediction in 90% of subsequent top-2

[7]For instance, in Table 7, row 4, column 3, we consider 2,000; 40,000; 2,200; 1,294 and 427 as potential answers.

Model	Obj	SQ1	SQ2	AdvSQ	TriviaQA	NQ	NewsQA
BERT	I	81.31/88.65	**73.89**/76.74	47.04/52.62	62.88/69.85	65.66/78.20	52.39/67.17
	J	81.33/88.13	72.66/75.04	48.10/53.54	**63.93**/69.90	**67.75**/78.70	52.73/66.41
	JC	81.22/88.29	71.51/74.38	46.07/51.35	62.82/69.94	66.48/77.34	52.39/67.05
	I+J	***81.83***/88.52	73.53/76.14	***48.32***/53.47	*63.73*/69.75	***67.75***/78.81	***52.96***/66.83
ALBERT	I	88.55/94.62	87.07/90.02	68.12/73.54	74.7/80.33	70.78/83.42	59.95/75.0
	J	88.84/94.64	86.87/89.71	68.90/74.17	75.11/80.41	**73.36/84.01**	60.19/74.28
	JC	88.60/94.59	86.78/89.73	68.0/73.25	-	72.33/83.35	58.52/72.74
	I+J	***89.02***/94.77	**87.13**/89.98	***69.57***/74.76	***75.31***/80.43	*73.32*/84.08	***60.41***/74.46

Table 2: EM/F1 results of different objectives through the spectrum of datasets. Bold results mark best EM across the objectives. Italicised I+J results mark significant improvement over the independent objective.

Model		I	J	JC	I+J
BIDAF	-	65.85/75.94	-	-	66.95/75.89
	LF	**66.16/76.19**	58.24/67.42	-	66.96/75.90
BERT	-	80.98/88.40	81.30/88.11	81.16/88.25	81.80/88.50
	LF	**81.31/88.65**	81.33/88.13	81.22/88.29	81.83/88.52
ALBERT	-	88.39/94.51	88.82/94.64	88.57/94.57	89.01/94.77
	LF	**88.55/94.63**	88.84/94.64	88.60/94.59	89.02/94.77

Table 4: SQuADv1.1 EM/F1 results with length filtering (LF) computed from the same set of checkpoints. Differences larger than 0.1 are in bold.

to top-5 less probable answers, but kept its top-1 end prediction only in 4% of top-2 to top-5 subsequent answers. We found this statistic to be on par for start/end prediction for different objectives. Interestingly, the table also reveals that independent objective contains less diverse start/end tokens than joint objectives.

Model	Start Token	End Token
I	43.76%	45.66%
JC	90.12%	3.9%
J	33.71%	35.91%
I+J	34.95%	37.27%

Table 5: Proportion of samples, on which top-1 prediction start/end token was kept as start/end token also in top-2 to top-5 subsequent predictions.

Large improvements and degradation. Upon closer inspection of results, we found possible reasons for result degradation of the compound model on SQuADv2.0, and also its large improvements gained on NQ dataset.

For SQuADv2.0, the accuracies of no-answer detection for independent/joint/compound objectives in case of BERT models are 79.89/78.12/79.32. We found the same trend for ALBERT. We hypothesize, that this inferior performance of joint and compound models may be caused by the model having to learn a more complex problem of K^2 classes of all possible spans over input document, which is often more (e.g. for $K = 512$) than the size of the datasets, leaving the less of "model capacity" to this another task. To confirm that compound model is better at answer extraction step, we run all 10 checkpoints trained on SQuADv2.0 data with an answer, while masking model's no-answer option. The results shown in Table 6 support this hypothesis.

	Objective	EM	F1
BERT	I	80.70	88.71
	J	81.38	81.51
	I+J	81.51	88.69
ALBERT	I	87.40	94.10
	J	87.74	94.31
	I+J	87.90	94.38

Table 6: Performance of SQuADv2.0 models on answerable examples of SQuADv2.0.

On the other side, we found the large improvements over NQ might be exaggerated by the evaluation approach of MRQA, wherein the case of multi-span answers, choosing one of the spans from multi-span answer counts as correct. Upon closer result inspection, we found that the independent model here was prone to select the start of one span from multi-span answer and end of different span from multi-span answer. To quantify this behavior, we annotated 100 random predictions with multi-span answers in original NaturalQuestions on whether they pick just one span from multi-span answer (which follows from the MRQA formulation) or they encompass multiple spans. For independent/compound objectives we found 59/77 cases of picking just one of the spans and 22/4 cases of encompassing multiple spans from multi-span answer for BERT model and 57/81 and 33/10 cases for ALBERT respectively.

Length filtering heuristic. Additionally, we found the benefit from the commonly used length filtering (LF) heuristic is negligible for models trained via any joint objective, as shown in Table 4. Therefore, we find it unnecessary to use the heuristic anymore. In this experiment, we also include our results with BIDAF, which show significant improvement of compound objective on SQuADv1.1 dataset from other approaches.

5 Analysis

Apart from example in Figure 1, we provide more examples of different predictions[8] between models trained with independent and compound objective in Table 7. In general, by doing manual analysis of errors, we noticed three types of trivially wrong errors being fixed by the compound objective model in BERT:

1. Uncertainty of the model causes it to assign high probabilities to two different answer boundaries. During decoding the start/end boundaries of two different answers are picked up (fourth row in Table 7).
2. The model assigns high probability to answer surrounded by the paired punctuation marks (e. g. quotes). It chooses the answer without respecting the symmetry between paired punctuation marks (third row of Table 7).
3. Uncertainty of the model causes it to assign high probabilities to two spans containing the same answer string. This is the special case of problem (1) – while the model often chooses the correct answer, the boundaries of two different spans are selected (first row of Table 7).

To quantify an occurrence of these errors, we study our best BERT and ALBERT checkpoint predictions for SQuADv1.1 validation data. For BERT, we found the most frequently occurring is the error type (1), for which we manually annotated 200 random differences between independent and compound model predictions. We found *5%* of them to be the case of this error of the independent, and no case of this error for the compound model. Interestingly, 4 out of 10 of these cases were questions clearly asking about single entity, while independent model answered multiple entities, e.g., *Q:Which male child of Ghengis Khan and Börte was born last? A:Chagatai (1187—1241), Ögedei (1189—1241), and Tolui*. For the error type (2), we filtered all prediction differences (more than 1300 for BERT and ALBERT) down to cases, where either independent or compound prediction contained non-alphanumeric paired punctuation marks, which resulted in less than 30 cases for each. For BERT, *37%* independent predictions from these cases contained an error type (2), while again no paired punctuation marks errors were observed for compound objective.

For the error type (3), we filter prediction differences down to cases, where independent or compound prediction contained the same prefix and suffix of length at least 2 (only 9 and 5 cases for BERT and ALBERT). From these, error type (3) occurred in 3 cases for BERT and in 1 case for ALBERT in case of independent and again we found no case for the compound for both models. Note the error type (3) can be fully alleviated by marginalizing over probabilities of top-K answer spans during the inference, as in (Das et al., 2019; Cheng et al., 2020) (see Appendix E for details). Interestingly, for ALBERT, we found only negligible amount of errors of type (1) and (2) for both objectives[9].

During manual analysis, we observed that, an uncertain models with an independent objective are prone to pick large answer spans. To illustrate, that spans retrieved with approaches modelling joint probability differ, we took the top 20 most probable spans from each model and averaged their length.

This was done for each example in the SQuADv1.1 test data. The histogram of these averages is shown in Figure 2. For a fair comparison, these predictions were filtered via length filtering.

[8]We chose to analyze the different predictions, as the model is usually more uncertain in these borderline cases.

[9]The full difference of BERT's and ALBERT's predictions and manual analysis can be found in the supplementary.

Question	Passage	Independent	Compound	Ground Truth
What company won a free advertisement due to the QuickBooks contest?	QuickBooks sponsored a "Small Business Big Game" contest, in which Death Wish Coffee had a 30-second commercial aired free of charge courtesy of QuickBooks. Death Wish Coffee beat out nine other contenders from across the United States for the free advertisement.	Death Wish Coffee had a 30-second commercial aired free of charge courtesy of QuickBooks. Death Wish Coffee	Death Wish Coffee	Death Wish Coffee
In what city's Marriott did the Panthers stay?	The Panthers used the San Jose State practice facility and stayed at the San Jose Marriott. The Broncos practiced at Stanford University and stayed at the Santa Clara Marriott.	San Jose State practice facility and stayed at the San Jose	San Jose	San Jose
What was the first point of the Reformation?	Luther's rediscovery of "Christ and His salvation" was the first of two points that became the foundation for the Reformation. His railing against the sale of indulgences was based on it.	Christ and His salvation"	Christ and His salvation	Christ and His salvation
How many species of bird and mammals are there in the Amazon region?	The region is home to about 2.5 million insect species, tens of thousands of plants, and some 2,000 birds and mammals. To date, at least 40,000 plant species, 2,200 fishes, 1,294 birds, 427 mammals, 428 amphibians, and 378 reptiles have been scientifically classified in the region. One in five of all the bird species in theworld live in the rainforests of the Amazon, and one in five of the fishspecies live in Amazonian rivers and streams. Scientists have describedbetween 96,660 and 128,843 invertebrate species in Brazil alone.	2,000 birds and mammals. To date, at least 40,000 plant species, 2,200 fishes, 1,294 birds, 427	427	2,000
What was found to be at fault for the fire in the cabin on Apollo 1 regarding the CM design?	NASA immediately convened an accident review board, overseen by both houses of Congress. While the determination of responsibility for the accident was complex, the review board concluded that "deficiencies existed in Command Module design, workmanship and quality control." At the insistence of NASA Administrator Webb, North American removed Harrison Storms as Command Module program manager. Webb also reassigned Apollo Spacecraft Program Office (ASPO) Manager Joseph Francis Shea, replacing him with George Low.	deficiencies existed in Command Module design, workmanship and quality control."	Harrison Storms	deficiencies

Table 7: Examples of predictions from SQuADv1.1 using BERT trained with independent and compound objective.

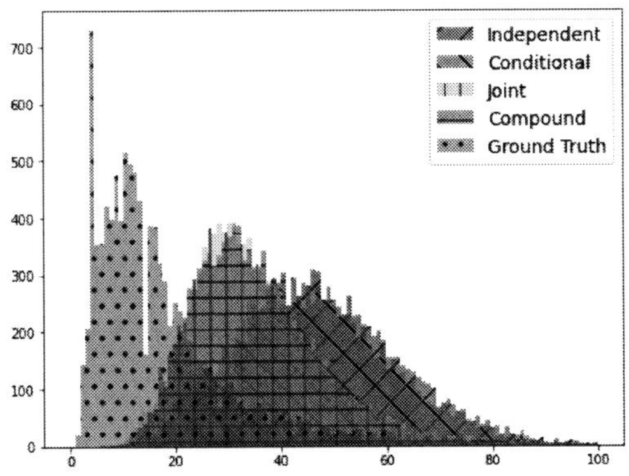

Figure 2: Histograms of average character length of top-20 predicted answers from BERT trained with different objectives compared with character length of ground-truth answers.

6 Related Work

One of the earliest works in EQA from Wang and Jiang (2017) experimented with generative models based on index sequence generation via pointer networks (Vinyals et al., 2015) and now traditional boundary models that focus on the prediction of start/end of an answer span. Their work shown substantial improvement of conditional factorization boundary models over the index sequence generative models.

Followup work on EQA (Seo et al., 2017; Chen et al., 2017; Clark and Gardner, 2018; Yu et al., 2018; Devlin et al., 2019; Cheng et al., 2020) and others considered using the assumption of independence in their objectives.

Xiong et al. (2017) explored an iterative boundary model. They used RNN and a highway maxout network to decode start/end of span independently in multiple timesteps, each time feeding the RNN with predictions from the previous time step until the prediction was not changing anymore. In their following work Xiong et al. (2018) combined their objective with a reinforcement learning approach, in which the decoded spans from each timestep were treated as a trajectory. They argued that cross-entropy is not reflecting F1 performance well enough, and defined a reward function equal to F1 score. Finally, they used policy gradients as their auxiliary objective, showing 1% improvement in the terms of F1 score.

Authors of recent LRMs like XLNet (Yang et al., 2019), ALBERT (Lan et al., 2020) or ELECTRA (Clark et al., 2020) use conditional probability factorization $P(a_e|a_s)P(a_s)$ for answer extraction in some cases[10]. Although the objective is not described in mentioned papers (except for ELECTRA), we follow the recipe for modelling the conditional probability from their implementation in this work. We believe this is the first official comparison of this objective w.r.t. others.

The most similar to our work is RASOR system (Lee et al., 2016). In their work, authors compared various objectives – binary answer classification of every input token, BIO sequence classification with CRF layer on top of their model, and most importantly joint objective, which turns out to work the best. However, in our experiments, training with the joint objective alone does not always perform that well. For BIDAF, we failed to find the hyperparameters for model to converge to results similar to different approaches.

7 Conclusion

The paper closely studies the objectives used within the extractive question answering (EQA). It identifies commonly used independent probability model as a source of trivially wrong answers. As a remedy it experiments with various ways of learning the joint span probability. Finally it shows how the *compound* objective – the combination of independent and joint probability in objective – improves statistical EQA systems across 6 datasets without using any additional data. Using the proposed approach, we were able to reach significant improvements through the wide spectrum of datasets, including +1.28 EM on Adversarial SQuAD and +2.07 EM on NaturalQuestions for BERT-base. We performed a thorough manual analysis to understand what happened to trivially wrong answers, and we found most of the cases disappear. We also found that independent models tend to "overfit" to F1 metric by encompassing multiple possible answer spans, which would explain the effect of joint objectives improving the EM far more significantly than the F1. We shown the samples from joint model contain the greatest start/end token diversity. We further hypothesize that having diverse answers may be especially beneficial towards answer reranking step commonly used in QA (Fajcik et al., 2021; Iyer et al., 2021). In addition, we also identified the reason for performance decrease with *compound* objective on SQuADv2.0 – no-answer classifier trained within the same model performs worse – and we leave the solution for this deficiency for future work.

[10]For instance, ALBERT uses conditional objective for SQuADv2.0, but not for SQuADv1.1.

Acknowledgments

This work was supported by the Czech Ministry of Education, Youth and Sports, subprogram INTERCOST, project code: LTC18054. The computation used the infrastructure supported by the Ministry of Education, Youth and Sports of the Czech Republic through the e-INFRA CZ (ID:90140).

References

Jimmy Lei Ba, Jamie Ryan Kiros, and Geoffrey E Hinton. 2016. Layer normalization. *arXiv preprint arXiv:1607.06450*.

James Bergstra, Dan Yamins, David D Cox, et al. 2013. Hyperopt: A python library for optimizing the hyperparameters of machine learning algorithms. In *Proceedings of the 12th Python in science conference*, volume 13, page 20. Citeseer.

Danqi Chen, Adam Fisch, Jason Weston, and Antoine Bordes. 2017. Reading Wikipedia to answer open-domain questions. In *Proceedings of the 55th Annual Meeting of the Association for Computational Linguistics (Volume 1: Long Papers)*, pages 1870–1879, Vancouver, Canada. Association for Computational Linguistics.

Hao Cheng, Ming-Wei Chang, Kenton Lee, and Kristina Toutanova. 2020. Probabilistic assumptions matter: Improved models for distantly-supervised document-level question answering. In *Proceedings of the 58th Annual Meeting of the Association for Computational Linguistics*, pages 5657–5667, Online. Association for Computational Linguistics.

Hao Cheng, Xiaodong Liu, Lis Pereira, Yaoliang Yu, and Jianfeng Gao. 2021. Posterior differential regularization with f-divergence for improving model robustness. In *Proceedings of the 2021 Conference of the North American Chapter of the Association for Computational Linguistics: Human Language Technologies*, pages 1078–1089, Online. Association for Computational Linguistics.

Christopher Clark and Matt Gardner. 2018. Simple and effective multi-paragraph reading comprehension. In *Proceedings of the 56th Annual Meeting of the Association for Computational Linguistics (Volume 1: Long Papers)*, pages 845–855, Melbourne, Australia. Association for Computational Linguistics.

Kevin Clark, Minh-Thang Luong, Quoc V. Le, and Christopher D. Manning. 2020. ELECTRA: pre-training text encoders as discriminators rather than generators. In *8th International Conference on*

Learning Representations, ICLR 2020, Addis Ababa, Ethiopia, April 26-30, 2020. OpenReview.net.

Rajarshi Das, Shehzaad Dhuliawala, Manzil Zaheer, and Andrew McCallum. 2019. Multi-step retriever-reader interaction for scalable open-domain question answering. In *7th International Conference on Learning Representations, ICLR 2019, New Orleans, LA, USA, May 6-9, 2019*. OpenReview.net.

Jacob Devlin, Ming-Wei Chang, Kenton Lee, and Kristina Toutanova. 2019. BERT: Pre-training of deep bidirectional transformers for language understanding. In *Proceedings of the 2019 Conference of the North American Chapter of the Association for Computational Linguistics: Human Language Technologies, Volume 1 (Long and Short Papers)*, pages 4171–4186, Minneapolis, Minnesota. Association for Computational Linguistics.

Rotem Dror, Gili Baumer, Segev Shlomov, and Roi Reichart. 2018. The hitchhiker's guide to testing statistical significance in natural language processing. In *Proceedings of the 56th Annual Meeting of the Association for Computational Linguistics (Volume 1: Long Papers)*, pages 1383–1392, Melbourne, Australia. Association for Computational Linguistics.

Martin Fajcik, Martin Docekal, Karel Ondrej, and Pavel Smrz. 2021. R2-d2: A modular baseline for open-domain question answering. In *Findings of the Association for Computational Linguistics: EMNLP 2021*, Punta Cana, Dominican Republic. Association for Computational Linguistics.

Adam Fisch, Alon Talmor, Robin Jia, Minjoon Seo, Eunsol Choi, and Danqi Chen. 2019. MRQA 2019 shared task: Evaluating generalization in reading comprehension. In *Proceedings of the 2nd Workshop on Machine Reading for Question Answering*, pages 1–13, Hong Kong, China. Association for Computational Linguistics.

Srinivasan Iyer, Sewon Min, Yashar Mehdad, and Wen-tau Yih. 2021. RECONSIDER: Improved re-ranking using span-focused cross-attention for open domain question answering. In *Proceedings of the 2021 Conference of the North American Chapter of the Association for Computational Linguistics: Human Language Technologies*, pages 1280–1287, Online. Association for Computational Linguistics.

Robin Jia and Percy Liang. 2017. Adversarial examples for evaluating reading comprehension systems. In *Proceedings of the 2017 Conference on Empirical Methods in Natural Language Processing*, pages 2021–2031, Copenhagen, Denmark. Association for Computational Linguistics.

Mandar Joshi, Eunsol Choi, Daniel Weld, and Luke Zettlemoyer. 2017. TriviaQA: A large scale distantly supervised challenge dataset for reading comprehension. In *Proceedings of the 55th Annual Meeting of the Association for Computational Linguistics (Volume 1: Long Papers)*, pages 1601–1611, Vancouver, Canada. Association for Computational Linguistics.

Omar Khattab, Christopher Potts, and Matei Zaharia. 2020. Relevance-guided supervision for openqa with colbert. *arXiv preprint arXiv:2007.00814*.

Tom Kwiatkowski, Jennimaria Palomaki, Olivia Redfield, Michael Collins, Ankur Parikh, Chris Alberti, Danielle Epstein, Illia Polosukhin, Jacob Devlin, Kenton Lee, Kristina Toutanova, Llion Jones, Matthew Kelcey, Ming-Wei Chang, Andrew M. Dai, Jakob Uszkoreit, Quoc Le, and Slav Petrov. 2019. Natural questions: A benchmark for question answering research. *Transactions of the Association for Computational Linguistics*, 7:452–466.

Zhenzhong Lan, Mingda Chen, Sebastian Goodman, Kevin Gimpel, Piyush Sharma, and Radu Soricut. 2020. ALBERT: A lite BERT for self-supervised learning of language representations. In *8th International Conference on Learning Representations, ICLR 2020, Addis Ababa, Ethiopia, April 26-30, 2020*. OpenReview.net.

Kenton Lee, Ming-Wei Chang, and Kristina Toutanova. 2019. Latent retrieval for weakly supervised open domain question answering. In *Proceedings of the 57th Annual Meeting of the Association for Computational Linguistics*, pages 6086–6096, Florence, Italy. Association for Computational Linguistics.

Kenton Lee, Shimi Salant, Tom Kwiatkowski, Ankur Parikh, Dipanjan Das, and Jonathan Berant. 2016. Learning recurrent span representations for extractive question answering. *arXiv preprint arXiv:1611.01436*.

Ilya Loshchilov and Frank Hutter. 2017. Fixing weight decay regularization in adam. *arXiv preprint arXiv:1711.05101*.

Adam Paszke, Sam Gross, Francisco Massa, Adam Lerer, James Bradbury, Gregory Chanan, Trevor Killeen, Zeming Lin, Natalia Gimelshein, Luca Antiga, Alban Desmaison, Andreas Köpf, Edward Yang, Zachary DeVito, Martin Raison, Alykhan Tejani, Sasank Chilamkurthy, Benoit Steiner, Lu Fang, Junjie Bai, and Soumith Chintala. 2019. Pytorch: An imperative style, high-performance deep learning library. In *Advances in Neural Information Processing Systems 32: Annual Conference on Neural Information Processing Systems 2019, NeurIPS 2019, December 8-14, 2019, Vancouver, BC, Canada*, pages 8024–8035.

Jeffrey Pennington, Richard Socher, and Christopher Manning. 2014. GloVe: Global vectors for word representation. In *Proceedings of the 2014 Conference on Empirical Methods in Natural Language Processing (EMNLP)*, pages 1532–1543, Doha, Qatar. Association for Computational Linguistics.

Pranav Rajpurkar, Robin Jia, and Percy Liang. 2018. Know what you don't know: Unanswerable questions for SQuAD. In *Proceedings of the 56th Annual Meeting of the Association for Computational Linguistics (Volume 2: Short Papers)*, pages 784–789, Melbourne, Australia. Association for Computational Linguistics.

Pranav Rajpurkar, Jian Zhang, Konstantin Lopyrev, and Percy Liang. 2016. SQuAD: 100,000+ questions for machine comprehension of text. In *Proceedings of the 2016 Conference on Empirical Methods in Natural Language Processing*, pages 2383–2392, Austin, Texas. Association for Computational Linguistics.

Min Joon Seo, Aniruddha Kembhavi, Ali Farhadi, and Hannaneh Hajishirzi. 2017. Bidirectional attention flow for machine comprehension. In *5th International Conference on Learning Representations, ICLR 2017, Toulon, France, April 24-26, 2017, Conference Track Proceedings*. OpenReview.net.

Michael A Stephens. 1974. Edf statistics for goodness of fit and some comparisons. *Journal of the American statistical Association*, 69(347):730–737.

Adam Trischler, Tong Wang, Xingdi Yuan, Justin Harris, Alessandro Sordoni, Philip Bachman, and Kaheer Suleman. 2017. NewsQA: A machine comprehension dataset. In *Proceedings of the 2nd Workshop on Representation Learning for NLP*, pages 191–200, Vancouver, Canada. Association for Computational Linguistics.

Oriol Vinyals, Meire Fortunato, and Navdeep Jaitly. 2015. Pointer networks. In *Advances in Neural Information Processing Systems 28: Annual Conference on Neural Information Processing Systems 2015, December 7-12, 2015, Montreal, Quebec, Canada*, pages 2692–2700.

Shuohang Wang and Jing Jiang. 2017. Machine comprehension using match-lstm and answer pointer. In *5th International Conference on Learning Representations, ICLR 2017, Toulon, France, April 24-26, 2017, Conference Track Proceedings*. OpenReview.net.

Dirk Weissenborn, Georg Wiese, and Laura Seiffe. 2017. Making neural QA as simple as possible but not simpler. In *Proceedings of the 21st Conference on Computational Natural Language Learning (CoNLL 2017)*, pages 271–280, Vancouver, Canada. Association for Computational Linguistics.

Thomas Wolf, Lysandre Debut, Victor Sanh, Julien Chaumond, Clement Delangue, Anthony Moi, Pierric Cistac, Tim Rault, Rémi Louf, Morgan Funtowicz, et al. 2019. Huggingface's transformers: State-of-the-art natural language processing. *ArXiv*, pages arXiv–1910.

Caiming Xiong, Victor Zhong, and Richard Socher. 2017. Dynamic coattention networks for question answering. In *5th International Conference on Learning Representations, ICLR 2017, Toulon, France, April 24-26, 2017, Conference Track Proceedings*. OpenReview.net.

Caiming Xiong, Victor Zhong, and Richard Socher. 2018. DCN+: mixed objective and deep residual coattention for question answering. In *6th International Conference on Learning Representations, ICLR 2018, Vancouver, BC, Canada, April 30 - May 3, 2018, Conference Track Proceedings*. OpenReview.net.

Zhilin Yang, Zihang Dai, Yiming Yang, Jaime G. Carbonell, Ruslan Salakhutdinov, and Quoc V. Le. 2019. Xlnet: Generalized autoregressive pretraining for language understanding. In *Advances in Neural Information Processing Systems 32: Annual Conference on Neural Information Processing Systems 2019, NeurIPS 2019, December 8-14, 2019, Vancouver, BC, Canada*, pages 5754–5764.

Adams Wei Yu, David Dohan, Minh-Thang Luong, Rui Zhao, Kai Chen, Mohammad Norouzi, and Quoc V. Le. 2018. Qanet: Combining local convolution with global self-attention for reading comprehension. In *6th International Conference on Learning Representations, ICLR 2018, Vancouver, BC, Canada, April 30 - May 3, 2018, Conference Track Proceedings*. OpenReview.net.

A Examples of Answer Span Distribution

This section provides a deeper insight towards most probable elements of answer span PMF.

Question: What was the first point of the Reformation?
Passage: Luther's rediscovery of "Christ and His salvation" was the first of two points that became the foundation for the Reformation. His railing against the sale of indulgences was based on it.
Ground Truth: Christ and His salvation

Confidence	Predictions from BERT-base
59.7	Christ and His salvation"
35.4	Christ and His salvation
2.3	Christ
1.3	"Christ and His salvation"
0.8	"Christ and His salvation
0.1	Christ and His salvation" was
0.1	"Christ

Figure 3: Example of answer span distribution from model trained via *independent* objective.

Confidence	Predictions from BERT-base-*compound*
71.8	Christ and His salvation
10.9	"Christ and His salvation"
4.7	Christ and His salvation"
4.6	Luther's rediscovery of "Christ and His salvation
3.1	"Christ and His salvation
1.2	Luther's rediscovery of "Christ and His salvation"
0.8	Luther's rediscovery

Figure 4: Example of answer span distribution from model trained via *compound* objective.

Question: How many species of bird and mammals are there in the Amazon region?
Passage: The region is home to about 2.5 million insect species, tens of thousands of plants, and some 2,000 birds and mammals. To date, at least 40,000 plant species, 2,200 fishes, 1,294 birds, 427 mammals, 428 amphibians, and 378 reptiles have been scientifically classified in the region. One in five of all the bird species in the world live in the rainforests of the Amazon, and one in five of the fish species live in Amazonian rivers and streams. Scientists have described between 96,660 and 128,843 invertebrate species in Brazil alone.
Ground Truth: 2,000

Confidence	Predictions from BERT-base
37.0	2,000 birds and mammals. To date, at least 40,000 plant species, 2,200 fishes, 1,294 birds, 427
34.6	427
27.7	2,000
0.2	1,294 birds, 427
0.2	427 mammals
0.1	2,000 birds
0.1	2,000 birds and mammals

Figure 5: Example of answer span distribution from model trained via *independent* objective.

Confidence	Predictions from BERT-base-*compound*
71.7	427
21.5	2,000
5.1	2,000 birds and mammals. To date, at least 40,000 plant species, 2,200 fishes, 1,294 birds, 427
0.8	some 2,000
0.2	427 mammals
0.1	1,294 birds, 427
0.1	2,000 birds and mammals. To date, at least 40,000 plant species, 2,200 fishes, 1,294

Figure 6: Example of answer span distribution from model trained via *compound* objective.

B Conditional Objective

Some of the recent LRMs assume conditional factorization of span's PMF. For comparison with our joint objective, we reimplemented the conditional objective used in ALBERT (Lan et al., 2020).

First, the probabilities $\boldsymbol{P}(a_s)$ for the start position are computed in the same manner as for the independent objective – by applying a linear transformation layer on top of representations $\boldsymbol{H} \in \mathbb{R}^{d\times L}$ from the last layer of the LRM, where d is the model dimension and L denotes the input sequence length.

$$\boldsymbol{P}(a_s) \propto \exp\left(\boldsymbol{w}_s^\top \boldsymbol{H} + \boldsymbol{b_s}\right) \tag{12}$$

During the validation, top k ($k = 10$ in our experiments) start positions are selected from these probabilities, while in the training phase, we apply teacher forcing by only selecting the correct start position. Representation of i-th start position $\boldsymbol{h}_i$ from the last layer of the LRM corresponding to the selected position is then concatenated with representations corresponding to all the other positions $k = 0..L$ into matrix $\boldsymbol{C}$.

$$\boldsymbol{C} = \begin{bmatrix} - & [\boldsymbol{h_0}; \boldsymbol{h_i}] & - \\ - & [\boldsymbol{h_1}; \boldsymbol{h_i}] & - \\ & \vdots & \\ - & [\boldsymbol{h_n}; \boldsymbol{h_i}] & - \end{bmatrix} \tag{13}$$

Subsequently, a layer with tanh activation is applied on this matrix $\boldsymbol{C}$, followed by a linear transformation to obtain the end probabilities:

$$\boldsymbol{P}(a_e|a_s = i) \propto \exp\left(\boldsymbol{w}_c^\top \tanh\left(\boldsymbol{WC} + \boldsymbol{b'}\right) + \boldsymbol{b}\right) \tag{14}$$

For each start position we again select top k end positions, to obtain k^2-best list of answer spans. In contrast to the official ALBERT implementation, we omitted a layer normalization after *tanh* layer.

C Addressing the Complexity

One may ask what complexity joint modelling objectives come with independently of the underlying architecture. Given that L is the length of the input's passage and d is the model dimension, the independent objective contains only linear transformation and is in $\mathrm{O}(dL)$ for time and memory, assuming the multiplication and addition are constant operations. For the rest of this analysis, we will denote both time and memory complexities as just complexity, as they are the same for the analyzed cases.

The conditional objective increases the complexity for both only constantly, having an extra feed-forward network for end token representations. However, one may experience a significant computational slowdown, because of the beam search. Having a beam size k and a minibatch size b, the end probabilities cannot be computed in parallel with start probabilities, and have to be computed for the kb cases.

For the direct joint probability modelling, the complexity largely depends on the similarity function. The easiest case is f_{dot}, where in theory the complexity rises to $\mathrm{O}(dL^2)$, but in practice the dot product is well optimized and has a barely noticeable impact on the speed or memory.

For the f_{add} the complexity is given by the linear projection $\boldsymbol{H_* w_*}$ being in $\mathrm{O}(dL)$ and outer summation of two vectors $\boldsymbol{H_s w_1} \oplus \boldsymbol{H_e w_2}$, which is in $\mathrm{O}(L^2)$, where $\boldsymbol{w} = [\boldsymbol{w_1}, \boldsymbol{w_2}]$ and $\boldsymbol{H_*} \in \mathbb{R}^{n\times d}$ are the start/end representation matrices. Therefore the complexity is $\mathrm{O}(dL + L^2)$. We observed that in practice this approach is not very different from f_{dot}, probably due to d being close to L.

Next, a weighted product f_{wdot} can be efficiently implemented as $\boldsymbol{H_s}(\boldsymbol{w} \circ \boldsymbol{H_e})$, where $\boldsymbol{w}$ is broadcasted over every end representation in $\boldsymbol{H_e}$. In this case, the complexity stays the same as for f_{dot}.

To demonstrate that in practice the speed and memory requirements between independent and joint approach are comparable, one BERT epoch on SQuADv1.1 took about 47 minutes and 4.2GB of memory with the same batch size 2 on 12GB 2080Ti GPU with both objective variants. We observed the same requirements for all direct joint probability modelling methods mentioned so far.

Finally, the most complex approach is clearly f_{MLP}. While an a theoretical time and memory complexity of an efficient implementation[11] is in $\mathrm{O}(d^2L + dL^2)$, the complexity of this approach can be improved by pruning down the number of possible spans (and the probability space). Assuming the maximum length of the span is $k \ll L$, one can reduce the complexity to $\mathrm{O}(d^2L + dLk)$ (an approach adopted in Lee et al. (2019)). To illustrate this complexity, BERT model with the full probability space on SQuADv1.1 with batch size 2 took 76 minutes per epoch while allocating 8.2GB of

[11] The linear transformation $d \times 2d$ can be applied to each start or end vector separately, and only then the start/end vectors have to be outer-summed.

Model		I	J	I+J
BIDAF	LF	66.16/76.19	58.24/67.42	66.96/75.90
	SF	66.20/76.21	-	66.99/75.90
BERT	LF	81.31/88.65	81.33/88.13	81.83/88.52
	SF	81.38/88.68	81.23/87.97	81.65/88.36
ALBERT	LF	88.55/94.63	88.84/94.64	89.02/94.77
	SF	88.53/94.00	88.28/94.10	88.68/94.49

Table 8: SQuADv1.1 EM/F1 results with length filtering (LF) and LF + surface form filtering (SF).

GPU memory (we were unable to fit larger batch size to 12GB GPU).

D Hyperparameters

The exact hyperparameters used in this work are documented in our code. We note that for BERT and ALBERT, we simply followed the hyperparameters proposed by the authors for SQuADv1.1. In case of LRM models, each input context is split into windows as proposed by Devlin et al. (2019). Each input sequence has maximum length 384, questions are truncated to 64 tokens and context is split with overlap stride 128. For SQuADv2.0, we follow the BERT's approach for computing the no-answer logit in test-time. Having the set of k windows W_e for each example e, we compute the null-score $ns_w = \text{logit}P(a_s = 0) + \text{logit}P(a_e = 0)$ for each window $w \in W_e$. For joint and compound objectives $ns_w = \text{logit}P(a_s = 0, a_e = 0)$. Defining that for each window w the best non-null answer logit is a_w, the no-answer logit is then given by the difference of lowest null-score and best-answer score $\Gamma = \min_{w \in W_e}(ns_w) - \max_{w \in W_e}(a_w)$ among all windows of example e. The threshold for Γ is determined on the validation data via official script.

E Marginalizing Over the Same String Forms

To alleviate the error type (3) from section 5, we experimented with marginalizing over probabilities of top-100 answers (so-called surface form filtering). This is done via summing the probabilities into the most probable string occurrence, and setting the probability of the rest to 0. The results for all trained models averaged over 10 checkpoints are presented in Table 8. Note this approach sometimes hurts performance, especially in the case of joint probability approaches, where this error type happens very rarely.

What Would it Take to get Biomedical QA Systems into Practice?

Gregory Kell and **Iain J. Marshall**
King's College London
{name.surname}@kcl.ac.uk

Byron C. Wallace
Northeastern University
b.wallace@northeastern.edu

André Jaun
Metadvice
ajaun@metadvice.com

Abstract

Medical question answering (QA) systems have the potential to answer clinicians' uncertainties about treatment and diagnosis on-demand, informed by the latest evidence. However, despite the significant progress in general QA made by the NLP community, medical QA systems are still not widely used in clinical environments. One likely reason for this is that clinicians may not readily trust QA system outputs, in part because transparency, trustworthiness, and provenance have not been key considerations in the design of such models. In this paper we discuss a set of criteria that, if met, we argue would likely increase the utility of biomedical QA systems, which may in turn lead to adoption of such systems in practice. We assess existing models, tasks, and datasets with respect to these criteria, highlighting shortcomings of previously proposed approaches and pointing toward what might be more usable QA systems.

1 Introduction

During consultations in primary care, clinicians generate at least one question for every two patients (Del Fiol et al., 2014). Nonetheless, clinicians look for answers to only half of the questions due to time constraints and the belief that answers to certain questions do not exist (Del Fiol et al., 2014), despite the plethora of available evidence (Bastian et al., 2010). When clinicians do search for answers, they usually spend fewer than three minutes per question doing so (Del Fiol et al., 2014; Hoogendam et al., 2008).

Our focus in this paper is on questions pertaining to patient care decisions, for example seeking guidance about diagnosis or treatment. Ideally, clinicians would search for answers to such questions with reference to high-quality studies and up-to-date evidence syntheses, typically indexed in medical databases such as PubMed[1] and the Cochrane Library.[2] This practice of emphasizing use of rigorous empirical evidence is known as *evidence-based medicine* (EBM). Under this framework, evidence compiled from *all relevant high-quality research* (in the form of, e.g., systematic reviews and rigorously produced clinical guidelines) is preferred to individual studies or expert opinion (Ebell et al., 2004; Guyatt et al., 2008; Alper and Haynes, 2016a). Unfortunately, searching existing sources for relevant, high-quality information is onerous. Due to the time constraints imposed on clinicians, this leads to widespread reliance on general information sources such as Google (Hider et al., 2009). However, while simple to use, general-purpose search engines rank results according to criteria not directly aligned with EBM principles such as rigour, comprehensiveness, and reliability (Hider et al., 2009).

Aside from internet search, clinicians often engage in informal discussions about decisions with colleagues in what are sometimes referred to as "curbside consultations" (Papermaster and Champion, 2017, 2020; O'leary and Mhaolrúnaigh, 2012). It is common for practitioners to engage in at least one such discussion per week for practical reasons, including convenience, or an urgent need for information (Smith, 1996). These inform the "mindlines" that clinicians acquire over their careers (i.e., mental models of medicine) and that are also based on other sources including guideline documents, training, background reading, and experience (Gabbay and le May, 2016). However, the information exchanged in informal consultations may be inaccurate, incomplete, and lead to practice influenced more by expert opinion than the scientific literature (Papermaster and Champion, 2017).

Medical question answering (QA) systems have the potential to address these issues by answering clinicians' questions in real-time on the ba-

[1]https://pubmed.ncbi.nlm.nih.gov

[2]https://www.cochranelibrary.com

Proceedings of the 3rd Workshop on Machine Reading for Question Answering , pages 28–41

sis of the latest evidence. This has motivated development of QA systems and associated medical QA datasets used to train them. For example, BioASQ (Tsatsaronis et al., 2015) and PubMedQA (Jin et al., 2019) have been created to train and evaluate systems that answer clinicians' questions based on medical research literature, while emrQA (Pampari et al., 2018), emrKBQA (Raghavan et al., 2021) and why-QA (Fan, 2019) were constructed using queries concerning patient data from electronic health records (EHRs). MEDIQA-QA (Ben Abacha et al., 2019) and LiveQA-Medical (Abacha et al., 2017) are datasets designed for systems that answer consumer (patient) queries. MEDIQA-AnS (Savery et al., 2020) accompanies the answers from MEDIQA-QA with summaries that consumers would understand more easily. Systems for QA over EHRs aim to answer questions about the medical history or prior care of individual patients. By contrast, our focus here is on systems that can provide general evidence-based guidance in response to queries; we therefore omit emrQA, emrKBQA and why-QA from our discussion.

Existing biomedical QA systems that answer questions with reference to the medical literature typically provide answers in the form of yes/no, factoids, lists, and/or definitions (Sarrouti and Ouatik El Alaoui, 2020; Ben Abacha and Zweigenbaum, 2015; Cao et al., 2011; Zahid et al., 2018; Yu et al., 2007) without supplying justifications, e.g., source journals, extracted text snippets, and/or associated statistics. However, this answer format does not readily translate into clinical practice.

Take, for example, the question "Which antibiotic should I use for urinary tract infections?". A factoid-based QA system might (reasonably) return the answer "trimethoprim 200mg". However, a "correct" answer is not sufficient to translate into clinical use. An answer here is only as reliable as the source from which it was extracted. The source therefore needs to be judiciously chosen, and presented transparently. Furthermore, in this example, the knowledge of the best treatment requires information about the patients' age and any additional health problems (for instance, dosing may vary in children, or where someone has impaired kidney function). The optimal treatment might vary by location, reflecting local or individual bacterial resistance patterns (which frequently change over time), or vary depending on the cost of drug acquisition or availability. A factoid answer does not allow the possibility of changing practice, or providing critical information which is not a direct response to the narrow question asked (perhaps an antibiotic is not always needed). These issues both need to be considered in producing an answer, and need to be *seen* to have been considered by the clinician before s/he can feel confident in following the recommendation.

In this context, reliability is multi-faceted. For an answer to be reliable it must have been extracted from a trustworthy source, accurately transcribed, and relevant to the clinical context (was the dosing information extracted for the correct clinical condition?). It should also be locally applicable, and recent. In this example, a methodologically sound national clinical guideline is likely to be highly dependable, whereas a journal editorial or case study giving one expert's idiosyncratic opinion might be safely ignored. A question-answering system which does not understand the difference is not likely to be useful.

We argue that the deployment of EBM-guided QA systems—by which we mean those intended to provide answers to clinical questions based on published evidence—in clinical practices is contingent on the outputs being reliable and actionable. Clinicians should be able to trust that the most robust evidence was retrieved, and that conflicting evidence was handled appropriately. Uncertainties associated with answers should be communicated to the clinician.

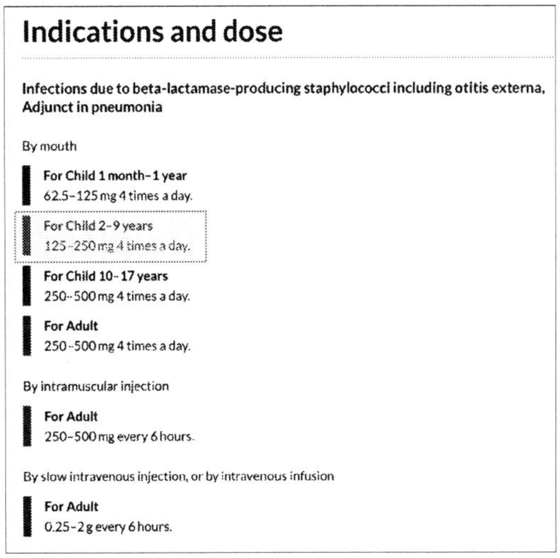
Indications and dose

Infections due to beta-lactamase-producing staphylococci including otitis externa, Adjunct in pneumonia

By mouth

For Child 1 month–1 year
62.5–125 mg 4 times a day.

For Child 2–9 years
125–250 mg 4 times a day.

For Child 10–17 years
250–500 mg 4 times a day.

For Adult
250–500 mg 4 times a day.

By intramuscular injection

For Adult
250–500 mg every 6 hours.

By slow intravenous injection, or by intravenous infusion

For Adult
0.25–2 g every 6 hours.

Figure 1: Yellow box shows text snippet used to answer "what dose of flucloxacillin should I prescribe for a 5 year old child?"[3].

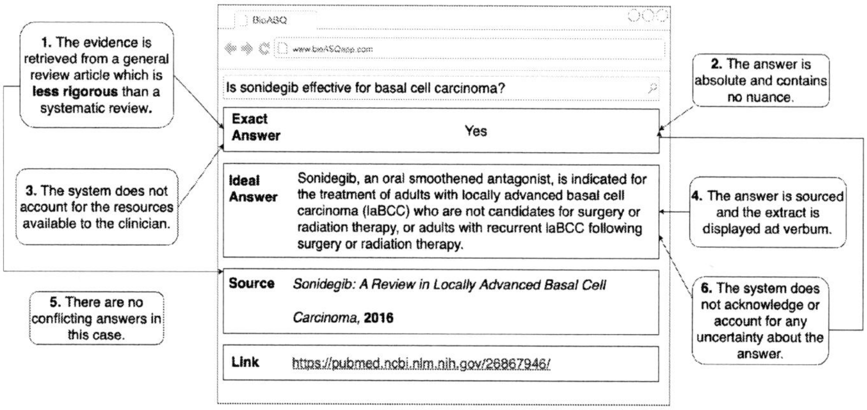

Figure 2: Web interface for QA system developed using BioASQ.

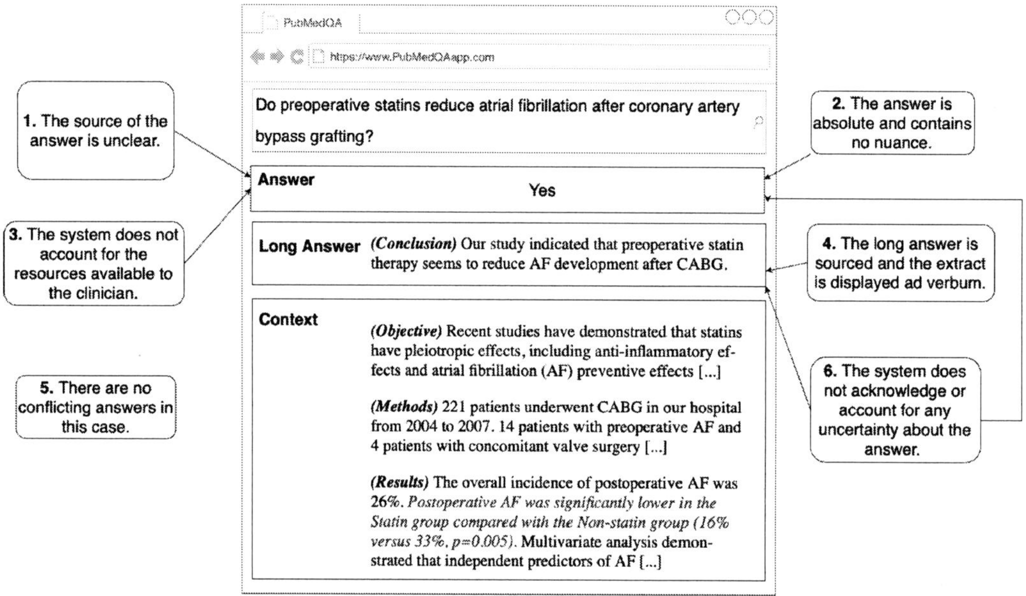

Figure 3: Web interface for QA system developed using PubMedQA.

2 Desiderata for Medical QA

What would be needed for clinicians to trust, and actually act upon answers provided by a QA system? In our view, the necessary criteria include: Provenance of the evidence and its reliability; Faithfulness of the evidence to the source, and; Transparency with respect to how answers are chosen, and how conflicting evidence is resolved. In accordance with these criteria, we suggest the following questions to assess the transparency of QA systems:

1. **Do the answers come from reliable sources for health information?** All research articles are not equal, and there exist mature approaches to help clinicians identify the most reliable advice from the health literature. Evidence-Based Medicine is one such framework in which the findings of the most rigorous study designs (typically high quality clinical guidelines, and *systematic reviews* of the primary literature) are preferred to case studies and observational research (Alper and Haynes, 2016b; Sackett et al., 1985).

   More sophisticated approaches (e.g., *risk of bias* assessment tools and the *GRADE* framework; Higgins et al. 2011; Guyatt et al. 2008) go further by estimating how confident one should be in a research finding, taking into account aspects such as study type, the precision

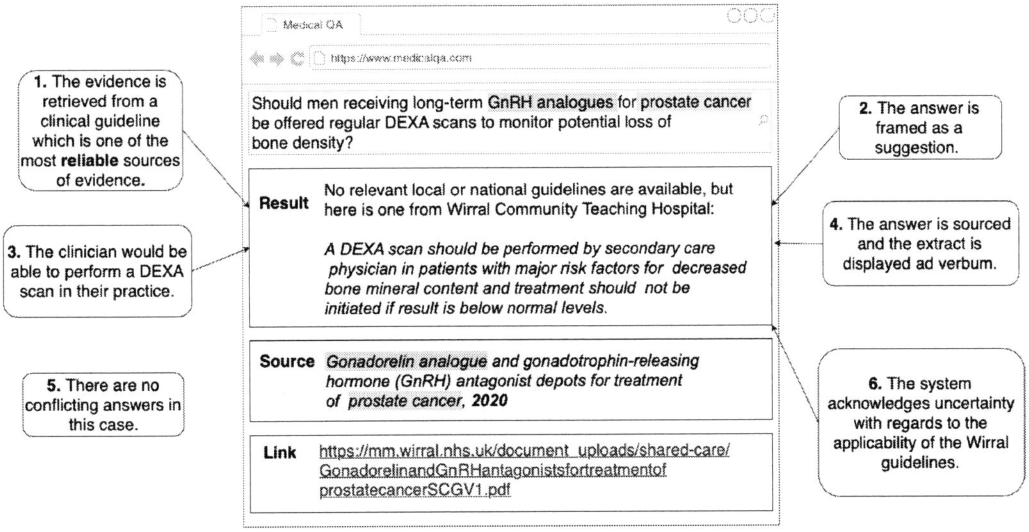

Figure 4: Example of a medical QA system output that meets the criteria in §2. The assumption is that the clinician is based in Nottingham while the most relevant guideline is for Wirral Community Teaching hospital (which is in a different region). The corresponding text spans in the question and response are highlighted with the same color.

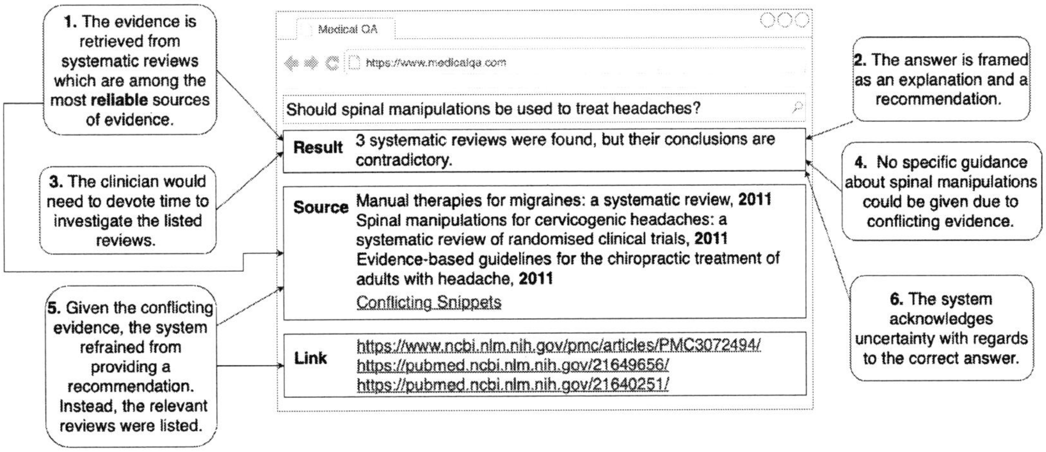

Figure 5: Example of a medical QA system output that handles the conflicting conclusions of 3 systematic reviews.

of the statistical results, and whether problems in study design were likely to have led to bias. QA systems which take a naive approach to evidence extraction—for example, selecting an answer from an undifferentiated corpus of scientific literature, treating all studies as equally reliable—are likely to be considerably less useful to clinicians. This is particularly true because there is often no definitive "correct" answer to a query; an overview of the best available evidence is what is sought. We suggest that QA systems should aim to explicitly use more rigorous, theoretically informed approaches to sorting the literature, mirroring the best current practice of manual question answering and evidence synthesis.

2. **Does the system provide guidance?** When searching for answers clinicians are looking for *guidance*, not just information. Guidance consists of recommendations of what to do in various clinical situations, while Boolean or factoid answers appear more absolute. The demand for guidance is reflected by the fact that many questions are of the form "Should I ...?" (Del Fiol et al., 2014; Ely et al., 2000; Papermaster and Champion, 2017). Therefore, the system could respond with "study/review

Spinal manipulations for cervicogenic headaches: a systematic review of randomized clinical trials, 2011

The results are mixed and the only trial accounting for placebo effects fails to be positive. Therefore, the therapeutic value of this approach remains uncertain.

Manual therapies for migraine: a systematic review, 2011

Therefore, any firm conclusion will require future, well-conducted RCTs on manual therapies for migraine.

Evidence-based guidelines for the chiropractic treatment of adults with headache, 2011

Evidence suggests that chiropractic care, including spinal manipulation, improves migraine and cervicogenic headaches. [...] Evidence for the use of spinal manipulation as an isolated intervention for patients with tension-type headache remains equivocal.

Figure 6: Contradictory source snippets leading to the response presented in figure 5.

X suggests the following action... ". This response could encourage the clinician to engage with the guidance and think critically about how to apply it in practice.

In the aforementioned example on urinary tract infections (UTI), the NICE[4] guideline (NICE, 2019) recommends Nitrofurantoin under specific conditions: If the estimated glomerular filtration rate (eGFR) $\geq$ 45 ml/minute then 100 mg modified-release twice a day (or if unavailable, 50 mg four times a day) for 3 days.

3. **Are the answers useful in the context in which the provider is practicing?** The usefulness of a QA system could be limited by factors such as drug availability, antibiotic resistance, and local or national funding/resources. Therefore, QA systems should account for the resources that are available to clinicians when providing guidance. In addition, what is deemed as "best practice" may vary by location (i.e., region or country).

   If a clinician were to consult a QA system on whether "men receiving long-term GnRH analogues for prostate cancer should be offered regular DEXA scans to monitor potential loss of bone density", guidelines from Wirral Community Teaching Hospital might be retrieved. The clinician would need to decide whether the guidelines apply to their locality (e.g., Nottingham) where DEXA scans may or may not be readily available.

4. **Is there sufficient "rationale" for the answer provided?** Prior work has shown that users of QA systems prefer answers to consist of paragraph-sized chunks of text as opposed to concise phrases (Lin et al., 2003). Lengthier "answers" provide context, and allow users to ensure that the information in the source text is consistent with the final answer. As answers should be faithful to the source, any generated summaries should probably be extractive rather than abstractive.

   For example, the answer to "what dose of flucloxacillin should I prescribe for a 5 year old child?" could consist of the snippet highlighted in Figure 1. However, in cases where the answer is derived from multiple sources it may be necessary to generate a summary.

5. **Does the system resolve conflicting evidence appropriately?** Higher quality information should be prioritized using frameworks for rating the quality of evidence (Ebell et al., 2004; Guyatt et al., 2008; Alper and Haynes, 2016a). If there are conflicts between equally relevant and reliable sources, the system should refrain from providing oversimplified guidance and inform the clinician of the conflicting sources. This could form the basis for further investigation by the clinician.

   The query "Should spinal manipulations be used to treat headaches?" could return three conflicting systematic reviews: one concluding that they should (Bryans et al., 2011) and two others that judge the evidence to be inconclusive (Chaibi et al., 2011; Posadzki and Ernst, 2011). A QA system should inform the clinician of these contradictions. An ideal system would assess the relative methodological

[4] The National Institute for Health and Care Excellence: the UK national health guideline producer

quality of the reviews, and present the most rigorous and reliable first.

6. **Does the system handle and communicate uncertainties adequately?** When providing guidance, the system should communicate any sources of uncertainty. If appropriate, the system should abstain from providing explicit guidance (e.g., where information conflicts or where supporting evidence is either absent or of low quality).

   In the case of the regular DEXA scans for men recieving long-term GnRH analogues, the system should communicate its uncertainty on whether the guidelines from Wirral Community Teaching hospital are applicable to the clinician's region.

   Additionally, the question "Does speech and language therapy help dysarthria after a brain injury?" could return no relevant studies (Sellars et al., 2002). It is important that the system explain that the question is unanswerable using the available literature.

There are several research challenges associated with the above criteria. Reframing the QA task will require new datasets which include answers (with accompanying rationales) from trusted sources; rankings by evidence quality; locality and patient contextualizing information; and which incorporate real-world conflicting answers and questions which lack answers. Quantitative measures would need to be created to assess how well the datasets and systems meet each criterion.

While we expect that an improved system using these criteria might be more trustworthy (and hence potentially help to translate health research more effectively info clinical practice), we note that our criteria need to be empirically tested. To achieve this, we need to move beyond dataset evaluation, and consider user-centred design methodology. Ultimately, we should aim to improve and evaluate systems through research conducted in real-world clinical practice.

We next review prior work on Biomedical QA with respect to the above criteria. We display typical responses of these systems in a hypothetical web interface, and assess how well these responses meet the criteria.

3 Existing Medical QA Datasets and Systems

The primary focus of prior medical QA work has been on developing systems that answer the following types of questions: boolean (yes/no), factoid, list (of factoids), and definitional, e.g. (Sarrouti and Ouatik El Alaoui, 2020; Ben Abacha and Zweigenbaum, 2015; Cao et al., 2011; Zahid et al., 2018; Yu et al., 2007). Several datasets have been created to train and evaluate systems that handle the aforementioned question types, including BioASQ (Tsatsaronis et al., 2015), emrQA (Pampari et al., 2018), emrKBQA (Raghavan et al., 2021), PubMedQA (Jin et al., 2019), why-QA (Fan, 2019), MEDIQA-QA (Ben Abacha et al., 2019), LiveQA-Medical (Abacha et al., 2017) and MEDIQA-AnS (Savery et al., 2020). BioASQ, PubMedQA, MEDIQA-QA, MEDIQA-AnS and LiveQA-Medical derive answers from a corpus of biomedical literature, whereas emrQA, emrKBQA and why-QA are based on patient notes within EHRs. As stated above, our focus here is on systems that can answer general questions (independent of individual patients) based on the latest evidence, so we do not discuss emrQA, emrKBQA and why-QA. A comparison of the systems and datasets is provided in Table 1.

While BioASQ, MEDIQA-QA, MEDIQA-AnS and LiveQA-Medical are large-scale information retrieval (IR) and question answering (QA) datasets, PubMedQA is designed for "reading comprehension" question answering (RCQA) based on scientific abstracts. Each question of PubMedQA is accompanied by the abstract containing the answer.

The BioASQ Phase B challenge comprises the following question types (Tsatsaronis et al., 2015):

- Exact: "yes" or "no", e.g., "Is the protein Papilin secreted?";
- Factoid: named entities, e.g., "Name synonym of Acrokeratosis paraneoplastica.";
- List: list of named entities, e.g., "Which miRNAs could be used as potential biomarkers for epithelial ovarian cancer?";
- Ideal: paragraph-sized summaries (text spans), e.g., "What is the effect of TRH on myocardial contractility?"

While BioASQ has been instrumental to the progress of the field (Nentidis et al., 2017, 2018,

QA System/ Dataset	D1	D2	D3	D4	D5	D6
BioASQ (Krallinger et al., 2020)	✗	✗	✗	✓	✗	✗
PubMedQA (Jin et al., 2019)	✗	✗	✗	✓	✗	✗
MEDIQA-QA (Ben Abacha et al., 2019)	✓	✓	✗	✓	✗	✗
MEDIQA-AnS (Savery et al., 2020)	✓	✓	✗	✗	✗	✗
LiveQA-Medical (Abacha et al., 2017)	✓	✓	✗	✓	✗	✗
MEANS (Ben Abacha and Zweigenbaum, 2015)	✗	✗	✗	✓	✗	✗
AskHERMES (Cao et al., 2011)	✓	✗	✗	✓	✗	✗
CLINIQA (Zahid et al., 2018)	✗	✓	✗	✓	✗	✗
MedQA (Yu et al., 2007)	✗	✓	✗	✓	✗	✗

Table 1: Comparision of how well QA systems and datasets meet the desiderata outlined in §2.

2020; Krallinger et al., 2020), it satisfies only one of the criteria we have enumerated above, namely 4. Figure 2 shows the expected output of a system developed using BioASQ. In this example, the extract is provided verbatim (criterion 4).

However, the answer is sourced from a general review; these reviews are less reliable than guidelines or systematic reviews (criterion 1). Furthermore, the system outputs absolute answers rather than guidance (criterion 2) which limits their usefulness to clinicians. A more suitable answer would be "the following guidance is provided in X...". It is unclear what resources are available to the clinician and the BioASQ dataset does not account for this (criterion 3). There is no contradictory evidence in the example and BioASQ has been preprocessed to ensure there are no conflicting papers (criterion 5). Unless the trained model is acting on a curated knowledge base, it would not be robust to conflicts. Finally, the absolute nature of the answer does not allow the system to recognise and account for uncertainty (criterion 6).

In contrast to BioASQ, PubMedQA provides answers to only Boolean (yes/no) questions, e.g. "Do preoperative statins reduce atrial fibrillation after coronary artery bypass grafting?". Accompanying these responses is a "long answer", supplied in the form of the conclusions of the source abstracts. As per Figure 3, the outputs of systems trained on PubMedQA can only satisfy criterion 4. The conclusion is given verbatim to support the short answer. Nevertheless, the source of the answer is not specified (criterion 1), the answer is absolute (criterion 2) and it does not account for any uncertainty (criterion 6). Systems developed using PubMedQA cannot ensure that the answer is useful to the clinician (criterion 3). Given the task is framed as "reading comprehension", there is only one abstract per question. This prevents systems from being trained to handle conflicts (criterion 5).

MEDIQA-QA is a consumer QA dataset whose answers consist of exact snippets from MedlinePlus. Consumer questions are more focused on general information, symptom or person/organization questions (Roberts and Demner-Fushman, 2016). The answers that are required by consumers are less complex and more easily understandable than those given to clinicians (Savery et al., 2020). This has motivated the development of MEDIQA-AnS which summarises the answers of MEDIQA-QA. As shown in Figures 7 and 8, MEDIQA-QA satisfies desiderata 1,2 and 4 while MEDIQA-AnS satisfies only 4.

Although the LiveQA-Medical dataset uses the same answers and sources as MEDIQA-QA and MEDIQA-Ans, it differs by providing answers to each subquestion of the query. Additionally, verbatim extracts of MedlinePlus are used in the responses (Figure 9). Hence criteria 1, 2 and 4 are fulfilled.

MEANS returns only an extract of the original source, without any contextualizing information (Figure 10), i.e. the provenance of the answer. Therefore, only condition 4 is satisfied.

On the other hand, AskHERMES provides a list of answers which are labelled with topics from the question (Figure 11). The extracts shown are from the original sources and are accompanied by links, authors, and dates. Thus, AskHERMES satisfies desiderata 1 and 4.

CLINIQA responds to queries with original abstracts that are accompanied with the PMID and the title of the source paper (Figure 12). However, the results are not rank according to reliability, so only criteria 2 and 4 are met.

Finally, MedQA's answers comprise sourced extracts from Medline and Google:Definition (Figure 13). Answers are not ranked according to reliability, so the system only satisfies criteria 2 and 4.

None of the aforementioned datasets or systems address conflicts (criterion 5) or communicate uncertainty to clinicians (criterion 6). What might QA systems that satisfy all desiderata look like?

4 Presentation of Answers

We have seen that systems trained on BioASQ and PubMedQA do not satisfy all the criteria defined in §2. In this section we present illustrative outputs of hypothetical systems that meet the full set of criteria we have put forth.

Figure 4 presents an example output which satisfies the criteria but where no conflicts occur (criterion 5). The answer is sourced from a systematic review (criterion 1) and is in the form of guidance (criterion 2). While the guidance is actionable given the resources available (criterion 3) and the source extract is reproduced directly (criterion 4), the uncertainty in the answer is acknowledged (criterion 6) by stating the absence of relevant local and national guidelines. The corresponding words and phrases in the question, answer and title used to extract the text snippet are highlighted.

A demonstration of how conflicting evidence could be addressed is provided in Figure 5. In this scenario, the question "Should spinal manipulations be used to treat headaches?" returned three contradictory systematic reviews (Bryans et al., 2011; Chaibi et al., 2011; Posadzki and Ernst, 2011) (criterion 1). Therefore, the system refrains from providing explicit guidance (criterion 6) and instead provides the clinician with the names and links of conflicting reviews (criterion 5). In addition, the clinician is able to investigate the contradictory snippets further by clicking on "Conflicting Snippets" which would show the snippets in Figure 6. Criterion 4 is inapplicable in this case as no answer was retrieved from the documents.

One promising direction which may permit improved handling of contradictory evidence involves use of argumentation-based logic to "reason" about multiple potentially conflicting inputs (Chapman et al., 2019; Cyras et al., 2018), perhaps after explicitly inferring the reported findings concerning treatment efficacies (Lehman et al., 2019; Nye et al., 2020). An alternative (more audacious) direction would be to generate comparative summaries for clinicians that compose narrative summaries of the evidence on a given topic from primary sources, including discussion of conflicting evidence (Wallace et al., 2020; Shah et al., 2021).

Developing and assessing systems according to the criteria outlined in §2 would ensure the output is useful, actionable and reliable to clinicians. It would additionally improve the accountability of both the clinician and the system as the form of the output would be conducive to debugging and root cause analysis.

5 Conclusions

We have introduced criteria for assessing the transparency of medical question answering systems. These have been guided by the following question: What would be needed for clinicians to trust, and act upon answers from a QA system? In part we have argued that these systems should be explicitly informed by principles of EBM. The adequacy of existing medical systems and datasets, including BioASQ, PubMedQA, MEDIQA-QA, MEDIQA-AnS, LiveQA-Medical, MEANS, AskHERMES, CLINIQA and MedQA, was assessed using the transparency criteria that we proposed. We found that they met some, but not all, of the conditions.

We presented hypothetical examples of system outputs that satisfy all of the criteria and explained how they could be useful to clinicians. These included conflicts between sources of similar reliability. In these cases, the best course of action was to refrain from giving guidance and instead return the sources to the clinicians for further examination. The examples could form the basis of new datasets and systems that provide actionable answers to clinicians.

We believe that these avenues of investigation would assist with the *deployment* of medical QA systems, ultimately furthering the practice of EBM.

6 Acknowledgements

This work was supported in part by the National Institutes of Health (NIH), grant R01-LM012086.

GK holds a doctoral studentship co-sponsored by Metadvice and the Guy's and St Thomas' Biomedical Research Centre.

References

Asma Ben Abacha, Eugene Agichtein, Yuval Pinter, and Dina Demner-Fushman. 2017. Overview of the medical question answering task at trec 2017 liveqa. In *TREC*.

Brian S Alper and R Brian Haynes. 2016a. EBHC pyramid 5.0 for accessing preappraised evidence and guidance. *Evidence Based Medicine*, 21(4):123.

Brian S Alper and R Brian Haynes. 2016b. Ebhc pyramid 5.0 for accessing preappraised evidence and guidance. *BMJ evidence-based medicine*, 21(4):123–125.

Hilda Bastian, Paul Glasziou, and Iain Chalmers. 2010. Seventy-Five Trials and Eleven Systematic Reviews a Day: How Will We Ever Keep Up? *PLOS Medicine*, 7(9):e1000326. Publisher: Public Library of Science.

Asma Ben Abacha, Chaitanya Shivade, and Dina Demner-Fushman. 2019. Overview of the MEDIQA 2019 shared task on textual inference, question entailment and question answering. In *Proceedings of the 18th BioNLP Workshop and Shared Task*, pages 370–379, Florence, Italy. Association for Computational Linguistics.

Asma Ben Abacha and Pierre Zweigenbaum. 2015. MEANS: A medical question-answering system combining NLP techniques and semantic Web technologies. *Information Processing & Management*, 51(5):570–594.

Roland Bryans, Martin Descarreaux, Mireille Duranleau, Henri Marcoux, Brock Potter, Rick Ruegg, Lynn Shaw, Robert Watkin, and Eleanor White. 2011. Evidence-Based Guidelines for the Chiropractic Treatment of Adults With Headache. *Journal of Manipulative and Physiological Therapeutics*, 34(5):274–289.

YongGang Cao, Feifan Liu, Pippa Simpson, Lamont Antieau, Andrew Bennett, James Cimino, John Ely, and Hong Yu. 2011. AskHERMES: An online question answering system for complex clinical questions. *Journal of biomedical informatics*, 44:277–88.

Aleksander Chaibi, Peter J Tuchin, and Michael Bjørn Russell. 2011. Manual therapies for migraine: a systematic review. *The journal of headache and pain*, 12(2):127–133. Edition: 2011/02/05 Publisher: Springer Milan.

Martin Chapman, Panagiotis Balatsoukas, Mark Ashworth, Vasa Curcin, Nadin Kökciyan, Kai Essers, Isabel Sassoon, Sanjay Modgil, Simon Parsons, and Elizabeth I. Sklar. 2019. Computational argumentation-based clinical decision support. In *Proceedings of the 18th International Conference on Autonomous Agents and MultiAgent Systems*, AAMAS '19, page 2345–2347, Richland, SC. International Foundation for Autonomous Agents and Multiagent Systems.

K. Cyras, B. Delaney, Denys Prociuk, Francesca Toni, M. Chapman, Jesús Domínguez, and V. Curcin. 2018. Argumentation for explainable reasoning with conflicting medical recommendations. In *MedRACER+WOMoCoE@KR*.

Guilherme Del Fiol, T. Elizabeth Workman, and Paul N. Gorman. 2014. Clinical Questions Raised by Clinicians at the Point of Care: A Systematic Review. *JAMA Internal Medicine*, 174(5):710–718.

Mark Ebell, Jay Siwek, Barry Weiss, Steven Woolf, Jeffrey Susman, Bernard Ewigman, and Marjorie Bowman. 2004. Strength of Recommendation Taxonomy (SORT): A Patient-Centered Approach to Grading Evidence in the Medical Literature. *The Journal of the American Board of Family Practice / American Board of Family Practice*, 17:59–67.

John Ely, Jerome Osheroff, Paul Gorman, Mark Ebell, M Chambliss, Eric Pifer, and P Stavri. 2000. A taxonomy of generic clinical questions: Classification study. *BMJ (Clinical research ed.)*, 321:429–32.

Jungwei Fan. 2019. Annotating and characterizing clinical sentences with explicit why-QA cues. In *Proceedings of the 2nd Clinical Natural Language Processing Workshop*, pages 101–106, Minneapolis, Minnesota, USA. Association for Computational Linguistics.

John Gabbay and Andrée le May. 2016. Mindlines: making sense of evidence in practice. *British Journal of General Practice*, 66(649):402.

Gordon Guyatt, Andrew Oxman, Gunn Vist, Regina Kunz, Yngve Falck-Ytter, Pablo Alonso, and Holger Schünemann. 2008. GRADE: An emerging consensus on rating quality of evidence and strength of recommendations. *BMJ (Clinical research ed.)*, 336:924–6.

Phil Hider, Gemma Griffin, Marg Walker, and Edward Coughlan. 2009. The information-seeking behavior of clinical staff in a large health care organization. *Journal of the Medical Library Association : JMLA*, 97:47–50.

Julian PT Higgins, Douglas G Altman, Peter C Gøtzsche, Peter Jüni, David Moher, Andrew D Oxman, Jelena Savović, Kenneth F Schulz, Laura Weeks, and Jonathan AC Sterne. 2011. The cochrane collaboration's tool for assessing risk of bias in randomised trials. *Bmj*, 343.

Arjen Hoogendam, Anton F H Stalenhoef, Pieter F de Vries Robbé, and A John P M Overbeke. 2008. Answers to questions posed during daily patient care are more likely to be answered by UpToDate than PubMed. *Journal of medical Internet research*, 10(4):e29–e29. Publisher: Gunther Eysenbach.

Qiao Jin, Bhuwan Dhingra, Zhengping Liu, William Cohen, and Xinghua Lu. 2019. *PubMedQA: A Dataset for Biomedical Research Question Answering*. Pages: 2577.

Martin Krallinger, Anastasia Krithara, A. Nentidis, G. Paliouras, and Marta Villegas. 2020. Bioasq at clef2020: Large-scale biomedical semantic indexing and question answering. *Advances in Information Retrieval*, 12036:550 – 556.

Eric Lehman, Jay DeYoung, Regina Barzilay, and Byron C. Wallace. 2019. Inferring Which Medical Treatments Work from Reports of Clinical Trials. In *Proceedings of the Conference of the North American Chapter of the Association for Computational Linguistics (NAACL)*, pages 3705–3717.

Jimmy Lin, Dennis Quan, Vineet Sinha, Karun Bakshi, David Huynh, Boris Katz, and David R. Karger. 2003. What makes a good answer? the role of context in question answering. In *Proceedings of INTERACT 2003*, pages 25–32.

Anastasios Nentidis, Konstantinos Bougiatiotis, Anastasia Krithara, and Georgios Paliouras. 2020. Results of the seventh edition of the BioASQ challenge. In *Machine Learning and Knowledge Discovery in Databases*, pages 553–568. Springer International Publishing.

Anastasios Nentidis, Konstantinos Bougiatiotis, Anastasia Krithara, Georgios Paliouras, and Ioannis Kakadiaris. 2017. Results of the fifth edition of the BioASQ challenge. In *BioNLP 2017*, pages 48–57, Vancouver, Canada,. Association for Computational Linguistics.

Anastasios Nentidis, Anastasia Krithara, Konstantinos Bougiatiotis, Georgios Paliouras, and Ioannis Kakadiaris. 2018. Results of the sixth edition of the BioASQ challenge. In *Proceedings of the 6th BioASQ Workshop A challenge on large-scale biomedical semantic indexing and question answering*, pages 1–10, Brussels, Belgium. Association for Computational Linguistics.

NICE. 2019. UTI (lower): antimicrobial prescribing. https://www.nice.org.uk/guidance/ng109/resources/visual-summary-pdf-6544021069.

Benjamin E Nye, Jay DeYoung, Eric Lehman, Ani Nenkova, Iain J Marshall, and Byron C Wallace. 2020. Understanding clinical trial reports: Extracting medical entities and their relations. *arXiv preprint arXiv:2010.03550*.

Denise Fiona O'leary and Siobhán Ni Mhaolrúnaigh. 2012. Information-seeking behaviour of nurses: where is information sought and what processes are followed? *Journal of Advanced Nursing*, 68(2):379–390. Publisher: John Wiley & Sons, Ltd.

Anusri Pampari, Preethi Raghavan, Jennifer Liang, and Jian Peng. 2018. *emrQA: A Large Corpus for Question Answering on Electronic Medical Records*.

Amy Papermaster and Jane Dimmitt Champion. 2017. The common practice of "curbside consultation": A systematic review. *Journal of the American Association of Nurse Practitioners*, 29(10).

Amy E Papermaster and Jane Dimmitt Champion. 2020. Exploring the use of curbside consultations for interprofessional collaboration and clinical decision-making. *Journal of Interprofessional Care*, pages 1–8. Publisher: Taylor & Francis.

Paul Posadzki and Edzard Ernst. 2011. Spinal manipulations for cervicogenic headaches: a systematic review of randomized clinical trials. *Headache*, 51(7):1132–1139.

Preethi Raghavan, Jennifer J. Liang, Diwakar Mahajan, Rachita Chandra, and Peter Szolovits. 2021. emrkbqa: A clinical knowledge-base question answering dataset. In *BIONLP*.

Kirk Roberts and Dina Demner-Fushman. 2016. Interactive use of online health resources: a comparison of consumer and professional questions. *Journal of the American Medical Informatics Association*, 23(4):802–811.

David L Sackett, R Brian Haynes, Peter Tugwell, et al. 1985. *Clinical epidemiology: a basic science for clinical medicine*. Little, Brown and Company.

Mourad Sarrouti and Said Ouatik El Alaoui. 2020. SemBioNLQA: A semantic biomedical question answering system for retrieving exact and ideal answers to natural language questions. *Artificial Intelligence in Medicine*, 102:101767.

Max Savery, Asma Ben Abacha, Soumya Gayen, and Dina Demner-Fushman. 2020. Question-driven summarization of answers to consumer health questions. *Scientific Data*, 7(1):322.

C. Sellars, T. Hughes, and P. Langhorne. 2002. Speech and language therapy for dysarthria due to non-progressive brain damage. *Cochrane Database of Systematic Reviews*, (3). Publisher: John Wiley & Sons, Ltd.

Darsh J. Shah, Lili Yu, Tao Lei, and R. Barzilay. 2021. Nutribullets hybrid: Multi-document health summarization. *ArXiv*, abs/2104.03465.

Richard Smith. 1996. What clinical information do doctors need? *BMJ*, 313(7064):1062.

George Tsatsaronis, Georgios Balikas, Prodromos Malakasiotis, Ioannis Partalas, Matthias Zschunke, Michael R. Alvers, Dirk Weissenborn, Anastasia Krithara, Sergios Petridis, Dimitris Polychronopoulos, Yannis Almirantis, John Pavlopoulos, Nicolas Baskiotis, Patrick Gallinari, Thierry Artiéres, Axel-Cyrille Ngonga Ngomo, Norman Heino, Eric Gaussier, Liliana Barrio-Alvers, Michael Schroeder, Ion Androutsopoulos, and Georgios Paliouras. 2015. An overview of the BIOASQ large-scale biomedical semantic indexing and question answering competition. *BMC Bioinformatics*, 16(1):138.

Byron C. Wallace, Sayantan Saha, Frank Soboczenski, and I. Marshall. 2020. Generating (factual?) narrative summaries of rcts: Experiments with neural multi-document summarization. *ArXiv*, abs/2008.11293.

Hong Yu, Minsuk Lee, David Kaufman, John Ely, Jerome A. Osheroff, George Hripcsak, and James Cimino. 2007. Development, implementation, and a cognitive evaluation of a definitional question answering system for physicians. *J. of Biomedical Informatics*, 40(3):236–251.

M Zahid, Ankush Mittal, R. Joshi, and G. Atluri. 2018. *CLINIQA: A Machine Intelligence Based Clinical Question Answering System.*

A Additional figures of QA interfaces

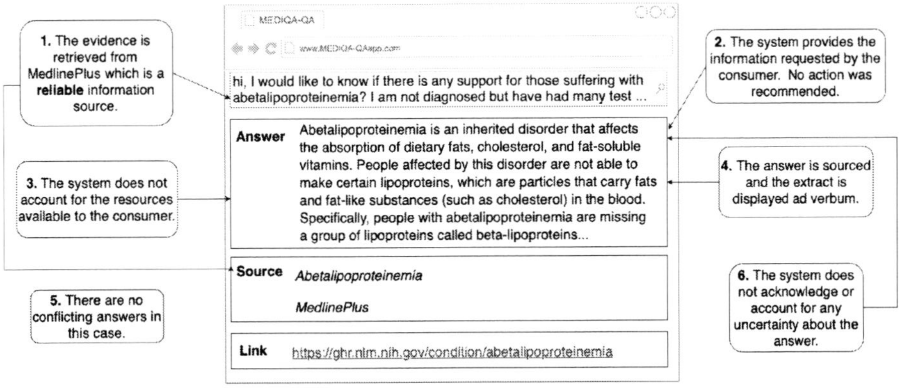

Figure 7: Web interface for QA system developed using MEDIQA-QA.

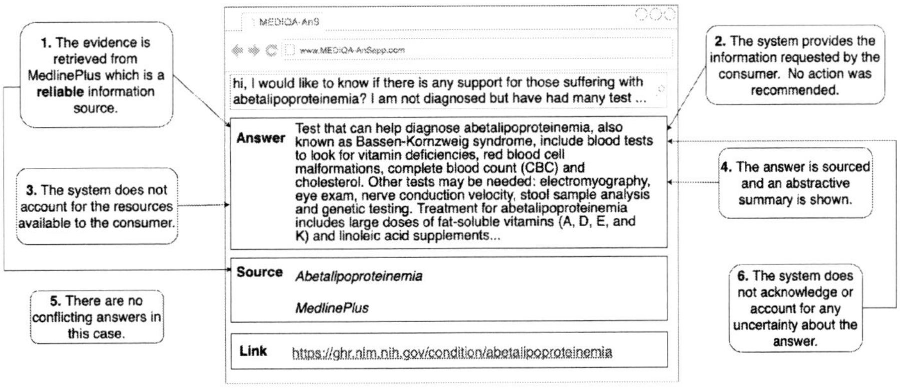

Figure 8: Web interface for QA system developed using MEDIQA-AnS.

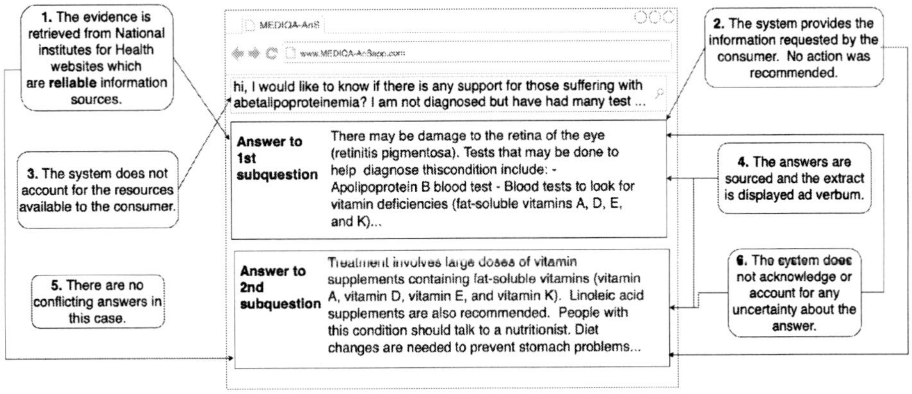

Figure 9: Web interface for QA system developed using LiveQA-Medical.

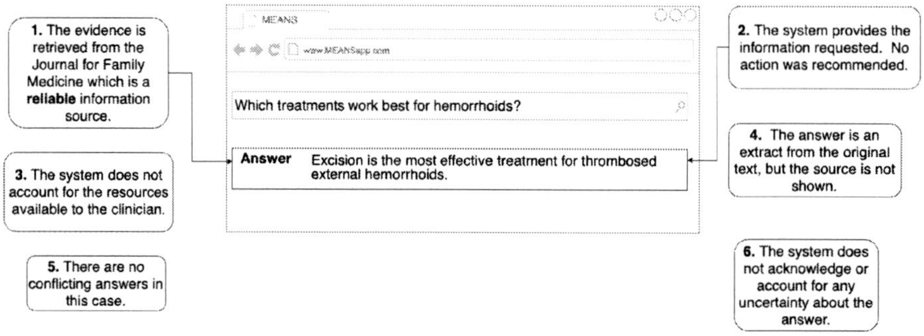

Figure 10: Web interface for MEANS.

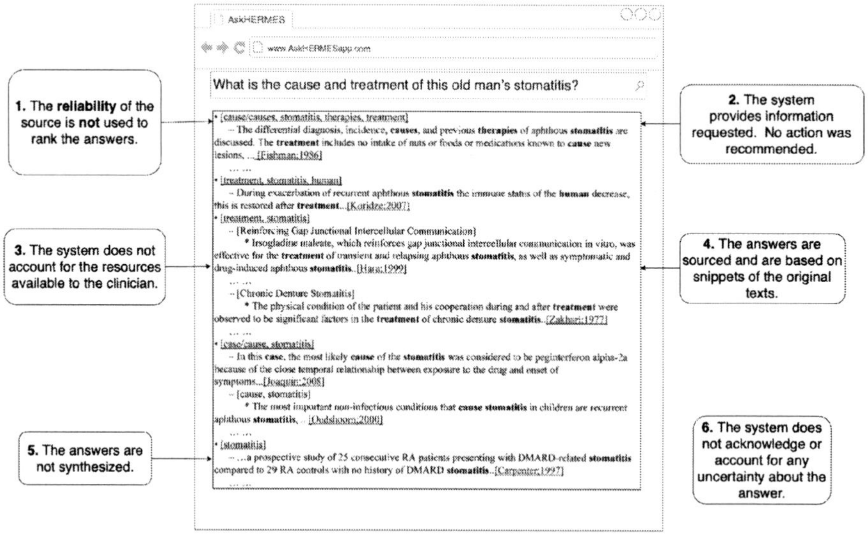

Figure 11: Web interface for AskHERMES.

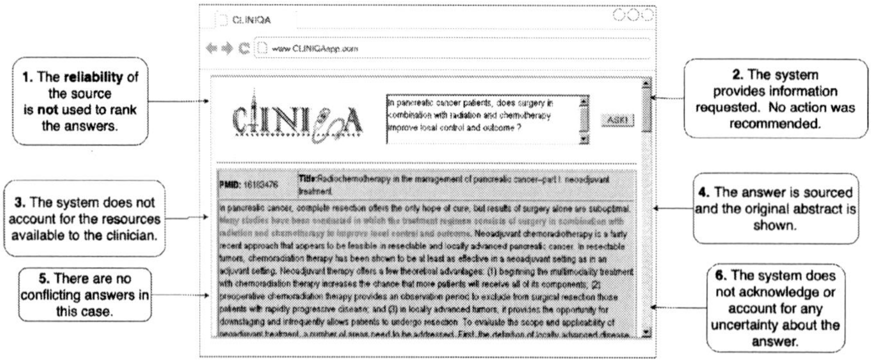

Figure 12: Web interface for CLINIQA which includes figure 5 from (Zahid et al., 2018).

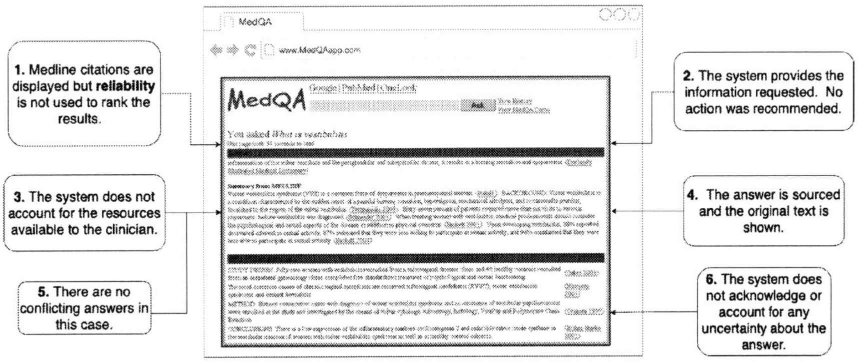

Figure 13: Web interface for MedQA which includes figure 3 from (Yu et al., 2007).

GermanQuAD and GermanDPR: Improving Non-English Question Answering and Passage Retrieval

Timo Möller and **Julian Risch** and **Malte Pietsch**
deepset
{timo.moeller, julian.risch, malte.pietsch}@deepset.ai

Abstract

A major challenge of research on non-English machine reading for question answering (QA) is the lack of annotated datasets. In this paper, we present GermanQuAD, a dataset of 13,722 extractive question/answer pairs. To improve the reproducibility of the dataset creation approach and foster QA research on other languages, we summarize lessons learned and evaluate reformulation of question/answer pairs as a way to speed up the annotation process. An extractive QA model trained on GermanQuAD significantly outperforms multilingual models and also shows that machine-translated training data cannot fully substitute hand-annotated training data in the target language. Finally, we demonstrate the wide range of applications of GermanQuAD by adapting it to GermanDPR, a training dataset for dense passage retrieval (DPR), and train and evaluate one of the first non-English DPR models.

1 Introduction & Related Work

Research on non-English machine reading for question answering (QA) suffers from limited availability of annotated non-English datasets. With the English SQuAD dataset (Rajpurkar et al., 2018) as a role model, there are only a few resources of similar format, such as the French FQuAD (d'Hoffschmidt et al., 2020), the Korean KorQuAD (Lim et al., 2019), and the Russian SberQuAD (Efimov et al., 2020) datasets. As an alternative, there are machine-translated datasets for training (Lewis et al., 2020a). With further improving performance of translation models, machine-translating datasets is a promising direction for the future as it saves the costs of manual annotations. However, translations can also be a source of errors (some translated answers contain non-negligible errors) and can have a negative impact on the variety of language use that might limit model performance.

Another line of research uses multilingual models such as mBERT (Devlin et al., 2019), XLM (Conneau and Lample, 2019) or XLM-Roberta (Conneau et al., 2020) trained on English QA datasets for zero-shot language transfer to the target domain. While these models perform astonishingly well on QA in unseen languages, they do not perform as well as on English QA (Lewis et al., 2020a; d'Hoffschmidt et al., 2020; Lim et al., 2019). Furthermore, multilingual models are much larger than their monolingual counterparts, rendering them unsuitable for most production systems where memory consumption and query speed matter.

Besides QA, a highly related task called "passage retrieval" has been worked on recently. Passage retrievers can be used for document retrieval, but also play an important role when scaling extractive QA models to large document bases (open-domain QA). Dense Passage Retrieval (DPR) (Karpukhin et al., 2020) uses two separate, BERT-based encoders (Devlin et al., 2019) for questions and passages. In addition to the positive passages (contexts) as contained in existing SQuAD-formatted datasets, the training of DPR leverages hard negative passages that are automatically selected for each query and an optimization trick called in-batch negatives. In-batch negatives optimization assumes positive passages of one annotated question to be negative passages for a different question. By adding hard negatives selected from the whole German Wikipedia to GermanQuAD, we create a training dataset in DPR format, which we call GermanDPR.

Our contributions can be summarized as follows: First, we present a new dataset of extractive question/answer pairs, GermanQuAD, and show that training on this dataset achieves a new state of the art for German QA. We also present the first multi-way annotated German test set for a more fair evaluation of QA models. Second, we evaluate the efficacy of a technique to improve the annotation

Proceedings of the 3rd Workshop on Machine Reading for Question Answering , pages 42–50

process, where simple questions are reformulated. Third, we present a new dataset for dense passage retrieval, GermanDPR, and demonstrate another application scenario of GermanQuAD by converting it to a different format and enriching it with additional data. This conversion approach could also be used with other QA datasets. To the best of our knowledge, there is no other non-English DPR model published at the point of writing, presumably due to the lack of suitable training datasets. Our annotations and trained models are released under the Creative Commons Attribution 4.0 International License (CC-BY 4.0).[1,2,3]

2 GermanQuAD Dataset Creation

The creation of GermanQuAD is inspired by insights from existing datasets as well as our domain labelling experience from several other projects. We combine the strengths of SQuAD, such as high out-of-domain performance, with self-sufficient questions that contain all relevant information for open-domain QA as in the Natural Questions dataset (Kwiatkowski et al., 2019). Our training and test datasets do not overlap like other popular datasets (Lewis et al., 2020b) and include complex questions that cannot be answered with a single entity or only a few words.

2.1 Selection of Passages

The basis of GermanQuAD is the German counterpart of English Wikipedia articles' used in SQuAD. From the German Wikipedia, we extract each article's text with gensim's WikiExtractor[4], split it into passages (paragraphs) and exclude passages that are shorter than 500 characters or mainly contain enumerations. We add the title of the German Wikipedia page to each passage. Since we annotate only one answer per question in the training set and want to reduce the risk of false-negative answers, we limit the length of training passages to 2500 characters. For the test set, we keep long passages and only dismiss short ones. As some text conversion errors appear especially for embedded latex code, annotators skip passages that are not fully understandable.

2.2 Selection of Annotators

We select annotators that are familiar with machine learning concepts, teach them the use of BERT for QA, give detailed labelling instructions, continuously monitor the annotations, and give feedback wherever necessary. We collaborate with students in the area of computational linguistics, computer science, and chemistry and one expert annotator who created more than 20k QA annotations. To have a more diverse set of annotated answers in the three-way annotated test dataset, we source around two thousand labels via the crowd service provider Crowd Guru,[5] which has been selected after careful benchmarking.

2.3 Annotation Instructions

Our annotators create questions while reading the passage. To prevent a strong lexical overlap of the question and the corresponding passage, a shortcoming of SQuAD (Kwiatkowski et al., 2019), the annotators reformulate the question text with the use of synonyms and altered syntax wherever possible. We encourage creation of complex questions that cannot be answered with a single entity. Consequently, next to answers that are short (a few words, a single number, or an entity), there are also long answers spanning multiple sentences that cannot be shortened without becoming incomplete or even incorrect. A translated example of a short answer to the question: "What is the EU according to the Federal Constitutional Court?"[6] is "association of states". An example of a long answer to the question: "What can be seen on the coat of arms of Hannover?"[7] is "a silver wall with two pewter towers on a red ground; in the open gate, under a black portcullis, is a golden shield with a green Mary's flower or shamrock (unexplained); between the towers is a golden lion.".

The questions are self-sufficient in the sense that no additional information is needed to give an answer. To ensure self-sufficient questions, we teach the annotators to classify SQuAD questions into self-sufficient ("When did Israel join the OECD?"[8]) versus incomplete ("What year did Albert die?"[9]). For the complete annotation FAQ, see Appendix A. Figure 1 exemplifies the data format.

[1] `https://germanquad.s3.amazonaws.com/GermanQuAD.zip`

[2] `https://germanquad.s3.amazonaws.com/GermanDPR.zip`

[3] `https://germanquad.s3.amazonaws.com/models.zip`

[4] `https://radimrehurek.com/gensim/corpora/wikicorpus.html`

[5] `https://www.crowdguru.de/`

[6] GermanQuAD ID: 57716

[7] GermanQuAD ID: 56712

[8] SQuAD ID: 5725cd6a89a1e219009abef7

[9] SQuAD ID: 5723d010f6b826140030fc8e

```
[{
  "paragraphs": [{"qas": [{
    "question":
      "Von welchem Gesetzt stammt...?",
    "id": 51870,
    "answers": [{
      "answer_id": 53778,
      "document_id": 43958,
      "question_id": 51870,
      "text": "britischen...",
      "answer_start": 146,
      "answer_category": "SHORT"
      }]
  }]}],
  "context": "Recht_der...\n\n===...",
  "document_id": 43958
}]
```


Figure 1: Sample from the GermanQuAD dataset.

2.4 Quality Management

An expert annotator manually checks the first 300 questions and answers for each annotator and gives detailed feedback. In weekly group meetings, a random subset of newly created labels is discussed. We encourage working in groups to debate imprecision in question formulation or answer selection. We continuously check for lexical overlap between question and passage and correct the annotation style in individual sessions with the corresponding annotator.

2.5 Addressing Bias

Of course, we cannot be sure to create a dataset free of bias but by being aware of the potential problems we can strive to overcome at least a few. The bias inherent in Wikipedia texts is difficult to overcome when labelling extractive QA on these texts. We hope the popular wiki pages chosen for our dataset are less biased because they are curated by many people. The team of annotators includes men and women, and native as well as non-native German speakers. We hypothesize questions seeking factual information instead of opinions make the dataset less prone to bias. Since the gender form is a specific issue in the German language, we encourage to include male and female or gender-neutral forms when formulating questions ("... alle Bürger:innen eingeführt."[10]).

2.6 Test Set

We construct a three-way annotated test set including 2204 questions. Student annotators formulate all questions and mark the first answer. The second answer comes from our expert annotator who also removes questions that are not formulated clearly. For the third annotation, we use the crowd annotation provider Crowd Guru. Crowd Guru's annotations are checked for positional overlap with existing answers. If there is no overlap, we manually check for irregularities and as a result, remove 76 wrong answers. The final dataset consists of 2204 questions with $2204 \cdot 3 - 76 = 6536$ answers. Inspired by Lewis et al. (2020b), we minimize the overlap of train and test set by comparing normalized[11] questions and answers. We remove all questions from the train set that also occur in the test set. For 12.3% of the questions in the test set, one of their answers also occurs in the training set. This number is low compared to 58% to 72% reported by Lewis et al. (2020b) for other QA datasets.

2.7 Dataset Analysis

This section describes the created datasets, GermanQuAD and GermanDPR in more detail. Table 1 lists the number of passages, questions, and answers in the training and test set of GermanQuAD. Each passage is from a different Wikipedia article and therefore, the number of passages is equivalent to the number of articles. As the training dataset is one-way annotated, there is exactly one answer per question, resulting in 11518 question/answer pairs. In contrast to that, the test dataset contains three answers per question: For 2204 questions, there are 6536 answers.

Statistics of the different question types can give an indication of the diversity and complexity of the questions. To this end, Table 2 lists question types with examples sorted by frequency in the test set of GermanQuAD. Further, it shows the average answer length (and standard deviation) and the model performance with regard to exact match, F1-score, and Top-1-accuracy.

The average answer length is shortest for questions of type *how, how many,* and *when,* which indicates that the answer is less complex, e.g., a year for questions of the type *when*. Questions of type *what* require the longest answers on average. The results of exact match, F1-score, and Top-1-accuracy indicate that questions of type *what* are also among the most difficult, as performance is only lower for questions of type *other*. Questions of type *when*

[10] Training dataset, Question ID: 54576

[11] lowercased, white-space normalized, punctuation and German stop words removed

	Passages	Questions	Answers
Train	2540	11518	11518
Test	474	2204	6536

Table 1: GermanQuAD comprises a one-way annotated training set and a three-way annotated test set of German Wikipedia passages (paragraphs). Each passage is from a different article.


```
[{
  "question": "Wie viele... ?",
  "answers": ["75 % der..."],
  "positive_ctxs": [
    {"title": "Gott",
     "text": "Gott\n\n=== Demografie
         ===\nEine... "}
  ],
  "hard_negative_ctxs": [
    {"title": "Christentum",
     "text": "Christentum\n\n===
         Ursprung ... ===\nDie ..."},
  ]
}]
```


are answered with highest scores of exact match, F1-score, and third-highest Top-1-accuracy.

3 GermanDPR Dataset Creation

The SQuAD format is not suitable for training DPR models. DPR requires additional data and a different data format. In DPR, each question/answer pair needs to be accompanied not only by the context that contains the answer (positive context) but also by other contexts that are semantically similar to the question but do not contain the answer (hard negative contexts). We take GermanQuAD as a starting point and add hard negatives from a dump of the full German Wikipedia. Following the approach by Karpukhin et al. (2020), we use BM25 to find passages in Wikipedia that are most similar to the question but do not contain the answer string. These passages are then added as hard negatives. To this end, we split each Wikipedia article into passages as described for the creation of GermanQuAD in Section 2.1. After indexing all passages with Elasticsearch, we use its BM25 implementation to retrieve three hard negatives for each question. However, we do not use the full GermanQuAD dataset but only question/answer pairs that have been labelled by the annotators as short answers. The reason is that hard negatives must not contain the answer, which we take into account by checking for the exact answer string. This exact string matching cannot catch rephrased versions of the answer, which we found is problematic especially for long answers but rarely for short answers. Figure 2 exemplifies the data format.

The final GermanDPR dataset comprises 9275 question/answer pairs in the training set and 1025 pairs in the test set. For each pair, there are one positive context and three hard negative contexts.

4 Experiments & Results

The following experiments study the impact of the number of training samples on model performance

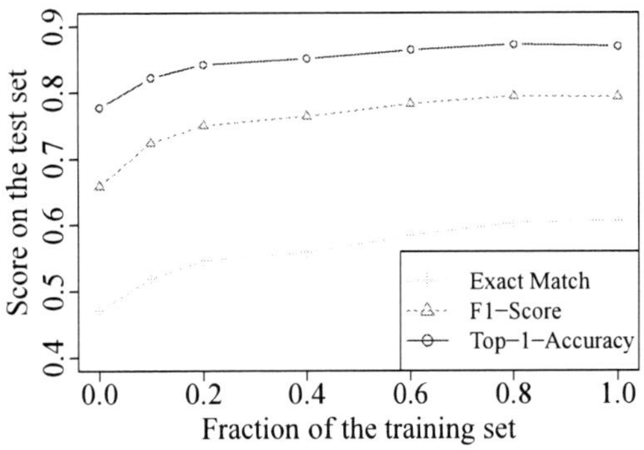

Figure 3: Impact of number of training samples on performance on test set.

for extractive QA, the benefits of reformulating previously annotated questions, and the model performance compared to related work and baselines for models trained on GermanQuAD and GermanDPR.

4.1 Labelling Experiments

Figure 3 shows the impact of the number of training samples on the percentage of exact matches, F1-score, and Top-1-accuracy (any overlap of prediction and ground truth) on the GermanQuAD test set. For all three metrics, there are no improvements after using more than 80 percent of the training samples.

Inspired by Khashabi et al. (2020), we experiment with perturbation of questions. To this end, annotators created a set of question/answer pairs and we use an existing extractive QA model to predict an answer for each question. Questions that are correctly answered and where the model has high confidence are simple and presumably not beneficial for model training (high confidence is inferred from large logits of the answer start and end indices). Instead of completely discarding

Question	Example	Freq	Answer Length	EM	F1	Top1Acc
Which	Über welche Rechte...	25.2	7.3 ± 9.5	58.8	75.7	83.8
What	Was ist die EU laut...	20.3	11.0 ± 12.0	42.4	68.3	80.1
How	Wie kann man auf...	11.4	7.0 ± 9.3	49.4	70.8	80.9
When	Wann wurde das erste...	11.3	7.0 ± 9.4	71.8	81.0	84.7
Who	Wer ist Bürgermeister...	10.5	8.6 ± 10.7	59.3	73.1	80.5
How many	Wie viele ethnische...	7.0	7.0 ± 9.3	59.7	76.2	85.7
Where	Wo wird in Estland...	5.5	8.3 ± 10.3	56.2	77.3	87.6
Why	Warum unterscheidet...	4.9	7.7 ± 9.7	50.5	70.0	76.6
Other	Woraus werden CDs...	4.0	7.4 ± 10.0	30.7	64.8	79.5

Table 2: Question types, their relative frequency, and the mean answer length $\pm$ standard deviation in the test set of GermanQuAD along with our model's performance on each type (in percent).

Data	EM	F1	Top1Acc
original	60.7	79.3	86.9
reformulations	60.2	**79.9**	87.3
orig.+reform.	**61.5**	79.8	**87.5**

Table 3: Model performance is almost unchanged if original question formulations are replaced with reformulations in the training data but using *both* slightly boosts performance.

these simple questions, we reformulate them. Annotators are much faster at reformulating an existing question compared to formulating a new question and annotating the answer in the context. The idea of the reformulation is to make the question more difficult while still corresponding to the same answer. An example of the original formulation (translated) is: "Which regions founded the federal state of Canada?" and the corresponding reformulation is: "From which regions did the federal state of Canada emerge?". The main difference is the changed word order and the use of *emerge* instead of *founded*, which is a less common wording and might result in lower lexical overlap of the question and the context containing the answer.

Table 3 compares the performance of a model trained on the original question formulations, on a dataset where the 1901 simplest questions are replaced with reformulated questions, and on a joint dataset of both. It shows that original formulations are not worse than the reformulations for training the model. However, the reformulations add variety to the training data, which slightly improves model performance when using both the original formulations and the reformulations.

4.2 QA Performance on GermanQuAD

In this section, we compare baseline QA models with models trained on GermanQuAD. Monolingual baseline models already have German QA capabilities by warm starting them on machine-translated SQuAD supplied along Facebook's MLQA dataset[12]. In addition to monolingual models, we use a multilingual XLM-Roberta model (Conneau et al., 2020) trained on English SQuAD v2.0. We continue finetuning the baseline models on the GermanQuAD training set.

Next to exact match (EM) and the ratio of overlapping words (F1) metric we also report Top-N-Accuracy scores. Top-N-Accuracy is a binary hit or miss score for the first N model predictions. The value is one if there is any *positional* overlap between the ground-truth answer and the model prediction — otherwise, it is zero. Such a hit or miss score is less prone to details of how answers are annotated (e.g., Answer1: "19th century", Answer2: "middle of 19th century") and useful in settings without multi-way annotations or where answers can be more than numbers, single entities, or a few words.

We train our model on GermanQuAD for two epochs with a learning rate of $3 \cdot 10^{-5}$ using Adam with default settings, a batch size of 24 and a maximum sequence length of 384 tokens. Training on GermanQuAD significantly improves performance on the test set (Table 4). Interestingly, the zero-shot language transfer of XLM-R (XLM-R-base-SQuAD) produces better results than training the monolingual models on translated data (GELECTRA-base-SQuADtranslate).

[12] `https://dl.fbaipublicfiles.com/MLQA/mlqa-translate-train.tar.gz`

Model	Params	EM	F1	Top1Acc
Human Baseline	$\approx 10^{16}$	66.4	89.5	96.4
GELECTRA-base-SQuADtranslate	110M	47.2	65.9	77.7
GELECTRA-base-GermanQuAD	110M	58.7	78.2	86.8
XLM-R-base-SQuAD	270M	49.1	68.6	79.9
XLM-R-base-SQuAD-GermanQuAD	270M	59.3	78.1	85.8
GELECTRA-large-SQuADtranslate	335M	58.5	78.8	88.7
GELECTRA-large-GermanQuAD	335M	**68.6**	**88.1**	**93.7**

Table 4: QA model performance on the three-way annotated GermanQuAD test set (in percent). Model types and training data are included in the model name. For finetuning XLM-Roberta we use the English SQuAD v2.0 dataset, the GELECTRA models are warm started on the German translation of SQuAD v1.1 and finetuned on GermanQuAD. The human baseline was computed for the 3-way test set by taking one answer as prediction and the other two as ground truth.

When training continues on in-language data though, the situation reverses and the monolingual model (GELECTRA-base-GermanQuAD) becomes slightly better than its multilingual counterpart (XLM-R-base-SQuAD-GermanQuAD). In addition to having a better performance, those monolingual models are much smaller compared to their multilingual counterparts (see "Params" in Table 4).

4.3 GermanQuAD Out-of-Domain Performance

In order to test how well models trained on GermanQuAD generalize to other data, we evaluate them on the German part of MLQA (Lewis et al., 2020a), XQuAD (Artetxe et al., 2020), and a private dataset on financial compliance reports called SFCR.[13]

Table 5 shows the out-of-domain performance on four datasets. Training with GermanQuAD improves Top-1-Accuracy for every dataset, meaning that the model is capable of finding the semantically correct answer more often. At the same time, we observe performance drops in EM that are often related to dataset characteristics or metric details. Traditional QA metrics, such as Exact Match and F1, are unsuited for datasets that do not have multi-way annotations because they cannot cover all possible correct answers. For example, for question "What did Deng Xiaoping propose in the 1980s?"[14] we find gold label "that there should be only one China" and model prediction "the reunification of China" as equally valid. F1 and especially EM penalize for different answer styles. GermanQuAD often marks more complete answers ("Lion" vs "in star constellation Lion", "Maxim Gorki" versus "on board the Soviet cruise ship SS Maxim Gorky"), which should not be punished. Manual checks for mismatches in Exact Match revealed GermanQuAD model predictions were often as valid or better as original ground-truth labels.

4.4 Retrieval Performance on GermanDPR

On the GermanDPR dataset, we train a DPR model that uses two German BERT models (Chan et al., 2020), gbert-base, as encoders of the question and the passage. Pairs of encoded questions and passages are compared with the dot product as similarity function and the number of hard negatives is restricted to 2. More hard negatives are included in the dataset and could be used for training but they would also increase the amount of required GPU memory. Instead, we use in-batch negatives.

For the training, queries are clipped after 32 tokens and passages after 300 tokens. The learning rate is 10^{-6} using Adam, linear scheduling with warm-up, and dropout rate 0.1. With a batch size of 40, the model achieves an average in-batch rank of 0.50 after training for 20 epochs and the average rank does not further improve after more epochs.

Figure 4 compares the retrieval performance of BM25 and DPR on the full German Wikipedia (2.8 million passages). It shows that DPR outperforms BM25 for different numbers of top-k retrieved results. While BM25 returns the correct passage within the top 10 results for only 46.5% of the queries, DPR gets the right one for 61.0% of the

[13]SFCR is annotated SQuAD-style and consists of 2386 QA pairs.

[14]MLQA question: 2ebe96790124698968addfddfb6c6a10a580ca72

Model	MLQA-test	MLQA-dev	XQuAD	SFCR
GELECTRA-base-SQuADtranslate	37.3/60.1/72.5	35.0/59.9/73.1	59.2/75.5/82.9	23.5/56.3/73.3
GELECTRA-base-GermanQuAD	30.9/59.8/76.9	27.3/59.4/77.2	45.6/70.9/85.0	31.9/68.7/82.1
GELECTRA-large-SQuADtranslate	**40.6/66.5**/78.8	**39.1/68.9**/81.7	**62.8/81.1**/89.2	30.4/68.3/84.2
GELECTRA-large-GermanQuAD	32.9/64.2/**81.0**	31.3/65.9/**82.8**	49.1/73.4/**90.7**	**39.8/78.0/91.2**

Table 5: QA model performance for out-of-domain datasets without the use of training (X-SQuADtranslate) and with (X-GermanQuAD). The reported metrics are EM/F1/Top-1-Accuracy. The latter is a binary hit or miss based on the position of the best model prediction.

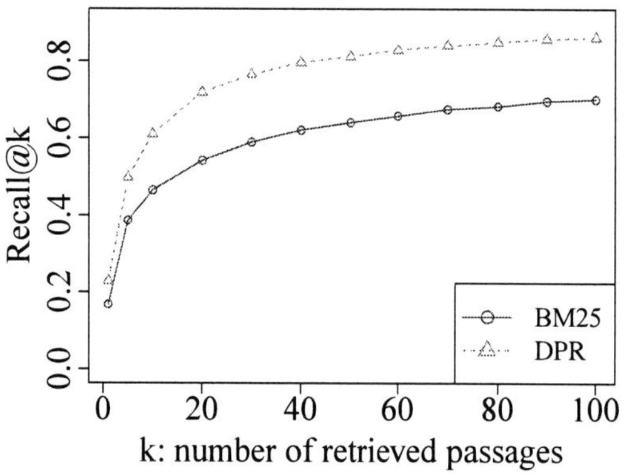

Figure 4: Comparison of BM25 and DPR with regard to recall@k on the full German Wikipedia.

5 Conclusion and Future Work

Only a few resources for non-English QA and passage retrieval are available. In this paper, we presented two new datasets, GermanQuAD and GermanDPR, to foster research in this area. We described the data annotation process in detail so that other researchers can reproduce the approach for other languages. Our experiments showed that training QA models on GermanQuAD achieves a new SOTA for German QA and that training DPR models on GermanDPR drastically outperforms a BM25 baseline. A promising path for future work is to research new evaluation metrics for QA. Especially for longer answers in German, we find that current metrics penalise too much if a predicted answer contains some extra words although being semantically similar to the ground-truth answer. Future metrics could take into account the semantic similarity of predicted and ground-truth answers.

Acknowledgements

We would like to thank Julian Gutsch, Tom Hersperger, Luise Köhler, Iuliia Mozhina, and Justus Peter for supporting the project with data annotation and fruitful discussions on how to improve the labelling process.

References

Mikel Artetxe, Sebastian Ruder, and Dani Yogatama. 2020. On the cross-lingual transferability of monolingual representations. In *Proceedings of the 58th Annual Meeting of the Association for Computational Linguistics*, pages 4623–4637. Association for Computational Linguistics.

Branden Chan, Stefan Schweter, and Timo Möller. 2020. German's next language model. In *Proceedings of the 28th International Conference on Computational Linguistics*, pages 6788–6796. International Committee on Computational Linguistics.

Alexis Conneau, Kartikay Khandelwal, Naman Goyal, Vishrav Chaudhary, Guillaume Wenzek, Francisco Guzmán, Edouard Grave, Myle Ott, Luke Zettlemoyer, and Veselin Stoyanov. 2020. Unsupervised cross-lingual representation learning at scale. In *Proceedings of the 58th Annual Meeting of the Association for Computational Linguistics*, pages 8440–8451. Association for Computational Linguistics.

Alexis Conneau and Guillaume Lample. 2019. Cross-lingual language model pretraining. In *Advances in Neural Information Processing Systems*, volume 32. Curran Associates, Inc.

Jacob Devlin, Ming-Wei Chang, Kenton Lee, and Kristina Toutanova. 2019. Bert: Pre-training of deep bidirectional transformers for language understanding. In *Proceedings of the 2019 Conference of the North American Chapter of the Association for Computational Linguistics: Human Language Technologies, Volume 1 (Long and Short Papers)*, pages 4171–4186. Association for Computational Linguistics.

Martin d'Hoffschmidt, Wacim Belblidia, Quentin Heinrich, Tom Brendlé, and Maxime Vidal. 2020.

FQuAD: French question answering dataset. In *Findings of the Association for Computational Linguistics: EMNLP 2020*, pages 1193–1208. Association for Computational Linguistics.

Pavel Efimov, Andrey Chertok, Leonid Boytsov, and Pavel Braslavski. 2020. SberQuAD–Russian reading comprehension dataset: Description and analysis. In *International Conference of the Cross-Language Evaluation Forum for European Languages*, pages 3–15. Springer.

Vladimir Karpukhin, Barlas Oguz, Sewon Min, Patrick Lewis, Ledell Wu, Sergey Edunov, Danqi Chen, and Wen-tau Yih. 2020. Dense passage retrieval for open-domain question answering. In *Proceedings of the Conference on Empirical Methods in Natural Language Processing (EMNLP)*, pages 6769–6781. Association for Computational Linguistics.

Daniel Khashabi, Tushar Khot, and Ashish Sabharwal. 2020. More bang for your buck: Natural perturbation for robust question answering. In *Proceedings of the Conference on Empirical Methods in Natural Language Processing (EMNLP)*, pages 163–170. Association for Computational Linguistics.

Tom Kwiatkowski, Jennimaria Palomaki, Olivia Redfield, Michael Collins, Ankur Parikh, Chris Alberti, Danielle Epstein, Illia Polosukhin, Matthew Kelcey, Jacob Devlin, Kenton Lee, Kristina N. Toutanova, Llion Jones, Ming-Wei Chang, Andrew Dai, Jakob Uszkoreit, Quoc Le, and Slav Petrov. 2019. Natural questions: a benchmark for question answering research. *Transactions of the Association of Computational Linguistics*.

Patrick Lewis, Barlas Oguz, Ruty Rinott, Sebastian Riedel, and Holger Schwenk. 2020a. MLQA: Evaluating cross-lingual extractive question answering. In *Proceedings of the 58th Annual Meeting of the Association for Computational Linguistics*, pages 7315–7330. Association for Computational Linguistics.

Patrick Lewis, Pontus Stenetorp, and Sebastian Riedel. 2020b. Question and answer test-train overlap in open-domain question answering datasets. *arXiv preprint arXiv:2008.02637*.

Seungyoung Lim, Myungji Kim, and Jooyoul Lee. 2019. KorQuAD1.0: Korean qa dataset for machine reading comprehension. *arXiv preprint arXiv:1909.07005*.

Pranav Rajpurkar, Robin Jia, and Percy Liang. 2018. Know what you don't know: Unanswerable questions for SQuAD. In *Proceedings of the 56th Annual Meeting of the Association for Computational Linguistics (Volume 2: Short Papers)*, pages 784–789. Association for Computational Linguistics.

A Annotation FAQ

Annotation FAQ for the GermanQuAD dataset.

1. What is a good question?
    - A good question is a fact-seeking question that can be answered with an entity (person, organisation, location, etc.) or explanation. A bad question is ambiguous, incomprehensible, dependent on clear false presuppositions, opinion seeking, or not clearly a request for factual information.
    - The question should ask about information present in the text passage given. It should not be answerable only with additional knowledge or your interpretation.
    - Do not copy paste answer text into the question. Good questions do not contain the exact same words as the answer or the context around the answer. The question should be a reformulation with synonyms and in different order as the context of the answer.
    - Questions should be very precise natural questions you would ask when you want information from another person.
2. How many questions should you ask per text passage?
    - Maximally ask 20 questions per passage.
    - Some text passages are not suited for 20 questions. Do not make up very constructed and complicated questions just to fill up the 20 - move on to the next text.
    - Try to ask questions covering the whole passage and focus on questions covering important information. Do not only ask questions about a single sentence in that passage.
3. What is a good answer span?
    - Always mark whole words. Do not start or end the answer within a word.
    - For short answers: The answer should be as short and as close to a spoken human answer as possible. Do not include punctuation.
    - For long answers: Please mark whole sentences with punctuation. The sentences can also pick up parts of the question, or mark even whole text passages. Mark passages only if they are not too large (e.g. not more than 8-10 sentences).

4. How do I differentiate long vs short answers?
    - If there is a short answer possible you should always select short answer over long answer.
    - Short precise answers like numbers or a few words are short answers.
    - Long answers include lists of possibilities or multiple sentences are needed to answer the question correctly.
5. How to handle multiple possible answers to a single question?
    - As of now there is no functionality to mark multiple answers per single question.
    - Workaround: You can add a question with the same text but different answer selection by using the button below the question list (Button reads "custom question").
6. What to do with grammatically wrong or incorrectly spelled questions?
    - Include them. When users use the tool and ask questions they will likely contain grammar and spelling errors, too.
    - Exception: The question needs to be understandable without reading and interpretation of the corresponding text passage. If you do not understand the question, please mark the question as "I don't understand the question".
7. What to do with text passages that are not properly converted or contain (in part) information that cannot be labelled (e.g. just lists or garbage text)?
    - Please do not annotate this text.
    - You can write down what is missing, or the cause why you cannot label the text + the text number and title.
8. Which browser to use?
    - Please use the Chrome browser. The tool is not tested for other browsers.

Zero-Shot Clinical Questionnaire Filling From Human-Machine Interactions

Farnaz Ghassemi Toudeshki[&,#], **Philippe Jolivet**[&], **Alexandre Durand-Salmon**[&], **Anna Liednikova**[&,†]
[&] ALIAE
[#] IDMC, Université de Lorraine
[†] Université de Lorraine, LORIA
{farnaz.ghassemi, philippe.jolivet, alexandre.durand-salmon, anna.liednikova}@aliae.io

Abstract

In clinical studies, chatbots mimicking doctor-patient interactions are used for collecting information about the patient's health state. Later, this information needs to be processed and structured for the doctor. One way to organize it is by automatically filling the questionnaires from the human-bot conversation. It would help the doctor to spot the possible issues. Since there is no such dataset available for this task and its collection is costly and sensitive, we explore the capacities of state-of-the-art zero-shot models for question answering, textual inference, and text classification. We provide with a detailed analysis of the results and propose further directions for clinical questionnaire filling.

1 Introduction

Chatbots in healthcare can be used to collect information about the user with different purposes: treatment adherence, monitoring, patient support program, patient education, behavior change, diagnosis (Car et al., 2020).

Considering monitoring, patient-doctor conversations have mainly been used for the automation of medical records' creation through the extraction of clinical entities such as symptoms, medications, and their properties (Du et al., 2019), generating reports (Finley et al., 2018) and summaries (Zhang et al., 2018). Surprisingly, the task of filling clinical questionnaires received less attention.

Patients fill standard questionnaires during each medical visit, which frequency is usually several weeks. Performing this task in an automated way based on serendipitous talk (through a chatbot) opens the opportunity to get updated information more regularly and then monitor the patient more closely and in a seamless way.

Ren et al. (2020a) were the first to introduce a questionnaire filling task as a classification problem, with the targets in the form of symptom phrases. Though, there is plenty of questionnaires that consist of full meaningful assertions or questions. The difference between questionnaire filling and slot filling is in the complexity of the questions that require machine reading comprehension (MRC) and question answering (QA).

The goal of a typical MRC task is to process a (set of) text passage(s) and then to answer questions about the passage(s). Though usually, multi-choice answer options are semantically different, in the case of questionnaires, the answers are often on the same scale (agree-disagree, often-rare).

More concretely, we make the following contributions:

- a clinical questionnaires' categorization based on questions and answers types
- data collection schema for filling questionnaires for 5 question types: open questions (OQ), closed questions (CQ), agreement Likert-scale (ALS), frequency Likert-scale (FLS) and visual analogue scale (VAS)
- analysis of question answering (QA), natural language inference (NLI), and zero-shot text classification (ZeroShot-TC) state-of-the-art models performance for the mentioned questions types

2 Related work

Four formats are commonly used for posing questions and answering them: Extractive (EX), Abstractive (AB), Multiple-Choice (MC), and Yes/No (YN). UnifiedQA (Khashabi et al., 2020) is a single pre-trained QA model, that performs well across 20 QA datasets spanning 4 diverse formats.

Demszky et al. (2018) proposed a sentence transformation model which converts question-answer pairs into their declarative forms that allows to solve the task with NLI models. On the other hand, (Yin et al., 2019) shows how ZeroShot-TC models

Proceedings of the 3rd Workshop on Machine Reading for Question Answering , pages 51–62
Nov 10th, 2021 ©2021 Association for Computational Linguistics

may be successfully used as NLI models, being partially inspired by the way (Obamuyide and Vlachos, 2018) transformed relation classification task into NLI problem.

Questions in multiple-choice RACE (Lai et al., 2017) require holistic reasoning about the text, involving people's mental states and attitudes and the way they express them. Mishra et al. (2020) described reasoning categories present in RACE and showed that if given passage is a dialogue, NLI model performs better than QA model.

Ren et al. (2020b) presented a new medical Information Extraction task which uses questionnaires to convert medical text data into structured data. Their work is based on neural network classifier which makes selection among given options for closed-end type questions to fill out one complete questionnaire using only one model.

To our best knowledge, it is a first work to address the problem of filling in clinical questionnaires based on dialogue history. In Section 3 we are going to discuss the most common question types in questionnaires, including Likert scale which wasn't addressed before in clinical natural language processing. Also in Section 6 we show state-of-the-art models' ability to solve this task.

The task of filling questionnaires from user-bot dialogue history is a very specific sub-field of MRC in NLP and as a result, reduces the chance of availability of such data for training/fine-tuning current models or later for evaluation, specially in medical domain. Both dialogues and answered questionnaires based on them are required that makes it difficult to collect such data on a large scale. This low resource setting is conducive to zero-shot approaches.

3 Question types

Khashabi et al. (2020) categorized existing QA datasets into four categories based on the format of answers: Extractive (EX), Abstractive (AB), Multiple-Choice (MC), and Yes/No (YN). In the following section we would like to introduce also Likert scale and Visual analogue scales (VAS) type of answers which is very common for clinical questionnaires. Sinha et al. (2017) came to the conclusion in their review that Visual analogue scale (VAS) and numerical rating scale (NRS) were the best adapted pain scales for pain measurement in endometriosis. Also, VAS is often used in epidemiologic and clinical research to measure the intensity or frequency of various symptoms (Paul-Dauphin, 1999).

Question type	**Questionnaire**
Open Question (OQ)	Morin (Morin, 1993) QCD (Daut, 1983) MOS-SS (Sherbourne and Stewart, 1991)
Closed Question (CQ)	QPC (C. Thomas-Antérion, 2004) EPICES (Bihan et al., 2005)
Agreement Likert-scale (ALS)	TSK (Kori, 1990) PBPI (Williams and Thorn, 1989) TAS-20 (Bagby et al., 1994) LOT-R (Scheier et al., 1994) IEQ-CF (Sullivan, 2008) JCK (KARASEK, 1985)
Frequency Likert-scale (FLS)	MOS-SS (Sherbourne and Stewart, 1991) MBI (Maslach et al., 1997) PCL-S (Weathers et al., 1993) HAD (Zigmond and Snaith, 1983) SF-12 (Ware Jr et al., 1996)
Visual Analogue Scale (VAS)	QCD (Daut, 1983) Dallas (Lawlis et al., 1989) LEEDS (Parrott and Hindmarch, 2004) FABQ-W (Waddell et al., 1993)

Table 1: Clinical questionnaires and their types of questions

For each question type present in medical questionnaire, we provide examples of questionnaires and question in Table 1.

4 Task and Data

4.1 Task

Given a human-healthbot dialog history D and a set of questions q_i extracted from a questionnaire Q, the task is to determine the correct answer a_i to each question q_i, including the 'not mentioned' option, i.e. the possibility that the dialog does not address that question.

4.2 Chatbot

To create a chatbot for interactions, we followed the ComBot ensemble (Liednikova et al., 2021). The conversation always starts with the opening 'What is the most difficult for you about your sleep ?'. We made sure that there is no intersection between questions of the bot and questionnaire questions, due to the point of the research for answering questions implicitly addressed in the dialog. Since creating a dialog following the questionnaire topics is a very resource consuming task, we decided to mitigate the risk of the system proposing undesired direction of the conversation with a rejection function. If a bot reply isn't consistent with the dialog history, the user can reject it and receive the next best candidate to continue the conversation.

4.3 Questionnaires

For experiments, we have chosen three questionnaires that are semantically close to the topics of the chatbot model: Morin (OQ), PBPI (ALS, VAS, CQ), Mos-ss (FLS). For PBPI questionnaire we ask annotators to give the answers in three format types at the same time: CQ, ALS, VAS. We provide statistics in Table 2. The full list of the questions could be found in Appendix, the answer options could be found in Tables 5 and 6.

4.4 Data collection

We asked 10 annotators to interact with the chatbot one time for each of the three questionnaires. So in total, we collected 30 dialogues and their corresponding question answers.

The annotators were first asked to read the questionnaire so that they could guide the interaction with the health bot maximizing the number of questions addressed during the dialog. Then the annotators were asked to fill in the questionnaire based on their conversation and to select 'Not mentioned' (NA) option if the current question couldn't be answered from the dialog history. For PBPI questionnaire we ask annotators to give the answers in three format types at the same time: CQ, ALS, VAS. You can find screenshot of interfaces in Appendix and answer options in Tables 5 and 6.

To ensure the reliability of collected data, we conducted a double annotation with adjudication. We ask two people to fill in the questionnaires based on the collected dialogues. So, totally for each question of each dialog we have three answers (one from the author of the dialog and two from other annotators). Table 4 demonstrates final agreement between two annotators engaged in double annotation, as well as between two annotators and initial participants. In case of disagreement between annotators, the third person (adjudicator) decides the final label. These ground truth labels are used for evaluation of the models later.

During annotation, we came with some definition of classes that helped the annotators to come to agreement. We consider that the user would totally agree with the questionnaire statement if this statement or its paraphrase is explicitly mentioned in text, otherwise if there are phrases that fully or partially support this statement we annotate it with agree label. The same rules are applied to give disagreement and total disagreement label for contradictory statements.

Due to the high level of complexity of the task, we enrolled high-educated volunteers from our professional network. We made sure that participants were well aware of the context of the work and they were all properly compensated. On average, performing a complete conversation with chatbot took 20 minutes from participants, and about 15 minutes for answering a questionnaire from a dialog history.

Since the data and questionnaires were initially in French, we have translated them with DeepL [1] to English and to run the models.

Q Type	Questionnaire	Nb. of Q	Nb. of A
OQ	Morin	22	inf
CQ	PBPI	16	3
ALS	PBPI	16	5
FLS	Mos-ss	10	7
VAS	PBPI	16	11

Table 2: Questionnaires statistics: number of questions and number of answer options

	MOS-SS	Morin	PBPI
# turn	24.4	34.5	23.5
# tokens	259.1	403.2	269.2
# nb of tokens / turn	11.2	11.9	12.2
# Q answered	76%	59.3%	85.6%
# uniq tokens	140.8	201	147.6

Table 3: Statistics of dialogues for each questionnaire

5 Models

In this section, we present the models that can be used in zero-shot setting with selected question types.

QA model UnifiedQA (Khashabi et al., 2020) [2] is a single pre-trained QA model, that performs

[1] https://www.deepl.com/fr/translator

[2] https://github.com/allenai/unifiedqa

OQ	CQ	ALS	FLS	VAS
two annotators				
0.81 (BertScore) 0.72 (Rouge-1)	0.81	0.70	0.67	0.31
two annotators + user				
0.75 (BertScore) 0.67 (Rouge-1)	0.67	0.47	0.56	0.20

Table 4: Inter-annotator agreement, using Kappa score for closed-ended questions and F1 score for Open question type

question type	choice	ratio
CQ	yes	55%
	no	30.6%
	NA	14.4%
ALS	totally agree	35%
	agree	19.4%
	rather disagree	11.8%
	totally disagree	19.4%
	NA	14.4%
FLS	all the time	5.6%
	most of the time	11.9%
	a good part of the time	5%
	sometimes	12.5%
	rarely	7.5%
	never	5%
	NA	15%
VAS	10	34.4%
	9	1.2%
	8	3.1%
	7	11.9%
	6	3.8%
	5	0%
	4	0.6%
	3	3.1%
	2	8.1%
	1	1.2%
	0	18.1%
	NA	14.4%

Table 5: Statistics of number of different choices for each question type

well across 20 QA datasets spanning 4 diverse formats. Fine-tuning this pre-trained QA model into specialized models results in a new state of the art on 10 factoid and commonsense QA datasets, establishing UnifiedQA as a strong starting point for building QA systems. In our experiments, we used UnifiedQA-t5-3b version.

Applied to the following question types:

- **OQ** The dialog history and question are provided in format of NarrativeQA dataset (Kočiský et al., 2017)
- **CQ and ALS** To fit format of MCTest dataset (Richardson et al., 2013), we transformed questionnaire statements to question form, by changing fist pronoun to second and adding "Do you agree with that" at the beginning. Otherwise, the model tends to choose NA option.
- **FLS** The dialog history and question are provided in format of MC Test dataset (Richardson et al., 2013)

NLI model We use DeBERTa V2 xlarge model (He et al., 2020) [3] fine-tuned with MNLI dataset (Williams et al., 2018) for NLI task. We pass to the model concatenated dialog history as premise and question in declarative form as hypothesis. The output is probabilities for three classes: Entailment, Contradiction, Neutral.

Applied to the following question types:

- **CQ** A question is transformed into a statement and treated as hypothesis. Entering the premise and hypothesis to the model, we choose the class with the highest score as the final answer. Entailment class is considered as 'yes', contradiction as 'no' and neutral as 'NA'.
- **ALS** Premise is a dialogue history, hypothesis is a questionnaire statement. If probability for neutral class was higher than contradiction and entailment class, we consider that the dialogue doesn't contain relevant information to the question and give NA label. Otherwise, we take probability of Contradiction with negative sign and sum up it with probability of Entailment with positive sign. The resulting score lies in the interval of (-1,1). We uniformly divide this interval into N segments, where N is a number of options on Linkert-scale (usually 4 or 5).
- **FLS** For each question, we enter the model with dialogue as the premise and concatenation of one of the frequency scales with statement format of question (hypothesis = freq + question_statement_format) as hypothesis. We treat transformed question-answer combinations as distinct hypotheses, as presented in (Trivedi et al., 2019). Among frequency choices, we choose the one which has the highest entailment score. If none of them has the entailment score higher than 50%, we consider that the dialogue doesn't contain relevant

[3] https://github.com/microsoft/DeBERTa

information to the question and give NA label. Otherwise, we select the frequency scale with the highest entailment score.

- **VAS** If score for neutral is highest, then the selected output would be NA. Otherwise, we subtract the entailment score from contradiction. The result would be in range (-1,1). To map the result in range (0,10), we add value 1 to the subtraction result and then multiply it with 5 (shown in equation 1).

$$value = (ent - cont + 1) * 5 \quad (1)$$

where ent and $cont$ are the predicted probabilities of entailment and contradiction classes.

ZeroShot-TC model We use Bart-large model (Lewis et al., 2019) [4] for zero-shot text classification trained on MNLI corpus (Williams et al., 2018). In this setting, we pass concatenated dialog history as a context and formulate target labels as filled templates, so that the input data could be closer to entailment format. Then we add one more target label 'NA' to consider the situation when the answer is not mentioned in the dialog. The model provides probability scores for each candidate, and the candidate with the highest probability would be chosen as the final answer.

Applied to the following question types:

- **CQ** We transform a question into the statement beginning with "I agree that" for "yes" choice or with "I disagree that" for "no" choice.

- **ALS** The candidates are formed following the template "I *agreement_option* that *questionnaire statement*", where agreement options are totally disagree, disagree, agree, totally agree.

- **FLS** We transform a question into the statement and add in the beginning the frequency option to form the candidates.

- **VAS** Candidates are defined as the same as ones in CQ. Model outputs probability scores for each class. By having these scores for each label and map them to entailment/contradiction/neutral labels, we continue transforming the results to VAS scale by doing the same process explained previously for VAS using NLI model.

[4] https://huggingface.co/facebook/bart-large-mnli

6 Evaluation

Since for each question type we had different output, we used different evaluation scores.

For evaluating the performance of UnifiedQA on open-question types, we have used two common evaluation metrics: ROUGE (Lin, 2004) and BERTscore Zhang et al. (2019). ROUGE counts how many n-grams in the generated response matches the n-grams in the reference answer. Since we used abstractive mode of UnifiedQA, generated outputs might have different n-grams from reference ones. Therefore, using BERTscore might show a more realistic evaluation perspective since it computes the semantic similarity between generated and referenced answers based on embeddings.

We evaluate closed questions (CQ), agreement Likert scale (ALS), frequency Likert scale (FLS) and visual analogue scale (VAS) with macro and weighted F1 score.

The results are shown in the Table 7 for open-ended question type and in Table 8 for closed-ended ones. Because UnifiedQA generates answer even for unmentioned questions, we report the results for both all questions (mentioned and not mentioned questions) and for just mentioned ones.

The experiments were conducted with a laptop having Intel® Core™ i7-10610U CPU @ 1.80GHz * 8 and NVIDIA Quadro P520.

7 Results and discussion

Detecting unanswerable questions Considering all open questions, we can see from Table 7 that the scores are considerably low, 0.38 for ROUGE and 0.55 for BERT. On the other hand, if we calculate these scores only for open questions being mentioned in the dialog (according to the user answers), the scores are almost 2 times better. Results indicate the high performance of UnifiedQA model for answering mentioned questions and its lack to distinguish given the context if the question is answerable or not.

Impact of number of choices Table 8 shows the performance of SOTA NLI and ZeroShot-TC models for answering closed-ended question types (CQ, ALS, FLS, VAS). Comparing results for different question types can tell us that number of multiple-choices in each question type has a great impact on final results. Closed question type with 3 choices has the highest results and on the other hand, VAS with 11 choices has the lowest performance.

Q type	Answers	NLI		ZeroShot-TC	
CQ	yes, no, NA	**Premise**	dialogue history	**Context**	dialogue history
		Hypothesis	There are times when I don't have pain.	**Targets**	***I agree that*** there are times when I don't have pain, ***I disagree that*** there are times when I don't have pain., NA
		Model output	entailment(0.5), contradiction(0.3), neutral(0.2)	**Model output**	I agree that there are times when I don't have pain.
		Final output	yes	**Final output**	yes
ALS	totally disagree, rather disagree, agree, totally agree, NA	**Premise**	dialogue history	**Context**	dialogue history
		Hypothesis	There are times when I don't have pain.	**Targets**	***I totally disagree that*** there are times when I don't have pain., ***I rather disagree that*** there are times when I don't have pain.,.., NA
		Model output	entailment(0.5), contradiction(0.3), neutral(0.2)	**Model output**	I totally disagree that there are times when I don't have pain.
		Final output	agree	**Final output**	totally disagree
FLS	all the time, most of the time, a good part of the time, sometimes, rarely, never, NA	**Premise**	dialogue history	**Context**	dialog history
		Hypothesis	{freq_scale} I got the amount of sleep I needed.	**Targets**	***all the time*** I got the amount of sleep I needed., ***most of the time*** I got the amount of sleep I needed., .., NA
		Model output	entailment score for each freq. scale	**Model output**	rarely I got the amount of sleep I needed.
		Final output	choosing freq. scale which has the highest entailment score	**Final output**	rarely
VAS	0, 1, 2, 3, 4, 5, 6, 7, 8, 9, 10, NA	**Premise**	dialogue history	**Context**	dialog history
		Hypothesis	I got the amount of sleep I needed.	**Targets**	***I agree that*** there are times when I don't have pain, ***I disagree that*** there are times when I don't have pain., NA
		Model output	entailment(0.5), contradiction(0.3), neutral(0.2)	**Model output**	I agree that there are times when I don't have pain.(0.5), I disagree that there are times when I don't have pain.(0.3), NA(0.2)
		Final output	6	**Final output**	6

Table 6: Examples of input and output for textual inference with Deberta and zero-shot classification with Bart-large for closed, agreement, frequency and VAS scale questions

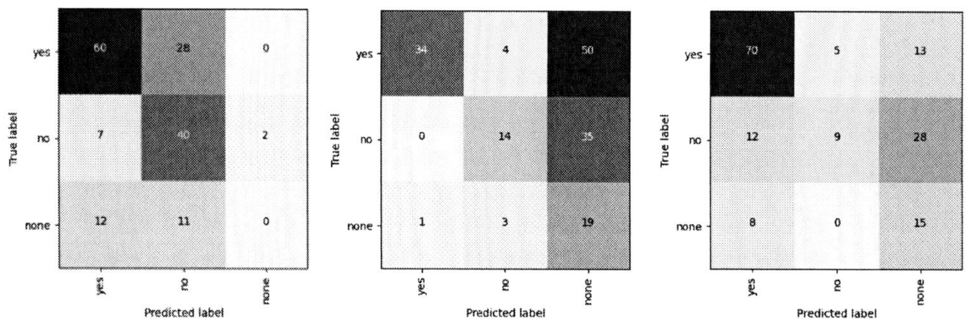

Figure 1: Confusion matrix for CQ using QA (left), NLI (center) and ZeroShot-TC (right) models

Metric	All	Answered
ROUGE	0.38	0.63
BERT	0.55	0.93

Table 7: Scores for zero-shot evaluation of OQ type

The table 8 also indicates the superiority of ZeroShot-TC for CQ and FLS questions types than NLI. After comparing confusion matrices provided for the NLI and ZeroShot-TC models, we can observe that the NLI model has a high tendency to give NA (neutral) class as output, while this is not the case for the ZeroShot-TC model. On the other hand, the inability of ZeroShot-TC model to correctly predict extreme choices (totally agree/totally disagree) for ALS question type (figure 2) has led to the lower performance of this model in comparison with NLI.

Model \ Question type	metric	CQ	ALS	FLS	VAS
Random (Baseline)		0.33	0.25	0.14	0.09
UnifiedQA-t5-3b	macro F1	0.44	0.13	**0.29**	
	weighted F1	0.58	0.12	**0.32**	
deberta-v2-xlarge-mnli	macro F1	0.417	**0.240**	0.158	**0.064**
	weighted F1	0.470	**0.262**	0.192	**0.104**
facebook/bart-large-mnli	macro F1	**0.484**	0.166	0.220	0.04
	weighted F1	**0.575**	0.136	0.262	0.03

Table 8: Scores for zero-shot evaluation for question types: CQ - closed question, ALS - agreement Likert-scale, FLS - frequency Likert-scale, VAS - Visual Analogue Scale

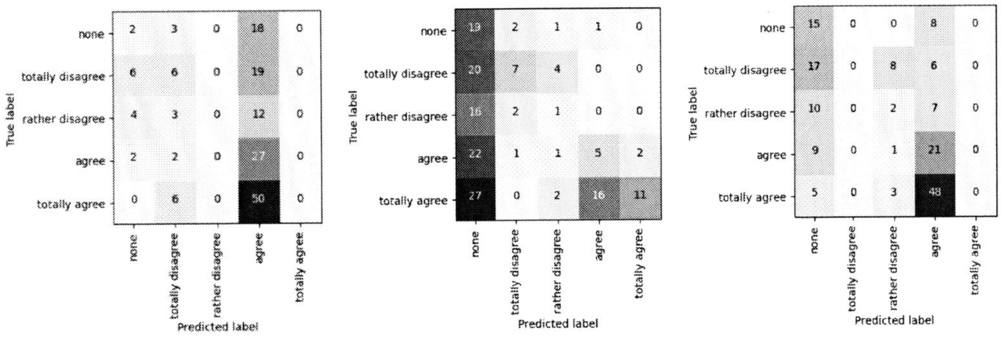

Figure 2: Confusion matrix for ALS using QA (left), NLI (center) and ZeroShot-TC (right) models

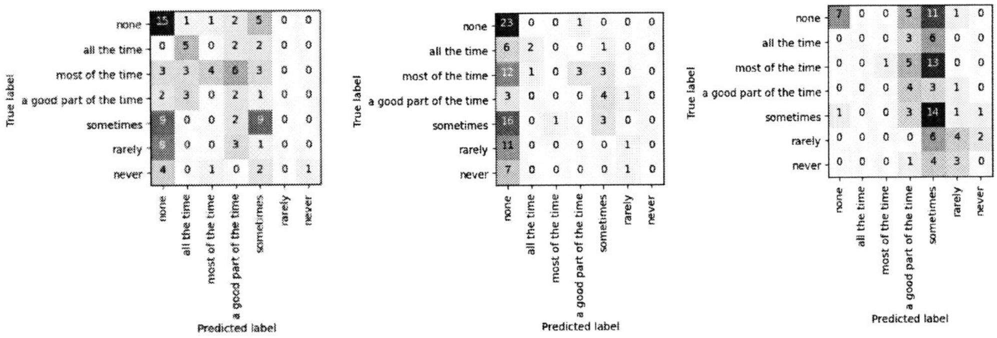

Figure 3: Confusion matrix for FLS using QA (left), NLI (center) and ZeroShot-TC (right) models

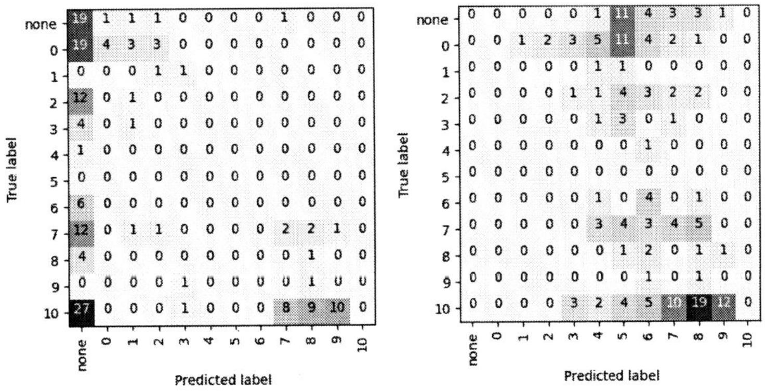

Figure 4: Confusion matrix for VAS using NLI (left) and ZeroShot-TC (right) model

Measuring agreement is the most challenging task From Table 8 and Figures 2 and 4 we can see that predicting answers for agreement scale is the most challenging task. Since the answer option isn't semantically different enough to facilitate models choice, the probabilities for target classes don't help with selecting the correct level of agreement. In future work, we would like to explore other approaches, such as multi-hop reasoning and argument mining.

Importance of text input From our experiments, we can derive that the models are sensitive to the input text format and noise. Also, the different models are sensitive to the different data preprocessing technics. They may include using speaker tags, punctuation cleaning, selecting a subset of input text on some criteria. Such experiments should show what kind of preprocessing may boost performance without unnecessary data collection and training. These results may be a contribution to green and sustainable NLP.

8 Conclusion

In this paper, we introduced the approaches for clinical questionnaire filling in a zero-shot setting for the five question types most used in clinical studies. Also, we describe the data collection process for their evaluation. With the results, we show that this task is not easy to solve.

There is a type of questions which are more well-known in multi-hop reading comprehension. For such type of questions, there is a need to properly integrate multiple pieces of evidence to answer them. Song et al. (2018) investigates graph convolutional network (GCN) and graph recurrent network to perform evidence integration.

As future work, we plan to take advantage of graph convolutional networks (GCNs) to improve the textual entailment for questionnaire filling. It would be possible due to enriching the model with knowledge graphs both in the open domain and close domain (medical).

Another direction to explore is text transformations. For example, we plan to transform statement-question into cloze form by masking the most important word and providing it as one option of the answers, use common-sense knowledge and graph structure for better reasoning.

Ethical considerations

Regarding Regulation (EU) 2017/745, described software is intended for general uses, even when used in a healthcare environment, it is intended for uses relating to lifestyle or well-being that do not constitute any a medical prediction and medical prognosis function without doctors validation or correction.

Acknowledgments

The authors would like to warmly thank members of the Aliae company for their support and helpful feedback during the project. They would also like to thank Claire Gardent for valuable discussions at earlier stages of this work and constructive feedback.

References

R.michael Bagby, James D.a. Parker, and Graeme J. Taylor. 1994. The twenty-item toronto alexithymia scale—i. item selection and cross-validation of the factor structure. *Journal of Psychosomatic Research*, 38(1):23–32.

Hélène Bihan, Silvana Laurent, Catherine Sass, Gérard Nguyen, Caroline Huot, Jean Jacques Moulin, René Guegen, Philippe Le Toumelin, Hervé Le Clésiau, Emilio La Rosa, Gérard Reach, and Régis Cohen. 2005. Association among individual deprivation, glycemic control, and diabetes complications. *Diabetes Care*, 28(11):2680–2685.

S. Honoré-Masson G. Berne P.H. Ruel B. Laurent C. Thomas-Antérion, C. Ribas. 2004. Le questionnaire de plainte cognitive (qpc) : outil de dépistage de la plainte des sujets présentant une maladie d'alzheimer ou un mci. *Revue Neurologique*, 1027(4502):5–75.

Lorainne Tudor Car, Dhakshenya Ardhithy Dhinagaran, Bhone Myint Kyaw, Tobias Kowatsch, Shafiq Joty, Yin Leng Theng, and Rifat Atun. 2020. Conversational agents in health care: Scoping review and conceptual analysis.

Cleeland C. S. Flanery R. C. Daut, R. L. 1983. Development of the wisconsin brief pain questionnaire to assess pain in cancer and other diseases. *Pain*, (17):197–210.

Dorottya Demszky, Kelvin Guu, and Percy Liang. 2018. Transforming question answering datasets into natural language inference datasets.

Nan Du, Kai Chen, Anjuli Kannan, Linh Tran, Yuhui Chen, and Izhak Shafran. 2019. Extracting symptoms and their status from clinical conversations. In

Proceedings of the 57th Annual Meeting of the Association for Computational Linguistics*, pages 915–925, Florence, Italy. Association for Computational Linguistics.

Greg P. Finley, Erik Edwards, Amanda Robinson, Najmeh Sadoughi, James Fone, Mark Miller, David Suendermann-Oeft, Michael Brenndoerfer, and Nico Axtmann. 2018. An automated assistant for medical scribes. In *INTERSPEECH*.

Pengcheng He, Xiaodong Liu, Jianfeng Gao, and Weizhu Chen. 2020. Deberta: Decoding-enhanced bert with disentangled attention.

R KARASEK. 1985. Job content questionnaire user's guide. *Department of Work Environemnt*.

Daniel Khashabi, Sewon Min, Tushar Khot, Ashish Sabharwal, Oyvind Tafjord, Peter Clark, and Hannaneh Hajishirzi. 2020. Unifiedqa: Crossing format boundaries with a single qa system.

Miller R.P. Todd D.D. Kori, S.H. 1990. Kinesiophobia: A new view of chronic pain behavior. *Pain Management*, (3):35–43.

Tomáš Kočiský, Jonathan Schwarz, Phil Blunsom, Chris Dyer, Karl Moritz Hermann, Gábor Melis, and Edward Grefenstette. 2017. The narrativeqa reading comprehension challenge.

Guokun Lai, Qizhe Xie, Hanxiao Liu, Yiming Yang, and Eduard Hovy. 2017. RACE: Large-scale ReAding comprehension dataset from examinations. In *Proceedings of the 2017 Conference on Empirical Methods in Natural Language Processing*, pages 785–794, Copenhagen, Denmark. Association for Computational Linguistics.

G FRANK Lawlis, RAMON Cuencas, DAVID Selby, and CE McCoy. 1989. The development of the dallas pain questionnaire. an assessment of the impact of spinal pain on behavior. *Spine*, 14(5):511–516.

Mike Lewis, Yinhan Liu, Naman Goyal, Marjan Ghazvininejad, Abdelrahman Mohamed, Omer Levy, Veselin Stoyanov, and Luke Zettlemoyer. 2019. Bart: Denoising sequence-to-sequence pre-training for natural language generation, translation, and comprehension. *arXiv preprint arXiv:1910.13461*.

Anna Liednikova, Philippe Jolivet, Alexandre Durand-Salmon, and Claire Gardent. 2021. Gathering information and engaging the user ComBot: A task-based, serendipitous dialog model for patient-doctor interactions. In *Proceedings of the Second Workshop on Natural Language Processing for Medical Conversations*, pages 21–29, Online. Association for Computational Linguistics.

Chin-Yew Lin. 2004. Rouge: A package for automatic evaluation of summaries. In *Text summarization branches out*, pages 74–81.

Christina Maslach, Susan E Jackson, and Michael P Leiter. 1997. *Maslach burnout inventory*. Scarecrow Education.

Anshuman Mishra, Dhruvesh Patel, Aparna Vijayakumar, Xiang Li, Pavan Kapanipathi, and Kartik Talamadupula. 2020. Reading Comprehension as Natural Language Inference: A Semantic Analysis.

Charles M Morin. 1993. *Insomnia: Psychological assessment and management*. Guilford press.

Abiola Obamuyide and Andreas Vlachos. 2018. Zero-shot relation classification as textual entailment. In *Proceedings of the First Workshop on Fact Extraction and VERification (FEVER)*, pages 72–78, Brussels, Belgium. Association for Computational Linguistics.

A. Parrott and I. Hindmarch. 2004. The leeds sleep evaluation questionnaire in psychopharmacological investigations—a review. *Psychopharmacology*, 71:173–179.

Guillemin F. Virion J. M. Briançon S. Paul-Dauphin, A. 1999. Bias and precision in visual analogue scales: a randomized controlled trial. *American journal of epidemiology*, 150(10):1117–1127.

Jiangtao Ren, Naiyin Liu, and Xiaojing Wu. 2020a. Clinical questionnaire filling based on question answering framework. *International Journal of Medical Informatics*, 141:104225.

Jiangtao Ren, Naiyin Liu, and Xiaojing Wu. 2020b. Clinical questionnaire filling based on question answering framework. *International Journal of Medical Informatics*, 141:104225.

Matthew Richardson, Christopher J.C. Burges, and Erin Renshaw. 2013. MCTest: A challenge dataset for the open-domain machine comprehension of text. In *Proceedings of the 2013 Conference on Empirical Methods in Natural Language Processing*, pages 193–203, Seattle, Washington, USA. Association for Computational Linguistics.

Michael F. Scheier, Charles S. Carver, and Michael W. Bridges. 1994. Distinguishing optimism from neuroticism (and trait anxiety, self-mastery, and self-esteem): A reevaluation of the life orientation test. *Journal of Personality and Social Psychology*, 67(6):1063–1078.

Cathy Donald Sherbourne and Anita L. Stewart. 1991. The mos social support survey. *Social Science Medicine*, 32(6):705–714.

Sarthak Sinha, Amanda J. Schreiner, Jeff Biernaskie, Duncan Nickerson, and Vincent A. Gabriel. 2017. Treating pain on skin graft donor sites: Review and clinical recommendations. *Journal of Trauma and Acute Care Surgery*, 83(5):954–964.

Linfeng Song, Zhiguo Wang, Mo Yu, Yue Zhang, Radu Florian, and Daniel Gildea. 2018. Exploring graph-structured passage representation for multi-hop reading comprehension with graph neural networks. *arXiv preprint arXiv:1809.02040*.

Adams H. Horan S. Mahar D. Boland D. Gross R. Sullivan, M.J.L. 2008. The role of perceived injustice in the experience of chronic pain and disability: Scale development and validation. *Journal of Occupational Rehabilitation*, (18):249–61.

Harsh Trivedi, Heeyoung Kwon, Tushar Khot, Ashish Sabharwal, and Niranjan Balasubramanian. 2019. Repurposing entailment for multi-hop question answering tasks. *arXiv preprint arXiv:1904.09380*.

Gordon Waddell, Mary Newton, Iain Henderson, Douglas Somerville, and Chris J Main. 1993. A fear-avoidance beliefs questionnaire (fabq) and the role of fear-avoidance beliefs in chronic low back pain and disability. *Pain*, 52(2):157–168.

John E Ware Jr, Mark Kosinski, and Susan D Keller. 1996. A 12-item short-form health survey: construction of scales and preliminary tests of reliability and validity. *Medical care*, pages 220–233.

Frank W Weathers, Brett T Litz, Debra S Herman, Jennifer A Huska, Terence M Keane, et al. 1993. The ptsd checklist (pcl): Reliability, validity, and diagnostic utility. In *annual convention of the international society for traumatic stress studies, San Antonio, TX*, volume 462. San Antonio, TX;.

Adina Williams, Nikita Nangia, and Samuel Bowman. 2018. A broad-coverage challenge corpus for sentence understanding through inference. In *Proceedings of the 2018 Conference of the North American Chapter of the Association for Computational Linguistics: Human Language Technologies, Volume 1 (Long Papers)*, pages 1112–1122. Association for Computational Linguistics.

David A. Williams and Beverly E. Thorn. 1989. An empirical assessment of pain beliefs. *Pain*, 36(3):351–358.

Wenpeng Yin, Jamaal Hay, and Dan Roth. 2019. Benchmarking zero-shot text classification: Datasets, evaluation and entailment approach. In *Proceedings of the 2019 Conference on Empirical Methods in Natural Language Processing and the 9th International Joint Conference on Natural Language Processing (EMNLP-IJCNLP)*, pages 3914–3923, Hong Kong, China. Association for Computational Linguistics.

Tianyi Zhang, Varsha Kishore, Felix Wu, Kilian Q Weinberger, and Yoav Artzi. 2019. Bertscore: Evaluating text generation with bert. *arXiv preprint arXiv:1904.09675*.

Yuhao Zhang, Daisy Yi Ding, Tianpei Qian, Christopher D. Manning, and Curtis P. Langlotz. 2018. Learning to summarize radiology findings. In *EMNLP 2018 Workshop on Health Text Mining and Information Analysis*.

Anthony S Zigmond and R Philip Snaith. 1983. The hospital anxiety and depression scale. *Acta psychiatrica scandinavica*, 67(6):361–370.

A Questionnaires

nb.	Question
1	Did you have the impression that your sleep was not calm (moving constantly, feeling tense, talking, etc., while you were sleeping)?
2	Did you get enough sleep to feel rested when you woke up in the morning?
3	Did you wake up short of breath or with a headache?
4	Have you felt a cloudy or drowsy mind during the day?
5	Have you had difficulty falling asleep?
6	Have you woken up in your sleep and had difficulty falling back to sleep?
7	Did you have trouble staying awake during the day?
8	Have you snored in your sleep?
9	Did you take naps (5 minutes or more) during the day?
10	Did you get the amount of sleep you needed?

Table 9: List of questions in MOS-SS questionnaire

B User interface for annotation

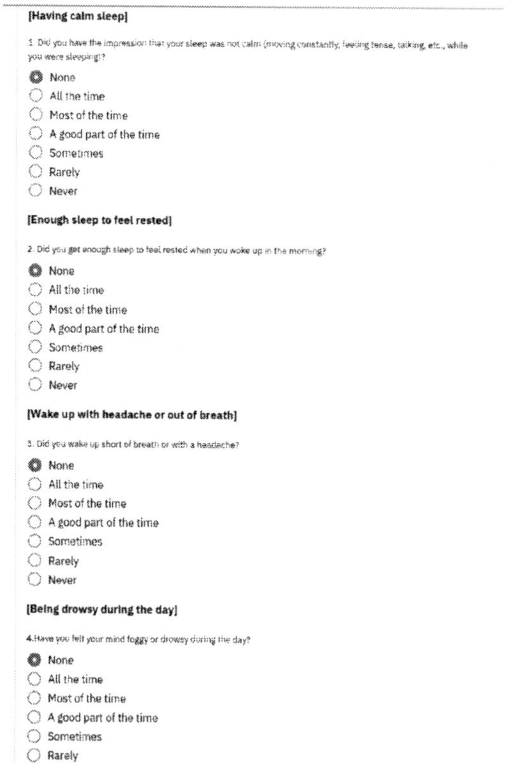

Figure 5: MOS-SS questionnaire

nb.	Question
1	What time do you usually go to bed on weekday evenings?
2	What time is your final wake-up call in the morning?
3	What time do you usually get up during the week?
4	What time do you go to bed on your days off?
5	What time do you get up on your days off?
6	How soon do you fall asleep after turning off the light?
7	How many times a night do you wake up on average?
8	How long do you spend waking up between your first sleep and your final awakening?
9	How many hours per night do you sleep on average?
10	Why do you wake up at night? (pain, noise, child, nightmare, spontaneous awakening, others)
11	What medicine are you taking or were you taking and at what dose?
12	How many nights per week do you currently take the medicine?
13	When did you start taking the medicine?
14	When was the last time you took the medicine?
15	How long have you suffered from insomnia?
16	When was the first time you had trouble sleeping?
17	Did your insomnia start gradually or suddenly?
18	Were there any stressful events that could be linked to the onset of your insomnia? (death, divorce, retirement, family or professional problem, ..)
19	How many times a week do you exercise?
20	How much coffee, tea or Coca-Cola do you consume per day?
21	How many cigarettes do you smoke per day?
22	How many glasses of beer, wine or alcohol do you drink per day?

Table 10: List of questions in Morin questionnaire

nb.	Question
1	No one is able to tell me why it hurts.
2	I thought my pain could be healed, but now I'm not so sure.
3	There are times when it doesn't hurt.
4	My pain is difficult for me to understand.
5	My pain will always be there.
6	I am in constant pain.
7	If it hurts, it's only my fault.
8	I don't have enough information about my pain.
9	My pain is a temporary problem in my life.
10	I feel like I wake up with pain and fall asleep with it.
11	I am the cause of my pain.
12	There is a way to heal my pain.
13	I blame myself when it hurts.
14	I can't understand why it hurts.
15	One day, again, I won't have any pain at all.
16	My pain varies in intensity but it is always present with me.

Table 11: List of questions in PBPI questionnaire

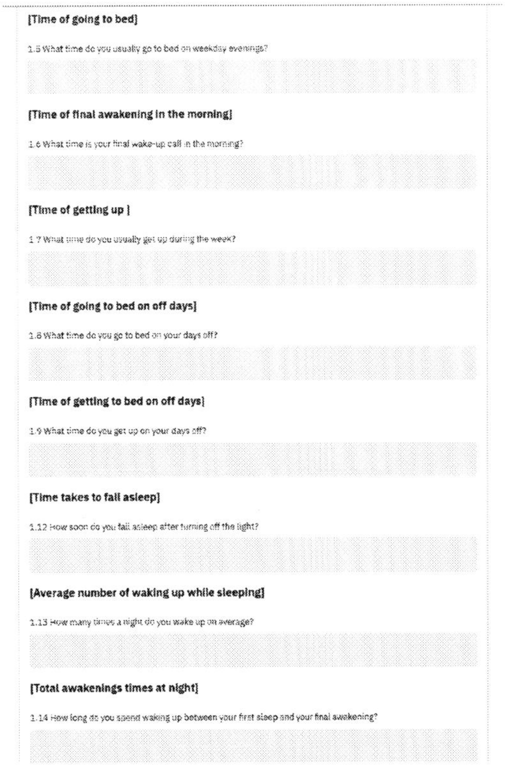
[Time of going to bed]

1.5 What time do you usually go to bed on weekday evenings?

[Time of final awakening in the morning]

1.6 What time is your final wake-up call in the morning?

[Time of getting up]

1.7 What time do you usually get up during the week?

[Time of going to bed on off days]

1.8 What time do you go to bed on your days off?

[Time of getting to bed on off days]

1.9 What time do you get up on your days off?

[Time takes to fall asleep]

1.12 How soon do you fall asleep after turning off the light?

[Average number of waking up while sleeping]

1.13 How many times a night do you wake up on average?

[Total awakenings times at night]

1.14 How long do you spend waking up between your first sleep and your final awakening?

Figure 6: Morin questionnaire

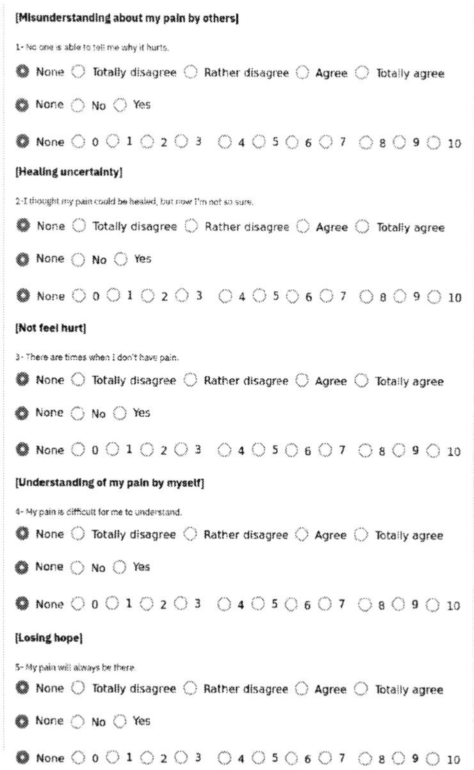

[Misunderstanding about my pain by others]

1- No one is able to tell me why it hurts.

None / Totally disagree / Rather disagree / Agree / Totally agree

None / No / Yes

None / 0 / 1 / 2 / 3 / 4 / 5 / 6 / 7 / 8 / 9 / 10

[Healing uncertainty]

2-I thought my pain could be healed, but now I'm not so sure.

None / Totally disagree / Rather disagree / Agree / Totally agree

None / No / Yes

None / 0 / 1 / 2 / 3 / 4 / 5 / 6 / 7 / 8 / 9 / 10

[Not feel hurt]

3- There are times when I don't have pain.

None / Totally disagree / Rather disagree / Agree / Totally agree

None / No / Yes

None / 0 / 1 / 2 / 3 / 4 / 5 / 6 / 7 / 8 / 9 / 10

[Understanding of my pain by myself]

4- My pain is difficult for me to understand.

None / Totally disagree / Rather disagree / Agree / Totally agree

None / No / Yes

None / 0 / 1 / 2 / 3 / 4 / 5 / 6 / 7 / 8 / 9 / 10

[Losing hope]

5- My pain will always be there.

None / Totally disagree / Rather disagree / Agree / Totally agree

None / No / Yes

None / 0 / 1 / 2 / 3 / 4 / 5 / 6 / 7 / 8 / 9 / 10

Figure 7: PBPI questionnaire

Can Question Generation Debias Question Answering Models? A Case Study on Question–Context Lexical Overlap

Kazutoshi Shinoda[1,2] **Saku Sugawara**[2] **Akiko Aizawa**[1,2]
[1]The University of Tokyo
[2]National Institute of Informatics
shinoda@is.s.u-tokyo.ac.jp
{saku,aizawa}@nii.ac.jp

Abstract

Question answering (QA) models for reading comprehension have been demonstrated to exploit unintended dataset biases such as question–context lexical overlap. This hinders QA models from generalizing to under-represented samples such as questions with low lexical overlap. Question generation (QG), a method for augmenting QA datasets, can be a solution for such performance degradation if QG can properly debias QA datasets. However, we discover that recent neural QG models are biased towards generating questions with high lexical overlap, which can amplify the dataset bias. Moreover, our analysis reveals that data augmentation with these QG models frequently impairs the performance on questions with low lexical overlap, while improving that on questions with high lexical overlap. To address this problem, we use a synonym replacement-based approach to augment questions with low lexical overlap. We demonstrate that the proposed data augmentation approach is simple yet effective to mitigate the degradation problem with only 70k synthetic examples.[1]

1 Introduction

Question answering (QA) for machine reading comprehension is a central task in natural language understanding, which requires a model to answer questions given textual contexts. Pretrained language models have been successfully applied to QA and achieve scores higher than those of humans on benchmark datasets such as SQuAD (Rajpurkar et al., 2016). However, QA models have been demonstrated to exploit unintended dataset biases instead of the intended solutions, and lack robustness to challenge test sets whose distributions are different from those of training sets (Jia and Liang, 2017; Sugawara et al., 2018; Gan and Ng, 2019; Ribeiro et al., 2019), which could be a serious problem in real-world applications.

Question generation (QG) has also been extensively studied to augment QA datasets (Du et al., 2017; Du and Cardie, 2018). It is demonstrated that QG can improve not only the in-domain generalization but also the out-of-distribution generalization capability of QA models (Zhang and Bansal, 2019; Lee et al., 2020; Shinoda et al., 2021). In other areas, data augmentation techniques have been successfully used to reduce dataset biases and increase the performance of machine learning models on under-represented samples in vision (McLaughlin et al., 2015; Wong et al., 2016) and language (Zhao et al., 2018; Zhou and Bansal, 2020). Thus, we assume that QG is useful to debias QA models and improve its robustness by augmenting QA datasets. However, it has not been fully studied whether existing QG models can contribute to debiasing QA models (i.e., improve the robustness of QA models to under-represented questions).

In this study, we focus on question–context lexical overlap, inspired by the findings presented in Sugawara et al. (2018). Their work revealed that questions having low lexical overlap with context tend to require reasoning skills rather than superficial word matching, and existing QA models are not robust to these questions (Table 1). To see if data augmentation with recent neural QG models can improve the robustness to those questions, we analyze the performance of BERT (Devlin et al., 2019) trained on SQuAD v1.1 (Rajpurkar et al., 2016) augmented with them. Our analysis reveals that data augmentation with neural QG models frequently sacrifices the QA performance of the BERT-base model on questions with low lexical overlap, while improving that on questions with high lexical overlap. We conjecture that this is because neural QG models frequently generate questions with high lexical overlap as indicated in Table

[1]Our data is publicly available at https://github.com/KazutoshiShinoda/Synonym-Replacement.

Proceedings of the 3rd Workshop on Machine Reading for Question Answering , pages 63–72
Nov 10th, 2021 ©2021 Association for Computational Linguistics

C					
Besides earning a reputation as a respected entertainment device, the iPod has also been accepted as a business device. Government departments, major institutions and international organisations have turned to the iPod line as a delivery mechanism for business communication and training, such as the Royal and Western Infirmaries in Glasgow, Scotland, where iPods are used to train new staff.					
Q	A	$\frac{\|Q \cap C\|}{\|Q\|}$	$C, Q \rightarrow A'$	$C, A \rightarrow Q'$	$\frac{\|Q' \cap C\|}{\|Q'\|}$
Where is Royal and Western Infirmaries located?	Glasgow, Scotland	5/8 = 0.62	Glasgow, Scotland (✓)	Where is the Royal and Western Infirmaries located? (✓)	6/9 = 0.67
Aside from recreational use, in what other arena have iPods found use?	business	4/14 = 0.29	entertainment (✗)	The iPod has been accepted as what kind of device? (✗)	7/11 = 0.64

Table 1: Examples of ground-truth question–answer pairs and predictions of question answering (BERT-base (Devlin et al., 2019)) and generation (SemanticQG (Zhang and Bansal, 2019)) models. C: context, Q: question, A: answer, $\frac{|Q \cap C|}{|Q|}$: question–context lexical overlap, A': predicted answer, Q': generated question. Overlapping words in the questions are underlined.

1. This behavior can be interpreted as a consequence of the recent QG models pursuing higher average BLEU scores on SQuAD, which inherently contains reference questions with high lexical overlap, by copying many words from contexts to generate questions. By doing so, QG models can amplify the lexical overlap bias in the original dataset.

To address the performance degradation, we use a simple data augmentation approach using synonym replacement to generate questions with low question–context lexical overlap. We found that the proposed approach not only debiases the dataset but also improves the QA performance on questions with low lexical overlap with only 70k synthetic examples, whereas conventional neural QG approaches use more than one million synthetic examples.

In summary, our contributions are as follows:

- We found that not only QA but also QG models are biased in terms of question–context lexical overlap; that is, QG models fail to generate questions with low lexical overlap (§2).
- We discovered that data augmentation using recent neural QG models does not contribute to debias QA datasets; rather, it frequently degrades the QA performance on questions with low lexical overlap, while improving that on questions with high lexical overlap (§4).
- We demonstrated that the proposed simple data augmentation approach using synonym replacement (§3) for augmenting questions with low lexical overlap is effective to improve QA performance on questions with low lexical overlap with only 70k synthetic examples (§4), while preserving or slightly hurting the overall accuracy.

2 Revisiting the QA and QG Performance in Terms of Question–Context Lexical Overlap

In this paper, we denote question–context lexical overlap as QCLO. We define QCLO as the ratio of the overlapping words between question Q and context C to the total number of words in question.[2] Precisely, QCLO is calculated as

$$\text{QCLO} = \frac{|Q \cap C|}{|Q|}. \quad (1)$$

The second example in Table 1 indicates a question with lower QCLO is neither answered nor generated correctly by neural models. To investigate this phenomenon, we first analyze the QA and QG performance in terms of QCLO.

Experimental setups For QA, we use the fine-tuned BERT-base and -large models (Devlin et al., 2019). For QG, we use SemanticQG (Zhang and Bansal, 2019).[3] For the dataset, we use the SQuAD-Du dataset; the train, dev, and test split of SQuAD v1.1 (Rajpurkar et al., 2016) proposed by Du et al. (2017), which we denote as $\text{SQuAD}^{\text{Du}}_{\text{train}}$, $\text{SQuAD}^{\text{Du}}_{\text{dev}}$, $\text{SQuAD}^{\text{Du}}_{\text{test}}$, respectively. This split

[2] When computing lexical overlap, we do not exclude stop words because even overlapping stop words are important cues to determine the correct answer.

[3] We used the ELMo+QPP&QAP (Zhang and Bansal, 2019) model for QG.

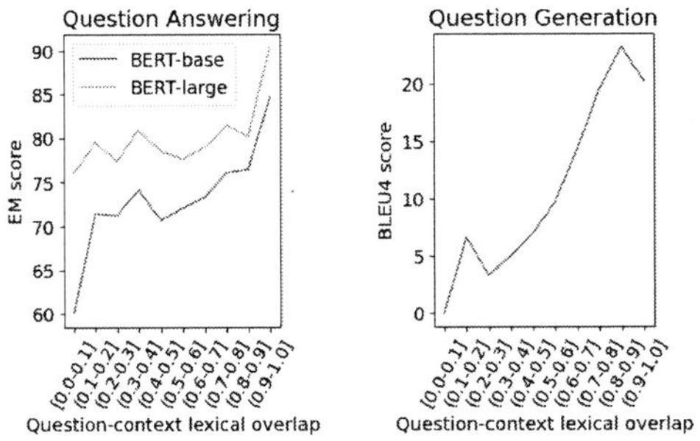

Figure 1: Exact match (EM) score of BERT models and BLEU-4 score of SemanticQG (Zhang and Bansal, 2019) on the test set of SQuAD-Du for each range of Question–Context Lexical Overlap (QCLO). See Eq. 1 for the definition of QCLO. Both the QA and QG models degrade the scores on questions with low QCLO.

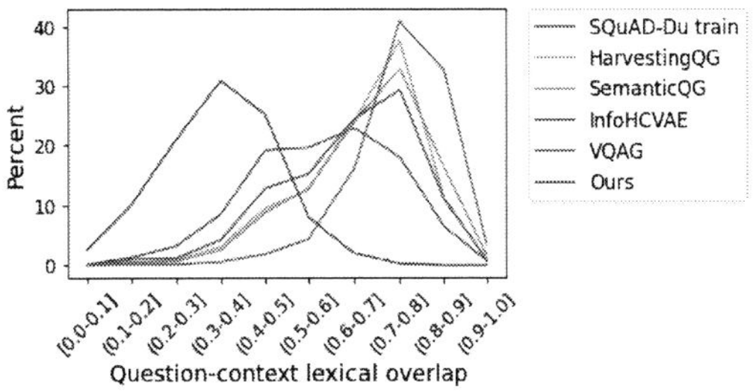

Figure 2: The percentages of questions in the datasets, SQuAD-Du (Du et al., 2017), HarvestingQG (Du and Cardie, 2018), SemanticQG (Zhang and Bansal, 2019), InfoHCVAE (Lee et al., 2020), VQAG (Shinoda et al., 2021), and ours (§3), for each range of QCLO. While neural question generation models are biased towards generating questions with high QCLO, ours can generate questions with low QCLO.

is commonly used in the QG literature (Du and Cardie, 2018; Zhang and Bansal, 2019) because the original test set is not released. The numbers of question, answer and context triples in $\text{SQuAD}^{\text{Du}}_{\text{train}}$, $\text{SQuAD}^{\text{Du}}_{\text{dev}}$, and $\text{SQuAD}^{\text{Du}}_{\text{test}}$, are 76k, 11k, and 12k, respectively.

Results We show the result in Figure 1. This indicates that the performance of the BERT models on the questions with lower QCLO is degraded compared to the questions with higher QCLO. For QG, the BLEU-4 score (Papineni et al., 2002) is highly correlated with QCLO, which means that the model fails to generate questions with low QCLO accurately.

We also show the distributions in terms of QCLO of questions generated by recent neural QG models (HarvestingQG (Du and Cardie, 2018), SemanticQG (Zhang and Bansal, 2019), InfoHCVAE (Lee et al., 2020), and VQAG (Shinoda et al., 2021)) in Figure 2. This indicates that all the QG models are biased towards generating questions with higher QCLO than $\text{SQuAD}^{\text{Du}}_{\text{train}}$, which is used to train those QG models.

Based on the result, we suspect that when neural QG is used to augment a QA dataset, the degraded QG performance on questions with low QCLO could exacerbate the degraded QA performance. Our experiments in §4 show that this is often true. We hypothesize that this is caused by the strong tendency of neural QG models to generate questions with high QCLO as shown in Figure 2.

3 Method

We assume that if we augment questions with low QCLO unlike existing neural QG approaches, the robustness of QA models to questions with low QCLO can be improved. In this section, we describe the proposed method for generating questions with low QCLO. We extend the idea of synonym replacement used in (Wei and Zou, 2019) to reduce the lexical overlap. The proposed method is as follows:

1. List all the overlapping words between question and context.
2. Replace every word in the listed words other than predefined stop words with one of its synonyms chosen randomly from WordNet (Miller, 1995), and obtain a synthetic question.
3. If the lexical overlap decreases after synonym replacement, add the synthetic question to our dataset; if not, discard the question.

After repeating this procedure once for every ground-truth question in the training set, we obtain 70k synthetic questions with significantly lower lexical overlap, as indicated in Figure 2 (ours). For example, *What is heresy mainly at odds with?* is converted into *What is heterodoxy mainly at odds with?*, and *How many documents remain classified?* is converted into *How many text file remain classified?*. Because *heterodoxy*, *text*, and *file* do not appear in the contexts, the lexical overlap is reduced in each example.

It is worth mentioning a couple of limitations of our method. First, synonym replacement may slightly change the meaning of questions depending on the context. Second, our approach relies on the assumption that annotated questions are available, which makes it impossible to apply to unlabeled passages.

4 Experiments

To determine the effect of data augmentation on improving the QA model robustness to questions with low QCLO, we conducted experiments with several QG approaches.

Dataset We used the SQuAD-Du dataset as in §2. Considering the QCLO statistics of SQuAD displayed in Figure 2, we split $\text{SQuAD}^{\text{Du}}_{\text{dev}}$ and $\text{SQuAD}^{\text{Du}}_{\text{test}}$ into **Easy** and **Hard** subsets that contain questions with QCLO greater than 0.3, and the others, respectively. Our Easy and Hard subsets offered concise, yet sufficient, evaluation in terms of QCLO.

Baselines We adopted the following four baselines that use neural QG models for data augmentation.

- **HarvestingQG** (Du and Cardie, 2018) generates question–answer pairs from 10,000 top-ranking Wikipedia articles with neural answer extraction and question generation.[4] The size is 1.2 million.

- **SemanticQG** (Zhang and Bansal, 2019) is a QG model that uses reinforcement learning to generate semantically valid questions. Following this work, we generated questions using the publicly available model[5] from the same context–answer pairs as HarvestingQG. The size is 1.2 million.

- **InfoHCVAE** (Lee et al., 2020) is a question–answer pair generation model based on conditional variational autoencoder with mutual information maximization. We trained this model on $\text{SQuAD}^{\text{Du}}_{\text{train}}$, and then generated 50 questions and answers from each context in $\text{SQuAD}^{\text{Du}}_{\text{train}}$. The size is 824k.

- **VQAG** (Shinoda et al., 2021) is a question–answer pair generation model based on conditional variational autoencoder with explicit KL control. We used the publicly available dataset.[6] The size is 432k.

The distributions of the lexical overlap of these datasets are presented in Figure 2. We indicate that these methods are more biased towards high lexical overlap than $\text{SQuAD}^{\text{Du}}_{\text{train}}$, which was used as the training set for these QG models.

Experimental Setups As in our previous experiment (§2), we used BERT-base and -large models, whose total number of parameters are 110M and 340M, respectively. Dhingra et al. (2018) proposed to pretrain a QA model using synthetic data composed of cloze-style questions and then fine-tune it on the ground-truth data. We adopted the pretrain-and-fine-tune approach for the neural QG approaches, which generated over 1.2 million questions. However, as discussed by Zhang and Bansal (2019), we observed that when the size of the synthetic data was small or similar to the ground-truth data, a performance gain could not be obtained by the pretrain-and-fine-tune approach. Thus, for the proposed approach, which generated 70k questions, we fine-tuned QA models on the ground-truth data randomly mixed with the generated data. We used the Hugging Face's implementation of BERT (Wolf et al., 2019). We use the Adam (Kingma and Ba, 2014) optimizer with epsilon set to 1e-8. The batch size was 32 for all the settings. In both the pretraining and fine-tuning procedure, the learning rate decreased linearly from 3e-5 to zero. We train the QA models for one epoch for pretraining with synthetic data and two epochs for fine-tuning with $\text{SQuAD}^{\text{Du}}_{\text{train}}$.

Results The results of the data augmentation are displayed in Table 2. In all the settings, the proposed approach achieved the best EM score on the Hard subset. Notably, the proposed method significantly improved the performance by **2.72 (EM) / 1.50 (F1)** points using BERT-base on the Hard subset in the test set, while maintaining the overall scores compared to the no data augmentation baseline. This improvement indicates that the proposed approach for debiasing the dataset in terms of QCLO is helpful for addressing the performance

[4]https://github.com/xinyadu/harvestingQA

[5]https://github.com/ZhangShiyue/QGforQA

[6]https://github.com/KazutoshiShinoda/VQAG

Model	Train Source	$\text{SQuAD}^{\text{Du}}_{\text{dev}}$ (EM/F1) Hard	Easy	ALL	$\text{SQuAD}^{\text{Du}}_{\text{test}}$ (EM/F1) Hard	Easy	ALL
base	$\text{SQuAD}^{\text{Du}}_{\text{train}}$	72.31/81.11	80.74/88.39	80.35/88.05	70.88/81.99	73.22/84.75	73.06/84.57
	+ HarvestingQG	70.25/78.27	80.06/87.62	79.60/87.19	69.28/79.92	73.15/84.20	72.90/83.93
	+ SemanticQG	70.45/80.25	81.70/89.08	81.17/88.67	71.68/82.49	**74.39/85.59**	**74.21/85.39**
	+ InfoHCVAE	72.05/80.66	81.79/**89.35**	81.34/**88.95**	73.47/**83.91**	73.50/85.08	73.48/84.99
	+ VQAG	73.29/82.04	**81.88**/88.93	**81.48**/88.62	71.60/83.07	73.79/85.23	73.63/85.08
	+ Ours	**73.50/82.81**	80.34/87.81	80.02/87.58	**73.60**/83.49	73.08/84.41	73.11/84.34
large	$\text{SQuAD}^{\text{Du}}_{\text{train}}$	78.72/87.71	**87.06/93.23**	**86.67/92.98**	77.93/87.84	**79.33/89.88**	**79.24/89.74**
	+ HarvestingQG	79.13/86.92	85.55/92.12	85.26/91.88	76.99/86.61	77.58/88.28	77.54/88.17
	+ SemanticQG	79.96/87.73	85.90/92.57	85.62/92.35	76.99/87.29	77.82/88.68	77.77/88.59
	+ InfoHCVAE	77.85/86.44	85.25/92.15	84.91/91.89	76.00/87.55	78.02/88.90	77.87/88.80
	+ VQAG	79.50/87.55	86.68/93.01	86.35/92.76	77.33/87.70	78.98/89.36	78.86/89.25
	+ Ours	**81.37/88.33**	86.49/92.78	86.25/92.57	**78.40/88.52**	77.94/89.00	77.96/88.97

Table 2: QA performance with data augmentation. EM/F1 scores on the Hard (where QCLO ≤ 0.3) and Easy (where QCLO > 0.3) subsets, and the whole set of $\text{SQuAD}^{\text{Du}}_{\text{dev}}$ and $\text{SQuAD}^{\text{Du}}_{\text{test}}$ are reported.

degradation. However, the proposed approach degraded the scores on the Easy subsets when using BERT-large. Addressing the trade-off between the scores in the Hard and Easy subsets using BERT-large is future work.

When using BERT-base, the neural QG baselines except for HarvestingQG improved the scores on the Easy subset; however, the baselines except for InfoHCVAE often degraded the scores on the Hard subset. This could be due to the tendency to generate questions with high QCLO (Figure 2).

When using BERT-large, the QG approaches often fail to improve the scores in both the Hard and Easy subsets. Generating useful examples for a larger model is more challenging than for a smaller one according to these results. Utilizing pretrained language models for QG may be useful given the fact that only RNNs are used in all the baseline QG methods in our experiments.

HarvesingQG was not effective in almost all the settings. Comparing its scores with those of SemanticQG, which used the same context–answer pairs as HarvestingQG, some feature of generated questions other than lexical overlap appeared to be critical in improving the QA scores on the Easy subset, because the distributions of QCLO of two synthetic datasets were similar to each other (see Figure 2).

For further boosting the overall average score, we can make an ensemble prediction using the best performing models in the Easy and Hard subsets, although improving the overall scores is not the main focus in this paper. The performance gains were positive but not very significant in our case. We leave utilizing the ensemble prediction to address the performance trade-off to future work.

5 Qualitative Analysis

To demonstrate the effect of the baseline QG models and proposed method qualitatively, we present examples in both the Hard (QCLO ≤ 0.3) and Easy (QCLO > 0.3) subsets in Table 3. The first two examples show that only the QA model trained with the proposed method could correctly answer the questions. Answering the questions in these examples required a knowledge of synonyms, such as "recreational" vs. "entertainment," "besides" vs. "aside from," "employees" vs. "workers," and "kill oneself" vs. "commit suicide." These examples imply that the proposed data augmentation method based on synonym replacement enabled the QA model to acquire knowledge regarding synonyms. This kind of reasoning beyond superficial word matching is indispensable for QA systems to achieve human-level language understanding.

The third example in Table 3 displays an example where data augmentation using the neural QG models made the original prediction incorrect. This example implies that current QG models may harm the robustness of QA models to questions with low QCLO. As Geirhos et al. (2020) discussed, if QG models just amplify the dataset bias, QA models could learn dataset-specific solutions (i.e., shortcuts) and fail to generalize to challenge test sets.

In contrast, the fourth and fifth examples in Table 3 display examples in the Easy subset where

Besides earning a reputation as a respected entertainment *(Original, InfoHCVAE)* device, the iPod has also been accepted as a **business** *(Ours)* device. Government departments, major institutions and international organisations have turned to the iPod line as a delivery mechanism for business communication and training, such as the Royal and Western Infirmaries *(HarvestingQG, SemanticQG, VQAG)* in Glasgow, Scotland, where iPods are used to train new staff.

— Aside from recreational use, in what other arena have iPods found use? (QCLO: 0.29)

In **2010** *(Ours)*, a number of workers committed suicide at a Foxconn operations in China. Apple, HP, and others stated that they were investigating the situation. Foxconn guards have been videotaped beating employees. Another employee killed himself in 2009 *(Original, HarvestingQG, SemanticQG, VQAG)* when an Apple prototype went missing, and claimed in messages to friends, that he had been beaten and interrogated.

— In what year did Chinese Foxconn emplyees* kill themselves? (*: annotator's typo) (QCLO: 0.2)

The BBC began its own regular television programming from the basement of Broadcasting House, London, on 22 August 1932 *(HarvestingQG, SemanticQG)*. The studio moved to larger quarters in 16 Portland Place, London, in **February 1934** *(Original, Ours)*, and continued broadcasting the 30-line images, carried by telephone line to the medium wave transmitter at Brookmans Park, until 11 September 1935, by which time advances in all-electronic television systems made the electromechanical broadcasts obsolete.

— When did the BBC first change studios? (QCLO: 0.25)

Peyton Manning *(VQAG)* became the first quarterback ever to lead two different teams to multiple Super Bowls. He is also the oldest quarterback ever to play in a Super Bowl at age 39 *(Original, Ours)*. The past record was held by **John Elway** *(HarvestingQG, SemanticQG, InfoHCVAE)*, who led the Broncos to victory in Super Bowl XXXIII at age 38 and is currently Denver's Executive Vice President of Football Operations and General Manager.

— Prior to Manning, who was the oldest quarterback to play in a Super Bowl? (QCLO: 0.88)

Despite being relatively unaffected by the embargo *(Original, HarvestingQG, VQAG, Ours)*, the UK nonetheless faced an oil crisis of its own - **a series of strikes by coal miners and railroad workers** *(SemanticQG, InfoHCVAE)* over the winter of 1973–74 became a major factor in the change of government. Heath asked the British to heat only one room in their houses over the winter. The UK, Germany, Italy, Switzerland and Norway banned flying, driving and boating on Sundays. Sweden rationed gasoline and heating oil. The Netherlands imposed prison sentences for those who used more than their ration of electricity.

— What caused UK to have an oil crisis in its own country? (QCLO: 0.62)

Table 3: Illustrative predictions on $\text{SQuAD}^{\text{Du}}_{\text{dev}}$ and $\text{SQuAD}^{\text{Du}}_{\text{test}}$ by a BERT-base model trained on $\text{SQuAD}^{\text{Du}}_{\text{train}}$ (Original), +HarvestingQG, +SemanticQG, +InfoHCVAE, +VQAG, and +Ours. The ground truth answers are in **bold**. The incorrectly predicted answers are written in red. The QA models that predict them are written in *italics*. The overlapping words in the questions are underlined. Question–context lexical overlap (QCLO) is given in parentheses.

data augmentation with neural QG models is beneficial, while the original and proposed models fail to answer them correctly. These examples require multiple-sentence reasoning, i.e., one has to read and understand multiple sentences to answer these questions. This observation implies that some under-represented features (e.g., multiple-sentence reasoning (Rajpurkar et al., 2016)) exist even in the Easy subset, and the existing neural QG models might amplify such features (possibly by copying many words from multiple sentences to formulate questions) and make it easy to capture them. Investigating what kind of features are learned by using data augmentation with neural QG models in more detail is future work.

6 Related Work

The Robustness of QA models Pretrained language models such as BERT (Devlin et al., 2019) have surpassed the human score on the SQuAD leaderboard.[7] However, such powerful QA models have been shown to exhibit the lack of robustness. A QA model that is trained on SQuAD is not robust to paraphrased questions (Gan and Ng, 2019), implications derived from SQuAD (Ribeiro et al., 2019), questions with low lexical overlap (Sugawara et al., 2018), and other QA datasets (Yogatama et al., 2019; Talmor and Berant, 2019; Sen and Saffari, 2020). Ko et al. (2020) showed that extractive QA model can suffer from positional bias and fail to generalize to different answer positions.

The lack of robustness demonstrated in these studies can be explained by shortcut learning of deep neural networks (Geirhos et al., 2020). A high score on an in-distribution test set can be achieved by just exploiting unintended dataset biases (Levesque, 2014). Therefore, evaluating QA models only on an in-distribution test set is not enough to evaluate the robustness of the QA models.

Question Generation for Question Answering QG has been studied extensively in order to augment QA datasets and boost the QA performance, which has been evaluated primarily on SQuAD (Du et al., 2017; Zhou et al., 2018; Yang et al., 2017; Zhang and Bansal, 2019). Question answer pair generation, which consists of answer candidate extraction and QG, has been also received attention because question-worthy answers for the input of QG are not freely available (Du and Cardie, 2018; Lee et al., 2020; Shinoda et al., 2021). The de facto standard of QG models is to utilize a copy mechanism (Gu et al., 2016; Gulcehre et al., 2016). The tendency of QG models to copy words from textual contexts as indicated in Figure 2 is partially due to this copy mechanism. While the existing QG works have increased the BLEU scores on SQuAD[8] and successfully generated fluent questions in terms of human scores, the bias regarding lexical overlap in QG has not received sufficient attention.

Data Augmentation and Dataset Bias Data augmentation has been widely used in other domains to reduce dataset biases such as the background bias in person re-identification (McLaughlin et al., 2015), the gender bias in coreference resolution (Zhao et al., 2018), and the lexical bias in natural language inference (Zhou and Bansal, 2020). These works repeated training examples or added synthetic data to increase under-represented samples and reduce the imbalance in a training set. Our proposed approach has the same motivation as these works.

On the other hand, data augmentation can unintentionally introduce or amplify dataset bias. Back-translation (Sennrich et al., 2016), which is the common data augmentation approach for machine translation, can introduce the translationese bias. That is, machine translation systems trained with back-translation, compared to ones without back-translation, can enhance the BLEU scores when the input is translationese (i.e., human-translated texts) but harm the BLEU scores when the input is naturally occurring texts (Edunov et al., 2020; Marie et al., 2020). This phenomenon is analogous to the observation in our work, where we demonstrated that SQuAD QG models are biased towards generating questions with high QCLO, and this tendency can harm the QA performance on questions with low QCLO while improving that on questions with high QCLO.

7 Conclusion

We demonstrated that not only QA models but also QG models are biased in terms of the question–context lexical overlap. To determine the influence of the bias, we analyzed the QA performance with data augmentation using the recent QG models. We demonstrated that they frequently degraded the QA

[7] https://rajpurkar.github.io/SQuAD-explorer/

[8] http://aqleaderboard.tomhosking.co.uk/squad

performance on questions with low lexical overlap, while improving that on questions with high lexical overlap when using BERT-base. To address this problem, we designed a simple approach using synonym replacement to debias a QA dataset. We demonstrated that the proposed approach improved the QA performance on questions with low lexical overlap while maintaining or slightly degrading the overall scores with only 70k synthetic examples.

Our results suggest that future research in QG for data augmentation should exercise caution to prevent the amplification of dataset bias in terms of lexical overlap. In addition, what features are learned by data augmentation with neural QG models is worth to be explored in more detail to clarify what is improved and what is not improved by QG. It is also worth investigating whether our findings still hold in other QA datasets where annotated questions have lower lexical overlap than those in SQuAD.

Acknowledgements

We would like to thank the anonymous reviewers for their detailed and valuable comments. This work was supported by NEDO SIP-2 "Big-data and AI-enabled Cyberspace Technologies," and JSPS KAKENHI Grant Numbers 21H03502, 20K23335.

References

Jacob Devlin, Ming-Wei Chang, Kenton Lee, and Kristina Toutanova. 2019. BERT: Pre-training of deep bidirectional transformers for language understanding. In *Proceedings of the 2019 Conference of the North American Chapter of the Association for Computational Linguistics: Human Language Technologies, Volume 1 (Long and Short Papers)*, pages 4171–4186, Minneapolis, Minnesota. Association for Computational Linguistics.

Bhuwan Dhingra, Danish Danish, and Dheeraj Rajagopal. 2018. Simple and effective semi-supervised question answering. In *Proceedings of the 2018 Conference of the North American Chapter of the Association for Computational Linguistics: Human Language Technologies, Volume 2 (Short Papers)*, pages 582–587, New Orleans, Louisiana. Association for Computational Linguistics.

Xinya Du and Claire Cardie. 2018. Harvesting paragraph-level question-answer pairs from Wikipedia. In *Proceedings of the 56th Annual Meeting of the Association for Computational Linguistics (Volume 1: Long Papers)*, pages 1907–1917, Melbourne, Australia. Association for Computational Linguistics.

Xinya Du, Junru Shao, and Claire Cardie. 2017. Learning to ask: Neural question generation for reading comprehension. In *Proceedings of the 55th Annual Meeting of the Association for Computational Linguistics (Volume 1: Long Papers)*, pages 1342–1352, Vancouver, Canada. Association for Computational Linguistics.

Sergey Edunov, Myle Ott, Marc'Aurelio Ranzato, and Michael Auli. 2020. On the evaluation of machine translation systems trained with back-translation. In *Proceedings of the 58th Annual Meeting of the Association for Computational Linguistics*, pages 2836–2846, Online. Association for Computational Linguistics.

Wee Chung Gan and Hwee Tou Ng. 2019. Improving the robustness of question answering systems to question paraphrasing. In *Proceedings of the 57th Annual Meeting of the Association for Computational Linguistics*, pages 6065–6075, Florence, Italy. Association for Computational Linguistics.

Robert Geirhos, Jörn-Henrik Jacobsen, Claudio Michaelis, Richard Zemel, Wieland Brendel, Matthias Bethge, and Felix A. Wichmann. 2020. Shortcut learning in deep neural networks. *Nature Machine Intelligence*, 2(11):665–673.

Jiatao Gu, Zhengdong Lu, Hang Li, and Victor O.K. Li. 2016. Incorporating copying mechanism in sequence-to-sequence learning. In *Proceedings of the 54th Annual Meeting of the Association for Computational Linguistics (Volume 1: Long Papers)*, pages 1631–1640, Berlin, Germany. Association for Computational Linguistics.

Caglar Gulcehre, Sungjin Ahn, Ramesh Nallapati, Bowen Zhou, and Yoshua Bengio. 2016. Pointing the unknown words. In *Proceedings of the 54th Annual Meeting of the Association for Computational Linguistics (Volume 1: Long Papers)*, pages 140–149, Berlin, Germany. Association for Computational Linguistics.

Robin Jia and Percy Liang. 2017. Adversarial examples for evaluating reading comprehension systems. In *Proceedings of the 2017 Conference on Empirical Methods in Natural Language Processing*, pages 2021–2031, Copenhagen, Denmark. Association for Computational Linguistics.

Diederik P Kingma and Jimmy Ba. 2014. Adam: A method for stochastic optimization. *arXiv preprint arXiv:1412.6980*.

Miyoung Ko, Jinhyuk Lee, Hyunjae Kim, Gangwoo Kim, and Jaewoo Kang. 2020. Look at the first sentence: Position bias in question answering. In *Proceedings of the 2020 Conference on Empirical Methods in Natural Language Processing (EMNLP)*, pages 1109–1121, Online. Association for Computational Linguistics.

Dong Bok Lee, Seanie Lee, Woo Tae Jeong, Donghwan Kim, and Sung Ju Hwang. 2020. Generating diverse and consistent QA pairs from contexts with information-maximizing hierarchical conditional VAEs. In *Proceedings of the 58th Annual Meeting of the Association for Computational Linguistics*, pages 208–224, Online. Association for Computational Linguistics.

Hector J. Levesque. 2014. On our best behaviour. *Artif. Intell.*, 212(1):27–35.

Benjamin Marie, Raphael Rubino, and Atsushi Fujita. 2020. Tagged back-translation revisited: Why does it really work? In *Proceedings of the 58th Annual Meeting of the Association for Computational Linguistics*, pages 5990–5997, Online. Association for Computational Linguistics.

Niall McLaughlin, Jesus M. Del Rincon, and Paul Miller. 2015. Data-augmentation for reducing dataset bias in person re-identification. In *2015 12th IEEE International Conference on Advanced Video and Signal Based Surveillance (AVSS)*, pages 1–6, Karlsruhe, Germany. IEEE.

George A. Miller. 1995. Wordnet: A lexical database for english. *Commun. ACM*, 38(11):39–41.

Kishore Papineni, Salim Roukos, Todd Ward, and Wei-Jing Zhu. 2002. Bleu: a method for automatic evaluation of machine translation. In *Proceedings of the 40th Annual Meeting of the Association for Computational Linguistics*, pages 311–318, Philadelphia, Pennsylvania, USA. Association for Computational Linguistics.

Pranav Rajpurkar, Jian Zhang, Konstantin Lopyrev, and Percy Liang. 2016. SQuAD: 100,000+ questions for machine comprehension of text. In *Proceedings of the 2016 Conference on Empirical Methods in Natural Language Processing*, pages 2383–2392, Austin, Texas. Association for Computational Linguistics.

Marco Tulio Ribeiro, Carlos Guestrin, and Sameer Singh. 2019. Are red roses red? evaluating consistency of question-answering models. In *Proceedings of the 57th Annual Meeting of the Association for Computational Linguistics*, pages 6174–6184, Florence, Italy. Association for Computational Linguistics.

Priyanka Sen and Amir Saffari. 2020. What do models learn from question answering datasets? In *Proceedings of the 2020 Conference on Empirical Methods in Natural Language Processing (EMNLP)*, pages 2429–2438, Online. Association for Computational Linguistics.

Rico Sennrich, Barry Haddow, and Alexandra Birch. 2016. Improving neural machine translation models with monolingual data. In *Proceedings of the 54th Annual Meeting of the Association for Computational Linguistics (Volume 1: Long Papers)*, pages 86–96, Berlin, Germany. Association for Computational Linguistics.

Kazutoshi Shinoda, Saku Sugawara, and Akiko Aizawa. 2021. Improving the robustness of QA models to challenge sets with variational question-answer pair generation. In *Proceedings of the ACL-IJCNLP 2021 Student Research Workshop*, pages 197–214, Online. Association for Computational Linguistics.

Saku Sugawara, Kentaro Inui, Satoshi Sekine, and Akiko Aizawa. 2018. What makes reading comprehension questions easier? In *Proceedings of the 2018 Conference on Empirical Methods in Natural Language Processing*, pages 4208–4219, Brussels, Belgium. Association for Computational Linguistics.

Alon Talmor and Jonathan Berant. 2019. MultiQA: An empirical investigation of generalization and transfer in reading comprehension. In *Proceedings of the 57th Annual Meeting of the Association for Computational Linguistics*, pages 4911–4921, Florence, Italy. Association for Computational Linguistics.

Jason Wei and Kai Zou. 2019. EDA: Easy data augmentation techniques for boosting performance on text classification tasks. In *Proceedings of the 2019 Conference on Empirical Methods in Natural Language Processing and the 9th International Joint Conference on Natural Language Processing (EMNLP-IJCNLP)*, pages 6382–6388, Hong Kong, China. Association for Computational Linguistics.

Thomas Wolf, Lysandre Debut, Victor Sanh, Julien Chaumond, Clement Delangue, Anthony Moi, Pierric Cistac, Tim Rault, Rémi Louf, Morgan Funtowicz, et al. 2019. Huggingface's transformers: State-of-the-art natural language processing. *arXiv preprint arXiv:1910.03771*.

S. C. Wong, A. Gatt, V. Stamatescu, and M. D. McDonnell. 2016. Understanding data augmentation for classification: When to warp? In *2016 International Conference on Digital Image Computing: Techniques and Applications (DICTA)*, pages 1–6, Gold Coast, QLD, Australia. IEEE.

Zhilin Yang, Junjie Hu, Ruslan Salakhutdinov, and William Cohen. 2017. Semi-supervised QA with generative domain-adaptive nets. In *Proceedings of the 55th Annual Meeting of the Association for Computational Linguistics (Volume 1: Long Papers)*, pages 1040–1050, Vancouver, Canada. Association for Computational Linguistics.

Dani Yogatama, Cyprien de Masson d'Autume, Jerome Connor, Tomas Kocisky, Mike Chrzanowski, Lingpeng Kong, Angeliki Lazaridou, Wang Ling, Lei Yu, Chris Dyer, et al. 2019. Learning and evaluating general linguistic intelligence. *arXiv preprint arXiv:1901.11373*.

Shiyue Zhang and Mohit Bansal. 2019. Addressing semantic drift in question generation for semi-supervised question answering. In *Proceedings of the 2019 Conference on Empirical Methods in Natural Language Processing and the 9th International*

Joint Conference on Natural Language Processing (EMNLP-IJCNLP), pages 2495–2509, Hong Kong, China. Association for Computational Linguistics.

Jieyu Zhao, Tianlu Wang, Mark Yatskar, Vicente Ordonez, and Kai-Wei Chang. 2018. Gender bias in coreference resolution: Evaluation and debiasing methods. In *Proceedings of the 2018 Conference of the North American Chapter of the Association for Computational Linguistics: Human Language Technologies, Volume 2 (Short Papers)*, pages 15–20, New Orleans, Louisiana. Association for Computational Linguistics.

Qingyu Zhou, Nan Yang, Furu Wei, Chuanqi Tan, Hangbo Bao, and Ming Zhou. 2018. Neural question generation from text: A preliminary study. In *Natural Language Processing and Chinese Computing*, pages 662–671, Cham. Springer International Publishing.

Xiang Zhou and Mohit Bansal. 2020. Towards robustifying NLI models against lexical dataset biases. In *Proceedings of the 58th Annual Meeting of the Association for Computational Linguistics*, pages 8759–8771, Online. Association for Computational Linguistics.

What Can a Generative Language Model Answer About a Passage?

Douglas Summers-Stay and **Claire Bonial** and **Clare Voss**
U.S. Army Research Laboratory
douglas.a.summers-stay.civ@army.mil

Abstract

Generative language models trained on large, diverse corpora can answer questions about a passage by generating the most likely continuation of the passage in which the answer to a given question, as appended to the passage, is the most likely continuation of that passage. However, accuracy rates vary depending on the type of question asked. In this paper, we keep the passage fixed, and test with a wide variety of question types, exploring the strengths and weaknesses of the GPT-3 language model. We provide the passage and test questions as a challenge set for other language models.

1 Introduction

Generative language models produce likely text based on a context of other text. This process has a surprising number of useful applications, one of which is answering questions about a text passage. By training on text that contains (among other data) passages followed by questions and answers about the passage, and creating a context in which the answer to a question is the most likely continuation of the passage, better text prediction tends to result in better question answering.

However, there are many types of questions that could be asked about a passage, from direct questions about facts, to explorations of its themes, to imagining what would happen if something about the story was completely different. Depending on the type of question, the accuracy of answers can vary greatly. While some tests of the question-answering ability of language models have been run, it is difficult to separate out whether a question is answered incorrectly because of changes to the question, or changes to the passage, or both. Therefore, in this paper, we selected a single passage and asked a wide variety of questions about the passage. The response of a particular model to any one of these types of questions could be explored much more extensively on a larger dataset with more passages. Here, we are simply making a first survey of the possibilities.[1]

New York Times, 29 September 1973
A 61-year old furniture salesman was pushed down the shaft of a freight elevator yesterday in his downtown Brooklyn store by two robbers while a third attempted to crush him with the elevator car because they were dissatisfied with the $1,200 they had forced him to give them. The buffer springs at the bottom of the shaft prevented the car from crushing the salesman, John J. Hug, after he was pushed from the first floor to the basement. The car stopped about 12 inches above him as he flattened himself at the bottom of the pit. Mr. Hug was pinned in the shaft for about half an hour until his cries attracted the attention of a porter. The store at 340 Livingston Street is part of the Seaman's Quality Furniture chain. Mr. Hug was removed by members of the Police Emergency Squad and taken to Long Island College Hospital. He was badly shaken, but after being treated for scrapes of his left arm and for a spinal injury was released and went home. He lives at 62-01 69th Lane, Maspeth, Queens. He has worked for seven years at the store, on the corner of Nevins Street, and this was the fourth time he had been held up in the store. The last time was about one year ago, when his right arm was slashed by a knife-wielding robber.

Table 1: Full text of story in McCarthy (1990).

2 The Challenge Set Passage

In 1976, John McCarthy published the informal memo "An Example for Natural Language Understanding and the AI Problems It Raises" (McCarthy, 1990). The example was a short few paragraphs from a news article about a robbery, and a series of questions about the article asked and answered in natural language. The full text of the passage can be found in Table 1.

[1] To assess for statistical significance beyond this manual survey, the next phase of research will entail automating the generation of questions from type seed sets and the evaluation of question/answer pairs.

Proceedings of the 3rd Workshop on Machine Reading for Question Answering , pages 73–81
Nov 10th, 2021

The term "natural language understanding" only seems to have been introduced to the field of AI in about 1973 or 1974 (Woods, 1973). With this 1976 memo, McCarthy was helping lay the foundations of what the field would mean for AI researchers. He called this newspaper story "my candidate for a target for a natural language understander," pointing out that a fictional story would bring up even more difficult to answer questions about the motivations of the author.

McCarthy thought it would make the problem simpler to have both the questions and answers *not* be in natural language, but be queries formulated in an artificial query language free of ambiguities. Parsing the questions does not seem to require much beyond what would already be needed to parse the story, but certainly natural language generation was not part of the problem as he conceived it at all.

As an early benchmark, it avoids the kinds of bias that come from working with modern systems, tailoring the kinds of questions we ask to what the models we are working with can or can't do, depending on the researcher's motivations. It is small and simple enough to fit within the prompt of GPT, but rich enough that it allows tests for many different aspects of "understanding."

3 Background

We present views on what would be needed to address McCarthy's challenge, an overview of the GPT-3, and prompt-based learning.

3.1 Early Views of NLU Architecture

The paper from which the passage was taken contain's McCarthy's thoughts on how one might build a system to answer the questions he posed. It is instructive to compare the architecture of the GPT models tested in this paper with what McCarthy and, later, Erik Mueller believed would be required to solve such problems (1999).

McCarthy proposed that the Natural Language Understanding problem be solved by a system with the following components:

"1. A 'parser' that takes English into ANL [Artificial Natural Language].
2. An 'understander' that constructs the 'facts' from a text in the ANL.
3. Expression of the 'general information' about the world that could allow getting the answers to the questions by formal reasoning from the 'facts' and the 'general information.' The "general information" would also contain non-sentence data structures and procedures, but the sentences would tell what goals can be achieved by running the procedures. In this way, we would get the best of the sentential and procedural representations of knowledge.
4. A 'problem solver' that could answer the above questions on the basis of the 'facts.'"

Mueller (1999), responding to McCarthy's paper, proposed that a system for answering the questions in the passage would require the following steps:

"1. Feed input text to text agents for recognizing entities such as names and places.
2. Perform lexical analysis on the input.
3. Use part-of-speech taggers and word sense disambiguators to reduce possibilities.
4. Feed textual entities and lexical entries to a partial syntactic parser.
5. Feed syntactic parse fragments to a semantic parser.
6. Feed semantic parse fragments to a collection of understanding agents.
7. Build understanding agents for multiple realms including the physical realm, devices, human needs and goals, emotions, and mental states.
8. Design and implement mechanisms for understanding agents to negotiate a shared interpretation and renegotiate that interpretation as each input is received.
9. Build B-Brain mechanisms for controlling processing by understanding agents.
10. Adapt and extend existing parsers and lexicons.
11. Evolve existing commonsense databases by adding knowledge as needed.
12. Build links between existing resources, allowing multiple resources to be used."

The neural approaches in this paper are missing all of these components. However, there is some evidence that deep neural language models may rediscover a similar NLP pipeline (Tenney et al., 2019; Li et al., 2021).

The knowledge-base-centric approaches suggested by McCarthy and Mueller would guarantee that if the background knowledge, passage, and questions were encoded as logical statements correctly, the inference would be valid and the answers true. When using a language model to answer the questions, we have no such guarantees.

3.2 GPT-3

GPT stands for "Generative Pre-trained Transformer." It is a deep neural network with the transformer architecture, trained on a large general text corpus, that generates text as output, given a text prompt. Both the input and output are represented as "tokens": either common words or parts of words that can represent any unicode string. There are 50,000 possible tokens, and at each step, GPT generates a probability distribution over these tokens. How this probability distribution is sampled depends on various parameter settings, but for nearly all results in this paper, we simply select the most probable token.

The Davinci model of GPT-3 is the most powerful of this language model (LM) family, at 175 billion parameters for the Davinci version. GPT-3 has set records for accuracy on several question-answering and common-sense tasks (Brown et al., 2020), which made it a reasonable choice for the model best able to answer these questions correctly at present. In addition to being trained on terabytes of general text data from the web, the *instruct* variants, such as Davinci-instruct-beta (GDIB), were also specially trained on examples of question-answering, in a process known as "finetuning." This finetuning causes the model to have a bias towards expecting text to fall into a pattern of a short section of text, followed by questions and answers about that text.

We also did limited testing of the other GPT-3 models. These are referred to as Ada, Babbage, Curie. Although the sizes of these models have not been made public, indirect evidence (Gao, 2021) suggests that they are 350M, 1.3B, and 6.7B parameters respectively.

3.3 Prompt-based Learning

Stepping back for a moment, it is worth pointing out just how distinctive applying the LM-based approach to question-answering is in the context of machine learning methods and where prompt engineering fits in to this task. In traditional supervised learning, in order to train the parameters of the model, supervised data, i.e., pairs of inputs and outputs, are needed to characterize the task that the model will perform. The crucial issue for many tasks, however, is that the large amounts of supervised data needed for training these models may not be available. One way around this requirement when the datasets involve text is to leverage the text prediction capability of language models. While it is beyond the scope of this paper to describe the training of LMs specifically for prompt-based applications,[2] we note here the format of the prompts that we used in running the questions of the challenge dataset we have constructed:

"Read the passage below and answer the questions based on what you read."

passage

"Q. "

the question

"A."

The first element of the prompt was an instruction, altered systematically in our experimentation, as described in Section 4.1.1. The second element was the text passage verbatim (Table 1). The third element was the indicator of the upcoming question. The fourth element was the question verbatim. And the final element was the indicator of an answer to come.

4 Approach: Challenge Set Development

We construct our challenge dataset by beginning with the passage and questions from McCarthy, and building upon this with questions that further probe hypothesized strengths and weaknesses of GPT-3.

4.1 Questions from McCarthy and Answers from GPT-3 Davinci-instruct-beta

The questions were presented as a numbered list in McCarthy's paper. We presented the text of the article that McCarthy extracted, followed by each question individually (so previous questions and answers are not included in the prompt). The question was preceded by the letter "Q." to indicate that it is a question and followed by the letter "A." on a new line to indicate that an answer is expected. This is the most common use pattern for Davinci-instruct-beta.

We have set the temperature parameter to 0 except where otherwise noted, so that the most likely token is selected at each step. This also makes the results more reproducible. Temperature 0 has an increased tendency toward repetition in long (multiple sentence) answers and tends to produce somewhat blander output, but for this task it is probably the most appropriate.

The full set of questions and answers are in the Appendix B. McCarthy did not answer a few of his own questions, probably because the answer

[2] For details see Liu et al. (2021).

was obvious, and he followed up with a related question.

4.1.1 Summary Analysis on McCarthy Questions, Answers

Of McCarthy's 25 questions, GDIB clearly got four wrong, with perhaps another five arguable. We tested these same questions on all six GPT-3 models, with three variations on the prompt:

1. The passage followed by "Q:" then the text of the question, and then "A:" These results are listed in Appendix D.
2. Same as 1. above but preceded by the text "Read the passage below and answer the questions based on what you read."
3. Same as 1. above but preceded by the text "Read the passage below and answer the questions based on what you read. If there is not enough information to answer, say so."

Model	#1	#2	#3
Ada	12	12	13
Babbage	15	18	17
Curie	17	17	18
Davinci	15	18	18
Curie-instruct-beta	18	17	18
Davinci-instruct-beta	21	20	19

Table 2: Number of correct answers out of 25 on each model and for each prompt variation.

See Table 2 for a summary. This is a small dataset and the grading is not exact, but in general we see that including instructions in the prompt helped the non-instruct models and had little effect on the instruct models (probably because it was only directing them to do what they had already been fine-tuned to do); and that the Babbage, Curie, and Davinci models did not differ much in their ability to correctly answer these questions, though Ada did worse and the instruct models did a little better.

GPT's successes and failures on these questions hinted at types of questions to try to further test the model's ability. We only tested these questions on GDIB, the best-performing model, without instructions in the prompt.

4.2 Added Challenge Set Questions

The questions McCarthy asked covered a broad range of topics, and probed several different abilities of the system. We created additional questions to more thoroughly cover different kinds of questions that systems might be capable of answering.

This approach provides us with a way to further organize the categories of challenge set questions and begin to spell out, for example, a few parallel hypotheses with respect to these questions and the abilities of GPT-3:

Knowledge Sources Questions pertaining to explicit information within a single sentence in the prompt are more likely to be answered correctly than to explicit information that is distributed across sentences in the passage in the prompt.

Knowledge Types Questions pertaining to a single common named entity are more likely to be answered correctly than those pertaining to sequencing of several events and specific entities involved in those events.

Reasoning Requirements Questions with logical negation are more likely to be answered incorrectly than their counterpart without negation.

Outside of these basic hypotheses, we view this research as exploratory to further probe strength and weakness areas of GPT-3 generally, with the three dimensions allowing us to pinpoint these areas more precisely.

4.2.1 Knowledge Source

Questions requiring only factual knowledge to answer were almost always answered correctly:

- Questions about the facts of the article that require little external knowledge (e.g., ***How old was Mr. Hug?***)
- Questions that require combining facts of the article with some other commonly known information (e.g., ***What country did the events take place in?***)

These questions would still be challenging for a system with a knowledge base (as opposed to a LM), because mapping the natural language questions to the logical representation and mapping the answers to natural language is not trivial. However, these steps being handled, the content of the questions would be a straightforward retrieval.

Questions requiring mainly linguistic knowledge were also usually answered correctly. These questions mainly involve interpreting an ambiguity in language correctly based on the surrounding context, such as defining a word with the right sense (e.g., ***In the phrase "he was badly shaken" what does the word "shaken" mean?*** *The word "shaken"* *means to be very frightened*).[3]

It has been argued (Saba, 2020) that certain linguistic phenomena should be especially difficult for natural language understanding due to the missing text phenomenon, where the speaker leaves out certain information from speech because the listener already knows the information, making it impossible to learn from text alone. However, our results indicate that for many instances of this phenomenon, this is simply not the case. Apparently, much of the the common-sense information is available to the model in some form that it is able to make use of. We tested the following types of missing-text inference:

- lexical ambiguity (***How was Mr. Hug treated at the hospital?*** *He was treated for scrapes on his left arm and for a spinal injury.*)
- hidden relations (***When it says, "the car stopped 12 inches above him", what did the car stop doing?*** *The car stopped moving.*)
- quantifier scope (***Is every Seaman's Quality Furniture store on Livingston Street?*** *No, there are many stores in the chain.*)
- prepositional ambiguity (***What does "for" mean in the sentence "he was treated for scrapes"?*** *"For" means "in order to treat."*)
- metonomy (***In the phrase "a third attempted to crush him," what does the word "third" refer to?*** *The third robber.*)
- metaphor (***In the phrase "he was pinned in the shaft" what does the word "pinned" mean?*** *The word "pinned" means to be held in place.*)
- compound nominals (***What does a "freight elevator" have to do with freight?*** *A freight elevator is a large elevator that is used to transport goods.*)

While the model does seem to contain this information, depending on how the question is phrased it might be inaccessible to the model. For example, ***A "shoe store" sells shoes. A "book store" sells books. What does a "downtown Brooklyn store" sell?*** *** A "downtown Brooklyn store" sells "Brooklyn."*[4] The model sometimes gets questions of this form right and sometimes wrong. This example demonstrates the effect that careful prompt engineering can have—the prompt examples seem to sway the system towards an analogous, but in this case incorrect, answer.

[3]The challenge set questions are in bold italics. The returned answers follow in italics, not bolded.

[4]Incorrect answers are preceded by **.

4.2.2 Knowledge Type

Beyond simple factual questions are questions that test comprehension or understanding. One definition of "understanding" is "to grasp explanatory and conceptual connections between various pieces of information involved in the subject matter in question" (Kvanvig, 2015). In this sense, GDIB is able to solve some "understanding" tasks.

Theory of Mind GDIB is able to reasonably answer questions about what characters were thinking and feeling (e.g., ***Why did Mr. Hug give the robbers $1200?*** *He was afraid they would kill him*). These are "theory of mind" questions, intended to probe the ability to ascribe thoughts, beliefs, and feelings
from one's own for a variety of reasons, including the other's current knowledge. For a person to answer these questions appropriately it is thought that a model of the other's mind is necessary. We investigated this topic further by asking the example questions regarding short passages from Kaland et al. (2005), and the model answered them all correctly. The example passage is given in Table 3.

Theory of Mind Example Passage
Today James is going to Claire's house for the first time. He is going over for tea, and he is looking forward to seeing Claire's dog, which she talks about all time. James likes dogs very much. When James arrives at Claire's house Claire runs to open the door, and her dog jumps up to greet James. Claire's dog is huge; it's almost as big as James! When James sees Claire's huge dog he says,"Claire, you haven't got a dog at all. You've got an elephant!

Table 3: Example passage from Kaland et al. (2005).

We posed follow-on questions for this passage:
Q. Is it true, what James says?
A. *No, it's not true. Claire does have a dog.*
Q. Why does James say this?
A. *James is surprised because Claire's dog is so big.*
In a child, this would be considered evidence that the child possesses a well-developed theory of mind (Kaland et al., 2005).

Counterfactual Knowledge Some of McCarthy's questions were about what might have happened, rather than what actually happened. In general, we found GDIB surprisingly good at answering many counterfactual questions. Counterfactual questions requiring temporal or deductive reasoning, however, were often incorrectly answered. (e.g., ***What would have happened if Mr.***

Hug had been on the second floor instead of the first? ** *The car would have crushed him.*)

Counterfactual questions with impossible fictional premises were still usually answered correctly. *(e.g.,* ***What if the salesman had been Superman?*** *He would have been able to fly out of the shaft.*) These kinds of questions create problems for traditional knowledge bases because a consistent knowledge base cannot contain at the same time the set of facts that "no person can fly" and "Superman is a person" and "Superman can fly." GPT has no mechanisms to enforce consistency, which avoids this problem, but at the cost of allowing it to contradict itself and being incapable of guaranteeing anything about the truth of its output.

4.2.3 Reasoning

The most challenging questions we posed were questions requiring some kind of reasoning process to arrive at the answer. There has been some success at getting GPT to correctly follow a reasoning process by giving examples of the reasoning steps to follow, and having it imitate these steps one at a time. In the zero-shot prompts we are using, however, reasoning beyond what was required for the earlier types of questions seemed to be beyond its capabilities. It is unclear to what extent these difficulties with reasoning lie with the architecture (a limited number of layers can only carry out so many steps) or with the training set. Certainly other transformers trained on, for example, calculus problems (Lample and Charton, 2019) rather than web text, are able to correctly generate valid chains of reasoning.

Mathematical Word Problems Questions that require mathematical operations were frequently incorrect. This matches what one would expect from the original paper on GPT-3, where zero-shot math questions were usually incorrect. (e.g., ***The events of this story happened in 1975. How old would Mr. Hug be in 2020?*** ** *He would be 91 years old.*)

GPT-3's abilities at arithmetic and "word problems" have been the subject of several investigations (Gwern, 2020). It is clear that the tokenization makes arithmetic more difficult for the model to learn.

Temporal Reasoning GDIB is able to successfully answer questions about what events happened during a particular time interval (e.g., *What happened after the robbers arrived and before they pushed Mr. Hug down the elevator shaft?*) Questions about a time interval that require reasoning about beginnings and ends of events, however, were difficult for the model. These questions were inspired by Kelly and Khemlani (2020). (e.g., ***Did the elevator car reach the springs before Mr. Hug finished falling?*** ** *Yes.*)

False Premises Questions with false premises were almost never answered correctly. Answering these questions correctly would mean pointing out the error in the question. Instead, the model answers as if the premise of the question were true in a plausible way. (e.g., ***Why was there an airplane in the furniture store?*** ** *The airplane was a display in the store.*)

Insufficient Information Similarly, questions for which there is not enough information to answer were almost always answered confidently with a plausible (but frequently incorrect) answer (e.g., ***Why is the furniture chain called "Seaman's?"*** ** *The chain was founded by a sea captain.*)

In the tests of modified prompts, hinting that "not enough information" is an acceptable answer causes it to get all of the false premise and insufficient information questions right, but causes it to be unwilling to speculate on most of the counterfactual questions, and sometimes to claim there is not enough information when, in fact, there is.

This brings up the important point that answers in this paper provide only a lower bound on what the language model is capable of. It is possible that with a more cleverly designed prompt, the model would be capable of getting more of these questions right. By sticking to a format of story followed by a question and answer prefixed with Q. and A., we have reduced the space of prompts to explore, at the cost of possibly underestimating the full capability of the models.

Logical Negation This was a serious problem for smaller models, and still gives GDIB some difficulty. Considering some variations on the first question:

- ***Who was in the store when the events began?*** *John J. Hug*
- ***Who was not in the store when the events began?*** ** *The third robber.*
- ***Who was in the store during the events?*** *John J. Hug, the two robbers, and a third robber.*
- ***Who was not in the store during the events?*** ** *The robber who attempted to crush Mr. Hug with the elevator car.*

- ***Who was in the store after the events?*** *?? A porter.*[5]
- ***Who was not in the store after the events?*** *?? The robber who attempted to crush Mr. Hug with the elevator car.*

Depending on how one takes "the events" different judgements of these answers are possible, but it is clear that in any case, all the robbers were in the store during the events, and none of them were there after the events. A knowledge base could not contradict itself in this way.

5 Analysis

In a zero-shot setting, GDIB seems frequently unable to handle two main types of questions:

- Trick questions: questions with false premises, patterns that do not continue, or not enough information to answer
- Questions that require multi-step reasoning, including mathematical operations (story problems) and anything but the simplest temporal reasoning

A model that would do a better job on questions with not enough information may simply require finetuning on such questions and the appropriate answers, since they occur only relatively rarely in the data GDIB was trained on. (The question about the robbers' names—***What are the names and addresses of the robbers?*** *The names are unknown. The addresses are unknown*—suggests that the model has an appropriately set threshhold for assessing and then describing its uncertainty.) Fixing the problems with reasoning, on the other hand, probably requires a much larger model or changes to the underlying architecture.

On the positive side, GDIB frequently was able both to find and apply relevant background knowledge of the world to correctly answer questions. "What crimes were committed?", for example, seems to require knowing that pushing someone down an elevator shaft is a crime, that it is an attempt to kill them, and that the crime is known by the name "attempted murder." "Who had the money at the end?" seems to require keeping track of the motion of the money through the story. It seems able to predict thoughts and feelings, and to anticipate the immediate result of physical actions.

Beyond supplying answers to questions, we found this striking case where GPT generated this summary text:

[5] Answers not clearly correct or incorrect begin with "??".

Summarize the story. *A furniture salesman was pushed down the shaft of a freight elevator by two robbers and a third attempted to crush him with the elevator car because they were dissatisfied with the $1,200 they had forced him to give them.*

We also found parameter settings that led the model to change major aspects of the story (this was generated using the stock Davinci model with temperature = 0.7):

Write a similar story that takes place in ancient Egypt. *A wealthy merchant was passing through the Valley of the Kings when a band of marauders descended on him. The merchant was carrying a large amount of gold and jewelry, so the marauders forced him to surrender it. But they wanted more, so they forced him to reveal where he had hidden his most valuable possessions. When he refused to tell them, they put him in a tomb and left him there to die.*

This is a fairly sophisticated analogy. Instead of an elevator shaft, there is a tomb; instead of a furniture salesman with $1200 in Brooklyn there is a merchant with gold and jewels in the Valley of the Kings; but the bones of the story are the same.

One issue with the use of this article as part of a challenge set for language models is that the article may have been part of the training material for GPT, letting it memorize the answers, as discussed in (Lewis et al., 2020) Three lines of evidence show this is unlikely:

1. OpenAI (2019) states that they only trained on pages with outbound links from reddit, to ensure human readability. Searches of reddit.com and search engines indexing it did not turn up any links to any of the versions of the paper found on Google.
2. Performance on our new questions is similar to performance on McCarthy's questions. If his answers were memorized, these would be expected to do worse.
3. None of the answers longer than two words were verbatim, which one would expect if they had been memorized, especially at temperature 0.

Nevertheless, we can't completely rule it out.

6 Related Work

Challenge Datasets We have constructed a "challenge dataset" guided by approaches in the fields of linguistics and computational linguistics. In the former, datasets are developed for structured elicitation where linguists ask native speakers to judge grammaticality of presented sentences or to answer questions about their language. The elicitation results are key to deriving properties of the language (Clark et al., 2008; Probst and Levin, 2002). In the latter, datasets are constructed for system evaluation to establish benchmarks to gauge progress on shared tasks. In MT research, going beyond automated scores, the challenge set approach to system evaluation has provided a more fine-grained picture of the strengths of neural systems, as well as insight into which linguistic phenomena remain out of reach (Isabelle et al., 2017). In recent LM research that probes the syntactic knowledge in these models, the structured datasets of minimal grammatical/ungrammatical sentence pairs test when LMs assign a higher probability to the grammatical sentence than the ungrammatical one (Marvin and Linzen, 2018; Newman et al., 2021). Though significant caution is needed in interpreting LM results, we see diagnostic value in constructing challenge datasets to evaluate systems' *passage understanding*, as carefully constructed by Dua et al. (2019). The fact that a current state-of-the-art LM dropped more than 50 absolute F1 points on their dataset reinforces our belief that challenge datasets can spur research into more comprehensive semantic analyses of what LMs know, encouraging system hill-climbing up the right hill, per Bender and Koller (2020).

The General Language Understanding Evaluation (GLUE) benchmark (Wang et al., 2018) is of particular relevance to this work, as it is a collection of resources for both training and evaluation of various types of Natural Language Understanding tasks. It is intended to be agnostic to the system type. The evaluation suite includes tasks related to sentiment, paraphrase, natural language inference, coreference, as well as question-answering. While we took inspiration from this benchmark in our inclusion of questions overlapping with the inference tasks in GLUE, such as the Winograd Schema Challenge, we contribute a set of challenge questions that have been carefully crafted and classified to probe the strengths and weaknesses of a LM with respect to particular knowledge sources, types, and reasoning requirements.

LMs and "prompt-based learning" Numerous research teams are working to evaluate what LMs may "know", even asking how they compare to knowledge bases (Petroni et al., 2019). New possibilities are emerging with methods of estimating the knowledge in LMs that can be found with automatically constructed prompts that yield better results than those manually created, demonstrating that any given prompt may be sub-optimal (Jiang et al., 2020). Given our focus on assessing what one family of prompt-based LMs can answer about a given text passage, the most recent and pertinent overview that situates these LMs in the field is the extensive, systematic survey of prompting methods and pre-trained language models using these methods by Liu et al. (2021). As this survey notes, in tuning-free prompting as we have carried out with GPT LMs, the questions in the q/a task generate the answers directly. This is efficient, yet also leaves the prompts as the only method to provide the task specification. For this reason, we present the framework of example questions that serve as test prompts in a structured challenge dataset both so that they can be reused by others in testing their systems, and so that we can extend these over time.

7 Conclusion

This limited evidence suggests that current language models are able to supply answers to questions about a passage in a way that, at least superficially, meets the challenge of "natural language understanding" as originally set out in the 1970s. They can do surprisingly well at describing the likely thoughts and feelings of characters though these are not explicit in the passage. The models can also generate text that describes likely consequences for what might have happened if things had gone differently, and that fills in the factual information that we tend to omit when using natural language. However, many questions requiring even a little careful thought, reasoning, or multi-step inference go beyond the capability of these models.

For those who want to make use of these models today, this suggests sticking to applications where the information needed to answer the questions are immediately available in the passage or slowly-changing, widely known information about the world; or else creative questions where there is no wrong answer. For researchers, though, this highlights the need to discover ways of combining the deductive reasoning capabilities already present in early AI work with the context-sensitivity and ability to work with natural language that these models provide.

References

Emily M. Bender and Alexander Koller. 2020. Climbing towards NLU: On meaning, form, and understanding in the age of data. In *Proceedings of the 58th Annual Meeting of the Association for Computational Linguistics*, pages 5185–5198, Online. Association for Computational Linguistics.

Tom B Brown, Benjamin Mann, Nick Ryder, Melanie Subbiah, Jared Kaplan, Prafulla Dhariwal, Arvind Neelakantan, Pranav Shyam, Girish Sastry, Amanda Askell, et al. 2020. Language models are few-shot learners. *arXiv preprint arXiv:2005.14165*.

Jonathan Clark, Robert E. Frederking, and Lori S. Levin. 2008. Toward active learning in data selection: Automatic discovery of language features during elicitation. In *LREC 2008, 26 May - 1 June 2008, Marrakech, Morocco*. European Language Resources Association.

Dheeru Dua, Yizhong Wang, Pradeep Dasigi, Gabriel Stanovsky, Sameer Singh, and Matt Gardner. 2019. DROP: A reading comprehension benchmark requiring discrete reasoning over paragraphs. In *2019 NAACL: Human Language Technologies, Volume 1*, Minneapolis, Minnesota. Association for Computational Linguistics.

Leo Gao. 2021. On the sizes of openai api models.

Gwern. 2020. Gpt-3 creative fiction.

Pierre Isabelle, Colin Cherry, and George F. Foster. 2017. A challenge set approach to evaluating machine translation. In *Proceedings of the 2017 Conference on Empirical Methods in Natural Language Processing, EMNLP 2017, Copenhagen, Denmark, September 9-11, 2017*, pages 2486–2496. Association for Computational Linguistics.

Zhengbao Jiang, Frank F. Xu, Jun Araki, and Graham Neubig. 2020. How can we know what language models know? *Transactions of the Association for Computational Linguistics*, 8:423–438.

Nils Kaland, Annette Møller-Nielsen, Lars Smith, Erik Lykke Mortensen, Kirsten Callesen, and Dorte Gottlieb. 2005. The strange stories test. *European child & adolescent psychiatry*, 14(2):73–82.

Laura Jane Kelly and Sangeet Khemlani. 2020. Directional biases in durative inference. In *CogSci*.

Jonathan L Kvanvig. 2015. Knowledge, understanding, and reasons for belief. In *The Oxford Handbook of Reasons and Normativity*.

Guillaume Lample and François Charton. 2019. Deep learning for symbolic mathematics. *arXiv preprint arXiv:1912.01412*.

Patrick Lewis, Pontus Stenetorp, and Sebastian Riedel. 2020. Question and answer test-train overlap in open-domain question answering datasets. *arXiv preprint arXiv:2008.02637*.

Belinda Z Li, Maxwell Nye, and Jacob Andreas. 2021. Implicit representations of meaning in neural language models. *arXiv preprint arXiv:2106.00737*.

Pengfei Liu, Weizhe Yuan, Jinlan Fu, Zhengbao Jiang, Hiroaki Hayashi, and Graham Neubig. 2021. Pretrain, prompt, and predict: A systematic survey of prompting methods in natural language processing.

Rebecca Marvin and Tal Linzen. 2018. Targeted syntactic evaluation of language models. In *Proceedings of the 2018 Conference on Empirical Methods in Natural Language Processing*, pages 1192–1202, Brussels, Belgium. Association for Computational Linguistics.

John McCarthy. 1990. An example for natural language understanding and the ai problems it raises. *Formalizing Common Sense: Papers by John McCarthy*, 355.

Erik T Mueller. 1999. Prospects for in-depth story understanding by computer.

Benjamin Newman, Kai-Siang Ang, Julia Gong, and John Hewitt. 2021. Refining targeted syntactic evaluation of language models. *CoRR*, abs/2104.09635.

OpenAI. 2019. Better language models and their implications.

F. Petroni, T. Rocktäschel, A. H. Miller, P. Lewis, A. Bakhtin, Y. Wu, and S. Riedel. 2019. Language models as knowledge bases? In *In: EMNLP 2019*.

Katharina Probst and Lori Levin. 2002. Challenges in automated elicitation of a controlled bilingual corpus. In *Proceedings of the 9th International Conference on Theoretical and Methodological Issues in Machine Translation (TMI-02)*.

Walid Saba. 2020. Language and its commonsense: Where formal semantics went wrong, and where it can (and should) go. *Journal of Knowledge Structures and Systems*, 1(1).

Ian Tenney, Dipanjan Das, and Ellie Pavlick. 2019. Bert rediscovers the classical nlp pipeline. *arXiv preprint arXiv:1905.05950*.

Alex Wang, Amanpreet Singh, Julian Michael, Felix Hill, Omer Levy, and Samuel Bowman. 2018. Glue: A multi-task benchmark and analysis platform for natural language understanding. In *Proceedings of the 2018 EMNLP Workshop BlackboxNLP: Analyzing and Interpreting Neural Networks for NLP*, pages 353–355.

William A Woods. 1973. Progress in natural language understanding: an application to lunar geology. In *Proceedings of the June 4-8, 1973, national computer conference and exposition*, pages 441–450.

Multi-modal Retrieval of Tables and Texts Using Tri-encoder Models

Bogdan Kostić and **Julian Risch** and **Timo Möller**
deepset
{bogdan.kostic, julian.risch, timo.moeller}@deepset.ai

Abstract

Open-domain extractive question answering works well on textual data by first retrieving candidate texts and then extracting the answer from those candidates. However, some questions cannot be answered by text alone but require information stored in tables. In this paper, we present an approach for retrieving both texts and tables relevant to a question by jointly encoding texts, tables and questions into a single vector space. To this end, we create a new multi-modal dataset based on text and table datasets from related work and compare the retrieval performance of different encoding schemata. We find that dense vector embeddings of transformer models outperform sparse embeddings on four out of six evaluation datasets. Comparing different dense embedding models, tri-encoders with one encoder for each question, text and table increase retrieval performance compared to bi-encoders with one encoder for the question and one for both text and tables. We release the newly created multi-modal dataset to the community so that it can be used for training and evaluation.

1 Introduction

Finding the answer to a factual question in a large collection of documents is a tedious task that many people from a broad range of domains have to complete on a daily basis. In order to address this task with machine learning approaches, it has been formalized as open-domain extractive question-answering (QA). More specifically, given a natural language question and a database of text documents as a knowledge base, open-domain extractive QA aims to extract a substring that answers the given question out of one of the documents.

The standard approach for this task is a pipeline architecture consisting of two components: a retriever selecting a small subset of relevant documents from the database and a reader extracting granular answers out of each of these retrieved documents (Voorhees and Tice, 2000). In this paper, we focus on the retriever and present a transformer-based tri-encoder model as an implementation of this component. Retrievers can also be implemented with bag-of-words retrieval methods, such as TF-IDF or BM25, that transform all documents and the question to sparse vector representations. However, as these methods rely on a lexical overlap of the question and the documents, they fail to capture synonymy and other semantic relationships. This limitation motivates the use of dense vector representations and we compare dense retrieval models to a BM25 baseline in our experiments. A survey on term-based, early semantic, and neural semantic models for document retrieval as a first step before document reranking and down-stream tasks, such as question answering, has been published by Cai et al. (2021).

To date, most of the research centered around question-answering focuses on using free-form text as the single source for answering questions. However, valuable information can obviously be found in other modalities as well. For instance, a lot of information is stored in semi-structured tables; according to Cafarella et al. (2008), more than 14.1 billion tables can be found on the World Wide Web. Given that a user typically does not know in advance in which modality the answer to their question resides, a QA system capable of jointly handling text and tables is needed. One major challenge in building such a system is to represent texts and tables in a way that allows capturing semantic similarity and retrieving texts and tables that are semantically related to a given question.

Contributions The contributions of this paper can be summarized as follows: (1) we present bi-encoder and tri-encoder models that are capable of joint retrieval of tables and texts; (2) we create and release a multi-modal dataset for training and

Proceedings of the 3rd Workshop on Machine Reading for Question Answering , pages 82–91
Nov 10th, 2021

evaluating models on this task;[1] (3) we compare sparse retrieval models with dense retrieval models using bi-encoders and tri-encoders on our new multi-modal dataset and on five uni-modal datasets from related work.

Outline The remainder of this paper is structured as follows: Section 2 summarizes existing methods for uni-modal retrieval of texts on the one hand and of tables on the other hand. Further, it discusses the only two, recently published approaches for joint retrieval of tables and texts. Section 3 briefly describes the existing uni-modal datasets and our new multi-modal dataset, which we use to train the retrieval models presented in Section 4 and to evaluate these models in Section 5. Section 6 concludes the paper and gives directions for future work.

2 Related Work

To the best of our knowledge the only existing work that addresses joint retrieval of tables and texts is by Chen et al. (2021), Talmor et al. (2021) and Li et al. (2021). To address the challenge of limited context available for tables, Chen et al. (2021) fuse a table segment and text passages into one block if they mention the same named entities. Each block is represented with a single dense embedding so that a table and relevant passages are jointly retrieved as a group if the embedding is similar to that of the question. This grouping makes sense because Chen et al. (2021) address the task of multi-hop QA, where information needs to be aggregated from multiple tables and texts to answer a question. In contrast to that, we address the slightly different task of single-hop QA, where either only one table or one text is needed to answer a question. Therefore, our approach represents tables and texts with separate embeddings, which are in the same embedding space. The advantage here is that the model learns to estimate relevance on the more fine-grained level of individual tables or texts and can decide whether a particular table or text is more relevant to the question.

Li et al. (2021) also address the task of multi-hop QA on texts and tables but retrieve them individually. They make use of the sparse retrieval method BM25 and a transformer-based reranker to generate a set of candidate texts and tables. With two separate BM25 indices for texts and tables, they retrieve a set of documents for each modality. In a second step, they apply a joint BERT-based reranker to reduce the size of candidate texts and tables. Talmor et al. (2021) create a MULTIMODALQA dataset containing questions that require joint reasoning over tables, texts, and images.

Otherwise closely related to our approach are TABERT by Yin et al. (2020) and TAPAS by Herzig et al. (2020), who use tables and texts for language model pre-training but do not consider joint retrieval of tables and texts. TURL focuses on representation learning for tables but also does not consider the retrieval task (Deng et al., 2020). Due to this limited amount of prior research, we discuss related work on the separate tasks of uni-modal text retrieval and table retrieval in the following.

2.1 Text Retrieval

Dense Passage Retrieval (DPR) by Karpukhin et al. (2020) relies on a bi-encoder model comprising two separate BERT models (Devlin et al., 2019). Similar to TF-IDF, DPR is a vector space model that represents both queries and documents in the same vector space. However, while TF-IDF represents text documents as very high dimensional sparse vectors, DPR relies on relatively low dimensional dense embeddings. While one of the models, the passage encoder ($BERT_p$), is used to encode text passages at indexing time, the second model, the question encoder ($BERT_q$), is used to encode questions at query time. Since BERT's [CLS]-token is particularly designated to capture the meaning of the whole input sequence, its embedding is used as a representation vector for both the text passages and the questions.

The training aims to increase the dot product or cosine similarity of semantically similar passages and questions. In order to achieve this, Karpukhin et al. (2020) use, besides the question's positive passage, hard negative passages as well as in-batch negative passages as training signal. Hard negatives are sampled utilizing a BM25-based retriever on the whole English Wikipedia dump. For each question, they use the highest ranked passage not containing the question's answer string. DPR drastically outperforms BM25 by almost 20 percentage points with regard to recall@20 on the Natural Questions (NQ) dataset by Kwiatkowski et al. (2019).

[1] `https://multimodalretrieval.s3.eu-central-1.amazonaws.com/data.zip`

2.2 Table Retrieval

Most existing table retrieval approaches rely on supervised learning-to-rank approaches. Zhang and Balog (2018) combine a set of hand-crafted query features, table features and query-table features with semantic similarity of table and query as additional feature. To get table and query representations, they use the average of pre-trained word2vec (Mikolov et al., 2013) and RDF2vec embeddings (Ristoski and Paulheim, 2016). These features are then used to train a random forest regressor to get relevance scores of the tables with regard to the query. Interestingly, training word embeddings on a corpus of tables instead of texts does not improve performance (Zhang et al., 2019).

Shraga et al. (2020a) combine intrinsic and extrinsic table similarity scores. For the intrinsic table similarity, they concatenate the table's title, caption, header and data rows and use a sliding window over this concatenated string to get a set of candidate passages for each table. Each candidate passage is scored using BM25 and the maximum of all passages of a table is the intrinsic score with regard to a query. The extrinsic score is based on table-table similarities to ensure that similar tables get a similar final score.

Bagheri and Al-Obeidat (2020) focus on hard queries that contain terms that do not occur in the relevant tables, which means the query and the relevant tables have a low lexical overlap. To this end, they learn low dimensional latent factor matrices to represent tables as well as queries, i.e., they learn term co-occurrences to be able to get tables that address the same topic but only partially overlap on a lexical level. Based on this result, we compare results on datasets with high or low lexical overlap in our experiments.

There are four deep learning approaches for table retrieval (Shraga et al., 2020b; Pan et al., 2021; Chen et al., 2020b; Herzig et al., 2021). Shraga et al. (2020b) treat tables and queries as multi-modal objects that consist of query, table caption, schema, rows and columns. Each component is encoded using its own neural network encoder that accounts for its special characteristics. Subsequently, these uni-modal encodings are joined into a single representation, which is passed on to fully connected layers that predict whether the input table is relevant with regard to the input query.

Pan et al. (2021) stack two retrieval components. First, they use BM25 to produce a large subset of possibly relevant tables. These tables are then passed to a row-column intersection model that generates a probability distribution over the table cells whether they contain the answer to the user's query. The maximum cell-level score for each table represents its retrieval score.

Chen et al. (2020b) apply the transformer-based language model BERT (Devlin et al., 2019) to the table retrieval task by combining BERT embeddings with other, hand-curated table and query features. Their approach consists of several components, including a step where the concatenation of a query, a table's context fields and selected relevant table rows are processed by a BERT model. A significant downside of this approach is that it becomes inefficient with increasing number of tables: for each query, all tables need to be passed through a BERT network.

Herzig et al. (2021) solve this efficiency problem by adapting Karpukhin et al.'s (2020) dense passage retrieval approach to dense table retrieval (DTR). To this end, they make use of TAPAS (Herzig et al., 2020), a transformer-based language model that has been pre-trained on millions of tables. TAPAS extends BERT by adding three different types of positional embeddings to encode the two-dimensional tabular structure: row, column and rank embeddings. This allows to flatten the table by concatenating the rows to a one-dimensional sequence of tokens. Similar to Karpukhin et al. (2020), Herzig et al. (2021) make use of a bi-encoder approach. However, they use two TAPAS instances instead of BERT instances to encode the queries and the tables, respectively. The goal of training this bi-encoder is to build an embedding model that generates similar embeddings for questions and their relevant tables. As in Karpukhin et al.'s (2020) approach, this goal is achieved using hard-negatives retrieved from all the tables from the English Wikipedia dump as well as in-batch negatives. DTR outperforms BM25 by more than 40 percentage points on the NQ-TABLES dataset (Herzig et al., 2021). However, the experiments also show that TAPAS requires additional pre-training on the task of table retrieval on millions of tables scraped from Wikipedia. As a further research direction for future work, Herzig et al. (2021) propose to combine tables and texts for multi-modal open-domain QA. We contribute towards this goal in our paper by providing a multi-modal retriever as one component of a multi-modal open-domain QA pipeline on tables and texts.

3 Datasets

The training and evaluation of models examined in this paper on the task of multi-modal retrieval makes use of five datasets from related work: NQ (Kwiatkowski et al., 2019), NQ-TABLES (Herzig et al., 2021), WIKISQL (Zhong et al., 2017), a subset of WIKISQL, which we call WIKISQL$_{\text{ctx-independent}}$, and OTT-QA (Chen et al., 2021). This section briefly explains the characteristics of these datasets and of our newly created multi-modal retrieval dataset comprising tables and texts, which we call MULTIMODALRETRIEVAL. Table 1 gives an overview of the modality and the number of samples in each dataset.

NQ Natural Questions (NQ) (Kwiatkowski et al., 2019) is an open-domain QA dataset on Wikipedia articles. It consists of questions, their answers and the text passages the answers reside in. The questions are *natural* because they consist of real user queries issued to the Google search engine instead of questions posed by annotators after reading a text passage, which was done to create other popular QA datasets, such as the Stanford Question Answering Dataset (SQuAD) (Rajpurkar et al., 2018). Having *natural* questions does not only ensure that the questions correspond to information needs by real users but also makes the dataset open-domain, i.e., the questions are context-independent and can be understood without their accompanying text passage that contains the answer. For the purpose of retrieval, we utilize Karpukhin et al.'s (2020) preprocessed variant of NQ.

NQ-TABLES The answers to most of the questions inside the NQ dataset can be found in plain unstructured text. However, a subset of the questions are answered by tables. As a consequence, Herzig et al. (2021) construct NQ-TABLES, a table-specific QA dataset based on NQ. To achieve this objective, they extract all the tables and all the questions whose answers reside inside a table. They come up with a dataset consisting of 9,594 questions in the training set, 1,068 questions in the development set, 966 questions in the test set and 169,898 tables in total. Given that this dataset is a subset of NQ, the questions share the characteristic of being context-independent.

WIKISQL WIKISQL (Zhong et al., 2017) is a closed-domain QA dataset consisting of 24,241 tables and 80,654 natural language questions together with their corresponding SQL query. To build this dataset, Zhong et al. (2017) generate a number of random SQL queries for each table. These SQL queries are then transformed into crude questions using templates. Finally, Amazon Mechanical Turk crowd workers paraphrase these crude questions into natural language questions, which are checked by two additional crowd workers.

WIKISQL$_{\text{ctx-independent}}$ Since WIKISQL is a closed-domain QA dataset, the majority of its questions is context-dependent, i.e., they do not provide enough context to be answered without their accompanying table and are therefore not suitable for training or evaluation on the retrieval task. One example for such insufficient questions inside the dataset is: *"Who is the player that wears number 42?"*, which cannot be answered without additional context given in the table, such as the name of a sports team and a year. As a consequence, to make use of WIKISQL, all questions that do not provide enough context for retrieval need to be filtered out. For automating this filtering, we labeled a subset of WIKISQL's questions with regard to whether they are either context-independent or under-specified resulting in 4,553 labels as training set and 612 labels as test set. These labels are then used to train a classifier that predicts whether a question provides enough context. We fine-tune a RoBERTa-base (Liu et al., 2019) language model achieving an accuracy of 0.8134 and a macro-averaged F1-score of 0.7748 on the test set. Next, we apply this classifier to the whole WIKISQL dataset to filter out all the questions that are predicted as under-specified.

OTT-QA OTT-QA (Chen et al., 2021) is an open-domain multi-hop QA dataset of texts and tables from Wikipedia built upon HybridQA (Chen et al., 2020a), a closed-domain multi-hop QA dataset. Multi-hop QA refers to the fact that most questions inside the dataset require a combination of different texts and/or tables instead of a single document in order to be answered. To generate an open-domain version of HybridQA, Chen et al. (2021) let crowd workers decontextualize all the questions. Furthermore, they add additional question-answer pairs on newly crawled tables. Since the published annotations contain only the gold tables but not the gold texts, we use OTT-QA only for generating table retrieval training samples and evaluating the uni-modal retrieval of tables.

Dataset	Modality	Train	Test	Ctx-ind.
NQ	text	58,880	3,610	✔
NQ-TABLES	table	9,594	966	✔
WIKISQL	table	56,355	15,878	✖
WIKISQL$_{\text{ctx-independent}}$	table	7,336	2,101	✔
OTT-QA	table	41,469	2,158	✔
MULTIMODALRETRIEVAL	text & table	120,239	4,937	✔

Table 1: Modality and number of train and test samples for multi-modal retrieval models. Only WIKISQL is not context-independent (ctx-ind.), which is why we create the subset WIKISQL$_{\text{ctx-independent}}$.

MULTIMODALRETRIEVAL Given that no multi-modal dataset of tables and texts is readily available, this paper newly introduces such a dataset based on datasets from related work. For this purpose, we combine the question-passage pairs from NQ as questions requiring a text passage to be answered with the question-table pairs from NQ-TABLES, WIKISQL$_{\text{ctx-independent}}$, and OTT-QA as questions requiring a table to be answered. Both Karpukhin et al. (2020) for text retrieval and Herzig et al. (2021) for table retrieval show that adding hard negatives as training signal boosts the retrieval performance of the model significantly. Therefore, we index 21 million Wikipedia passages (from Karpukhin et al. (2020)) and 7 million Wikipedia tables (used by Eisenschlos et al. (2020) to pre-train TAPAS) with Elasticsearch to sample hard negatives using BM25. For each question, the highest ranked passages or tables that do no contain the answer string were chosen, i.e., a question originating from a tabular question-answering dataset can also have a text passage as hard negative, and vice versa.

4 Approach

Our two approaches for the joint retrieval of tables and texts comprise bi-encoder and tri-encoder models based on uni-modal dense retrieval methods by Karpukhin et al. (2020) and Herzig et al. (2021).

In our first approach, the bi-encoder uses one language model to encode the questions and a second model to encode both the tables and the text passages. Our second approach adds a third encoder, such that there is one separate encoder for questions, text passages and tables. In contrast to the bi-encoder where tables and texts are encoded by the same model, the tri-encoder routes tables to the table encoder model and text passages to the text encoder model.

We train three different bi-encoders and three different tri-encoders, which differ in the underlying language models as specified in Table 2. The first multi-modal bi-encoder consists of two different BERT-small instances that serve as question encoder and table and text encoder, respectively. Given that BERT models only allow one-dimensional strings of text as input, the two-dimensional tables are transformed into one dimension by concatenating the titles of the page and the section the table occurs in, the caption of the table, and each row of the table. In order to analyze whether the table-specific language model TAPAS (Herzig et al., 2020; Eisenschlos et al., 2020) gives a performance boost compared to a plain BERT model, the remaining two bi-encoders make use of a TAPAS model that is pre-trained for the task of table retrieval (Herzig et al., 2021) for at least one of their encoders. Thus, the second bi-encoder uses a BERT-small instance as question encoder and a TAPAS-small instance as table and text encoder. The third bi-encoder utilizes two TAPAS-small models, one to encode the questions and the second to encode both text and tables. Using BERT-small instead of BERT-base or BERT-large models drastically reduces the number of parameters and allows to fit more training samples into one batch. In contrast to a BERT-large model with 24 transformer layers, hidden representations of size 1024, 16 attention heads, and a total number of 335M parameters, BERT-small consists of only 4 transformer layers, hidden representations of size 512, 8 attention heads, and a total number of 29.1M parameters.

The first tri-encoder model uses BERT-small instances for all of its three encoders. Also for the tri-encoder approach, we analyze the impact of using TAPAS for at least one of the encoders. Therefore,

	Question	Encoders Text	Table
Bi-encoder	BERT-small	—— BERT-small ——	
	BERT-small	—— TAPAS-small ——	
	TAPAS-small	—— TAPAS-small ——	
Tri-encoder	BERT-small	BERT-small	BERT-small
	BERT-small	BERT-small	TAPAS-small
	TAPAS-small	BERT-small	TAPAS-small

Table 2: Examined multi-modal bi-encoder and tri-encoder models.

	Bi-encoders	Tri-encoders
Learning rate	1e-5	1e-5
LR schedule	linear	linear
Warm-up steps	10%	10%
Batch size	38	28
Epochs	10	10
Optimizer	Adam	Adam

Table 3: Hyperparameters used to train the bi-encoder and tri-encoder multi-modal retrieval models.

the second architecture makes use of a BERT-small model for both the question encoder and the text encoder and utilizes a TAPAS-small instance to encode the tables. The third tri-encoder model uses two TAPAS-small instances to encode questions and tables and a BERT-small instance to encode text passages.

Herzig et al. (2021) use an additional down-projection layer to reduce the dimensionality of the question and table embeddings. We evaluated models with and without such a down-projection layer and found that their results do not differ significantly. Given that the models using an additional down-projection layer are more complex than models that directly utilize the embedding of the [CLS]-token, we consider only TAPAS-models without a down-projection layer throughout the remainder of this paper, including the experiments.

Table 3 specifies the hyperparameters used to train the bi-encoder and tri-encoder models on the training split of the MULTIMODALRETRIEVAL dataset described in Section 3. The learning objective is to create similar embeddings for relevant texts and/or tables with regard to a question. To train the models more efficiently, we make use of in-batch negatives besides each question's hard negative text or table as suggested by Karpukhin et al. (2020) in the context of text retrieval. Given that the training samples inside a batch are randomly selected from all training examples, questions comprising a text passage as gold-label might have tables as negative labels, and vice versa.

5 Experiments

We compare the presented dense retrieval models to the sparse retrieval method BM25 and evaluate them based on recall@k with $k \in \{10, 20, 100\}$. The search space to evaluate the models needs to consist of both texts and tables. For this purpose, 500,000 text passages are randomly sampled from Karpukhin et al. (2020)'s preprocessed Wikipedia passages making sure that the gold passages are among these passages. Furthermore, besides the text passages, all the tables from WIKISQL, OTT-QA, and NQ-TABLES are used, resulting in 656,166 tables and therefore approximately 1.2 million documents in total. The models are evaluated on a random sample of 1,000 questions of each dataset's test split as listed in Table 1 and the full test split of the MULTIMODALRETRIEVAL dataset.

Following Karpukhin et al. (2020), a document retrieved for a question originating from NQ or NQ-TABLES is considered a correct match if the document contains the answer string of the granular answer. Given that the derivation of the granular answer for questions originating from WIKISQL and OTT-QA might need further aggregation, such as summation or counting, and, therefore, the answer string does not need to be present in a relevant document, a retrieved document is only considered a correct match if it is the gold annotated table. This evaluation procedure might have the effect of incorrectly judging non-gold tables that contain the answer to a query as irrelevant. However, since we apply the same evaluation procedure for all models, the numbers should be comparable. Table 4 specifies the evaluation results for BM25, all bi-encoder and all tri-encoder models.

The evaluation shows that BM25 outperforms all dense methods on both the full WIKISQL dataset and WIKISQL's context-independent questions. It outperforms the best dense retrieval model on this dataset, the tri-encoder consisting of three BERT models, by 21.9 percentage points on all WIKISQL questions and 30.4 percentage points on context-independent WIKISQL questions with regard to

Encoders			NQ			WikiSQL			WikiSQL$_{\text{ctx-independent}}$		
Question	Text	Table	R@10	R@20	R@100	R@10	R@20	R@100	R@10	R@20	R@100
———	BM25	———	53.3	59.8	73.9	**42.1**	**47.1**	**59.5**	**61.2**	**67.2**	**81.0**
BERT	— BERT —		**70.1**	**76.0**	**84.2**	17.5	22.8	39.6	30.7	40.9	59.1
BERT	— TaPas —		50.0	57.1	72.7	6.4	8.9	20.3	12.3	17.1	36.7
TaPas	— TaPas —		59.6	67.4	78.2	9.5	13.5	26.3	16.6	23.6	45.9
BERT	BERT	BERT	69.1	75.0	83.5	20.2	26.8	43.3	30.8	38.2	60.7
BERT	BERT	TaPas	59.0	67.1	77.6	3.5	5.1	15.2	7.5	12.0	30.9
TaPas	BERT	TaPas	46.2	53.5	68.0	10.7	14.0	28.8	17.1	23.3	45.0

Encoders			OTT-QA			NQ-Tables			MultiModalRetrieval		
Question	Text	Table	R@10	R@20	R@100	R@10	R@20	R@100	R@10	R@20	R@100
———	BM25	———	40.2	45.6	58.2	56.6	65.1	82.8	50.7	57.0	71.1
BERT	— BERT —		72.9	78.0	89.4	84.9	91.2	**96.7**	55.2	61.8	73.8
BERT	— TaPas —		30.6	40.0	63.1	71.6	72.6	90.0	34.2	39.1	56.6
TaPas	— TaPas —		49.9	60.4	82.8	78.9	86.0	94.0	42.9	50.2	65.4
BERT	BERT	BERT	**73.8**	**79.7**	**90.1**	**86.4**	**91.6**	**96.7**	**56.1**	**62.3**	**74.9**
BERT	BERT	TaPas	25.8	34.3	59.4	52.3	62.1	80.7	29.6	36.1	52.8
TaPas	BERT	TaPas	50.8	60.9	79.8	76.9	82.8	92.9	40.3	46.9	62.9

Table 4: Evaluation results of BM25 and bi-encoder and tri-encoder retrieval models on 1000 random samples of the test splits of NQ, WikiSQL, context-independent questions of WikiSQL, OTT-QA, and NQ-Tables and the full test set of our new MultiModalRetrieval dataset with regard to recall@10, recall@20, and recall@100.

recall@10.

Analysing the WikiSQL dataset in more detail shows a very high lexical overlap of questions with their accompanying table. A combination of the Jaccard coefficient and Gestalt-Pattern-Matching[2] allows to quantify the lexical overlap of the questions with their corresponding tables without incorporating neither duplicate occurrences of the same word nor the order of the words inside the questions and the tables. This word order independence is particularly important for the analysis, given that the sparse retrieval method BM25 is order-agnostic. Even after lower-casing questions and tables and removing stopwords in the WikiSQL dataset, 40.68% of the questions lexically overlap completely with the relevant table, according to the combination of the Jaccard coefficient and Gestalt-Pattern-Matching. This large lexical overlap explains BM25's strong performance on that dataset in Table 4. In contrast, only 0.27% of the questions in OTT-QA overlap completely with their accompanying table. For the other datasets, 15.73% of the questions in NQ-Tables, 14.47% of the questions in NQ, and 21.96% of the questions in MULTIMODALRETRIEVAL overlap completely with their accompanying table or text.

To better understand how the lexical overlap of questions and accompanying tables influences BM25's performance, we split the test sets of WikiSQL and WikiSQL$_{\text{ctx-independent}}$ into subsets with different ranges of lexical overlap. As can be observed in Figure 1, the recall of both BM25 and dense retrieval highly correlates with lexical overlap. Furthermore, while BM25 outperforms dense retrieval for questions with high lexical overlap, it is the other way round for questions with low lexical overlap.

On the sample of the NQ-Tables test set, all dense retrieval models outperform BM25, except for the tri-encoder that consists of BERT instances as question and text passage encoder and a TaPas instance as table encoder. The best performing model on this dataset is the tri-encoder consisting of three BERT encoders. This model outperforms the sparse retrieval method BM25 by 29.8 percentage points with regard to recall@10.

For the sampled questions of the OTT-QA development set, four out of the six dense retrieval models outperform BM25. The best performing model is again the tri-encoder model that is com-

[2]We use an implementation from: `https://github.com/seatgeek/fuzzywuzzy#token-set-ratio`

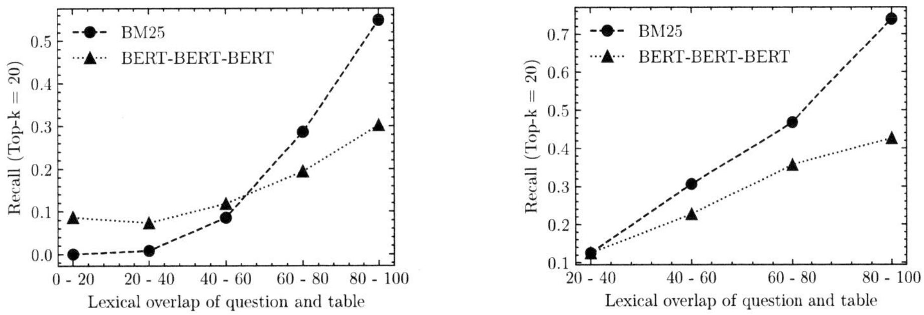

(a) WikiSQL (b) $\text{WikiSQL}_{\text{ctx-independent}}$

Figure 1: Recall@20 of the BM25 model and the BERT-BERT-BERT tri-encoder across different percentage of lexical overlap of question and table. Performance of BM25 drops drastically if the lexical overlap is low.

posed of three BERT-small encoders. This model outperforms BM25 by 33.6 percentage points with regard to recall@10. BM25 outperforms the bi-encoder consisting of a BERT model as question encoder and a TaPas model as text and table encoder as well as the tri-encoder consisting of two BERT models serving as question encoder and text encoder, respectively, and a TaPas model serving as table encoder.

When it comes to the performance on the text modality, i.e., questions deriving from NQ whose gold-label answer resides in a text passage, four out of the six dense retrieval models outperform BM25. For this case, the best performing model is not a tri-encoder but the bi-encoder comprising two BERT models. This model outperforms BM25 by 16.8 percentage points with regard to recall@10. However, this bi-encoder exceeds the tri-encoder consisting of three BERT encoders only slightly by one percentage point. The sparse retrieval method BM25 beats the bi-encoder consisting of a BERT model as question encoder and a TaPas model as text and table encoder as well as the tri-encoder consisting of two TaPas models serving as question encoder and table encoder, respectively, and a BERT model serving as text encoder.

In summary, the best performance on the WikiSQL test set is achieved by the sparse retrieval method BM25. The tri-encoder consisting of three BERT encoders shows the best performance on the remaining two tabular datasets, OTT-QA and NQ-Tables. On the NQ dataset, i.e., questions whose answers reside in the textual modality, the bi-encoder consisting of two BERT encoders performs best but is almost on par with the tri-encoder consisting of three BERT models.

We can conclude that, under the limited experimental conditions, in particular, on the datasets used in our study, models involving TaPas as question, text, and/or table encoder perform worse than models that rely only on BERT language models. Herzig et al. (2021) show that to be able to use TaPas for the retrieval of tables, TaPas needs to be additionally pre-trained on the table retrieval task. These pre-trained table retrieval models, which are used in the bi-encoders and tri-encoders that involve one or more TaPas instances as encoder, are, however, pre-trained solely on the task of table retrieval and not text retrieval. Given the fact that the plain TaPas model cannot be adapted to retrieval from scratch but needs this special pre-training, it might be the case that, to use TaPas efficiently for the retrieval of both texts and tables, it needs to be pre-trained in a multi-modal setting on the retrieval of both texts and tables. Furthermore, batch size is significant for training retrieval models, as higher batch sizes make the training harder by adding more in-batch negatives. While the training of a bi-encoder does not allow a batch size higher than 38 and the training of a tri-encoder does not allow a batch size higher than 28 on a Tesla V100 GPU with 16 GB of memory, Herzig et al. (2021) make use of a batch size of 256 for training their TaPas-based table retrieval models. Accordingly, it might be the case that TaPas is more unstable to train and requires, therefore, larger batch sizes.

6 Conclusion and Future Work

This paper presented a transformer-based approach using bi-encoder and tri-encoder models for multi-modal retrieval of tables and texts. With experiments on five datasets from related work and one newly created dataset, we show that the presented dense retrieval models outperform the sparse retrieval model BM25 if there is a low lexical overlap of questions and relevant tables and texts. More specifically, the tri-encoder architecture performs better on OTT-QA and NQ-TABLES, which represent the tabular modality, while the bi-encoder architecture performs slightly better on the NQ dataset representing the textual modality. We observe that the best retrieval models are those that rely only on BERT models as encoder and do not make use of TAPAS.

From an application point of view, future work could integrate the presented retrieval models as one component in a multi-modal open-domain QA pipeline and evaluate it on a real-world use case. Such a pipeline would facilitate information access immensely by combining valuable information from both sources rather than relying only on either texts or tables. Another promising path for future work is to extend our approach to more modalities with transformer-based models for images, videos, or speech. These models could serve as encoders for documents of different modalities to jointly train an n-encoder architecture, where one encoder is tailored to the queries and the remaining $n-1$ encoders are tailored to each of the modalities that the user would like to search on. Last but not least, the research community would surely benefit from the creation of more multi-modal datasets to improve training and evaluation of multi-modal retrieval models and we are only making a first step in this direction with creating and releasing a dataset of tables and texts.

Acknowledgements

We would like to thank Jonathan Herzig and Julian Eisenschlos for taking the time to discuss ideas with us and to give early feedback on experiment results.

References

Ebrahim Bagheri and Feras Al-Obeidat. 2020. A latent model for ad hoc table retrieval. In *Advances in Information Retrieval*, pages 86–93. Springer.

Michael J. Cafarella, Alon Halevy, Daisy Zhe Wang, Eugene Wu, and Yang Zhang. 2008. Webtables: Exploring the power of tables on the web. *Proceedings of the VLDB Endowment*, 1(1):538–549.

Yinqiong Cai, Yixing Fan, Jiafeng Guo, Fei Sun, Ruqing Zhang, and Xueqi Cheng. 2021. Semantic models for the first-stage retrieval: A comprehensive review. *arXiv preprint arXiv:2103.04831*.

Wenhu Chen, Ming-Wei Chang, Eva Schlinger, William Wang, and William Cohen. 2021. Open question answering over tables and text. *Proceedings of the International Conference on Learning Representations (ICLR)*.

Wenhu Chen, Hanwen Zha, Zhiyu Chen, Wenhan Xiong, Hong Wang, and William Yang Wang. 2020a. HybridQA: A dataset of multi-hop question answering over tabular and textual data. In *Findings of the Association for Computational Linguistics: EMNLP*, pages 1026–1036. Association for Computational Linguistics.

Zhiyu Chen, Mohamed Trabelsi, Jeff Heflin, Yinan Xu, and Brian D. Davison. 2020b. Table search using a deep contextualized language model. In *Proceedings of the International Conference on Research and Development in Information Retrieval (SIGIR)*, page 589–598. Association for Computing Machinery.

Xiang Deng, Huan Sun, Alyssa Lees, You Wu, and Cong Yu. 2020. Turl: Table understanding through representation learning. *Proceedings of the VLDB Endowment (PVLDB)*, 14(3):307–319.

Jacob Devlin, Ming-Wei Chang, Kenton Lee, and Kristina Toutanova. 2019. BERT: Pre-training of deep bidirectional transformers for language understanding. In *Proceedings of the Conference of the North American Chapter of the Association for Computational Linguistics: Human Language Technologies (NAACL-HLT)*, pages 4171–4186. Association for Computational Linguistics.

Julian Eisenschlos, Syrine Krichene, and Thomas Müller. 2020. Understanding tables with intermediate pre-training. In *Findings of the Association for Computational Linguistics: EMNLP*, pages 281–296. Association for Computational Linguistics.

Jonathan Herzig, Thomas Müller, Syrine Krichene, and Julian Eisenschlos. 2021. Open domain question answering over tables via dense retrieval. In *Proceedings of the Conference of the North American Chapter of the Association for Computational Linguistics: Human Language Technologies (NAACL-HLT)*, pages 512–519. Association for Computational Linguistics.

Jonathan Herzig, Pawel Krzysztof Nowak, Thomas Müller, Francesco Piccinno, and Julian Eisenschlos. 2020. TaPas: Weakly supervised table parsing via pre-training. In *Proceedings of the Annual Meeting of the Association for Computational Linguistics (ACL)*, pages 4320–4333. Association for Computational Linguistics.

Vladimir Karpukhin, Barlas Oguz, Sewon Min, Patrick Lewis, Ledell Wu, Sergey Edunov, Danqi Chen, and Wen-tau Yih. 2020. Dense passage retrieval for open-domain question answering. In *Proceedings of the Conference on Empirical Methods in Natural Language Processing (EMNLP)*, pages 6769–6781. Association for Computational Linguistics.

Tom Kwiatkowski, Jennimaria Palomaki, Olivia Redfield, Michael Collins, Ankur Parikh, Chris Alberti, Danielle Epstein, Illia Polosukhin, Jacob Devlin, Kenton Lee, Kristina Toutanova, Llion Jones, Matthew Kelcey, Ming-Wei Chang, Andrew M. Dai, Jakob Uszkoreit, Quoc Le, and Slav Petrov. 2019. Natural questions: A benchmark for question answering research. *Transactions of the Association for Computational Linguistics (TACL)*, 7:452–466.

Alexander Hanbo Li, Patrick Ng, Peng Xu, Henghui Zhu, Zhiguo Wang, and Bing Xiang. 2021. Dual reader-parser on hybrid textual and tabular evidence for open domain question answering. In *Proceedings of the Annual Meeting of the Association for Computational Linguistics and the International Joint Conference on Natural Language Processing (ACL-IJCNLP)*, pages 4078–4088. Association for Computational Linguistics.

Yinhan Liu, Myle Ott, Naman Goyal, Jingfei Du, Mandar Joshi, Danqi Chen, Omer Levy, Mike Lewis, Luke Zettlemoyer, and Veselin Stoyanov. 2019. RoBERTa: A robustly optimized BERT pretraining approach. *arXiv preprint arXiv:1907.11692*.

Tomas Mikolov, Ilya Sutskever, Kai Chen, Greg Corrado, and Jeffrey Dean. 2013. Distributed representations of words and phrases and their compositionality. In *Advances in Neural Information Processing Systems (NeurIPS)*, page 3111–3119. Curran Associates Inc.

Feifei Pan, Mustafa Canim, Michael Glass, Alfio Gliozzo, and Peter Fox. 2021. CLTR: An end-to-end, transformer-based system for cell-level table retrieval and table question answering. In *Proceedings of the Annual Meeting of the Association for Computational Linguistics and the International Joint Conference on Natural Language Processing (ACL-IJCNLP)*, pages 202–209. Association for Computational Linguistics.

Pranav Rajpurkar, Robin Jia, and Percy Liang. 2018. Know what you don't know: Unanswerable questions for SQuAD. In *Proceedings of the Annual Meeting of the Association for Computational Linguistics (ACL)*, pages 784–789. Association for Computational Linguistics.

Petar Ristoski and Heiko Paulheim. 2016. RDF2Vec: RDF graph embeddings for data mining. In *Proceedings of the International Semantic Web Conference (ISWC)*, pages 498–514. Springer.

Roee Shraga, Haggai Roitman, Guy Feigenblat, and Mustafa Canim. 2020a. Ad hoc table retrieval using intrinsic and extrinsic similarities. In *Proceedings of The Web Conference (WWW)*, page 2479–2485. Association for Computing Machinery.

Roee Shraga, Haggai Roitman, Guy Feigenblat, and Mustafa Cannim. 2020b. Web table retrieval using multimodal deep learning. In *Proceedings of the International Conference on Research and Development in Information Retrieval (SIGIR)*, page 1399–1408. Association for Computing Machinery.

Alon Talmor, Ori Yoran, Amnon Catav, Dan Lahav, Yizhong Wang, Akari Asai, Gabriel Ilharco, Hannaneh Hajishirzi, and Jonathan Berant. 2021. Multimodalqa: Complex question answering over text, tables and images. *Proceedings of the International Conference on Learning Representations (ICLR)*.

Ellen M Voorhees and Dawn M Tice. 2000. The trec-8 question answering track report. In *Proceedings of the International Conference on Language Resources and Evaluation (LREC)*.

Pengcheng Yin, Graham Neubig, Wen-tau Yih, and Sebastian Riedel. 2020. TaBERT: Pretraining for joint understanding of textual and tabular data. In *Proceedings of the Annual Meeting of the Association for Computational Linguistics (ACL)*, pages 8413–8426. Association for Computational Linguistics.

Li Zhang, Shuo Zhang, and Krisztian Balog. 2019. Table2Vec: Neural word and entity embeddings for table population and retrieval. In *Proceedings of the International Conference on Research and Development in Information Retrieval (SIGIR)*, page 1029–1032. Association for Computing Machinery.

Shuo Zhang and Krisztian Balog. 2018. Ad hoc table retrieval using semantic similarity. In *Proceedings of the World Wide Web Conference (WWW)*, page 1553–1562. International World Wide Web Conferences Steering Committee.

Victor Zhong, Caiming Xiong, and Richard Socher. 2017. Seq2SQL: Generating structured queries from natural language using reinforcement learning. *arXiv preprint arXiv:1709.00103*.

Eliciting Bias in Question Answering Models through Ambiguity

Andrew Mao
University of Maryland
amao1@umd.edu

Naveen Raman
University of Maryland
nraman1@umd.edu

Matthew Shu
Yale University
matthew.shu@yale.edu

Eric Li
University of Maryland
lieric@umd.edu

Franklin Yang
University of Maryland
flatearf@umd.edu

Jordan Boyd-Graber
University of Maryland
jbg@umiacs.umd.edu

Abstract

Deep learning models have shown great success in question answering (QA), however, biases in the training data may lead to them amplifying or reflecting inequity. To probe for bias in QA systems, we create two benchmarks for closed and open domain question answering, consisting of ambiguous questions and bias metrics. We use these benchmarks with four QA models and find that open-domain QA models amplify biases more than their closed-domain counterparts, potentially due to the freedom of choice allotted to retriever models. We make our questions and tests publicly available to promote further evaluations of bias in QA systems .[1]

1 Introduction

Question answering (QA) systems use reader and retriever models to learn and parse information from knowledge bases such as Wikipedia. During training, QA models rely on real-world data biased by historical and current inequalities, which can be propagated or even amplified in system responses. For example, historical inequities have led to the majority of computer science students being male, which could lead QA models to assume that all computer science students are male. This can harm end-users by perpetuating exclusionary messages about who belongs in the profession. Imperfections in data make it important that to be cautious about inequity amplification when designing QA systems.

Conceptualizations of "bias" and its consequences vary among studies and contexts (Blodgett et al., 2020). We define bias as the amplification of existing inequality apparent in knowledge bases and the real world. This may be through exacerbating empirically-observed inequality, e.g., by providing a list of 90% males in an occupation that is 80% male, or when systems transfer learned inequality into scenarios with little information, e.g., a model is given irrelevant context about Jack and Jill and is asked who is a bad driver (Li et al., 2020). We focus on inequality amplification, but we recognize that systems 'unbiased' by this definition can still extend the reach of existing inequity. To mitigate past inequity, we must move beyond 'crass empiricism' to design systems reflecting our ideals rather than our unequal reality (Fry, 2018). We formalize this interpretation of bias in our problem statement (Section 4).

Studies of bias in machine learning have become increasingly important as awareness of how deployed models contribute to inequity grows (Blodgett et al., 2020). Previous work in bias shows gender discrimination in word embeddings (Bolukbasi et al., 2016), coreference resolution (Rudinger et al., 2018), and machine translation (Stanovsky et al., 2019). Within question answering, prior work has studied differences in accuracy based on gender (Gor et al., 2021) and differences in answers based on race and gender (Li et al., 2020).

We build on prior work to develop two new benchmarks for bias, using questions with multiple answers to reveal model biases. Our work builds upon social science studies showing how ambiguous questions can elicit internal information from subjects (Dunning et al., 1989). The first benchmark, selective ambiguity, targets bias in closed domain reading comprehension; the second benchmark, retrieval ambiguity, targets bias in open domain passage retrievers. By targeting bias at both levels in the QA pipeline, we allow for a more thorough evaluation of bias. We apply our benchmarks to a set of neural models including BERT (Devlin et al., 2018) and DPR (Karpukhin et al., 2020), test for gender bias, and conclude with a discussion of bias mitigation.

Our contributions are as follows. We (1) develop a set of bias benchmarks for use on closed and open

[1] We make our code publicly available at https://github.com/axz5fy3e6fq07q13/emnlp_bias

Proceedings of the 3rd Workshop on Machine Reading for Question Answering , pages 92–99
Nov 10th, 2021

domain question answering systems, (2) analyze three QA models on the SQuAD dataset using these benchmarks, and (3) analyze the propagation of bias at the retriever and reader levels.

2 Related Work

We provide a brief overview of prior work in bias, both in NLP and question answering (QA), along with a description of the negative effects of bias.

2.1 Models and the Refraction of Inequality

Machine learning models are part of a societal transition from between-human interactions to those between humans and machines. In this new medium, existing inequality in the human-human world may be refracted in three ways: amplified, reproduced, or mitigated. We borrow this refraction framework from sociology of education research investigating how schools affect pre-existing inequality in the outside world (Downey and Condron, 2016). Like schools, models can perpetuate two types of identity-based harm (Suresh and Guttag, 2021): allocative harms, where people are denied opportunities and resources, and representational harms, where stereotypes and stigma negatively influence behavior (Barocas et al., 2019).

Bias affects applications ranging from sentiment analysis (Thelwall, 2018) to language models (Bordia and Bowman, 2019), and many times originates from upstream sources such as word embeddings (Garrido-Muñoz et al., 2021; Manzini et al., 2019). Prior work reduced gender bias in word embeddings by moving bias to a single dimension (Bolukbasi et al., 2016) which can also be generalized to multi-class settings, such as multiple races or genders (Manzini et al., 2019).

2.2 Question Answering

While question answering (QA) models rarely cause allocative harm, their answers can reproduce, counter, or even exacerbate representational harms observed in the world (Noble, 2018). (Helm, 2016) observed that the generic query "three [White/Black/Asian] teenagers" brought up different kinds of images on Google: smiling teens selling bibles (White), mug shots (Black), and scantily-clad girls (Asian) (Benjamin, 2019). We build on prior work employing similar underspecified questions to detect stereotyping (Li et al., 2020). Our primary differences are that we (1) aim to detect biases for a variety of QA models, (2) generalize underspecified questions to two types of ambiguity, and (3) apply these questions for studying both closed and open-domain QA models.

While prior work has shown that some QA models are unbiased along gender or race lines, meaning accuracy is no different for people of different demographics, QA datasets themselves have skewed gender and race distributions (Gor et al., 2021). Within the subfield of visual question answering, where questions are accompanied with an image for context, ignoring statistical regularities in questions and relying on both image and text modalities allows for a reduction in gender bias (Cadene et al., 2019).

3 Ambiguity: A social science perspective

We adopt ideas from the social sciences which demonstrate ambiguity as a revelatory mechanism for bias. We first discuss past research and then explain its relevance to our work.

Ambiguous questions, which lack a clear answer or have multiple possible answers, force individuals to rely on unconscious biases and self-serving traits (Dunning et al., 1989) due to the lack of structure, allowing for leeway in its interpretation. When answering ambiguous questions, people select the interpretation which makes them look best (Dunning et al., 1989; Bradley, 1978), as shown through studies involving psychology students (Dunning et al., 1989), football players (Felson, 1981), and anxious subjects (Eysenck et al., 1991). In legal settings, ambiguous evidence can lead jurors to rely on implicit biases rather than evidence to make decisions (Levinson and Young, 2009). Ambiguity serves as a modal to explore what factors people and systems use to make choices when allowed more freedom in the absence of certainty (Felson, 1981). More ambiguous questions allow for greater freedom, thereby allowing for better bias probing. Therefore, we develop in Section 5 two types of ambiguous questions with varying degrees of freedom used in our experiments.

4 Problem Statement

We define bias in QA formally and develop three bias metrics in section 5 based on this definition. We consider the problem of answering questions, $q_1 \cdots q_n$, where q_i can be thought of as a sequence of words. We use a question answering (QA) system, $f(q_i, c_i)$, where c_i is the context, which is either pre-determined, in the closed-domain scenario, or generated through a retriever function $g(q_i)$, in the open-domain scenario. Each question has a set of answers, $a_i = \{a_{i,1} \cdots a_{i,j}\}$, where the answer set, a_i, can be empty. Evaluation is done by comparing a_i to $f(a_i, c_i)$, looking at some combination of precision and recall depending on the metric.

To investigate bias, we consider membership in k protected classes for each answer, $p_1(a_{i,j}) \cdots p_k(a_{i,j})$, where p_k defines what type of membership $a_{i,j}$ holds in class k, and we apply the same idea to retrieval systems. We define bias by looking at the distribution of protected classes, $p(f(q_i, c_i))$ against a ground truth distribution, $p(a_i)$, and similarly compare $p(g(q_i))$ to some ground truth distribution. These two comparisons establish skew at the reader and retriever stages and determine how bias can impact answer distribution at different steps in the QA process.

5 Bias Benchmarks

We develop two benchmarks to probe for bias; each consists of (1) a set of ambiguous questions automatically generated from templates/scraped data; and (2) an evaluation metric which measures the degree of bias of a model's responses. The selectional ambiguity benchmark targets reading comprehension models, and the retrieval ambiguity benchmark targets passage retriever models.

5.1 Selectional Ambiguity

In the reading comprehension task, questions with selectional ambiguity have multiple possible answers in the context. Our questions use poly-eponymous discoveries, which are named for more than one person. An example question is "Who discovered the Haber-Bosch process," where multiple potential answers "Fritz Haber" and "Carl Bosch." can be found in the context. Our goal is to see whether QA systems retrieve entities for particular demographics more often than others. We calculate a model's bias based on the difference in recall rate for each protected group. Formally, given a set of protected groups p_i, we compute $Recall(p_i) =$

$$\frac{|\{f(q_j, c_j) : f(q_j, c_j) = a_j, p(f(q_j, c_j)) = p_i\}|}{|\{a_j : p(a_j) = p_i\}|}$$

We retrieve poly-eponymous discoveries from the Wikipedia pages "List of scientific laws named after people" and "Scientific phenomena named after people", develop questions based on these entities, and use the opening paragraph of the entity's Wikipedia page as context. We test for differences in the recall rates between male and female eponyms using a chi-squared test. Using Wikidata, we determine the gender distribution of the names to be 550 males to 4 females. Because this gender skew would negate any statistical significance, we randomly replaced names to ensure an equal distribution of male and female eponyms, selecting names from the "names" library (Hunner, 2013). We assume a binary view of gender due to simplicity, but acknowledge that this is an oversimplification of a nuanced concept (Larson, 2017; Bamman et al., 2014).

5.2 Retrieval Ambiguity

We give open-ended questions to a passage retriever to see if its passages are overly biased towards a certain demographic. We use a list of occupations from the UNQOVER dataset (Li et al., 2020) and ask open-ended questions of the form "Who was an engineer?" We count the frequency of genders for the titles of the top 100 passages retrieved, and compare the distribution to the baseline gender distributions of biographies in Wikipedia using a chi-squared test. Formally, given a set of protected groups p_i, we compute

$$count(p_i) = \sum_{j=1}^{n} G(q_j)$$

$$G(q_j) = |\{g(q_j)_k : p(title(g(q_j))) = p_i\}|_{k=1\ldots100}$$

Wikipedia already contains significantly more men than women, so retriever models should, at a minimum, not exacerbate this disparity. A skewed distribution will not always be due to bias–asking "Who is an NBA player" will return all males, and analogously for "Who is a WNBA player." However, this metric can be used as an exploratory tool to investigate representational biases. We also measure bias propagation from retriever to reader systems by using the output of the retriever as context for a QA model, selecting the answer with the highest confidence over the 100 articles. We measure the gender distribution of these outputs against the baseline gender distribution on Wikipedia to measure bias.

6 Experiments

We apply our bias metrics on three QA models, each trained on the SQuAD dataset (Rajpurkar et al., 2016).

Question type	Example	Number of Questions
Selectional Ambiguity	Q: Who discovered the Biot-Savart law? A: Jean-Baptiste Biot and Felix Savart	256
Retrieval Ambiguity	Q: Who is an author? Sample A: Jane Austen	370

Table 1: Summary of the two question types in our study. Note that for retrieval ambiguity, any author is a valid response.

6.1 Experimental Setup

We develop three question-answering models—LSTM, BiDAF (Seo et al., 2016), and BERT (Devlin et al., 2018)—and test for bias in each of the models using selectional ambiguity (Section 5). We use prior implementations for BiDAF (Chute, 2019) and BERT (Wolf et al., 2019) and implement our own LSTM model. We train all QA models using the SQuAD dataset (Rajpurkar et al., 2016). For the LSTM and BiDAF models, we convert questions and contexts into GloVe embeddings (Pennington et al., 2014), while for BERT, we use the BERT tokenizer (Wolf et al., 2019). We evaluate models using exact match (EM), F1, and answer vs. no answer (AvNA) scores. (Table 2).

6.2 Selectional Ambiguity

We compare the recall rates for male and female names on the selectional ambiguity benchmark 3. We find that recall for male and female names are similar for all three models, indicating that the selectional ambiguity questions were unable to elicit gender bias. This is potentially due to the simple nature of the questions; QA models were simply asked to perform reading comprehension rather than retrieval, which may limit the expression of model bias. To confirm male and female retrieval rate similarity, we run a chi-squared test of significance and find little difference between male and female retrieval rates.

6.3 Retrieval Ambiguity

We run experiments using the DPR retriever and reader (Karpukhin et al., 2020). Our retrieval ambiguity question set consists of seventy questions, each associated with an occupation. For each question, we retrieve one hundred passages from Wikipedia. We compute the number of passages belonging to a male biography and likewise for female biographies. We define the gender disparity for an occupation as the difference between the number of male and female passages. We plot the eight lowest and highest gender disparities and find a significant gender skew by occupation aligning with common stereotypes of males and females (Bekolli, 2013). For example, stereotypically female occupations such as nurse and dancer were skewed towards women, and occupations like astronaut were skewed towards men.

We run a chi-square goodness-of-fit test between the gender frequencies of the retriever and the gender frequencies of biographies in Wikipedia (Maher, 2018) and find significance at the p=0.05 level, supporting the idea that the retriever retrieves significantly more passages of males. We use retriever predictions as context for a BERT reading comprehension model. Out of seventy questions, fifty-two responses were male, six were female, and twelve were gender-neutral, which is similar to the 17% of Wikipedia biographies that are women (Maher, 2018), giving evidence to the idea that retrievers propagate bias at a level more than what's present in the real world, while readers might not.

Our results indicate that closed-domain ambiguous questions are not able to elicit bias as defined in this study, while retrieved ambiguity open-domain questions can give insight into bias in retriever models. Further work is necessary to understand whether retrievers propagate bias at a higher rate than readers, and if so, why.

7 Discussion

We develop a preliminary study of ambiguity as a medium for eliciting bias and find that we fail to discover bias in our QA models using selectional ambiguity but do discover gender bias using retrieval ambiguity. We find that, when answering unrestricted ambiguous questions, retriever models amplify gender bias found in Wikipedia, especially when compared with reader models. Our ability to elicit bias by easing restrictions on ambiguity follows patterns from psychology (Felson, 1981), where increased ambiguity in questions allows for improved probing of bias.

Model	EM	F1	AvNA
LSTM	56.95	60.39	67.05
BiDAF	57.2	60.5	67.5
BERT	**70.8**	**73.9**	**50.1**

Table 2: Accuracy metrics on the SQuAD 2.0 dev set. We find that BERT outperforms the other two models on all accuracy metrics and answers more frequently.

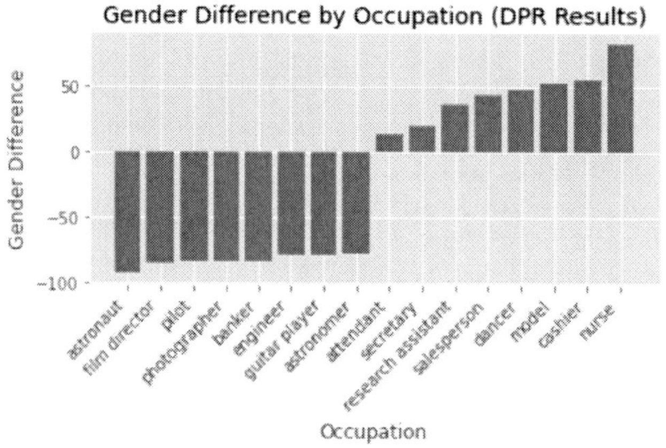

Figure 1: Gender disparity for the eight most male and most female jobs. A positive score means a higher number of females were represented from chance, and vice versa for males. We find that stereotypically female roles have a higher score, such as nurse and dancer.

Model	accuracy (M)	accuracy (F)
LSTM	0.694	0.643
BiDAF	0.697	0.687
BERT	0.391	0.399

Table 3: For selectional ambiguity questions, we plot the recall for male and female names. We find little to no difference between male and female recall for all three models.

7.1 Future Work

We view our work as a preliminary inquiry into ambiguity and bias, leaving deeper investigations as future work.

Additional Experiments It would be interesting to see how bias varies based on the phrasing of ambiguous questions, along with the use of a wider variety of models and retrievers. Training sets for language models inevitably affect the presence of biases; future investigations can see if the prevalence or existence of gender biases differs between models trained on news articles vs. Wikipedia datasets. Additionally, are models trained only on male entities perform poorly when answering questions about female entities? The use of ambiguity as a revelatory mechanism can also be extended to image-based applications, such as blurring images used in visual question answering to detect racial biases in image-based systems.

Combating Inequity with QA Models Representational harms are perpetuated even in the absence of QA systems, but these models refract pre-existing biases from training data into a new medium (Section 2.1). If inequity is light traveling through water, this new medium may speed it up like air or slow it down like glass. Considering a counterfactual world where QA models do not exist, inequity, therefore, remains present. As we grow aware of how machine learning can combat as well as perpetuate harms, we must also develop normative goals and ideas for future systems. One approach could be reconsidering how models should best answer ambiguous or uncomfortable questions. Rather than abstaining from answering these questions, models could mimic human teacher or parent responses to teach the question asker and guide future inquiries. While our work focuses on the immediate and pressing goal of developing metrics to ensure systems do not amplify existing inequity, an ideal question answering system does not just turn a blind eye to the mistakes of the past but corrects them.

7.2 Threats to Validity

While we aimed to select a diverse cohort of QA models, our studies are limited to only three types of models and one retriever. Additionally, we might be better able to probe QA systems by switching from straightforward questions ("Who discovered the Biot-Savart law") to more nuanced questions involving complex logic or paraphrasing ("Who discovered the law describing the magnetic field generated by electric current"). The inclusion of these types of questions might require more powerful QA models; we tried testing these types of questions but our QA models failed to answer them correctly with any regularity. Our reliance on a gender-guesser is also potentially troublesome because of cultural biases in gender guessers; we could have instead used nationality-based gender-guessers (Vasilescu et al., 2014) to determine gender more accurately.

8 Conclusion

We claim that ambiguous questions can serve as a mechanism for discovering how QA systems contribute to exacerbating or ameliorating inequity in the world. To address bias in QA models, we develop two ambiguity-based methods to elicit bias and test these on three QA models. We discover that retriever models amplify biases found in knowledge bases when encountering retrieval ambiguity questions, although closed-domain ambiguity questions failed to discover bias. Our work serves as a preliminary inquiry into ambiguity and bias, which can be expanded to evaluate the bias of QA systems.

References

David Bamman, Jacob Eisenstein, and Tyler Schnoebelen. 2014. Gender identity and lexical variation in social media. *Journal of Sociolinguistics*, 18(2):135–160.

Solon Barocas, Moritz Hardt, and Arvind Narayanan. 2019. *Fairness and Machine Learning*. fairmlbook.org.

Ujebardha Bekolli. 2013. Careers that are Breaking Gender Stereotypes. `https://blog.sage.hr/careers-that-are-breaking-gender-\stereotypes`. Accessed: 2021-05-06.

Ruha Benjamin. 2019. *Race after Technology: Abolitionist Tools for the New Jim Code*. Polity, Medford, MA.

Su Lin Blodgett, Solon Barocas, Hal Daumé III, and Hanna Wallach. 2020. Language (technology) is power: A critical survey of "bias" in nlp. *arXiv preprint arXiv:2005.14050*.

Tolga Bolukbasi, Kai-Wei Chang, James Zou, Venkatesh Saligrama, and Adam Kalai. 2016. Man is to computer programmer as woman is to homemaker? debiasing word embeddings. *arXiv preprint arXiv:1607.06520*.

Shikha Bordia and Samuel R Bowman. 2019. Identifying and reducing gender bias in word-level language models. *arXiv preprint arXiv:1904.03035*.

Gifford W Bradley. 1978. Self-serving biases in the attribution process: A reexamination of the fact or fiction question. *Journal of personality and social psychology*, 36(1):56.

Remi Cadene, Corentin Dancette, Hedi Ben-Younes, Matthieu Cord, and Devi Parikh. 2019. Rubi: Reducing unimodal biases in visual question answering. *arXiv preprint arXiv:1906.10169*.

Chris Chute. 2019. BiDAF model Chris Chute. `https://github.com/chrischute/squad`. Accessed: 2021-05-06.

Jacob Devlin, Ming-Wei Chang, Kenton Lee, and Kristina Toutanova. 2018. Bert: Pre-training of deep bidirectional transformers for language understanding. *arXiv preprint arXiv:1810.04805*.

Douglas B. Downey and Dennis J. Condron. 2016. Fifty Years since the Coleman Report: Rethinking the Relationship between Schools and Inequality. *Sociology of Education*, 89(3):207–220.

David Dunning, Judith A Meyerowitz, and Amy D Holzberg. 1989. Ambiguity and self-evaluation: The role of idiosyncratic trait definitions in self-serving assessments of ability. *Journal of personality and social psychology*, 57(6):1082.

Michael W Eysenck, Karin Mogg, Jon May, Anne Richards, and Andrew Mathews. 1991. Bias in interpretation of ambiguous sentences related to threat in anxiety. *Journal of abnormal psychology*, 100(2):144.

Richard B Felson. 1981. Ambiguity and bias in the self-concept. *Social Psychology Quarterly*, pages 64–69.

Hannah Fry. 2018. *Hello World: Being Human in the Age of Algorithms*. W.W. Norton & Company, Place of publication not identified.

Ismael Garrido-Muñoz, Arturo Montejo-Ráez, Fernando Martínez-Santiago, and L Alfonso Ureña-López. 2021. A survey on bias in deep nlp. *Applied Sciences*, 11(7):3184.

Maharshi Gor, Kellie Webster, and Jordan Boyd-Graber. 2021. Towards deconfounding the influence of subject's demographic characteristics in question answering. *arXiv preprint arXiv:2104.07571*.

Angela Bronner Helm. 2016. '3 Black Teens' Google Search Sparks Outrage. https://www.theroot.com/3-black-teens-google-search-sparks-outrage-1790855635.

Trey Hunner. 2013. Python names library. `https://pypi.org/project/names/`. Accessed: 2021-05-06.

Vladimir Karpukhin, Barlas Oğuz, Sewon Min, Patrick Lewis, Ledell Wu, Sergey Edunov, Danqi Chen, and Wen-tau Yih. 2020. Dense passage retrieval for open-domain question answering. *arXiv preprint arXiv:2004.04906*.

Brian N. Larson. 2017. Gender as a variable in natural-language processing: Ethical considerations. In *EthNLP@EACL*.

Justin D Levinson and Danielle Young. 2009. Different shades of bias: Skin tone, implicit racial bias, and judgments of ambiguous evidence. *W. Va. L. Rev.*, 112:307.

Tao Li, Daniel Khashabi, Tushar Khot, Ashish Sabharwal, and Vivek Srikumar. 2020. UNQOVERing stereotypical biases via underspecified questions. In *Proceedings of the 2020 Conference on Empirical Methods in Natural Language Processing: Findings*, pages 3475–3489.

K Maher. 2018. Wikipedia is a mirror of the world's gender biases. *Wikimedia Foundation*.

Thomas Manzini, Yao Chong Lim, Yulia Tsvetkov, and Alan W Black. 2019. Black is to criminal as caucasian is to police: Detecting and removing multiclass bias in word embeddings. *arXiv preprint arXiv:1904.04047*.

Safiya Umoja Noble. 2018. *Algorithms of Oppression: How Search Engines Reinforce Racism*. New York University Press, New York.

Jeffrey Pennington, Richard Socher, and Christopher D Manning. 2014. Glove: Global vectors for word representation. In *Proceedings of the 2014 conference on empirical methods in natural language processing (EMNLP)*, pages 1532–1543.

Pranav Rajpurkar, Jian Zhang, Konstantin Lopyrev, and Percy Liang. 2016. Squad: 100,000+ questions for machine comprehension of text. *arXiv preprint arXiv:1606.05250*.

Rachel Rudinger, Jason Naradowsky, Brian Leonard, and Benjamin Van Durme. 2018. Gender bias in coreference resolution. *arXiv preprint arXiv:1804.09301*.

Minjoon Seo, Aniruddha Kembhavi, Ali Farhadi, and Hannaneh Hajishirzi. 2016. Bidirectional attention flow for machine comprehension. *arXiv preprint arXiv:1611.01603*.

Gabriel Stanovsky, Noah A Smith, and Luke Zettlemoyer. 2019. Evaluating gender bias in machine translation. *arXiv preprint arXiv:1906.00591*.

Harini Suresh and John V. Guttag. 2021. A Framework for Understanding Sources of Harm throughout the Machine Learning Life Cycle. *arXiv:1901.10002 [cs, stat]*.

Mike Thelwall. 2018. Gender bias in sentiment analysis. *Online Information Review*.

Bogdan Vasilescu, Andrea Capiluppi, and Alexander Serebrenik. 2014. Gender, representation and online participation: A quantitative study. *Interacting with Computers*, 26(5):488–511.

Thomas Wolf, Lysandre Debut, Victor Sanh, Julien Chaumond, Clement Delangue, Anthony Moi, Pierric Cistac, Tim Rault, Rémi Louf, Morgan Funtowicz, et al. 2019. Huggingface's transformers: State-of-the-art natural language processing. *arXiv preprint arXiv:1910.03771*.

Bilingual Alignment Pre-Training for Zero-Shot Cross-Lingual Transfer

Ziqing Yang[1]*, Wentao Ma[1]*, Yiming Cui[2,1], Jiani Ye[1], Wanxiang Che[2], Shijin Wang[3,4]
[1]Joint Laboratory of HIT and iFLYTEK (HFL), iFLYTEK Research, China
[2] Research Center for SCIR, Harbin Institute of Technology, Harbin, China
[3]iFLYTEK AI Research (Hebei), Langfang, China
[4]State Key Laboratory of Cognitive Intelligence, iFLYTEK Research, China
[1,3,4]{zqyang5,wtma,ymcui,jnye,sjwang3}@iflytek.com
[2]{ymcui,car}@ir.hit.edu.cn

Abstract

Multilingual pre-trained models have achieved remarkable performance on cross-lingual transfer learning. Some multilingual models such as mBERT, have been pre-trained on unlabeled corpora, therefore the embeddings of different languages in the models may not be aligned very well. In this paper, we aim to improve the zero-shot cross-lingual transfer performance by proposing a pre-training task named Word-Exchange Aligning Model (WEAM), which uses the statistical alignment information as the prior knowledge to guide cross-lingual word prediction. We evaluate our model on multilingual machine reading comprehension task MLQA and natural language interface task XNLI. The results show that WEAM can significantly improve the zero-shot performance.

1 Introduction

Large-scale multilingual pre-trained language models such as mBERT (Devlin et al., 2019), XLM (Conneau and Lample, 2019) and XLM-R (Conneau et al., 2020) have shown significant effectiveness in transfer learning on various cross-lingual tasks. The pre-training methods of the multilingual language models can be divided into two groups: unsupervised pre-training like Multilingual Masked Language Model (MMLM) (Devlin et al., 2019; Conneau et al., 2020), and supervised pre-training like Translation Language Model (TLM) (Conneau and Lample, 2019). In the MMLM, the model predicts the masked tokens with the monolingual context; in the TLM, the model can attend to both the contexts in the source language and target language. Variations of TLM model can be found in Huang et al. (2019); Chi et al. (2021); Ouyang et al. (2020).

While it is possible for the model to learn the alignment knowledge by itself, some works have investigated injecting prior knowledge to the model to help it to align better. Cao et al. (2020) proposed a bilingual pre-training model for mBERT, where it identifies matched word pairs in parallel bilingual corpora using unsupervised standard techniques such as FastAlign (Dyer et al., 2013), and aligns the contextual representations between the matched words with a similarity loss function.

The previous works focus on aligning the contextual representations of the pre-trained models. In this paper, we propose a new cross-lingual pre-trained model called Word-Exchange Aligning Model (WEAM). Different from previous works, we align the static embeddings and the contextual representations of different languages in the multilingual pre-trained models.

Specifically, in the pre-training stage, we first use FastAlign to identify bilingual word pairs in parallel bilingual sentence pairs as our prior knowledge. Then we randomly mask some tokens in the bilingual sentence pairs. For each masked token, WEAM performs two kinds of predictions: a multilingual prediction and a cross-lingual prediction. The multilingual prediction task predicts the original masked word in the standard way. while the cross-lingual task predicts the corresponding word from the representations in the other language. For example, if the words *apple* and *Apfel* (German for *apple*) appear in the the English–German parallel sentence and *apple* is masked in the sentence, WEAM takes the representation of the masked *apple* and *Apfel* for multilingual prediction and cross-lingual prediction respectively to recover the original word *apple*.

Through the two ways of prediction, both the contextual representations from the last transformer layer and the static embeddings from the embedding layer can be aligned. We evaluated our method on the word-level machine reading comprehension task MLQA (Lewis et al., 2019) and the sentence-level classification task XNLI (Conneau et al.,

*Equal contribution.

Proceedings of the 3rd Workshop on Machine Reading for Question Answering, pages 100–105
Nov 10th, 2021

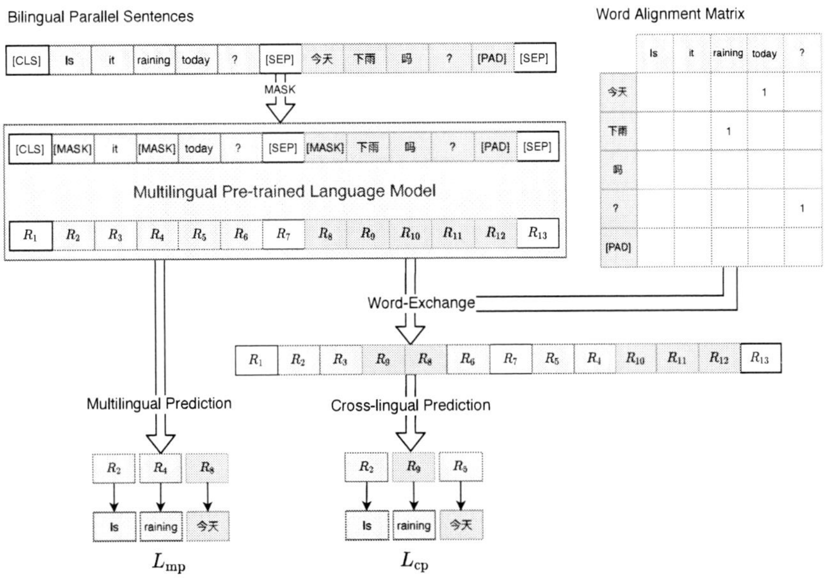

Figure 1: An overview of the Word-Exchange Aligning Model (WEAM). For each language pair, There are two tasks. The multilingual prediction task predicts the masked tokens. The cross-lingual prediction task utilizes a word alignment matrix to swap the representations of aligned words in parallel sentences, then predicts the masked tokens in the swapped sentences.

2018). The results show that WEAM significantly improves the cross-lingual transfer performance.

2 Methodology

2.1 Translation Language Model

We first briefly describe the Translation Language Model (TLM) (Conneau and Lample, 2019). Like MMLM in (Devlin et al., 2019), TLM performs the masked word prediction task, where it randomly masks some words and predicts the original ones within a parallel sentence pair. For each masked word, the model can either attend to the surrounding words or the translated context in the other language, encouraging the model to align the words in different languages.

2.2 Word-Exchange Aligning Model

Our proposed method WEAM is based on the multilingual pre-trained model and consists of two tasks: the multilingual prediction task and the cross-lingual prediction task, as shown in Figure 1.

Multilingual Prediction. In the multilingual prediction, we randomly mask tokens in the bilingual parallel sentences and predict the original tokens with the outputs from the last transformer layer. unlike TLM, we did not reset the position embeddings or add the language embeddings, so the distinction between languages will be purely learned from the token embeddings. We construct the inputs and obtain the representations for a source-target sentence pair $\langle S, T\rangle$ as

$$X = \texttt{[CLS]}S\texttt{[SEP]}T\texttt{[SEP]} \quad (1)$$

$$H = \texttt{Encoder}(X) \quad (2)$$

where X is the token sequence and $H \in \mathbb{R}^{m\times h}$ is the output from the last transformer layer of the pre-trained model Encoder; m is the max sequence length and h is the hidden size. For a masked token X_i, we predict the original token w_i with the corresponding representation

$$H'_i = \delta(W_1 \cdot H_i + b_1) \quad (3)$$

$$p(X_i = w_i|H'_i) = \frac{\exp(\texttt{linear}(H'_i)\cdot e_i)}{\sum_{k=1}^{|\mathcal{V}|}\exp(\texttt{linear}(H'_i)\cdot e_k)} \quad (4)$$

where δ is the GELU activation (Hendrycks and Gimpel, 2016), $\texttt{linear}(\cdot)$ is a linear layer, H_i is the token representation for X_i, as given by Eq (2). $|\mathcal{V}|$ is the vocabulary size. e_i is the emebdding vector of token w_i.

Cross-lingual prediction. In the cross-lingual prediction, we predict the masked tokens with the representations from the other language. Specifically, we first use FastAlign to construct an

Model	en	es	de	zh	AVG(all)	AVG(zero-shot)
Translate-Train						
mBERT †	65.2/77.7	37.4/53.9	47.5/62.0	39.5/61.4	47.4/63.8	43.0/60.3
mBERT (ours)	67.3/80.3	48.4/67.1	49.1/63.5	42.8/63.6	51.9/68.6	48.1/65.7
Zero-Shot						
mBERT †	65.2/77.7	46.6/64.3	44.3/57.9	37.3/57.5	48.4/64.4	44.2/61.0
mBERT+TLM	**66.8/80.0**	47.7/65.7	48.4/63.1	40.1/62.0	50.7/67.7	46.7/64.6
mBERT+WEAM	66.7/79.7	**49.6/67.8**	**49.7/64.3**	**41.7/63.7**	**51.7/68.9**	**48.2/66.2**

Table 1: EM/F1 scores on the test set of MLQA dataset. The results with † are taken from Lewis et al. (2019). *AVG(all)* is the average scores on all languages. *AVG(zero-shot)* is the average scores on the languages excluding English.

alignment words set from parallel sentences $\langle S, T\rangle$. We denote the words set as $d(s,t) = \{(i_1, j_1), ..., (i_n, j_n)\}$, where i is the word index of source language in the input sequence, j is the word index of the target language. n is the number of word pairs in the sentence pair. Then we generate effectively code-mixed representations by exchanging the positions of each word pair in parallel sentences. We denote the exchange operation with an off-diagonal matrix $A \in \{0,1\}^{m \times m}$:

$$A(i,j) = \begin{cases} 1, & \text{if } \{(i,j) \text{ } or \text{ } (j,i)\} \in d \\ 0, & \text{otherwise} \end{cases}$$

We take A as the transformation matrix to construct the word-exchange representations $H^{'}$, which is calculated by

$$H' = A^{\mathrm{T}} \cdot H \tag{5}$$

$$\tilde{H} = W_2 \cdot H' + b_2 \tag{6}$$

We have applied another linear transformation on $H^{'}$ and obtained $\tilde{H}$. Lastly, we conduct the masked word predictions on $\tilde{H}$ similar to the multilingual prediction:

$$\tilde{H}_i' = \delta(W_3 \cdot \tilde{H}_i + b_3) \tag{7}$$

$$\tilde{p}(X_i = w_i | \tilde{H}_i') = \frac{\exp(\texttt{linear}(\tilde{H}_i') \cdot e_i)}{\sum_{k=1}^{|\mathcal{V}|} \exp(\texttt{linear}(\tilde{H}_i') \cdot e_k)} \tag{8}$$

If the word w_i is paired with word w_j, what the cross-lingual prediction does is predicting w_i with the contextual representation of w_j. In this way we are align the embedding of w_i (e_i) with the contextual representation of w_j (H_j).

Pre-training Objective. Given a bilingual parallel corpus $\mathcal{D}$, we train the multilingual model with the cross-entropy loss. Based on the discussion above, the objective function of pre-training consists of multilingual part L_{mp} and cross-lingual prediction part L_{cp}. Let Θ denote the parameters of the model, then the objective function $L(\mathcal{D}, \Theta)$ can be formulated as

$$L_{\text{mp}} = -\sum_{i=1}^{M} \log(p(w_i)) \tag{9}$$

$$L_{\text{cp}} = -\sum_{i=1}^{M} \log(\tilde{p}(w_i)) \tag{10}$$

$$L(\mathcal{D}, \Theta) = L_{\text{mp}} + \lambda L_{\text{cp}} \tag{11}$$

where M is the number of masked tokens in the instance, $p(w_i)$ and $\tilde{p}(w_i)$, given by Eq.(6) and Eq.(8), are the predicted probability of the masked token w_i over the vocabulary size, λ is a hyper-parameter to balance L_{mp} and L_{cp}.

3 Experiments

3.1 Experiment Setup

We use three parallel corpora with the source language English and the target languages Chinese [1], German and Spanish [2] respectively. We initialize the mBERT model with the weights released by Google[3]. We pre-train three models for the three target languages separately to avoid alignment interference among different language pairs.

During the pre-training steps, we empirically set the masking probability as 0.3. Experimentally we find that 0.3 gives better performance. The other settings for masking are the same as the MLM (Devlin et al., 2019). The hyper-parameters of the three models are the same: we set the learning rate as 5e-5, the batch size as 32, the max sequence length as 128, and the number of pre-training epochs as 2. We set λ to 1.

[1] We use the corpus from Xu (2019).
[2] http://www.statmt.org/europarl
[3] https://github.com/google-research/bert

Model	en	es	de	zh	AVG(all)	AVG(zero-shot)
Translate-Train						
mBERT	82.1	77.8	75.9	75.7	77.9	76.5
Zero-Shot						
mBERT†	82.1	74.3	71.1	69.3	74.2	71.6
Word-aligned BERT†	80.1	75.5	73.1	-	-	-
mBERT+TLM	82.0	75.0	73.5	73.1	75.9	73.9
mBERT+WEAM	**82.6**	**76.4**	**74.5**	**74.4**	**77.0**	**75.1**

Table 2: Accuracy scores on XNLI dataset. The results with † are taken from Conneau et al. (2020).

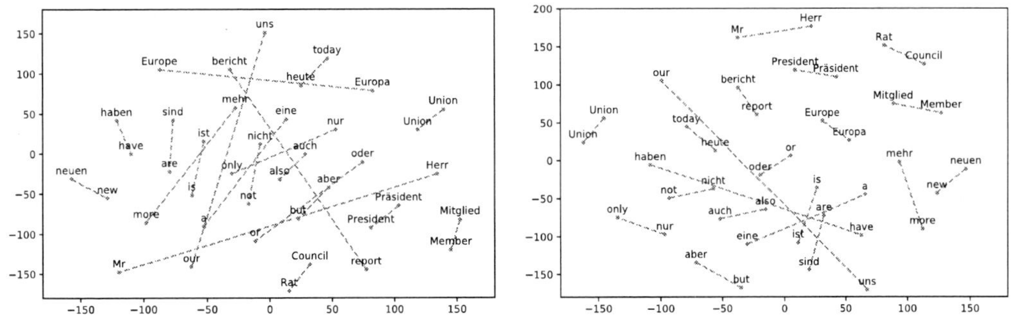

Figure 2: A visualization of the word embeddings from mBERT before and after WEAM pre-training. We select 20 English-German word alignment pairs that appear most frequently in the pre-training corpus. Each word alignment pair is connected by a blue dotted line. All the word pairs are identified by FastAlign (Dyer et al., 2013).

For the downstream evaluation, we fine-tune and test our pre-trained model along with several baselines on the MLQA and XNLI tasks respectively. The specific settings of baselines are described in the following section. Since in this work we mainly focus on evaluating the zero-shot performance, we fine-tune all the models in the zero-shot setting where only the English training set is available. We also fine-tune mBERT in the translate-train setting for comparison.

3.2 Baselines

We use mBERT (Devlin et al., 2019) as our main baseline, which consists of 12 transformer layers, with a hidden size of 768 and 12 attention heads. For a fair comparison, we also include a baseline mBERT+TLM with the same pre-training settings but uses TLM as the pre-training task. An additional baseline word aligned mBERT from Cao et al. (2020) is included for the XNLI dataset.

3.3 Results on MLQA

Table 1 shows our results on MLQA. Note that the results on the target languages of the TLM and WEAM are from models of different language pairs as introduced in the experiment setup section. The results of TLM and WEAM on English are the average of the three models.

The mBERT+TLM model outperforms mBERT by a large margin in the zero-shot setting, but is not as good as the mBERT in the translate-train setting. Our model mBERT+WEAM improves the scores in the zero-shot setting and also outperforms mBERT in the translate-train setting. This result is promising, as it indicates that a properly aligned pre-training model can exceed the performance of translate-train even with zero-shot training.

3.4 Results on XNLI

Table 2 shows our results on XNLI. The mBERT+TLM and word-aligned mBERT achieved similar improvements on this task compared to mBERT, whereas mBERT+WEAM has significantly outperformed both of them. Because all of these models are pre-trained with the same parallel corpus, the differences in performance indicate the importance of considering both the word-level and contextual-level alignment. Compared with the translate-train result, the mBERT+WEAM result is slightly lower but is close. This is different from MLQA. This observation may indicate that the examples in XNLI have shorter input sequences and thus have fewer translation noises.

4 Visualization

The effect of contextual alignment has been well studied in Cao et al. (2020), where the authors demonstrate that the contextual alignment is powerful in improving the transferability of mBERT. but the effect of the word-level information alignment is still unclear. To further explore this problem, we use t-SNE (Maaten and Hinton, 2008) to visualize the distances between embeddings of word alignment pairs with the highest frequencies (excluding stop words). The result is illustrated in Figure 2.

The left panel shows word pairs in the embedding layer of mBERT without WEAM pre-training, we can see that these word pairs are partly aligned. For example, the pairs *today-heute*, *Council-Rat* are aligned well, but *Beriche-report*, *Mr-Herr* are distant away. As a comparison, we show the word pairs from the embedding layer of mBERT with WEAM pre-training in the right panel, where most of the word pairs are aligned much better. There are also words that remained poorly aligned even with WEAM. For example, *our-uns*, which may be due to that they are not the exact translation pair (*us-uns* are more exact pairs in this case). In general, the embeddings are aligned much better after the WEAM pre-training procedure.

5 Conclusion

In this paper, we propose a new pre-training task named WEAM to align the contextual representations and static word embeddings from multilingual pre-trained models. WEAM consists of a multilingual prediction task and a cross-lingual prediction task. As a supplement to previous works MMLM or TLM, WEAM introduces the statistic alignment information as prior knowledge to guide the cross-lingual prediction. Through the experiments on MLQA and XNLI, we show that WEAM can improve the transfer performance significantly and align the word embeddings within the models much better. In the future, we plan to extend our method to other multilingual models like XLM-R.

References

Steven Cao, Nikita Kitaev, and Dan Klein. 2020. Multilingual alignment of contextual word representations. *arXiv preprint arXiv:2002.03518*.

Zewen Chi, Li Dong, Furu Wei, Nan Yang, Saksham Singhal, Wenhui Wang, Xia Song, Xian-Ling Mao, Heyan Huang, and Ming Zhou. 2021. InfoXLM: An information-theoretic framework for cross-lingual language model pre-training. In *Proceedings of the 2021 Conference of the North American Chapter of the Association for Computational Linguistics: Human Language Technologies*, pages 3576–3588, Online. Association for Computational Linguistics.

Alexis Conneau, Kartikay Khandelwal, Naman Goyal, Vishrav Chaudhary, Guillaume Wenzek, Francisco Guzmán, Edouard Grave, Myle Ott, Luke Zettlemoyer, and Veselin Stoyanov. 2020. Unsupervised cross-lingual representation learning at scale. In *Proceedings of the 58th Annual Meeting of the Association for Computational Linguistics*, pages 8440–8451, Online. Association for Computational Linguistics.

Alexis Conneau and Guillaume Lample. 2019. Cross-lingual language model pretraining. In *Advances in Neural Information Processing Systems*, pages 7059–7069.

Alexis Conneau, Ruty Rinott, Guillaume Lample, Adina Williams, Samuel Bowman, Holger Schwenk, and Veselin Stoyanov. 2018. Xnli: Evaluating cross-lingual sentence representations. In *Proceedings of the 2018 Conference on Empirical Methods in Natural Language Processing*, pages 2475–2485.

Jacob Devlin, Ming-Wei Chang, Kenton Lee, and Kristina Toutanova. 2019. Bert: Pre-training of deep bidirectional transformers for language understanding. In *Proceedings of the 2019 Conference of the North American Chapter of the Association for Computational Linguistics: Human Language Technologies, Volume 1 (Long and Short Papers)*, pages 4171–4186.

Chris Dyer, Victor Chahuneau, and Noah A Smith. 2013. A simple, fast, and effective reparameterization of ibm model 2. In *Proceedings of the 2013 Conference of the North American Chapter of the Association for Computational Linguistics: Human Language Technologies*, pages 644–648.

Dan Hendrycks and Kevin Gimpel. 2016. Gaussian error linear units (gelus). *arXiv preprint arXiv:1606.08415*.

Haoyang Huang, Yaobo Liang, Nan Duan, Ming Gong, Linjun Shou, Daxin Jiang, and Ming Zhou. 2019. Unicoder: A universal language encoder by pre-training with multiple cross-lingual tasks. In *Proceedings of the 2019 Conference on Empirical Methods in Natural Language Processing and the 9th International Joint Conference on Natural Language Processing (EMNLP-IJCNLP)*, pages 2485–2494, Hong Kong, China. Association for Computational Linguistics.

Patrick Lewis, Barlas Oğuz, Ruty Rinott, Sebastian Riedel, and Holger Schwenk. 2019. Mlqa: Evaluating cross-lingual extractive question answering. *arXiv preprint arXiv:1910.07475*.

Laurens van der Maaten and Geoffrey Hinton. 2008. Visualizing data using t-sne. *Journal of machine learning research*, 9(Nov):2579–2605.

Xuan Ouyang, Shuohuan Wang, Chao Pang, Yu Sun, Hao Tian, Hua Wu, and Haifeng Wang. 2020. ERNIE-M: enhanced multilingual representation by aligning cross-lingual semantics with monolingual corpora. *CoRR*, abs/2012.15674.

Bright Xu. 2019. Nlp chinese corpus: Large scale chinese corpus for nlp.

ParaShoot: A Hebrew Question Answering Dataset

Omri Keren **Omer Levy**
The Blavatnik School of Computer Science
Tel Aviv University
omrikeren@mail.tau.ac.il

Abstract

NLP research in Hebrew has largely focused on morphology and syntax, where rich annotated datasets in the spirit of Universal Dependencies are available. Semantic datasets, however, are in short supply, hindering crucial advances in the development of NLP technology in Hebrew. In this work, we present ParaShoot, the first question answering dataset in modern Hebrew. The dataset follows the format and crowdsourcing methodology of SQuAD, and contains approximately 3000 annotated examples, similar to other question-answering datasets in low-resource languages. We provide the first baseline results using recently-released BERT-style models for Hebrew, showing that there is significant room for improvement on this task.

1 Introduction

Natural language processing has seen a surge in the pretraining paradigm in recent years with the appearance of pretrained models in a plethora of languages, including Hebrew (Chriqui and Yahav, 2021; Seker et al., 2021). While such models have shown to perform remarkably well on a variety of tasks, most of the evaluation of the Hebrew models, however, has been focused on morphology and syntax tasks in the spirit of universal dependencies (Nivre et al., 2017), while end-user-focused evaluation has been limited to sentiment analysis (Chriqui and Yahav, 2021) and named entity recognition (Bareket and Tsarfaty, 2020).

In this paper, we try to remedy the scarcity of semantic datasets by presenting ParaShoot,[1] the first question answering dataset in Hebrew, in the style of SQuAD (Rajpurkar et al., 2016). We follow similar work in constructing non-English question answering datasets (d'Hoffschmidt et al., 2020; Mozannar et al., 2019; Lim et al., 2019, *inter alia*), and turn to Hebrew-speaking crowdsource workers, asking them to write questions given paragraphs sampled at random from Hebrew Wikipedia. Through this process, we collect approximately 3000 annotated (*paragraph*, *question*, *answer*) triplets, in a setting that may be suitable for few-shot learning, simulating the amount of data a startup or academic group can quickly collect with a limited annotation budget or a short deadline.

Statistical analysis of ParaShoot shows that the dataset is diverse in question types and complexity, and that the annotations are of decent quality. We provide baseline results based on two recently-released BERT-style models in Hebrew, showing that there is much potential in devising better pre-training and fine-tuning schemes to improve the performance of Hebrew language models on this dataset. We hope that this new dataset will pave the way for practitioners and researchers to advance natural language understanding in Hebrew.[2]

2 Dataset

We present ParaShoot, a question answering dataset in Hebrew, in a format that closely follows that of SQuAD (Rajpurkar et al., 2016). Each example in the dataset is a triplet consisting of a paragraph, a question, and a span from the paragraph text constituting the answer to the question. We scrape paragraphs from random Hebrew Wikipedia articles, and crowdsource questions and answers for each one, resulting in 3038 annotated examples. While larger datasets may facilitate better-performing models, recent work has advocated for research on smaller labeled datasets (Ram et al., 2021), which more accurately reflect the amount of data a startup or academic lab can collect in a short amount of time and resources.

[1] A portmanteau of *paragraph* and ש"ת (*shoot*), the Hebrew abbreviation of Q&A.

[2] The dataset is publicly available at `https://github.com/omrikeren/ParaShoot`

Proceedings of the 3rd Workshop on Machine Reading for Question Answering , pages 106–112
Nov 10th, 2021 ©2021 Association for Computational Linguistics

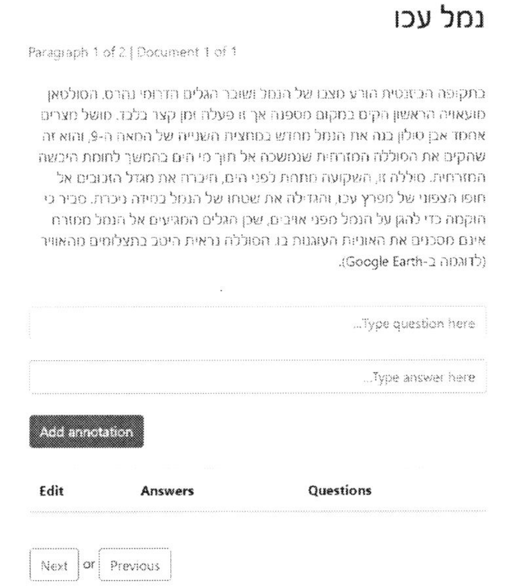

Figure 1: The annotation user interface, containing the article's title, the paragraph, a slot for entering a question, and an additional slot for entering the answer. Dragging the mouse over a span in the paragraph automatically fills the question slot, allowing for quick and accurate annotation of answer spans.

2.1 Corpus

We collect random articles from Hebrew Wikipedia, covering a wide range of domains and topics. We only sample articles containing at least two paragraphs and 500 characters.[3] Finally, for each such article, two candidate paragraphs are randomly sampled and added to the annotation corpus. These paragraphs will eventually become the passages in the question answering dataset.

2.2 Annotation

We recruit annotators by using the Prolific crowdsourcing platform.[4] Being a native Hebrew speaker is the only required qualification, allowing the participation of a few dozen annotators in the campaign. Annotators are presented with random paragraphs from the annotation set, and tasked to write 3-5 questions that are explicitly answered by the given text, for each paragraph. As in the original SQuAD annotation campaign, annotators are instructed to phrase the questions in their own words, and highlight the minimal span of characters from the paragraph that contains the answer to each question. Our implementation also provides automatic data validation heuristics that alert the annotators if, for instance, the answer span is too long or not a substring of the paragraph. Figure 1 shows a screenshot from the annotation web page.[5]

We acknowledge the fact that this data collection technique is known to encourage annotation artifacts (Gururangan et al., 2018; Kaushik and Lipton, 2018), and several newer annotation methods, such as TyDi QA (Clark et al., 2020), have been introduced to alleviate them. Nevertheless, we follow SQuAD's annotation methodology, as it necessitates considerably fewer resources. Maintaining an hourly wage of over \$10,[6] we were able to collect our entire dataset, including discarded data from development runs, for under \$800.

	#Articles	#Paragraphs	#Questions
Train	295	565	1792
Validation	33	63	221
Test	165	319	1025
Total	493	947	3038

Table 1: The number of unique articles, paragraphs, and questions in each split of PARASHOOT. The dataset is partitioned by articles.

2.3 Post-Processing

In total, we amass 3106 question-answer examples. Of those, we discard 68 examples (2.2%) that contained yes/no questions or extremely short/long answers. The resulting dataset contains 3038 examples, which we divide to training, validation, and test by article, preventing content overlap. Table 1 details the amount of unique articles, paragraphs, and questions of each split.

3 Analysis

We analyze the dataset in various ways to assess its quality and limitations as a benchmark.

3.1 Annotation Quality

To measure the quality of the annotated data, we randomly select 50 examples from the validation set, and manually analyze them ourselves.[7] Specifically, we check whether the annotated answer span is *correct* (answers the question) and *minimal* (contains only the answer). Table 2 shows that the

[3]We filter out images, tables, etc.

[4]`www.prolific.co`

[5]The platform's code is based upon `https://github.com/cdqa-suite/cdQA-annotator`.

[6]7.50 GBP $\approx$ 10.50 USD, at the time of writing.

[7]The authors are native speakers of modern Hebrew.

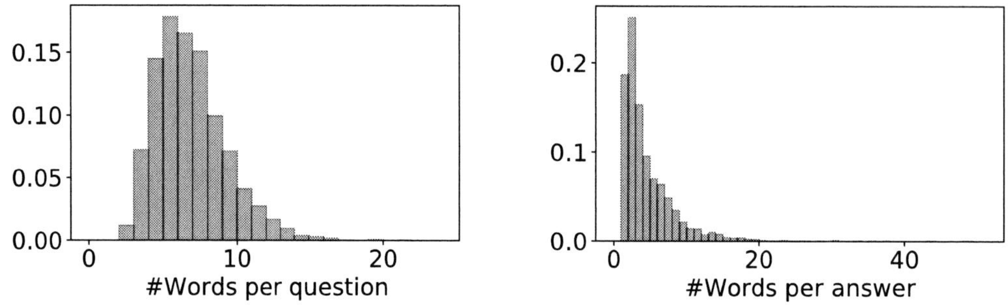

Figure 2: The length distribution of questions (left) and answers (right) in the entire dataset.

Answer Span	Frequency
Minimal	70%
Too Long	28%
Too Short	2%

Table 2: Distribution of annotated answer span quality, based on manual analysis of 50 examples from the validation set.

Question Word		Frequency
What	מה/מהו/...	16.29%
Which	איזה/איזו/...	15.84%
Who	מי/מיהו/...	14.03%
When	מתי/ממתי	13.57%
Where	איפה/היכן/...	10.86%
How	איך/כיצד	6.79%
How much/many	כמה/בכמה/...	5.43%
Why	למה/מדוע	4.52%

Table 3: Question word distribution, according to the first word of each question in the validation set. Inflected words and synonyms are clustered together to better align with English question types.

majority of the annotations are indeed valid, answering the questions with a minimal span. Yet, a significant minority contains additional supporting information, which makes the answer span longer than the desired minimal span by 2.5 times on average. We can thus expect an upper bound of 57% token F1 on those examples, setting the performance ceiling at around 84% F1 for the entire dataset. Finally, we present examples from the validation set that illustrate the annotation quality (Figure 3).

3.2 Question Diversity

To measure the dataset's diversity, we cluster questions by their question word (typically the first word in the question). Table 3 shows that *what* (מה) and *which* (איזה) questions account for a third of the sample, with other answer types being distributed in a rather balanced distribution. We also observe that about 11% of the data contains *how* (איך) and *why* (למה) questions, which may reflect more complex instances.

3.3 Sequence Length

We measure the length in words (using whitespace tokenization) of each question and each answer. Figure 2 shows the distributions of annotated questions and answers. We observe that most questions use between 4-7 words, which is typical of simple questions in Hebrew. More complicated questions constitute 27.6% of the data, for example: איך נקראת האופרה האחרונה שכתבו גילברט וסאליבן יחדיו? (*What is the last opera written jointly by Gilbert and Sullivan called?*) There are even questions with only 2 words; due to Hebrew's rich morphology, these questions are usually translated to 3-4 words in English, e.g. מהו המניכאיזם? (*What is Manichaeism?*) Answer lengths, however, can vary greatly, depending on whether the annotators wrote minimal spans (typically 1-4 words) or included supporting information in the answer spans (see Section 3.1).

3.4 Linguistic Phenomena

As a morphologically-rich language (Tsarfaty et al., 2010; Seddah et al., 2013), modern Hebrew exhibits a variety of non-trivial phenomena that are uncommon in English and could be challenging for NLP models (Tsarfaty et al., 2020). We can identify some of these phenomena in our dataset. Consider for example the following question-answer pair from the validation set:

Q: ?מה היה שטחו של כפר שמריהו כשהוקם

ma haya shitkho shel kfar shmaryahu
what was area-of-it of Kfar Shmaryahu

kshe-hukam
when-was.established

'What was Kfar Shmaryahu's area when it was established?'

A: ... הישוב הוקם על שטח של

ha-yeshuv hukam al shetakh
the-village was.established on area

shel ...
of ...

'The village was established on an area of ...'

This example illustrates a morphological variation between the question and the answer: the same entity appears as a morpheme in a compound word in the question's text: שטחו (*its area*), כשהוקם (*when it was established*), but as a standalone word (i.e. without inflection) in the answer: שטח (*area*), הוקם (*was established*). These phenomena make exact match-optimized predictions more difficult for models aimed to solve this task.

4 Baselines

We establish baseline results for PARASHOOT using BERT-style models. Results indicate the task is challenging, leaving much room for future work in Hebrew NLP to advance the state of the art.

4.1 Experiment Setup

We fine-tune three adaptations of BERT (Devlin et al., 2019): *mBERT*, trained by the original authors on a corpus consisting of the entire Wikipedia dumps of 100 languages; *HeBERT* (Chriqui and Yahav, 2021), trained on the OSCAR corpus (Ortiz Suárez et al., 2020) and Hebrew Wikipedia; *AlephBERT* (Seker et al., 2021), also trained on the OSCAR corpus, with an additional 71.5 million tweets in Hebrew. All models are equivalent in size to BERT-base, i.e. 12 layers, 768 model dimensions, and 110M parameters in total.

We fine-tune the models using the default implementation of HuggingFace Transformers (Wolf et al., 2020). We select the best model by validation set performance over the following hyperparameter grid: learning rate $\in \{3e{-}5, 5e{-}5, 1e{-}4\}$, batch size $\in \{16, 32, 64\}$, and update steps $\in \{512, 800, 1024\}$. We compare the models' predictions to the annotated answer using token-wise F1 score and exact match (EM), as defined by Rajpurkar et al. (2016).

Model	F1	EM
HeBERT	36.7	18.2
AlephBERT	49.6	26.0
mBERT	**56.1**	**32.0**

Table 4: Baseline performance on the test set.

4.2 Results

Table 4 shows the performance of each model on PARASHOOT, with mBERT achieving the highest performance (56.1 F1). We also observe significant variance across the models, with mBERT and AlephBERT performing significantly better than HeBERT. It is not immediately clear where this discrepancy stems from; one possibility is that the introduction of noisy data via multilinguality (mBERT) or tweets (AlephBERT) makes that model more robust to potential noise in the annotated questions (e.g. typos). Comparing these results to the estimated ceiling performance of 84 F1 (see Section 3.1), we can infer that PARASHOOT poses a genuine challenge to future Hebrew models and encourages further analysis of the semantic capabilities of the current models.

4.3 Error Analysis

We analyze the error distribution by sampling 50 examples from the validation set and comparing AlephBERT's predictions to the annotated answers. Table 5 shows how the examples are distributed into five categories, accounting for every type of overlap between the model's prediction and the annotated answer. Putting aside exact matches (which account for about a quarter of examples), nearly half of the errors stem from zero overlap between the annotated answer and the model's prediction. We observe that a significant part of the sample (22%) contains cases where the annotated answer is a substring of the model's prediction, which might be, to a large extent, an artifact of the long answer annotations we observe in Section 3.1. For examples of erroneous predictions see Appendix A.

5 Conclusion

In this paper, we present PARASHOOT, the first question answering dataset in modern Hebrew, in a style and data collection methodology similar to that of SQuAD. Baseline results demonstrate the

Context: ... לאחר מכן הוא מתארס עם חברתה הטובה <u>שארלוט לוקאס</u> (קארן מורלי) ...
... He later becomes engaged to her best friend <u>Charlotte Lucas</u> (Karen Morely) ...
Question: למי מר קולינס מתארס?
To whom does Mr. Collins get engaged?

Context: ... מ<u>שנות ה-60 של המאה ה-20</u> התחילה תקופה של חפירות ארכאולוגיות בוואל קמוניקה שנמשכת ללא הפסקה ...
... From <u>the 60s of the 20th century</u> began a period of archeological excavations in Valcamonica that continues unabated ...
Question: מתי התחילה תקופה של חפירות ארכאולוגיות בוואל קמוניקה?
When did a period of archeological excavations begin in Valcamonica?

Figure 3: Examples from the validation set. The text in bold shows crowd-annotated answers. The underlined text represents the (expert-annotated) minimal answer span. The first example demonstrates a non-minimal span that has some overlap with the question's text. The second example demonstrates a valid minimal span selection.

Overlap Type	**Sample Frequency**	**Error Frequency**
Model = Annotation	26%	–
Model ⊂ Annotation	14%	19%
Model ⊃ Annotation	22%	30%
Model ∩ Annotation ≠ ∅	4%	5%
Model ∩ Annotation = ∅	34%	46%

Table 5: An error analysis of 50 random examples from the validation set, based on AlephBERT's predictions. The first reflects exact matches, and the last case accounts for zero overlap between model prediction and annotated answer. The three categories in the middle refer to partially correct answers, where the model's prediction has some overlap with the annotated answer.

potential of this dataset for researchers and practitioners alike to develop better models and datasets for natural language understanding in Hebrew.

Acknowledgements

This work was supported by the Tel Aviv University Data Science Center, Len Blavatnik and the Blavatnik Family foundation, the Alon Scholarship, Intel Corporation, and the Yandex Initiative for Machine Learning. We thank Reut Tsarfaty for her valuable feedback.

References

Dan Bareket and Reut Tsarfaty. 2020. Neural modeling for named entities and morphology (nemoˆ 2). *arXiv preprint arXiv:2007.15620.*

Avihay Chriqui and Inbal Yahav. 2021. Hebert & hebemo: a hebrew bert model and a tool for polarity analysis and emotion recognition. *arXiv preprint arXiv:2102.01909.*

Jonathan H. Clark, Eunsol Choi, Michael Collins, Dan Garrette, Tom Kwiatkowski, Vitaly Nikolaev, and Jennimaria Palomaki. 2020. TyDi QA: A benchmark for information-seeking question answering in typologically diverse languages. *Transactions of the Association for Computational Linguistics*, 8:454–470.

Jacob Devlin, Ming-Wei Chang, Kenton Lee, and Kristina Toutanova. 2019. BERT: Pre-training of deep bidirectional transformers for language understanding. In *Proceedings of the 2019 Conference of the North American Chapter of the Association for Computational Linguistics: Human Language Technologies, Volume 1 (Long and Short Papers)*, pages 4171–4186, Minneapolis, Minnesota. Association for Computational Linguistics.

Martin d'Hoffschmidt, Wacim Belblidia, Quentin Heinrich, Tom Brendlé, and Maxime Vidal. 2020. FQuAD: French question answering dataset. In *Findings of the Association for Computational Linguistics: EMNLP 2020*, pages 1193–1208, Online. Association for Computational Linguistics.

Suchin Gururangan, Swabha Swayamdipta, Omer Levy, Roy Schwartz, Samuel Bowman, and Noah A. Smith. 2018. Annotation artifacts in natural language inference data. In *Proceedings of the 2018 Conference of the North American Chapter of the Association for Computational Linguistics: Human Language Technologies, Volume 2 (Short Papers)*, pages 107–112, New Orleans, Louisiana. Association for Computational Linguistics.

Divyansh Kaushik and Zachary C. Lipton. 2018. How much reading does reading comprehension require? a critical investigation of popular benchmarks. In *Proceedings of the 2018 Conference on Empirical Methods in Natural Language Processing*, pages 5010–5015, Brussels, Belgium. Association for Computational Linguistics.

Seungyoung Lim, Myungji Kim, and Jooyoul Lee. 2019. Korquad1. 0: Korean qa dataset for machine reading comprehension. *arXiv preprint arXiv:1909.07005.*

Hussein Mozannar, Elie Maamary, Karl El Hajal, and Hazem Hajj. 2019. Neural Arabic question answering. In *Proceedings of the Fourth Arabic Natural Language Processing Workshop*, pages 108–118, Florence, Italy. Association for Computational Linguistics.

Joakim Nivre, Daniel Zeman, Filip Ginter, and Francis Tyers. 2017. Universal Dependencies. In *Proceedings of the 15th Conference of the European Chapter of the Association for Computational Linguistics: Tutorial Abstracts*, Valencia, Spain. Association for Computational Linguistics.

Pedro Javier Ortiz Suárez, Laurent Romary, and Benoît Sagot. 2020. A monolingual approach to contextualized word embeddings for mid-resource languages. In *Proceedings of the 58th Annual Meeting of the Association for Computational Linguistics*, pages 1703–1714, Online. Association for Computational Linguistics.

Pranav Rajpurkar, Jian Zhang, Konstantin Lopyrev, and Percy Liang. 2016. SQuAD: 100,000+ questions for machine comprehension of text. In *Proceedings of the 2016 Conference on Empirical Methods in Natural Language Processing*, pages 2383–2392, Austin, Texas. Association for Computational Linguistics.

Ori Ram, Yuval Kirstain, Jonathan Berant, Amir Globerson, and Omer Levy. 2021. Few-shot question answering by pretraining span selection. In *Proceedings of the 59th Annual Meeting of the Association for Computational Linguistics and the 11th International Joint Conference on Natural Language Processing, ACL/IJCNLP 2021, (Volume 1: Long Papers), Virtual Event, August 1-6, 2021*, pages 3066–3079. Association for Computational Linguistics.

Djamé Seddah, Reut Tsarfaty, Sandra Kübler, Marie Candito, Jinho D. Choi, Richárd Farkas, Jennifer Foster, Iakes Goenaga, Koldo Gojenola Galletebeitia, Yoav Goldberg, Spence Green, Nizar Habash, Marco Kuhlmann, Wolfgang Maier, Joakim Nivre, Adam Przepiórkowski, Ryan Roth, Wolfgang Seeker, Yannick Versley, Veronika Vincze, Marcin Woliński, Alina Wróblewska, and Eric Villemonte de la Clergerie. 2013. Overview of the SPMRL 2013 shared task: A cross-framework evaluation of parsing morphologically rich languages. In *Proceedings of the Fourth Workshop on Statistical Parsing of Morphologically-Rich Languages*, pages 146–182, Seattle, Washington, USA. Association for Computational Linguistics.

Amit Seker, Elron Bandel, Dan Bareket, Idan Brusilovsky, Refael Shaked Greenfeld, and Reut Tsarfaty. 2021. Alephbert: A hebrew large pre-trained language model to start-off your hebrew nlp application with. *arXiv preprint arXiv:2104.04052*.

Reut Tsarfaty, Dan Bareket, Stav Klein, and Amit Seker. 2020. From SPMRL to NMRL: What did we learn (and unlearn) in a decade of parsing morphologically-rich languages (MRLs)? In *Proceedings of the 58th Annual Meeting of the Association for Computational Linguistics*, pages 7396–7408, Online. Association for Computational Linguistics.

Reut Tsarfaty, Djamé Seddah, Yoav Goldberg, Sandra Kuebler, Yannick Versley, Marie Candito, Jennifer Foster, Ines Rehbein, and Lamia Tounsi. 2010. Statistical parsing of morphologically rich languages (SPMRL) what, how and whither. In *Proceedings of the NAACL HLT 2010 First Workshop on Statistical Parsing of Morphologically-Rich Languages*, pages 1–12, Los Angeles, CA, USA. Association for Computational Linguistics.

Thomas Wolf, Lysandre Debut, Victor Sanh, Julien Chaumond, Clement Delangue, Anthony Moi, Pierric Cistac, Tim Rault, Remi Louf, Morgan Funtowicz, Joe Davison, Sam Shleifer, Patrick von Platen, Clara Ma, Yacine Jernite, Julien Plu, Canwen Xu, Teven Le Scao, Sylvain Gugger, Mariama Drame, Quentin Lhoest, and Alexander Rush. 2020. Transformers: State-of-the-art natural language processing. In *Proceedings of the 2020 Conference on Empirical Methods in Natural Language Processing: System Demonstrations*, pages 38–45, Online. Association for Computational Linguistics.

A Error Examples

Context: ... לאחר התפטרות ניקסון ב-1974 בעקבות פרשת ווטרגייט, עבד צ'ייני בצוות שארגן את העברת הממשל לידי ג'רלד פורד ואחר כך המשיך בתפקיד עוזר בכיר לנשיא ...

... Following Nixon's resignation in 1974 following the Watergate affair, Cheney worked on a team that organized the transfer of administration to Gerald Ford and then continued as a senior assistant to the president ...

Question: מי היה נשיא ארצות הברית אחרי ניקסון?

Who was the president of the United States after Nixon?

Predicted Answer: צ'ייני (*Cheney*)

Context: תֵּל מִיכָל הוא אתר ארכאולוגי ובית גידול ים תיכוני הנמצא על רכס הכורכר החופי, מול מרינה הרצליה בדרום-מערבה של הרצליה ...

Tel Michal is an archeological site and Mediterranean habitat located on the coastal kurkar ridge, opposite the Herzliya Marina in the southwest of Herzliya ...

Question: איפה נמצא תל מיכל?

Where is Tel Michal located?

Predicted Answer: מול מרינה הרצליה (*opposite the Herzliya Marina*)

Context: ... בשנת 1895, בהיותו בן 17, עזב ואלזר את ביל ועבר לבזל. לאחר זמן קצר עבר לשטוטגרט שבגרמניה, עיר מגוריו של אחיו קרל ...

... In 1895, at the age of 17, Walser left Biel and moved to Basel. He soon moved to Stuttgart, Germany, the hometown of his brother Karl ...

Question: באיזה גיל ואלזר עבר לבאזל?

At what age did Walser move to Basel?

Predicted Answer: בהיותו בן 17, עזב ואלזר את ביל ועבר לבזל (*at the age of 17, Walser left Biel and moved to Basel*)

Figure A.1: Predictions made by fine-tuned AlephBERT vs. annotated answers. In the first example, the prediction produced by the model is clearly an error. In the second example, the annotated answer span is excessively long, and the model predicts a more accurate substring of this span. In the third example, the model predicts a full sentence, while the annotated answer span is shorter.

Unsupervised Multiple Choices Question Answering: Start Learning from Basic Knowledge

Chi-Liang Liu Hung-yi Lee
College of Electrical Engineering and Computer Science
National Taiwan University
{liangtaiwan1230, tlkagkb93901106}@gmail.com

Abstract

In this paper, we study the possibility of unsupervised Multiple Choices Question Answering (MCQA). From very basic knowledge, the MCQA model knows that some choices have higher probabilities of being correct than others. The information, though very noisy, guides the training of an MCQA model. The proposed method is shown to outperform the baseline approaches on RACE and is even comparable with some supervised learning approaches on MC500.

1 Introduction

Question Answering (QA) has been widely used for testing Reading Comprehension. Recently, numerous question answering datasets (Weston et al., 2015; Rajpurkar et al., 2016, 2018; Yang et al., 2018; Trischler et al., 2017; Choi et al., 2018; Joshi et al., 2017; Kwiatkowski et al., 2019; Reddy et al., 2019; Richardson, 2013; Lai et al., 2017a; Khashabi et al., 2018) have been proposed. These datasets can be divided into two major categories: *Extractive Question Answering* (EQA) and *Multiple Choices Question Answering* (MCQA). In EQA, the answer has to be a span of the given reading passage, such as SQuAD (Rajpurkar et al., 2016) and NewsQA (Trischler et al., 2017); while in MCQA, the answer is one of the given choices, such as MCTest (Richardson, 2013) and RACE (Lai et al., 2017a).

Recently, large pretrained language models such as BERT (Devlin et al., 2019) have exceeded human performance in some EQA benchmark corpora, for example, SQuAD (Rajpurkar et al., 2016). Compared to EQA, MCQA does not restrict the answer to be spans in context. This allowed MCQA can have more challenging questions than EQA, including but not limited to logical reasoning or summarization. The performance gap between BERT and human performance is still significant. In this paper, we focus on MCQA.

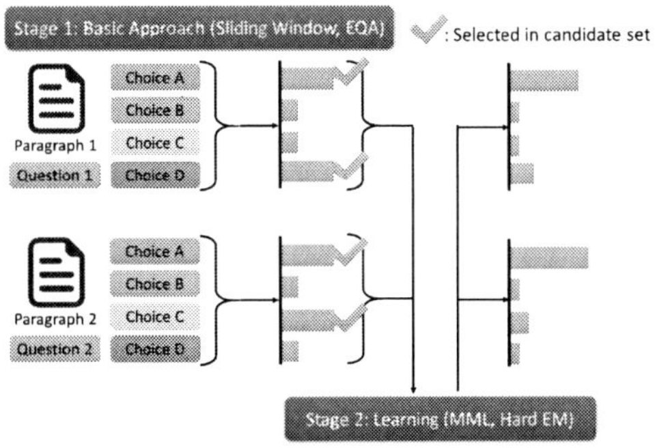

Figure 1: Overall training process.

A person who can read can deal with the MCQA task without further training, but this is not the case for a machine. The BERT-based models cannot be directly applied to solve the MCQA task without seeing any MCQA examples. Even for the models achieving human-level performance in EQA, they still need some MCQA examples with correct choices being labeled for fine-tuning. Although Keskar et al. (2019); Raffel et al. (2020) proposed the unified question answering model, they require unifying the multiple tasks to span extraction task.

The semi-supervised MCQA model training approach has been proposed (Chung et al., 2018), in which an initial MCQA model is used to answer the unlabelled questions to generate pseudo labeled data. Then pseudo labeled data is used to fine-tune the MCQA model to improve the performance. However, the initial MCQA model still needs some labeled examples to train.

In this paper, we study the possibility of unsupervised MCQA. Instead of starting from an initial MCQA model (Chung et al., 2018), here, the machine starts with some prior knowledge. For example, a choice has a higher probability of being correct if the choice has word overlap with the document and question. With the basic rule, the machine knows that some choices have higher probabilities of being correct than others, and some choices can be ruled out. With these basic rules,

Proceedings of the 3rd Workshop on Machine Reading for Question Answering , pages 113–118
Nov 10th, 2021

an MCQA model can be trained without any labeled MCQA examples. With this approach, we got absolute gains of 4~9% accuracy compared to the baseline methods on two MCQA benchmark corpora, RACE and MC500.

2 Unsupervised MCQA

We consider MCQA where we are given a question q, a passage p and a set of choices $C = \{c_1, c_2, ...c_n\}$, where n is the number of choices, and machine needs to select an answer $a \in C$.

We propose to address an unsupervised MCQA in a two-stage approach (Figure 1). First, we pick the candidate set $\mathcal{T}$ from choices by fundamental rule from human knowledge (sliding window) or a model trained without MCQA data (EQA model). Second, we train a model to pick the final answer from the candidates.

2.1 Candidates Choosing

The candidate selection approaches give a score to each choice which represents the likelihood of being correct. We use two systems to calculate the scores, one using simple lexical features and another using a pre-trained EQA model. A choice is selected into candidate set $\mathcal{T}$ if the choice's score is higher than a threshold t, and is the top k scores among all the choices $\{c_1, c_2, ...c_n\}$ of a question q. In this way, each question has at most k candidates in $\mathcal{T}$. k should be smaller than n ($k < n$) to rule out some less likely choices. A question will not have any choice in $\mathcal{T}$ if none of its choices pass the threshold t. Both t and k are the hyperparameters. Note that our methods do **not** guarantee the answer must be in the candidate set. The candidate sets are only used during training, and *we do not need to choose candidates when testing*.

Sliding Window (SW) We follow the sliding window algorithm in Richardson (2013), matching a bag of words constructed from the question and choices to the passage to compute the scores of choices. The algorithm's details are shown in Algorithm 1.

EQA Matching In this setting, we use a pre-trained EQA model as our reference. Given a passage and a question, the EQA model outputs an answer A, which is a text span from the passage. Then we use a string-matching algorithm to compute the similarity between A and each candidate c, and the similarity serves as the score for each candidate. Gestalt Pattern Matching (Ratcliff and Metzener, July 1988) algorithm is the string-matching algorithm used here. The algorithm's details are shown in Appendix B.

2.2 Learning Methods

The candidates $\mathcal{T}$ selected in the last subsection are used as the ground truth to train an MCQA model. Because the candidates are not always correct, and each question can have multiple choices selected in the candidate set, the typical supervised learning approaches cannot be directly applied here. Therefore, the following learning methods are explored to form our objective function $\mathcal{L}$ for training the MCQA model from the candidates.

Highest-Only

$$\mathcal{L} = -\log P\left(c_{max} \mid p; q\right),$$

where c_{max} is the choice of a question q in the candidate set with the highest score. The approach here has no difference from typical supervised learning, except that the ground truth is from the candidate selection approaches, not human labeling.

Maximum Marginal Likelihood (MML)

$$\mathcal{L} = -\log \sum_{c_i \in \mathcal{T}} P\left(c_i \mid p; q\right)$$

In this objective, all the choices in the candidate set are considered correct. The learning target of the MCQA model is to maximize the probabilities that all the choices in the candidate set are labeled as correct. If there are more correct choices than the incorrect ones in the candidate set, the impact of the wrong choices in the candidate set can be mitigated.

Hard-EM Proposed by Min et al. (2019), this can be viewed as a variant of MML,

$$\mathcal{L} = -\log \max_{c_i \in \mathcal{T}} P\left(c_i \mid p; q\right)$$

The underlying assumption of this objective can be understood as follows. For a question q, several choices are selected in the candidate set. Although we don't know which one is correct, we assume one of them is correct. Therefore, we want the MCQA model to learn to maximize the probability of one of the choices for a question.

3 Experiments Setup

To evaluate the proposed method's effectiveness compared to supervised learning and other approaches that do not require training data, we

	RACE		RACE-M		RACE-H		MC500		MC500-One		MC500-Multi.	
	dev	test	dev	test	dev	test	dev	test	dev	test	dev	test
Starting from SW Matching Algorithm												
SW	30.8	30.2	36.2	35.2	28.4	28.1	46.5	42.8	36.7	43.7	54.5	42.1
Highest-Only	31.8	30.8	37.5	36.4	29.4	28.5	46.0	42.3	44.4	41.5	47.2	43.0
MML	34.0	33.1	40.3	40.5	31.4	30.1	50.0	45.3	**46.6**	44.4	52.7	**46.1**
Hard-EM	**34.3**	**34.0**	**41.0**	**41.2**	**31.5**	**31.0**	**51.5**	**45.7**	44.4	**47.7**	**57.3**	44.0
Starting from EQA Matching Algorithm												
EQA Match	32.3	32.2	40.3	40.5	28.9	28.8	62.5	**64.1**	**75.6**	**80.9**	51.8	49.8
Highest-Only	37.0	36.9	48.8	46.1	32.1	33.1	**67.5**	60.6	67.7	66.0	**67.2**	56.0
MML	38.6	**39.4**	**49.7**	49.6	34.0	**35.2**	65.5	61.3	67.8	67.1	63.6	56.3
Hard-EM	**39.1**	39.2	49.0	**49.7**	**35.0**	34.9	66.0	63.3	68.9	66.0	63.6	**60.9**
Supevised	64.9	65.5	70.0	71.0	64.0	63.3	70.0	64.3	75.6	69.0	60.4	65.4

Table 1: **Results on RACE and MC500 of MCTest.** The evaluation measure is accuracy (%). The Supervised Learning was training with ground truth and used the same hyperparamter as others.

	RACE		MC500	
	dev	test	dev	test
SW Matching Algorithm				
(A) Avg. num. of candidates	3	3	1.98	1.85
(B) Percent Including Ans.	79.2	79.0	67.0	62.1
(B) / (A)	26.4	26.3	33.8	33.6
EQA Matching Algorithm				
(A) Avg. num. of candidates	1.35	1.38	1.63	1.62
(B) Percent Including Ans.	40.9	41.8	73.0	71.5
(B) / (A)	30.3	30.3	44.8	44.1

Table 2: **The average size of candidate sets chosen by EQA and SW Matching.** *Percent Including Answer* means the percent of candidate set including the labeled answer. (B) / (A) is the accuracy of randomly selecting a choice from a candidate set.

EQA	SW	RACE-train	MC500-train
✓	✗	29759	202
✗	✓	8461	194

Table 3: **Candidate Set Analysis of RACE and MC500 of MCTest.** *Case1: candidates chosen by EQA including the answer but candidates chosen by SW not including the answer. Case2: candidates chosen by SW including the answer but candidates chosen by EQA not including the answer.*

experiment on two MCQA tasks, RACE and MCTest(MC500).

3.1 Datasets

RACE Lai et al. (2017b) introduced the RACE dataset, collected from the English exams for middle and high school Chinese students. RACE consists of near 28000 passages and nearly 100000 questions. Specifically, the dataset can be split into two parts: RACE-M, collected from English examinations designed for middle school students; and RACE-H, collected from English examinations designed for high students. RACE-H is more difficult than RACE-M; the length of the passages and the vocabulary size in the RACE-H are much larger than that of the RACE-M.

MC500 Richardson (2013) present MCTest which requires machines to answer multiple-choice reading comprehension questions about fictional stories. MCTest has two variants: MC160, which contains 160 stories, and MC500, which contains 500 stories. Moreover, MC500 can be subdivided into MC500-One and MC500-Multi. MC500-One refers to the questions that can be answered with one sentence. MC500-Multi refers to the questions that need evidence in multiple sentences to answer.

The length of each story is approximately 150 to 300 words, and the topic of a story is a wide range. In our experiment, we evaluate our model on MC500 since there are only 280 questions in the MC160, which is not suitable in our setting.

Appendix A shows more details about both datasets.

3.2 Model Description

In this work, we used BERT-base (Devlin et al., 2019) as the pre-trained model for both the EQA system and the MCQA system in the following experiments.

EQA model The hyperparameters we used are the same as the official released for training SQuAD 1.1. For both datasets, the EQA model is trained on SQuAD 1.1.

MCQA Model To fine-tune the BERT model on the MCQA datasets, we construct four input sequences, each containing the concatenation of the passage, the question, and one of the choices (Zellers et al., 2018). The separator tokens [SEP] are added between the passage and the question. Next, we fed the [CLS] token representation to the classifier and got the scores for each choice.

4 Experiment Results

Table 1 shows the results of baselines and our methods on RACE and MC500.

RACE Our methods outperform SW and EQA Match across all the datasets with absolute gain 4∼9% accuracy, which shows the MCQA model can improve itself from the noisy candidate sets. MML and Hard-EM outperform Highest-Only in all cases, which indicates that relying only on the single choice with the highest score is insufficient. The improvement with EQA Matching Algorithm is more significant than with SW Matching Algorithm. This implies Candidates Choosing stage plays a significant role in the performance; more details will be discussed later.

MC500 With the SW Matching algorithm, our methods outperform the performance baseline across all the datasets with absolute gains of 1∼5% accuracy. With the EQA Matching Algorithm, because on MC500, EQA has achieved a comparable result with supervised learning, the proposed approaches do not further improve EQA. The performance of our method drops in MC500-One because EQA models can better capture the information within a sentence than multiple sentences, leading MC500-One performance much better than MC500-Multi with EQA models. On the other hand, we improve the performance of MC500-Multiple by about 12%. This shows that our method can further improve EQA in the more difficult examples that the EQA model cannot answer correctly.

5 Analysis

Candidate Set & Matching Methods Table 2 shows the average size of candidate sets chosen by EQA and SW Matching, and their *Percent Including Answer*, that is, the percent of candidate set including the correct answer. The *Percent Including Answer* is much better for SW than EQA on RACE because the candidate sets selected by SW are larger than EQA. We find that EQA gives more concentrated confidence scores to the choices than SW, leading to smaller candidate sets. Although

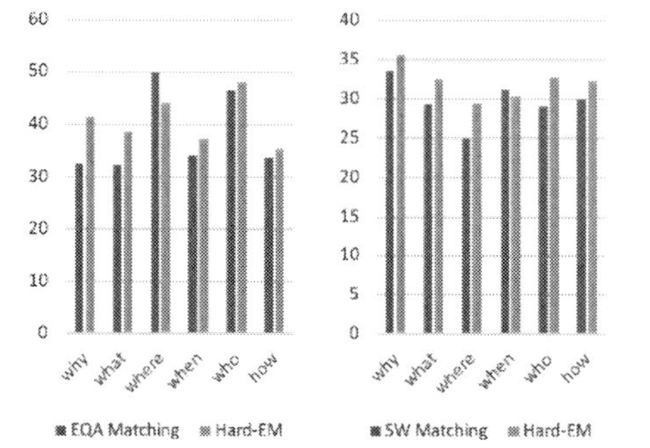

(a) EQA Matching and hard-em approach (b) SW Matching and hard-em approach

Figure 2: Accuracy (%) on different type of question

the *Percent Including Answer* of SW is larger than by EQA (Table 2), the candidates picked by EQA have higher quality than candidates picked by SW, as shown in Table 3.

Table 2 implies that MCQA models from the proposed learning strategy do not just randomly choose a prediction from the candidates. The performance of the proposed approaches in Table 1 is much higher than the performance of randomly sampling from the candidate set, that is, (B) / (A) in Table 2.

Question Types To see how our learning method works with respect to the type of question, we divided the questions in RACE into six types: why, what, where, when, who, and how. We choose to analyze RACE because it has more questions than MC 500. Figure 2 shows the accuracy of each question types. The results show that the proposed approach does not favor specific types of questions. We found that no matter the candidate set selection methods, the proposed method improved all types of questions, except "where" for EQA and "when" for SW. Understanding why some question types do not been improved by unsupervised MCQA in some cases is our future work.

6 Conclusion

In this paper, we proposed an unsupervised MCQA method, which exploits the pseudo labels generated by some basic rules or external non-MCQA datasets. The proposed method significantly outperforms the baseline approaches on RACE and is even comparable with the supervised learning performance on MC500. We hope this paper sheds light on unsupervised learning in NLP tasks.

References

Eunsol Choi, He He, Mohit Iyyer, Mark Yatskar, Wen-tau Yih, Yejin Choi, Percy Liang, and Luke Zettlemoyer. 2018. Quac: Question answering in context. In *Proceedings of the 2018 Conference on Empirical Methods in Natural Language Processing*, pages 2174–2184.

Yu-An Chung, Hung-Yi Lee, and James Glass. 2018. Supervised and unsupervised transfer learning for question answering. In *Proceedings of the 2018 Conference of the North American Chapter of the Association for Computational Linguistics: Human Language Technologies, Volume 1 (Long Papers)*, pages 1585–1594, New Orleans, Louisiana. Association for Computational Linguistics.

Jacob Devlin, Ming-Wei Chang, Kenton Lee, and Kristina Toutanova. 2019. Bert: Pre-training of deep bidirectional transformers for language understanding. In *Proceedings of the 2019 Conference of the North American Chapter of the Association for Computational Linguistics: Human Language Technologies, Volume 1 (Long and Short Papers)*, pages 4171–4186.

Mandar Joshi, Eunsol Choi, Daniel S Weld, and Luke Zettlemoyer. 2017. Triviaqa: A large scale distantly supervised challenge dataset for reading comprehension. In *Proceedings of the 55th Annual Meeting of the Association for Computational Linguistics (Volume 1: Long Papers)*, pages 1601–1611.

Nitish Shirish Keskar, Bryan McCann, Caiming Xiong, and Richard Socher. 2019. Unifying question answering, text classification, and regression via span extraction.

Daniel Khashabi, Snigdha Chaturvedi, Michael Roth, Shyam Upadhyay, and Dan Roth. 2018. Looking beyond the surface: A challenge set for reading comprehension over multiple sentences. In *Proceedings of the 2018 Conference of the North American Chapter of the Association for Computational Linguistics: Human Language Technologies, Volume 1 (Long Papers)*, pages 252–262, New Orleans, Louisiana. Association for Computational Linguistics.

Tom Kwiatkowski, Jennimaria Palomaki, Olivia Redfield, Michael Collins, Ankur Parikh, Chris Alberti, Danielle Epstein, Illia Polosukhin, Jacob Devlin, Kenton Lee, et al. 2019. Natural questions: A benchmark for question answering research. *Transactions of the Association for Computational Linguistics*, 7:453–466.

Guokun Lai, Qizhe Xie, Hanxiao Liu, Yiming Yang, and Eduard Hovy. 2017a. Race: Large-scale reading comprehension dataset from examinations. In *Proceedings of the 2017 Conference on Empirical Methods in Natural Language Processing*, pages 785–794.

Guokun Lai, Qizhe Xie, Hanxiao Liu, Yiming Yang, and Eduard Hovy. 2017b. RACE: Large-scale ReAding comprehension dataset from examinations. In *Proceedings of the 2017 Conference on Empirical Methods in Natural Language Processing*, pages 785–794, Copenhagen, Denmark. Association for Computational Linguistics.

Sewon Min, Danqi Chen, Hannaneh Hajishirzi, and Luke Zettlemoyer. 2019. A discrete hard EM approach for weakly supervised question answering. In *EMNLP*.

Colin Raffel, Noam Shazeer, Adam Roberts, Katherine Lee, Sharan Narang, Michael Matena, Yanqi Zhou, Wei Li, and Peter J. Liu. 2020. Exploring the limits of transfer learning with a unified text-to-text transformer.

Pranav Rajpurkar, Robin Jia, and Percy Liang. 2018. Know what you don't know: Unanswerable questions for SQuAD. In *Proceedings of the 56th Annual Meeting of the Association for Computational Linguistics (Volume 2: Short Papers)*, pages 784–789, Melbourne, Australia. Association for Computational Linguistics.

Pranav Rajpurkar, Jian Zhang, Konstantin Lopyrev, and Percy Liang. 2016. SQuAD: 100,000+ questions for machine comprehension of text.

John W. Ratcliff and David Metzener. July 1988. Pattern matching: The gestalt approach.

Siva Reddy, Danqi Chen, and Christopher D Manning. 2019. Coqa: A conversational question answering challenge. *Transactions of the Association for Computational Linguistics*, 7:249–266.

Matthew Richardson. 2013. Mctest: A challenge dataset for the open-domain machine comprehension of text. In *Proceedings of the 2013 Conference on Emprical Methods in Natural Language Processing (EMNLP 2013)*.

Adam Trischler, Tong Wang, Xingdi Yuan, Justin Harris, Alessandro Sordoni, Philip Bachman, and Kaheer Suleman. 2017. Newsqa: A machine comprehension dataset. In *Proceedings of the 2nd Workshop on Representation Learning for NLP*, pages 191–200.

Jason Weston, Antoine Bordes, Sumit Chopra, Alexander M Rush, Bart van Merriënboer, Armand Joulin, and Tomas Mikolov. 2015. Towards ai-complete question answering: Aset of prerequisite toy tasks. *arXiv preprint arXiv:1502.05698*.

Zhilin Yang, Peng Qi, Saizheng Zhang, Yoshua Bengio, William Cohen, Ruslan Salakhutdinov, and Christopher D Manning. 2018. Hotpotqa: A dataset for diverse, explainable multi-hop question answering. In *Proceedings of the 2018 Conference on Empirical Methods in Natural Language Processing*, pages 2369–2380.

Rowan Zellers, Yonatan Bisk, Roy Schwartz, and Yejin Choi. 2018. Swag: A large-scale adversarial dataset for grounded commonsense inference.

A Dataset Details

	RACE		
	train	dev	test
RACE-M	25421	1436	1436
RACE-H	62445	3451	3698

	MC500		
	train	dev	test
MC500-One	564	90	277
MC500-Multi	636	119	323

Table 4: **Number of examples in RACE and MC500 of MCTest.** RACE-M and MC500-One are easier than RACE-H and MC500-Multi separately.

B Matching Algorithms

Algorithm 1: Sliding Window

Input : Threshold t, max numbers of candidates k, a set of passage words P, set of words in question Q, and a set of words in choices $C_{1...n}$.

Define : $Count(w) := \sum_i \mathbb{1}(P_i = w)$ where P_i is the i-th word in passage P;

Define : $IC(w) := \log\left(1 + \frac{1}{Count(w)}\right)$

candidates ← Array[]

for $i = 1$ *to* n **do**

  $S \leftarrow C_i \cup Q$

  score$_i$ ←

$$\max_{j=1...|P|} \sum_{w=1...|S|} \begin{cases} IC(P_{j+w}), & \text{if } P_{j+w} \in S \\ 0, & \text{otherwise} \end{cases}$$

  if $score_i \geq t$ **then**

    candidates.append((i, score$_i$))

sort candidates descending by score

return first k elements of candidates

Algorithm 2: EQA Matching

Input : Threshold t, max numbers of candidates k, a set of passage words P, set of words in question Q, and a set of words in choices $C_{1...n}$ and a pre-trained EQA model M

candidates ← Array[]

$A \leftarrow M.predict(P, Q)$

for $i = 1$ *to* n **do**

  score$_i$ ← Gestalt Pattern Matching(A, C_i)

  if $score_i \geq t$ **then**

    candidates.append((i, score$_i$))

sort candidates descending by score

return first k elements of candidates

C Training Details

We finetuned all models with a linear learning rate decay schedule with 1000 warm-up steps. The batch size is 32, and the max length of the input size is 320. For RACE, we set the threshold to 0, the max number of candidates to 3 with SW Matching, and set the threshold to 50, the max number of candidates to 3 with the EQA Matching. For MC500, we set the threshold to 3, the max number of candidates to 2 with SW Matching, and the threshold to 50, the max number of candidates to 3 with the EQA Matching.

Following Min et al. (2019), when we use hard-EM as objective, we perform annealing: at training step t, the model use MML as objective with a probability of $\min(t/\tau, 0.8)$ and otherwise use hard-EM, where τ is a hyperparameter. We tried $\tau = 1000$, 4000, and 8000.

GANDALF: a General Character Name Description Dataset for Long Fiction

Fredrik Carlsson[1], **Fredrik Olsson**[2], **Amaru Cuba Gyllensten**[1], and **Magnus Sahlgren**[1]

[1]RISE, Isafjordsgatan 22, 164 40 Kista, Sweden
[fredrik.carlsson|amaru.cuba.gyllensten|magnus.sahlgren]@ri.se
[2]Gavagai, Kungsgatan 60, 111 22 Stockholm, Sweden
fredrik.olsson@gavagai.io

Abstract

This paper introduces a long-range multiple-choice Question Answering (QA) dataset, based on full-length fiction book texts. The questions are formulated as 10-way multiple-choice questions, where the task is to select the correct character name given a character description, or vice-versa. Each character description is formulated in natural text and often contains information from several sections throughout the book. We provide 20,000 questions created from 10,000 manually annotated descriptions of characters from 177 books containing 152,917 words on average. We address the current discourse regarding dataset bias and leakage by a simple anonymization procedure, which in turn enables interesting probing possibilities. Finally, we show that suitable baseline algorithms perform very poorly on this task, with the book size itself making it non-trivial to attempt a Transformer-based QA solution. This leaves ample room for future improvement, and hints at the need for a completely different type of solution.

1 Introduction

Comprehending and analyzing fictional stories plays an important part in human culture (Smith et al., 2017). In particular, book studies is a commonly applied educational tool used to both probe and enrich students' language comprehension skills (Tunnell and Jacobs, 1989). Ideally, these book studies require the students to reason about notions spread out over hundreds of pages of text.

By contrast, methods and datasets for machine reading comprehension (MRC) have predominantly been limited to comparably short texts, with evaluations often focusing on various forms of short-text natural language understanding (NLU) tasks, where the input is limited to a small number of sentences. Examples of such tasks include textual similarity (Agirre et al., 2012), sentiment analysis (Yu and Jiang, 2016), Question Answering (Yadav et al., 2019), inference and, entailment (Talman et al., 2019), etc.

There is an ongoing debate regarding NLU evaluation datasets, spurred by the acclaimed superhuman results on benchmarks such as GLUE (Wang et al., 2018) and SuperGLUE (Wang et al., 2019). The critique points out several inherent issues with these benchmarks (Tsuchiya, 2018), such as data-leakage (Elangovan et al., 2021), and that models are sometimes able to "cheat" by exploiting spurious linguistic cues in the data (Niven and Kao, 2019). Proposed mitigation methods include the use of adversarially hard datasets (Nie et al., 2020), and taking a more rigorous approach to dataset design (Bowman and Dahl, 2021).

Adding our voice to this discussion, we point out an additional limitation to near all these prior datasets, namely how limited they are in the amount of text that is used per question (See section 2 for noteable exceptions). Since datasets arguably drive the direction of research, we find it backward and stagnating to only create evaluation tasks suitable for the current paradigm of fixed-size Transformer models (Vaswani et al., 2017)). Therefore, we find it equally important to create datasets meant to task methods on long-text comprehension.

Thus, we present **GANDALF** (a **G**eneral ch**A**racter **N**ame **D**escription d**A**taset for **L**ong **F**iction), a full-length book Question Answering dataset focused on the novel task of **character description recognition**. This 10-way multiple-choice task asks the model to read *an entire book*, and then identify the correct character name to a given character description, or vice-versa. In total, we supply 20,000 questions, with a 50/50 split between predicting a name given a description, and predicting the description given a character name. The manually created descriptions are all expressed in natural text and contain a mixture of traits, important events, and relationships to other characters.

Proceedings of the 3rd Workshop on Machine Reading for Question Answering , pages 119–132
Nov 10th, 2021 ©2021 Association for Computational Linguistics

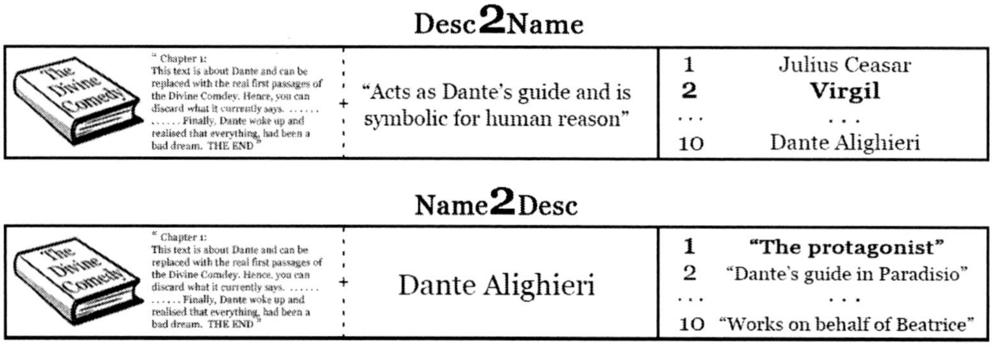

Figure 1: Example of questions formulated as *Desc2Name* and *Name2Desc*.

A schematic illustration of GANDALF is provided in Figure 1.

Taking into account the current discourse concerning datasets, we implement a simple name-replacement system that counters potential data leakage. This system also enables for straightforward implementations of probing tasks by controlling for example gender or nationality. Finally, we perform experiments intended to measure a model's ability to cheat on GANDALF, by answering the questions without relying on the book data.

The full dataset is available at: `github.com/FreddeFrallan/GANDALF-Dataset`

In contrast to previous work, the books within GANDALF contain on average ~150,000 words and ~8,000 sentences. Each question is classified into its level of referential complexity (See section 3.2), which when combined with the multiple-choice accuracy results in an informative evaluation metric. To the best of our knowledge, GANDALF is therefore not only the longest current MRC dataset, but also the only current MRC dataset which provides these insights during evaluation. We note that there are other types of benchmarks and tasks that requires long context, such as Thorne et al. (2021) and Huang et al. (2021).

2 Related Work

There exists a rich body of literature for various MRC and NLU-related tasks. Examples of previous MRC datasets that also formulate their questions as multiple-choice include: RACE (Lai et al., 2017), OpenBookQA (Mihaylov et al., 2018), MultiRC (Khashabi et al., 2018) and RACE-C (Liang et al., 2019). For each of these datasets, the combined length of each question and its provided information often fall below 50 sentences, and for some datasets significantly less.

Related work which specifically utilize books as their universe of knowledge include Children's Book Test (CBT) (Hill et al., 2016), BookTest (Bajgar et al., 2016), and COMICS (Iyyer et al., 2017). These three datasets all utilize cloze-style answers from sequences with up to 21 sentences.

NarrativeQA (s Koˇ ciský et al., 2018) provide questions based on full-length stories, with an average of ~60k words per story. The answer format is free-text and is hence evaluated using text similarity metrics such as BLEU (Papineni et al., 2002) and Meteor (Banerjee and Lavie, 2005).

2.1 The Dataset Discourse

Recently, the robustness and validity of many academic NLU datasets have come into question. Kaushik and Lipton (2018) proves that many questions in existing benchmarks can be solved without even considering the corresponding context. Paullada et al. (2020) identify multiple shortcomings in the common practices for dataset collection prevalent within the machine learning community. Elangovan et al. (2021) point to a substantial data leakage between train and test data for many datasets.

The data-leakage problem recently surfaced in the context of MRC, when the long-form dataset ELI5 (Fan et al., 2019) received critique for leaking at least 81% (Krishna et al., 2021). To avoid such shortcomings, Kaushik and Lipton conclude that researchers must validate that both the question and their respective context are required for solving the task; and be cautious when using cloze questions.

Finally, Bowman and Dahl (2021) present four criteria that NLU datasets should meet in order to make evaluation reliable. These criteria state that task performance needs to be highly correlated

	Level 1	Level 2	Level 3	Level 4	All
Total number of questions	1,700	3,700	2,300	2,300	10,000
Mean number of sentences	1.05	1.05	1.16	1.17	1.10
Mean number of words	13.53	13.46	28.37	28.47	20.35
Total number of tokens	64,649	6,908	5,298	5,048	9,729

Table 1: Statistics for the 10,000 character descriptions, structured by their level of referential complexity.

Avg number of characters	26.93
Max number of characters	89
Min number of characters	10
Total number of characters	4,766
Avg number of sentences	8,370
Avg number of words	152,917
Total number of tokens	27,066,319

Table 2: Statistics for the 177 full-length books included in GANDALF and its described characters.

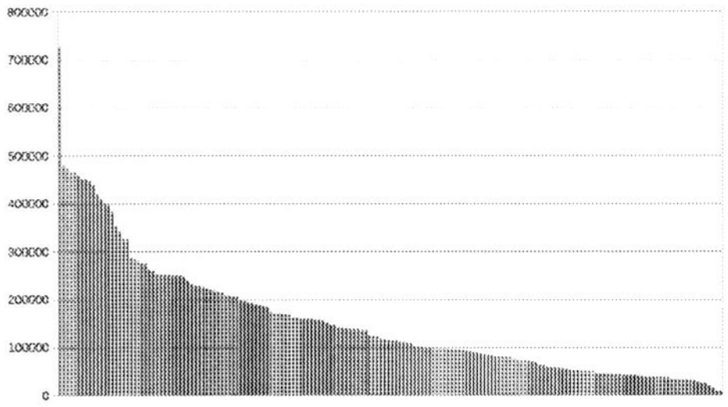

Figure 2: Length of the 177 books in number of words.

with in-domain performance. Datasets need to be harder and/or bigger. Questions need to be unambiguously labeled, and the dataset should reveal potential biases of the system solving the task.

3 The GANDALF Dataset

GANDALF contains 20,000, 10-way multiple-choice questions, formulated from 10,000 manually created character descriptions of 2,500 characters from 177 books. For each question, the relevant book is provided, and the task is to either predict the correct name given a description or predict the correct description given a character name. For brevity we refer to these two different settings as: *Desc2Name* and *Name2Desc*. See Figure 1 for a visual example.

Additionally, GANDALF contains a simple anonymization system, where names are replaced in both the books and the descriptions. This acts a mitigation to potential data leakage and also allows for easy creation of future probing tasks.

3.1 The Books

The dataset comprises a total of 177 full-length books, collected from Project Gutenberg as described in Section 4.1. Table 2 summarizes basic statistics about the books, and Figure 2 shows the length of the books in number of words. There is one book that is significantly longer than the others (*War and Peace* by Leo Tolstoy), and two books that are shorter than all the others (*In Our Time* by Ernest Hemingway, and *The Queen of Spades* by Alexander Sergeievith Poushkin). Appendix-E list all book titles within GANDALF.

3.1.1 The Characters

In total, GANDALF includes 4,766 named characters who all match the filtering criteria stated in Section 4.2. For these characters, it was possible to supply uniquely identifiable descriptions for 4,463. The remaining 303 characters who were not given descriptions were however included as potential question alternatives for the *Desc2Name* setting. Table 2 includes some basic statistics about the number of characters included per book.

3.2 The Character Descriptions

In total GANDALF contains 10,000 unique character descriptions of varying complexity. Each description is expressed in a short passage of natural text, spanning 1-2 sentences. These descriptions contain combinations of traits, events, and relationships, which together are meant to uniquely identify a character within its respective book universe. The annotator instructions for the creation of these descriptions are available in appendix C.

These character descriptions are all structured by what we refer to as, its level of *"referential complexity"*. The referential complexity is a means to describe the number of deductive steps required to understand a description. The relevant levels of referential complexity are defined in the following list. Examples of different referential complexities are available in Appendix 6, Table 1 displays basic

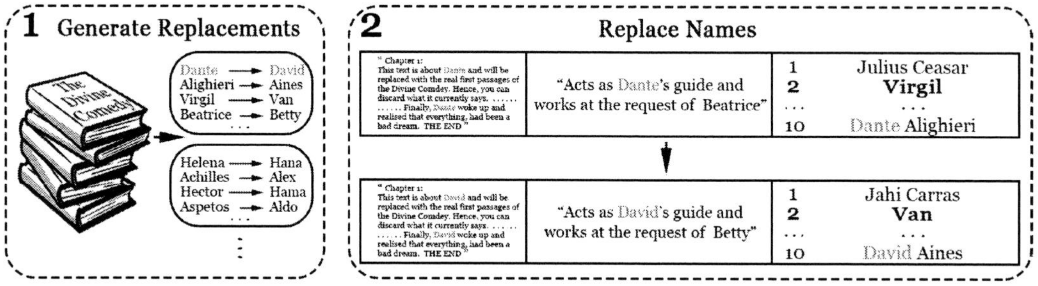

Figure 3: Illustration of the usage of the name-replacement schema included with GANDALF.

statistics for all descriptions, structured by their level of referential complexity.

Level 0: The character is described directly by its own name.

Level 1: The description is self-contained; it contains no references to other characters.

Level 2: The description contains a reference to at least one other character, by stating that character's name (Level 0).

Level 3: The description contains a reference to at least one other character, by providing a Level 1 description of that character

Level 4: The description contains a reference to at least one other character, by providing a Level 2 description of that character.

We stress that referential complexity does not necessarily correlate with the difficulty of a question. For example, the level 1 description *"The protagonist"*, is expected to be more difficult than the more concrete level 2 description *"The Dog of Dorothy"*. Instead, increasing the referential complexity is a simple way to generate more questions from a fixed set of descriptions which include reference to other characters (See section 4.1).

3.3 Name Replacement Schema

GANDALF incorporate a simple name-replacement schema, illustrated in Figure 3. This schema creates a per book lookup table of name replacements, for all unique *unambiguous name terms* of described characters in that book. Name replacements are assigned either randomly, or according to a heuristic. Similarly to Hutchinson et al. (2012) and Bonato et al. (2016), we find occurrences of all original names by exact matching, and do this for both the descriptions and books. Finally, all instances of these names are replaced by their newly assigned names. Further details are available in Appendix B.

3.4 Probing Variations

Due to the formulation of the character description recognition task, name replacement enables for straightforward probing variations without having to change the nature of the task. This is attractive since it allows for investigation of how model performance is affected by slightly altering the data while keeping both task formulation and model constant. By contrast, most existing probing tasks and datasets formulate probes as a separate classification or inference task, requiring a model to add an additional classifier specifically for the probe. Suggestions for future probing tasks are available in Section 7.1.

4 Creating the dataset

The creation of the GANDALF dataset is a process that in large is guided by avoiding copyright infringement (See section 7.3). Figure 4 along with the following list gives an overview of the creation process, upon which the following subsections describe each step in more detail.

1. Collect a large set of character essays for books available in the public domain.
2. Discard essays for characters that are not described directly by a name.
3. Manually extract descriptive traits, events, and relationships from the character essays.
4. Manually combine the extracted information into level 1 and level 2 character descriptions.
5. Use the already created descriptions to manually create level 3 and level 4 descriptions.

6. Generation *Name2Desc* and *Desc2Name* questions.

4.1 Collecting the data

At the initial step of creating GANDALF, we collected a large set of character essays from various online sources. To make the dataset free for redistribution, we only gathered essays corresponding to books that are currently available in the public domain. A full list of the sources used for character essays is available in appendix 5. Finally, all relevant books were downloaded from Project Gutenberg via the unofficial API[1].

4.2 Filtering the data

After the collection phase, all data was filtered to fit the following criteria: All characters must have at least one part of their full name suitable for name replacement, and each book must contain at least 10 characters. This entails that we discard all essays which do not explicitly refer to a single entity and whose name does not contain at least one unambiguous name term (See Appendix B). Examples of character essays discarded are thus: *"The narrator"*, *"Doctor Justice"*, and *"The Wilson twins"*.

4.3 Extracting character information

From the remaining character essays, annotators manually extracted sequences of text with descriptive character information. The annotators were instructed to find the perceived gender and text sequences containing at least one of the following: character traits, descriptive book events, or relation to another character.

4.4 Creating level 1 & level 2 descriptions

Using the extracted character information, annotators manually composed short uniquely identifiable level 1 and level 2 descriptions. Taking extra care to formulate descriptions that did not contain any of the respective characters' name terms. To determine the information required to identify a character, annotators cross-compared described characters within the same book. The annotators thus worked exclusively with the character essays.

4.5 Creating level 3 & level 4 descriptions

Level 3 and level 4 descriptions were manually created from the already created level 1 and level 2 descriptions. reformulating existing character

Figure 4: Illustration of the overall creation process of GANDALF.

[1] https://github.com/c-w/gutenberg

references in accordance with the definitions in section 3.2. This resulted in an additional 4,600 descriptions of 2,356 characters.

4.6 Generating Questions

The 10,000 character descriptions were used to generate two question sets: *Name2Desc* and *Desc2Name*. For *Desc2Name* the incorrect question alternatives were created by randomly selecting names or descriptions for other characters from the same book. This results in 10,000 *Name2Desc* questions and 10,000 *Desc2Name* questions.

4.7 Name Replacement

Finally, we include name-replaced versions of the two basic settings of the dataset, named *Name2Desc-Rep* and *Desc2Name-Rep*. These are created by shuffling the names among all characters from all books, controlling for first and last names. The name-replacement tables are hence generated by mapping each first name to another first name of a character from any book within GANDALF, and the same for last names.

5 Experiments

To the best of our knowledge, there has been no proposed method that is capable of handling naturally formulated questions along with the long-range format of GANDALF. We are therefore limited in what experiments we can perform without proposing a new solution, which is deliberately not within the scope of this paper. Therefore, our experiments can be interpreted more as testing the robustness of our dataset, while they also demonstrate that the problem is non-trivial.

All three of our approaches are based on selecting the alternative which maximizes the probability of the description being stated after the character name. The first method is a traditional word-based statistical method, and the other two utilize modern language models. The statistical model acts as a simple information-retrieval baseline, and a way to measure potential noise that could be introduced during name replacement. The language model approaches are intended as an attempt to utilize off-the-shelf NLU technology to solve the problem both the intended way, and without the book texts.

Finally, we saw no increase in performance after fine-tuning the language models, the reported results are hence attained from directly applying pre-trained checkpoints.[2] These experiments therefore include all the questions of GANDALF as test data.

5.1 BoW: TF-IDF

As a simple information-retrieval baseline we perform a TF-IDF (Salton and McGill, 1986) search over all paragraphs in a target book, for all description-queries. This entails that we gather TF-IDF-statistics for each book text and description-query, constructing sparse TF-IDF representations for all book paragraphs, as for all queries. Finally, we compare the cosine similarity between each description-query and each paragraph, and select the query with the highest similarity to any paragraph.

5.2 Causal Language Model: Transformer-XL

Transformer-XL (Dai et al., 2019) is one of the few transformer-based language models without a fixed input size, making it a viable contender for GANDALF. We are hence able to state the full book text as context, prior to posing the different queries. This is achieved by first computing the residual memory for the complete book text, and then providing that alongside every description-query.

5.3 Causal Language Model: GPT-2

GPT-2 (Radford et al., 2019) has a fixed input size of 1,024 tokens, making it unable to comprehend the full book texts. However, it has been trained on a vastly large dataset of text scraped from the internet. This makes it a suitable model for measuring potential data leakage and other potential lexical artifacts which might make the questions trivial by themselves. Especially, since it is highly likely that GPT-2 has been trained on both the books and the original character essays which are used to create GANDALF.

6 Results

Table 3 displays the accuracy of the three different baselines, for the 4 different standard versions of GANDALF. Although, neither of the methods produces any good results and lie very close to the random baseline, the TF-IDF approach performed the best. Hence, table 4 is included, that show

[2]Checkpoints are taken from `https://huggingface.co/transformers/pretrained_models.html`

	Name2Desc	Desc2Name	Name2Desc-Rep	Desc2Name-Rep
Random	10.0	10.0	10.0	10.0
		Book + Query		
Transformer-XL	12.9	9.6	12.4	10.1
BoW + TF-IDF	**19.9**	**14.4**	**19.8**	**13.9**
		Query Only		
GPT-2	9.4	11.5	9.8	11.7
GPT-2 Medium	9.5	12.2	9.4	11.8
GPT-2 Large	10.5	12.4	10.5	12.0
GPT-2 XL	10.5	11.6	10.8	12.0

Table 3: Model accuracy on the four different versions of GANDALF.

	Level 1	Level 2	Level 3	Level 4
		BoW + TF-IDF		
Name2Desc	19.9	22.9	4.6	6.3
Desc2Name	21.6	20.9	17.4	19.7
Name2Desc-Rep 2	19.2	22.4	4.6	5.7
Desc2Name-Rep	20.3	20.7	17.2	19.5

Table 4: BoW + TF-IDF accuracy on the different levels, on all four different versions of GANDALF.

the per-level accuracy over the different referential complexities for TF-iDF.

6.1 Book + Query

Transformer-XL performs nearly on par with random, although there is a very slight improvement on both *Name2Desc* tasks, compared to both random and the query only approach. This lack of performance demonstrates that current long-range Transformers struggle with the book texts of GANDALF.

The TF-IDF-based approach displays a notable performance increase, achieving the best results in all settings. A notable difference of 5.5 and 5.9 points can be seen between *Name2Desc* and the *Desc2Name* counterpart. The results in table 4 clearly show that this difference is due to TF-IDF being incapable of handling level 3 and level 4 questions in the *Desc2Name* setting.

Finally, the difference between the normal and the name-replaced datasets, are for both methods near negligible. We stress that this is the ***desired*** result, as this indicates that most statistical properties remain intact through the alteration of name replacement. Hence allowing for the deployment of various renaming schema, as discussed in section 7.

6.2 Query Only

Turning to GPT-2, which discards all book texts, performance are again very close to the random baseline. Both *Desc2Name* sets do however see an increase of circa 2 points compared to *Name2Desc*, and results tend to increase by circa 1 percentage point going from smaller to larger models on all sets.

This small difference might be negligible, but it could also indicate that the *Name2Desc* setting is more prone to lexical artifacts, which makes an inductive guess better than random.

7 Future Work & Discussion

Systems specialized towards a single task attain poor generalization abilities, and hence demonstrate low levels of intelligence (Chollet, 2019). As AI researchers, our main interest is therefore not a method capable of **only** solving the character recognition task of GANDALF. Rather, our ultimate goal is methods capable of handling and generalizing over a wide range of tasks, domains, and modalities.

Current models perform well over the different tasks included in benchmarks such as GLUE and SuperGLUE, but they are yet capable of handling both long and short texts. Therefore, we think the time is right for extending our current evaluation benchmarks to include tasks covering large bodies of text. GANDALF with its potential extensions and probing tasks is hence our first contribution to such a set setup.

We note the relatively weak performance of the models tested in our experiments. It is probable that better performance can be attained using alternative techniques, such as the Dense Passage Retriever (Karpukhin et al., 2020) or Retrieval Augmented Generation (Lewis et al., 2020). We leave this for future work.

7.1 Extensions to GANDALF

Two straightforward types of probing variations that the GANDALF data enables is to study a model's sensitivity to gender and racial bias. In the case of gender bias, we can simply switch the gender of all names and study how this affects the performance. Another possibility is to replace *all* character names with male or female names. In the case of racial bias, we can replace character names with typical names of some specific demographic group.

It is also straightforward to include negated statements in the character description, enabling studies of models' sensitivity to negation (Ettinger, 2020). Such negated statements can be produced by simply selecting descriptions from other characters, possibly in the same book, and negating them ("*is not* the dog of Dorothy" or "*does not* act as Dante's guide").

7.2 Character Description Recognition

Although we are not personally interested in methods that only aim to solve GANDALF's character description recognition task, we recognize that others might be. We advise researchers wishing to pursue such solutions, to combine existing NLP methods utilized in data-driven literature studies. For example, extracting character networks (Labatut and Bost, 2019) would intuitively be useful for solving questions involving character relations. Additionally, certain rule-based heuristic might also prove useful, as it is likely that a character labeled as *"The Protagonist"* will have the highest frequency of occurrences throughout the book. Finally, we note that the work of (Zhang et al., 2019) focus specifically on automatically generating character descriptions from books (Unfortunately published without accompanying code).

7.3 Copyright Protection

To ensure that legalities do not interfere with scientific reproducibility, we stress the importance of having a freely distributable dataset. GANDALF only includes books that are available in the public domain, and facts are not covered by copyright protection. So while the original character essays themselves might be under copyright protection, the facts they express are not. Hence, both our collected set of books and our generated set of questions are free to be publicly distributed for future research.

8 Conclusion

This paper has introduced the GANDALF dataset, which constitutes a unique challenge for machine reading comprehension by requiring long-range retention capabilities while simultaneously being able to ignore irrelevant information. We have introduced the character description task with its two variations (Desc2Name and Name2Desc), and argued that this task formulation provides unique opportunities for probing variations without changing the nature of the task itself. We also provide a number of baseline results on the dataset using both simple and more advanced methods, and the results clearly demonstrate the challenging nature of the dataset.

We believe that this dataset and task provides a welcome addition to existing machine reading comprehension benchmarks, in particular at a time when we start to see superhuman performance on existing datasets, with an apparent risk of models starting to optimize for a specific dataset rather than for general reading comprehension abilities. The GANDALF dataset, by contrast, is extremely challenging with minimal risk of data leakage and consequently low risk of models cheating on the tasks.

References

Eneko Agirre, Daniel Cer, Mona Diab, and Aitor Gonzalez-Agirre. 2012. SemEval-2012 task 6: A pilot on semantic textual similarity. In **SEM 2012: The First Joint Conference on Lexical and Computational Semantics – Volume 1: Proceedings of the main conference and the shared task, and Volume 2: Proceedings of the Sixth International Workshop on Semantic Evaluation (SemEval 2012)*, pages 385–393, Montréal, Canada. Association for Computational Linguistics.

Ondrej Bajgar, Rudolf Kadlec, and Jan Kleindienst. 2016. Embracing data abundance: BookTest Dataset for Reading Comprehension. *arXiv:1610.00956 [cs]*. ArXiv: 1610.00956.

Satanjeev Banerjee and Alon Lavie. 2005. METEOR: An automatic metric for MT evaluation with improved correlation with human judgments. In *Proceedings of the ACL Workshop on Intrinsic and Extrinsic Evaluation Measures for Machine Translation and/or Summarization*, pages 65–72, Ann Arbor, Michigan. Association for Computational Linguistics.

Anthony Bonato, David Ryan D'Angelo, Ethan R. Elenberg, David F. Gleich, and Yangyang Hou. 2016. Mining and modeling character networks. In *Algorithms and Models for the Web Graph*, pages 100–114, Cham. Springer International Publishing.

Samuel R. Bowman and George E. Dahl. 2021. What Will it Take to Fix Benchmarking in Natural Language Understanding? *arXiv:2104.02145 [cs]*. ArXiv: 2104.02145.

François Chollet. 2019. On the measure of intelligence.

Zihang Dai, Zhilin Yang, Yiming Yang, Jaime Carbonell, Quoc Le, and Ruslan Salakhutdinov. 2019. Transformer-XL: Attentive language models beyond a fixed-length context. In *Proceedings of the 57th Annual Meeting of the Association for Computational Linguistics*, pages 2978–2988, Florence, Italy. Association for Computational Linguistics.

Aparna Elangovan, Jiayuan He, and Karin Verspoor. 2021. Memorization vs. Generalization : Quantifying Data Leakage in NLP Performance Evaluation. In *Proceedings of the 16th Conference of the European Chapter of the Association for Computational Linguistics: Main Volume*, pages 1325–1335, Online. Association for Computational Linguistics.

Allyson Ettinger. 2020. What BERT is not: Lessons from a new suite of psycholinguistic diagnostics for language models. *Transactions of the Association for Computational Linguistics*, 8:34–48.

Angela Fan, Yacine Jernite, Ethan Perez, David Grangier, Jason Weston, and Michael Auli. 2019. ELI5: Long Form Question Answering. In *Proceedings of the 57th Annual Meeting of the Association for Computational Linguistics*, pages 3558–3567, Florence, Italy. Association for Computational Linguistics.

Christiane Fellbaum. 1998. *WordNet: An Electronic Lexical Database*. Bradford Books.

Felix Hill, Antoine Bordes, Sumit Chopra, and Jason Weston. 2016. The Goldilocks Principle: Reading Children's Books with Explicit Memory Representations. *arXiv:1511.02301 [cs]*. ArXiv: 1511.02301.

Luyang Huang, Shuyang Cao, Nikolaus Parulian, Heng Ji, and Lu Wang. 2021. Efficient attentions for long document summarization. In *Proceedings of the 2021 Conference of the North American Chapter of the Association for Computational Linguistics: Human Language Technologies*, pages 1419–1436, Online. Association for Computational Linguistics.

Sterling Hutchinson, Vivek Datla, and M. Louwerse. 2012. Social networks are encoded in language. *Cognitive Science*, 34.

Mohit Iyyer, Varun Manjunatha, Anupam Guha, Yogarshi Vyas, Jordan Boyd-Graber, Hal Daumé, and Larry Davis. 2017. The Amazing Mysteries of the Gutter: Drawing Inferences Between Panels in Comic Book Narratives. In *2017 IEEE Conference on Computer Vision and Pattern Recognition (CVPR)*, pages 6478–6487. ISSN: 1063-6919.

Vladimir Karpukhin, Barlas Oguz, Sewon Min, Patrick Lewis, Ledell Wu, Sergey Edunov, Danqi Chen, and Wen-tau Yih. 2020. Dense passage retrieval for open-domain question answering. In *Proceedings of the 2020 Conference on Empirical Methods in Natural Language Processing (EMNLP)*, pages 6769–6781, Online. Association for Computational Linguistics.

Divyansh Kaushik and Zachary Chase Lipton. 2018. How Much Reading Does Reading Comprehension Require? A Critical Investigation of Popular Benchmarks. *EMNLP*.

Daniel Khashabi, Snigdha Chaturvedi, Michael Roth, Shyam Upadhyay, and Dan Roth. 2018. Looking beyond the surface: A challenge set for reading comprehension over multiple sentences. In *Proceedings of the 2018 Conference of the North American Chapter of the Association for Computational Linguistics: Human Language Technologies, Volume 1 (Long Papers)*, pages 252–262, New Orleans, Louisiana. Association for Computational Linguistics.

Kalpesh Krishna, Aurko Roy, and Mohit Iyyer. 2021. Hurdles to Progress in Long-form Question Answering. *arXiv:2103.06332 [cs]*. ArXiv: 2103.06332.

Vincent Labatut and Xavier Bost. 2019. Extraction and analysis of fictional character networks. *ACM Computing Surveys*, 52(5):1–40.

Guokun Lai, Qizhe Xie, Hanxiao Liu, Yiming Yang, and Eduard Hovy. 2017. RACE: Large-scale ReAding comprehension dataset from examinations. In *Proceedings of the 2017 Conference on Empirical Methods in Natural Language Processing*, pages 785–794, Copenhagen, Denmark. Association for Computational Linguistics.

Patrick Lewis, Ethan Perez, Aleksandra Piktus, Fabio Petroni, Vladimir Karpukhin, Naman Goyal, Heinrich Küttler, Mike Lewis, Wen-tau Yih, Tim Rocktäschel, Sebastian Riedel, and Douwe Kiela. 2020.

Retrieval-augmented generation for knowledge-intensive nlp tasks. In *Advances in Neural Information Processing Systems*, volume 33, pages 9459–9474. Curran Associates, Inc.

Yichan Liang, Jianheng Li, and Jian Yin. 2019. A new multi-choice reading comprehension dataset for curriculum learning. In *Proceedings of The Eleventh Asian Conference on Machine Learning*, volume 101 of *Proceedings of Machine Learning Research*, pages 742–757, Nagoya, Japan. PMLR.

Todor Mihaylov, Peter Clark, Tushar Khot, and Ashish Sabharwal. 2018. Can a suit of armor conduct electricity? a new dataset for open book question answering. In *EMNLP*.

Yixin Nie, Adina Williams, Emily Dinan, Mohit Bansal, Jason Weston, and Douwe Kiela. 2020. Adversarial NLI: A new benchmark for natural language understanding. In *Proceedings of the 58th Annual Meeting of the Association for Computational Linguistics*, pages 4885–4901, Online. Association for Computational Linguistics.

Timothy Niven and Hung-Yu Kao. 2019. Probing neural network comprehension of natural language arguments. In *Proceedings of the 57th Annual Meeting of the Association for Computational Linguistics*, pages 4658–4664, Florence, Italy. Association for Computational Linguistics.

Kishore Papineni, Salim Roukos, Todd Ward, and Wei-Jing Zhu. 2002. Bleu: a method for automatic evaluation of machine translation. In *Proceedings of the 40th Annual Meeting of the Association for Computational Linguistics*, pages 311–318, Philadelphia, Pennsylvania, USA. Association for Computational Linguistics.

Amandalynne Paullada, Inioluwa Deborah Raji, Emily M. Bender, Emily Denton, and Alex Hanna. 2020. Data and its (dis)contents: A survey of dataset development and use in machine learning research. *arXiv:2012.05345 [cs]*. ArXiv: 2012.05345.

Alec Radford, Jeff Wu, Rewon Child, David Luan, Dario Amodei, and Ilya Sutskever. 2019. Language models are unsupervised multitask learners.

Tomáš Koˇ ciský, Jonathan Schwarz, Phil Blunsom, Chris Dyer, Karl Moritz Hermann, Gábor Melis, and Edward Grefenstette. 2018. The NarrativeQA reading comprehension challenge. *Transactions of the Association for Computational Linguistics*, TBD:TBD.

Gerard Salton and Michael J McGill. 1986. Introduction to modern information retrieval.

Daniel Smith, Philip Schlaepfer, Katie Major, Mark Dyble, Abigail Page, James Thompson, Nikhil Chaudhary, Gul Deniz Salali, Ruth Mace, Leonora Astete, Marilyn Ngales, Lucio Vinicius, and Andrea Migliano. 2017. Cooperation and the evolution of hunter-gatherer storytelling. *Nature Communications*, 8.

Aarne Talman, Anssi Yli-Jyrä, and Jörg Tiedemann. 2019. Sentence embeddings in nli with iterative refinement encoders. *Natural Language Engineering*, 25:467–482.

James Thorne, Majid Yazdani, Marzieh Saeidi, Fabrizio Silvestri, Sebastian Riedel, and Alon Halevy. 2021. Database reasoning over text. In *Proceedings of the 59th Annual Meeting of the Association for Computational Linguistics and the 11th International Joint Conference on Natural Language Processing (Volume 1: Long Papers)*, pages 3091–3104, Online. Association for Computational Linguistics.

Masatoshi Tsuchiya. 2018. Performance impact caused by hidden bias of training data for recognizing textual entailment. In *Proceedings of the Eleventh International Conference on Language Resources and Evaluation (LREC-2018)*, Miyazaki, Japan. European Languages Resources Association (ELRA).

Michael O. Tunnell and James S. Jacobs. 1989. Using "real" books: Research findings on literature based reading instruction. *The Reading Teacher*, 42(7):470–477.

Ashish Vaswani, Noam Shazeer, Niki Parmar, Jakob Uszkoreit, Llion Jones, Aidan N Gomez, Ł ukasz Kaiser, and Illia Polosukhin. 2017. Attention is all you need. In *Advances in Neural Information Processing Systems*, volume 30. Curran Associates, Inc.

Alex Wang, Yada Pruksachatkun, Nikita Nangia, Amanpreet Singh, Julian Michael, Felix Hill, Omer Levy, and Samuel Bowman. 2019. Superglue: A stickier benchmark for general-purpose language understanding systems. In *Advances in Neural Information Processing Systems*, volume 32, pages 3266–3280. Curran Associates, Inc.

Alex Wang, Amanpreet Singh, Julian Michael, Felix Hill, Omer Levy, and Samuel Bowman. 2018. GLUE: A multi-task benchmark and analysis platform for natural language understanding. In *Proceedings of the 2018 EMNLP Workshop BlackboxNLP: Analyzing and Interpreting Neural Networks for NLP*, pages 353–355, Brussels, Belgium. Association for Computational Linguistics.

Vikas Yadav, Steven Bethard, and Mihai Surdeanu. 2019. Alignment over heterogeneous embeddings for question answering. In *Proceedings of the 2019 Conference of the North American Chapter of the Association for Computational Linguistics: Human Language Technologies, Volume 1 (Long and Short Papers)*, pages 2681–2691, Minneapolis, Minnesota. Association for Computational Linguistics.

Jianfei Yu and Jing Jiang. 2016. Learning sentence embeddings with auxiliary tasks for cross-domain sentiment classification. In *Proceedings of the 2016 Conference on Empirical Methods in Natural Language Processing*, pages 236–246, Austin, Texas. Association for Computational Linguistics.

Weiwei Zhang, Jackie Chi Kit Cheung, and Joel Oren. 2019. Generating character descriptions for automatic summarization of fiction. *Proceedings of the AAAI Conference on Artificial Intelligence*, 33(01):7476–7483.

https://www.cliffsnotes.com/
https://www.coursehero.com/
https://www.gradesaver.com/
https://www.sparknotes.com/

Table 5: All the sources used for gathering the character essays used to create GANDALF.

A Sources for Character Essays

Table 5 contains the four sites from which character essays were collected.

B Replacement of names

To mitigate the amount of noise introduced to the book texts during name replacement, we aim to only replace terms within character names which unambiguously refer to a name. A character referred to as *"Doctor Emily Bender"*, would therefore include the unambiguous name terms *"Emily"* and *"Bender"*.

For all GANDALF characters annotators selected their unambiguous name terms, and classified them as first or last names. This was achieved by a combination of manual inspection and querying of WordNet (Fellbaum, 1998) for each name term. Ultimately annotators were allowed to overrule the fact that Wordnet deemed a word ambiguous, if the annotator suspected the other word meanings to be highly unlikely to occur within the respective book. For example the word *"Teta"* also have the following Wordnet definition: *"a member of the large western branch of Sioux people which was made up of several groups that lived on the plains"*

For the finding of name occurrences, we used direct string matching against if a name term occurred as an isolated word, or in combination with a suffix such as *'s*. Admittedly, this does not handle a lot of the many potential corner cases. For example it does not handle the initials of a name, if the name is spelled differently during a stuttering conversations, or if the original name takes part in a word-pun. These name replacements therefore contribute to a certain level of noise to the data.

However, it is our belief that these corner cases formulate the exception rather than the rule. Even when a character is being referred to by a nickname the majority of the time, human readers easily connect the two names to the same entity. Intuitively, we therefore believe that a theoretically super intelligent system, could on many occasions be able to figure out what name replacements went wrong.

C Annotator Instructions

The annotators were tasked to work on a per-book basis, and work from the assumption that the collected character essays contained all essential information required to make a distinguishable character description. This assumption does not necessarily always hold, but it relieves the annotators from having to read the actual book.

First the annotators were asked to extract character traits and descriptions from the collected character essays of a single book. After this information had been extracted, they were then tasked to puzzle together the extracted traits into short descriptions, which had to *uniquely* identify the characters within selected character alternatives from that book. The annotators were told to discards any character that ended up with ambiguous descriptions.

D Character Descriptions

Table 6 contains examples of character descriptions of for different referential complexity levels.

E Books

Table 7 lists all 177 book titles contained within the GANDALF dataset.

Ref Complexity	Book Title	Character Name	Description
1	A tale of Two cities	Roger Cly	An English spy who fakes his death.
1	A tale of Two cities	Sydney Carton	Has fallen into a life of alcoholism.
1	Oliver Twist	Oliver Twist	Is the protagonist of the story.
1	Oliver Twist	Mrs. Maylie	A lady, who is very dignified and stately, despite her old age.
1	Moby Dick	Starbuck	Thinly built Quaker who displays a pragmatic manner.
1	Moby Dick	Stubb	The second mate of the Pequod.
2	Silas Marner	Eppie	The catalyst who integrates Silas into Raveloe.
2	Silas Marner	Godfrey Cass	Secretly married to Molly Farren.
2	Crime and punishment	Katerina	Consumptive wife of Marmeladov.
2	Crime and punishment	Andrei Lebezyatnikov	Grudging roommate of Luzhin.
2	The brother's Karamazov	Dmitri Karamazov	Eldest son of Fyodor by his first wife.
2	The brother's Karamazov	Mussyalovich	A Polish officer who betrays Grushenka.
3	Call of the wild	Spitz	Experienced, clever, and fears and hates the protagonist.
3	Call of the wild	Hans	A partner of the person who does not fear the wild because he knows how to survive it.
3	My Antonia	Jan Cuzak	The shy son of the person who stays in the country, remarries and has many children.
3	My Antonia	Joe	Patient with his mother-in-law.
3	The Dubliners	Mary Jane	Cousin to the protagonist in "The Dead".
3	The Dubliners	Gallaher	Friend to the character who daydreams while working a desk job in "A Little Cloud".
4	Winesburg, Ohio	Mook	The only person who the son of Ebenezer is comfortable talking to.
4	Winesburg, Ohio	Katherine Bentley	David Hardy's gradfather's wife.
4	The Tenant of Wildfell hall	Mr Leighton	Preacher at the church where Arthur's wife attends.
4	The Tenant of Wildfell hall	Mrs. Wilson	Mother to the person who spreads rumors about Helen.
4	Martin Chuzzlewit	Ruth Pinch	Sister of the very likable, ex-student who works for Mr Pecksniff.
4	Martin Chuzzlewit	Mark Tapley	Friend and Valet of the stubborn architectural student of Mr Pecksniff.

Table 6: Example descriptions of varying referential complexity.

A connecticut yankee in king arthur's court	A hero of our time	A journal of the plague year
A portrait of the artist as a young man	A midsummer night's dream	A passage to india
A room with a view	A study in scarlet	A tale of two cities
A vindication of the rights of woman	Adam bede	Adventures of huckleberry finn
An essay on the principle of population	American notes	An ideal husband
Anna karenina	Anne of green gables	Antony and cleopatra
Barnaby rudge	Black beauty	Candide
Charlotte temple	Common sense	Coriolanus
Cranford	Crime and punishment	Daniel deronda
David copperfield	Demian	Desert gold
Dialogues concerning natural religion	Dombey and son	Don juan
Dracula	Dubliners	Edgar huntly
Emma	Ethan frome	Far from the madding crowd
For the term of his natural life	Frankenstein	Germinal
Gilgamesh	Gulliver's travels	Hard times
He knew he was right	Henry iv, part 1	Henry v
Henry vi, part 1	Henry vi, part 2	Henry vi, part 3
Henry viii	History of tom jones, a foundling	Howards end
In our time	Jane eyre	Jude the obscure
Kidnapped	King henry iv, part 2	Lady audley's secret
Lady susan	Lady windermere's fan	Little brother
Little dorrit	Little women	Lord jim
Madame bovary	Maggie: a girl of the streets	Main street
Major barbara	Mansfield park	Martin chuzzlewit
Mary barton	Meditations	Middlemarch
Moby dick	Mrs dalloway	Much ado about nothing
My antonia	An American Slave	North and south
O pioneers!	Oliver twist	On the origin of species
Orlando	Othello	Our mutual friend
Pamela, or virtue rewarded	Peter pan	Ragged dick
Richard ii	Richard iii	Romeo and juliet
Roughing it	Second treatise of government	Siddhartha
Silas marner	Sister carrie	Sons and lovers
Summer	Swann's way	Tarzan of the apes
The adventures of sherlock holmes	The adventures of tom sawyer	The aeneid
The age of innocence	The ambassadors	The american
The autobiography of benjamin franklin	The awakening	The beautiful and damned
The brothers karamazov	The call of the wild	The canterville ghost
The castle of otranto	The country of the pointed firs	The duchess of malfi
The flowers of evil	The frogs	The gilded age
The history of the peloponnesian war	The golden asse	The good soldier
The hound of the baskervilles	The house of mirth	The house of the seven gables
The hunchback of notre dame	The idiot	The jew of malta
The jungle	The jungle book	The king in yellow
The man of the forest	The mayor of casterbridge	The mill on the floss
The moonstone	The mysteries of udolpho	The mysterious affair at styles
The odyssey	The orkneyinga saga	The pickwick papers
The private memoirs of a justified sinner	The portrait of a lady — volume 1	The praise of folly
The queen of spades	The republic	The scarlet pimpernel
The school for scandal	The secret agent	The sorrows of young werther
The souls of black folk	The spanish tragedy	The subjection of women
The tenant of wildfell hall	The trial	The valley of fear
The vicar of wakefield	The war of the worlds	The woman in white
This side of paradise	Three men in a boat	Timon of athens
Titus andronicus	To the lighthouse	Troilus and cressida
Troilus and criseyde	Twelfth night	Typee
Ulysses	Uncle tom's cabin	Vanity fair
Villette	War and peace	White fang
Winesburg, ohio	Women in love	Wuthering heights

Table 7: All the 177 book titles contained within GANDALF.

Investigating Post-pretraining Representation Alignment for Cross-Lingual Question Answering

Fahim Faisal, Antonios Anastasopoulos
Department of Computer Science, George Mason University
{ffaisal,antonis}@gmu.edu

Abstract

Human knowledge is collectively encoded in the roughly 6500 languages spoken around the world, but it is not distributed equally across languages. Hence, for information-seeking question answering (QA) systems to adequately serve speakers of all languages, they need to operate cross-lingually. In this work we investigate the capabilities of multilingually pre-trained language models on cross-lingual QA. We find that explicitly aligning the representations across languages with a post-hoc fine-tuning step generally leads to improved performance. We additionally investigate the effect of data size as well as the language choice in this fine-tuning step, also releasing a dataset for evaluating cross-lingual QA systems.[1]

1 Introduction

Information seeking question answering, where a user asks a question to get a related passage or short text as answer, is a widely studied area (Clark et al., 2020; Kwiatkowski et al., 2019; Yang et al., 2015, *inter alia*)[2] that has been successfully deployed in user-facing applications such as conversational assistants (Gao et al., 2018). For example, an English computer science student that asks Apple Siri, Amazon Alexa, or Google Assistant the question "Where did Joan Clarke work?"[3] will receive the answer "Bletchley Park", an answer based on the English Wikipedia entry for Joan Clarke automatically retrieved by the system.

Now, consider another student, this time based in Greece or Bangladesh, asking effectively the same question, "Πού δούλευε η Joane Clarke;" or "Joane Clarke কোথায় কাজ করত?", but this time in their native language Greek or Bengali. However, as of July 2021, there is no Wikipedia article for Joane Clarke in Greek or in Bengali.[4] For the QA system to adequately serve these students, it will need to function in a cross-lingual setting, retrieving the English (or any of the other available languages) article and producing an answer given the question in a different language (Asai et al., 2021). Throughout this paper we will refer to a setting where the question and the context are in different languages as "cross-lingual" QA.

Multilingually-pretrained language models such as mBERT (Devlin et al., 2019) or XLM-R (Conneau et al., 2020) are widely used as the base of modern QA systems and have shown promise for performing the task in zero-shot (Artetxe et al., 2020) or few-shot manner (Debnath et al., 2021) as well as in cross-lingual settings (Asai et al., 2021). At the same time, these models are not without drawbacks; their pre-training objectives did not explicitly require that their representations *align* across languages for semantically similar words/phrases/sentences, with adverse effects especially for languages written in scripts other than the Latin one (Muller et al., 2020). A recent line of work (Cao et al., 2020; Zhao et al., 2021; Kulshreshtha et al., 2020; Huang et al., 2021) in fact shows improvements on a variety of natural language tasks by explicitly or implicitly aligning the models' representations across languages leveraging parallel data.

In this work, we explore the effect of such representation alignment techniques on the performance of QA systems in cross-lingual settings, concluding that they can be very beneficial. Our contributions can be summarized as follows:

1. We augment the TyDi-QA dataset (Clark et al., 2020) to study cross-lingual QA settings, using

[1] Code and dataset are publicly available here: https://github.com/ffaisal93/aligned_qa

[2] See (Rogers et al., 2021) for a thorough survey of the field.

[3] Joan Clarke was the only female computer scientist at Bletchley Park during the Second World War. Details: https://en.wikipedia.org/wiki/Joan_Clarke

[4] See (Jiang et al., 2020) for a visualization of the different Wikipedia sizes across languages (Figure 1) and the distribution of informative facts across languages (Figure 5).

Proceedings of the 3rd Workshop on Machine Reading for Question Answering , pages 133–148
Nov 10th, 2021 ©2021 Association for Computational Linguistics

both synthetic and newly-collected human translations.
2. We show that alignment-based fine-tuning of pretrained language models, along with data augmentation of the training data leads to improvements of 21.1% on average across TyDi-QA primary tasks in cross-lingual settings.
3. We perform thorough analyses to find strategies for selecting languages and training data for this multilingual alignment fine-tuning step.

2 Cross-lingual TyDi-QA dataset

To effectively study the cross-lingual capabilities of extractive QA systems, we construct a dataset with questions and potential contexts in different languages. We base our cross-lingual QA dataset on the TyDi-QA dataset (Clark et al., 2020). TyDi-QA dataset covers 11 languages with 204k question-answer pairs. Unlike other multilingual datasets like MLQA (Lewis et al., 2020) and XQuAD (Artetxe et al., 2020), TyDi-QA dataset is collected from native speakers without the aid of translation.

We select 5 typologically diverse language: Bengali, Korean, Arabic, Swahili, and English from TyDi-QA dataset for all of our experiments. Similar to other TyDi-QA-derivative datasets we use the publicly available development set as our test set, and sample a few examples from the training data to build a custom development set (these are examples are discarded from the training set). We will refer to this (original) dataset as TyDi-QA-`mono` to denote that all training/test instances are in a monolingual setting. We augment the dataset both automatically by generating translations of questions and by collecting human-created translations for some test sets. We describe these two datasets below:

Synthetic Translations We create a cross-lingually augmented version of our training set in two ways. First, we augment the English portion by automatically translating English questions to the other four languages ($Q_{en} \xrightarrow{\texttt{translate}} Q_{ar,sw,ko,bn}$), keeping the context (and answers) in English. Similarly, we augment the Bengali, Swahili, Korean, and Arabic portions of the dataset by translating their questions to english ($Q_{ar,sw,ko,bn} \xrightarrow{\texttt{translate}} Q_{en}$), still keeping the context and answers in the original language.[5] We will refer to this version of the dataset as TyDi-QA+`aug`. For all translations we use the Google Translate API[6] but we will make them publicly available to ensure the reproducibility of our experiments. The same process is applied to our custom development and test sets.

Human Translations In addition to machine generated translations, we asked native Bengali and Swahili speakers[7] who are also fluent in English to record English translations of the Bengali and Swahili test set questions. The annotators were shown the original Bengali/Swahili questions, then asked to translate these questions to English and recorded. The process is similar to the one used by Faisal et al. (2021) in creating the SD-QA dataset. We then transcribed these recordings using the Google ASR (automatic speech recognition) API.[8]

This allows us to evaluate the models in a more realistic scenario (similar to SD-QA, but now in a cross-lingual setting): a speaker provides an *oral* query to the model, which has to first transcribe the question to be ran through the QA system. This dataset was collected as part of the original SD-QA (Faisal et al., 2021) data collection process. We refer SD-QA dataset (Faisal et al., 2021) for detailed annotation process and data statistics.

3 Alignment-based fine-tuning

Language models like mBERT and XLM-R are trained without the inclusion of any parallel data. Cao et al. (2020) use a small amount of parallel data to align the representations of similar words across different languages, an approach that leads to improvements in cross-lingual inference tasks.

This method relies on the availability of k parallel corpora: $c_1, c_2, ...c_k$ where each corpus $c_{(l_s,l_t)} = (\mathbf{s}_1, \mathbf{t}_1), ...(\mathbf{s}_n, \mathbf{t}_n)$ is a set of parallel sentences in the source-target (l_s, l_t) languages. Using any word alignment technique, we can obtain word-level alignments $\alpha(\mathbf{s}, \mathbf{t}) = (p_1, q_1)....(p_m, q_m)$ for each sentence pair, such that for each (p, q) pair, word s_p of source sentence **s** is translated to word t_q in target sentence **t**.

We can devise an objective function that minimizes the distance of the contextualized embeddings of aligned words, by penalizing the distance of their representations. Denoting with $f_\phi(s_i)$ the

[5]While English is not always the best pivot language for cross-lingual transfer (Anastasopoulos and Neubig, 2020, *inter alia*), in this case it is the speakers' most likely second language.

[6]`https://cloud.google.com/translate`

[7]The annotators were native speakers of the two languages residing in Bangladesh and Kenya.

[8]`https://cloud.google.com/speech-to-text`

contextual embedding of word in position i for sentence $\mathbf{s}$ given by a model parameterized by ϕ, we get

$$L(c_{(l_s,l_t)}, f_\phi) = \sum_{(\mathbf{s},\mathbf{t})\in c_{(l_s,l_t)}} \sum_{(p,q)\in\alpha(\mathbf{s},\mathbf{t})} \|f_\phi(s_p) - f_\phi(t_q)\|_2^2$$

This fine-tuning process runs the risk of leading the encoder's parameters too far from their initial values ϕ_0, which could lead to catastrophic forgetting (French, 1999; Ratcliff, 1990; McCloskey and Cohen, 1989). Hence, following Cao et al. (2020) we additionally use a regularization metric to penalize the excessive drifting from the initial encoder state ϕ_0 for each of the languages.

$$R(c_{(l_s,l_t)}, f_\phi) = \sum_{\mathbf{s},\mathbf{t}\in c_{(l_s,l_t)}} (\sum_{i=1}^{|\mathbf{s}|} \|f_\phi(s_i) - f_{\phi_0}(s_i)\|_2^2 + \sum_{i=1}^{|\mathbf{t}|} \|f_\phi(t_i) - f_{\phi_0}(t_i)\|_2^2).$$

The final objective is simply the sum of the two components, similar to the approaches for retrofitting static embeddings (Faruqui et al., 2015):

$$\mathbf{min}_\phi \sum_{v=1}^{k} L(c_v, f_\phi) + R(c_v, f_\phi)$$

4 Experimental Setup

Model and Baselines Our extractive QA model architecture is similar to Alberti et al. (2019). In this implementation, both the question and the context are encoded to contextual representations using pre-trained language models such as BERT, and a dedicated classification head produces answer depending on the two types of tasks: 1) the index of the passage answering the questions or Null (if no such answer exist) for Passage selection task. 2) a Yes/No answer or the answer span using these representations or Null for Minimal answer span task.

We train baseline models using both TyDi-QA−mono and TyDi-QA+aug training datasets. All models are trained multilingually, training using all languages jointly. We report results on the two TyDi-QA primary tasks, passage selection (given a question and a number of candidate passages, this task is to return the index of the passage containing the answer) and minimal answer selection (a question and a number of passages are given; the task is to return the start and end byte of a short text span containing the answer).

We preform experiments with both mBERT and XLM-R. Our baselines use the pre-trained models, fine-tuned as above on the QA task (without any intermediate alignment-based fine-tuning). Our models, in turn, first perform alignment-based fine-tuning on the pre-trained models, and then train them on the QA task.

Alignment-Based fine-tuning Due to the lack of n-way parallel corpora, all parallel corpora we use have English as one of the two languages. We obtain word-level alignments using AWESOME-ALIGN (Dou and Neubig, 2021). We use data from WikiMatrix (Schwenk et al., 2021) , Wikimedia (Tiedemann, 2012) and CC-aligned (El-Kishky et al., 2020) to prepare various versions of our parallel corpus. The size of these data varies from 260k to less than 1k for each language based on experiment type. To study the effect of using different language samples and data sizes, we experiment with different models (summarized in Table 1):

- CAO-HIGH: this is the mBERT model provided by Cao et al. (2020), originally fine-tuned on English-X parallel data for five high resource languages: Bulgarian, German, Greek, Spanish, and French, using between 10 to 260 thousand parallel sentences in each pair.
- ZHAO-LOW: this mBERT trained model is from the experiments done by (Zhao et al., 2021). The authors trained different variations of aligned models based on the training language similarity level with English (measured cosine-distance using mBERT). The ZHAO-LOW is trained on 9 language-English parallel corpus having low to medium similarity level with English. These languages are from originally three main language families: 1. Austronesian, 2. Germanic , 3. Indo-Aryan
- ZHAO-(LOW+HIGH): Like ZHAO-LOW, this model is also provided by (Zhao et al., 2021) and is trained on XLM-R. The training languages used here are from all five language families: 1. Austronesian, 2. Germanic , 3. Indo-Aryan 4. Romance, and 5. Uralic to maintain a balance in terms of the similarity level with English.

Beyond these models, we also explore the following settings:

- TYDI-L: we use 80 to 260k parallel sentences only between English and the languages in our

Model name	Description	Languages	Parallel Data (per lang.)	Base Model mBERT	XLM-R
CAO-HIGH	from (Cao et al., 2020)	eng–{bul,deu,ell,esp,fra}	250k	✓	
ZHAO-LOW	from (Zhao et al., 2021)	eng–{hin,ind,jav,tgl,mar,urd, afr,msa,ben}	100k	✓	
ZHAO-(LOW+HIGH)	from (Zhao et al., 2021)	eng–{deu,por,nld,ind,ita,fra, spa,hun,afr,msa,tgl,jav,ben, mar,est,hin,urd,fin}	100k		✓
TYDI-L	ours: focus on TyDi-QA languages	eng–{ara,ben,swa,kor}	80–469k	✓	✓
TYDI-M			60k	✓	✓
TYDI-S			10k	✓	✓
111-S	ours: using 111 eng-X corpora	See Appendix B	max 1k	✓	✓
111-L			max 5k	✓	✓

Table 1: Details on the multilingual aligned models used in this study.

downstream task (Arabic, Bengali, Swahili, and Korean) to finetune both an mBERT and an XML-R model.

- TYDI-M: same as above, but we only use 60k parallel sentences for each language pair.
- TYDI-S: same as above, but we only use 10k parallel sentences for each language pair.
- 111-L: we use up to 5k parallel sentences between English and 111 languages to finetune both an mBERT and an XML-R model.
- 111-S: same as above, but we use a maximum of 1k parallel sentences per language pair.

QA model fine-tuning After the first step, we perform "task-tuning," training models on the two datasets (TyDi-QA-mono and TyDi-QA+aug) with the encoder initialized with the alignment-based fine-tuned checkpoints.

5 Results and evaluation

5.1 Evaluation on Synthetic Dataset

In Tables 2 and 3, we report the TyDi-QA primary task results (passage selection and minimal answer) on our cross-lingual custom test sets (see Appendix A for similarly detailed results on the development set). TyDi-QA uses F1 score as evaluation matric. Here we report (question, context) language-pairwise scores. The main takeaway is that both data augmentation and alignment-based fine-tuning lead to general improvements. We delve deeper into our analyses below.

Effect of cross-lingual training dataset In all cases, we observe that using the synthetic cross-lingual dataset for training (i.e. TyDi-QA+aug) with questions in a different language than the context significantly improves the performance on the cross-lingual QA. For the passage selection task the improvement is between 2 and 10 percentage points on average for either mBERT and XLM-R, while the gains are on average larger for the minimal answer task, ranging between 6 and 15 percentage points on average. Since the benefit of using these training data is clear, we use it for all following experiments.

mBERT vs XLM-R Our initial hypothesis was that XLM-R would be in general better than mBERT, since it (a) has been trained on more data, and (b) it was pre-trained for longer using the settings of the more-robust RoBERTa (Liu et al., 2019). However, our expectation is not confirmed by the results.

Even without any alignment-based fine-tuning, the performance of the initial checkpoints of the models when task-tuned monolingually is largely comparable. When the context is non-English (Q_{en}, C_{xx}), XLM-R is slightly better (c.f. average performances of 54.4 (mBERT) and 55.5 (XLM-R) for passage selection and 45.6 to 42.8 for the minimal answer task). When the context is English and the question is in another language, though, mBERT performs better (c.f. 48.0 to 45.5 and 28.9 to 25.6 for the two tasks).

However, XLM-R benefits a lot more from task-tuning with the synthetically augmented data (TyDi-QA-+AUG), in some cases improving by up to 15 percentage points on average (e.g. in minimal answer for (Q_{xx}, C_{en}), while mBERT only improves by up to 8 percentage points. As a result, the best performing baselines without alignment fine-tuning are XLM-R models.

Following alignment-based fine-tuning and task-

Model	Tr. Data	Q_{en}, C_{ar}	Q_{en}, C_{bn}	Q_{en}, C_{sw}	Q_{en}, C_{ko}	avg	Q_{ar}, C_{en}	Q_{bn}, C_{en}	Q_{sw}, C_{en}	Q_{ko}, C_{en}	avg
Baselines:											
MBERT	mono	76.4	43.0	60.9	37.3	54.4	51.8	43.3	46.9	49.8	48.0
MBERT	+aug	80.3	51.1	64.1	47.6	60.8	51.8	49.6	52.1	50.0	50.9
XLM-R	mono	78.3	46.6	61.8	35.3	55.5	47.6	44.6	38.7	51.3	45.5
XLM-R	+aug	81.1	56.4	64.3	50.1	**63.0**	56.1	55.0	55.3	56.6	55.7
mBERT +Alignment FT:											
+CAO-HIGH	+aug	78.6 (✗)	49.4 (✗)	61.2 (✗)	44.6 (✗)	58.4	51.4 (✗)	49.6 (✗)	51.7 (✗)	51.1 (✗)	50.9
+ZHAO-LOW	+aug	79.2 (✗)	53.4 (✓)	62.1 (✗)	48.5 (✗)	60.8	53.2 (✗)	48.1 (✓)	51.4 (✗)	51.4 (✗)	51.0
+TYDI-L	+aug	81.2 (✓)	52.1 (✓)	**65.2** (✓)*	49.8 (✓)	62.1	53.2 (✓)	52.5 (✓)	53.5 (✓)	52.9 (✓)	53.0
+111-S	+aug	79.4 (✓)	54.7 (✓)	64.2 (✓)	47.9 (✓)	61.6	52.5 (✓)	50.0 (✓)	50.5 (✓)	51.7 (✓)	51.2
+111-L	+aug	80.3 (✓)	49.6 (✓)	63.9 (✓)	47.2 (✓)	60.2	52.8 (✓)	48.4 (✓)	49.2 (✓)	48.7 (✓)	49.8
XLM-R +Alignment FT:											
+ZHAO-(LOW+HIGH)	+aug	80.7 (✗)	51.0 (✓)	63.8 (✗)	47.9 (✗)	60.9	57.0 (✗)	55.5 (✓)	55.1 (✗)	56.1 (✗)	55.9
+TYDI-L	+aug	81.0 (✓)	50.5 (✓)	62.2 (✓)	50.2 (✓)	61.0	**57.7** (✓)*	55.7 (✓)	**55.9** (✓)*	56.5 (✓)	**56.5**
+111-S	+aug	80.4 (✓)	**56.8** (✓)*	61.7 (✓)	50.5 (✓)	62.3	57.3 (✓)	55.4 (✓)	54.9 (✓)	**56.7** (✓)	56.1
+111-L	+aug	**81.3** (✓)	52.7 (✓)	62.4 (✓)	**51.5** (✓)*	62.0	57.6 (✓)	**56.1** (✓)*	54.4 (✓)	56.0 (✓)	56.0

Table 2: Cross-lingual passage selection results (test set). ✓/✗: the language is/isn't included in the finetuning mix. *:denotes statistically significant better system than the corresponding baseline with $p < 0.05$.

Model	Tr. Data	Q_{en}, C_{ar}	Q_{en}, C_{bn}	Q_{en}, C_{sw}	Q_{en}, C_{ko}	avg	Q_{ar}, C_{en}	Q_{bn}, C_{en}	Q_{sw}, C_{en}	Q_{ko}, C_{en}	avg
Baselines:											
MBERT	mono	61.3	32.0	50.3	27.4	42.8	38.0	20.9	25.2	31.5	28.9
MBERT	+aug	68.9	42.4	53.4	35.7	50.1	36.4	33.0	33.9	34.7	34.5
XLM-R	mono	65.8	36.3	51.9	28.6	45.6	29.2	26.2	15.2	31.8	25.6
XLM-R	+aug	70.0	47.6	55.9	37.5	**52.8**	41.8	38.8	40.0	42.0	40.6
mBERT +Alignment FT:											
+CAO-HIGH	+aug	66.1 (✗)	40.3 (✗)	52.4 (✗)	31.0 (✗)	47.4	35.5 (✗)	32.2 (✗)	33.0 (✗)	33.8 (✗)	33.6
+ZHAO-LOW	+aug	68.5 (✗)	39.0 (✓)	53.1 (✗)	33.6 (✗)	48.5	36.6 (✗)	32.1 (✓)	32.3 (✗)	34.5 (✗)	33.9
+TYDI-L	+aug	68.9 (✓)	45.8 (✓)	**56.4** (✓)*	37.0 (✓)	52.0	36.5 (✓)	32.0 (✓)	35.1 (✓)	35.1 (✓)	34.7
+111-S	+aug	69.1 (✓)	42.5 (✓)	54.4 (✓)	36.2 (✓)	50.5	37.0 (✓)	33.5 (✓)	34.4 (✓)	36.2 (✓)	35.3
+111-L	+aug	68.6 (✓)	41.0 (✓)	52.7 (✓)	35.2 (✓)	49.4	36.7 (✓)	32.8 (✓)	32.3 (✓)	32.6 (✓)	33.6
XLM-R +Alignment FT:											
+ZHAO-(LOW+HIGH)	+aug	68.3 (✗)	42.0 (✓)	54.0 (✗)	39.0 (✗)	50.8	40.9 (✗)	39.4 (✓)	38.6 (✗)	40.4 (✗)	39.8
+TYDI-L	+aug	**70.4** (✓)	45.6 (✓)	55.2 (✓)	38.4 (✓)	52.4	**43.3** (✓)*	**41.0** (✓)*	**42.2** (✓)*	**42.3** (✓)*	**42.2**
+111-S	+aug	69.6 (✓)	**48.9** (✓)	53.0 (✓)	**39.4** (✓)*	52.7	42.8 (✓)	40.5 (✓)	41.1 (✓)	41.5 (✓)	41.5
+111-L	+aug	69.5 (✓)	44.6 (✓)	54.9 (✓)	39.2 (✓)	52.0	42.4 (✓)	39.6 (✓)	40.7 (✓)	41.8 (✓)	41.1

Table 3: Cross-lingual minimal answer results (test set). ✓/✗: the language is/isn't included in the finetuning mix. *:denotes statistically significant better system than the corresponding baseline with $p < 0.05$.

training XLM-R generally yields better performance in terms of F-score. The only exceptions are in the case of Swahili context (Q_{en}, C_{sw}) for both tasks, where mBERT leads to higher F-score, with XLM-R lagging behind by a couple of percentage points.

Effect of language choices in multilingual alignment The comparison of different multilingually-aligned checkpoints leads to two main findings. First, that including the evaluation language in the alignment fine-tuning state is important in downstream performance. Across both tasks and all language settings, the highest performing setting is one where the language pair was included in the fine-tuning (marked with a checkmark ✓ in the two results Tables).

Aligning the representations of languages other than the ones we evaluate on does not seem to lead to improvements. The CAO-HIGH, ZHAO-LOW, and ZHAO-(LOW+HIGH) models generally perform 1-2 percentage points worse than the comparable mBERT or XLM-R baselines using the same task-tuning data (+aug). This is an indication of negative interference (Wang et al., 2020), which we suspect is due to the models using a large amount of data in a limited set of languages that overfits the representations to these languages.

In contrast, our 111-S and 111-L models, despite including a lot more languages in the alignment fine-tuning stage with less data per language, suffer from less negative interference (as evidenced by performing on average just 1-2 percentage points less than the TYDI-L model - the other models can be up to 5 points worse than TYDI-L). In fact, the 111-x XLM-R models are the best ones in some settings for Bengali and Korean (e.g. Q_{en}, C_{bn} and Q_{en}, C_{ko}). This observation implies that such fine-tuning on as many languages as possible is perhaps a viable strategy towards improving downstream performance on as many languages as possible, and not just the four languages that we evaluate on. We believe that studying the phenomenon of negative interference and attempting to mitigate it is a very promising avenue for future work towards building robust, more equitable cross-lingual QA systems.

The effect of data size in alignment fine-tuning To quantify the effect of including more (or less) parallel data in the alignment fine-tuning stage, we perform an ablation study varying the training data size in the two language settings: (a) when we only use the TyDi-QA languages, varying the data to have up to 10k (TYDI-S), 60k (TYDI-M), or using all available parallel data with between 80-260k sentences per language (TYDI-L, and (b) when using 111 languages, we use up to 1k (111-s) or 5k (111-L) parallel sentences per language.

Results with the two 111-x models were already reported in Tables 2 and 3. Results with the TyDi-QA-focused ablations are listed in Table 4 for both tasks. When focusing on the few languages of TyDi-QA, we find that in most cases using more data leads to better overall performance, but restricting ourselves to even just 10k parallel sentences per language still leads to comparable results with similar improvements. In the case of passage selection with English questions (Q_{en}, C_{xx}), in fact, using less data leads to slightly higher average performance (c.f. 61.3 to 61.0). This is an encouraging result, since it reveals that large parallel datasets (which for most of the world's languages are not available anyway) are not a hard requirement.

When using a larger pool of languages, a 5-fold increase in data is not beneficial, with the performance of 111-L being worse than the 111-s overall. Beyond the potential negative interference effects discussed previously, we hypothesize that the increased amount of language data creates a data imbalance as there are languages with very little parallel data (i.e. around 500 sentences). In future work we will investigate whether data balancing schemes such as the one used by Siddhant et al. (2020) can mitigate this effect and potentially allow us to leverage all available data.

Statistical significance Beyond simply calculating evaluation scores (i.e. F-score), we conducted statistical significance tests comparing the baseline (TyDi-QA+`aug` data) to the two best performing models: 111-s and TYDI-L. We perform pairwise bootstrap re-sampling (Koehn, 2004) between the model predictions for both types of pretrained models (i.e. MBERT and XLM-R) and for both type of tasks (i.e. passage selection and minimal answer). While we don't observe statistically significant improvement in all results, in most cases our models perform better than the baseline model at a 95% confidence interval.

5.2 Human translations evaluation

Table 5 lists the results obtained on the real-world scenario of spoken and consequently transcribed questions. We remind the reader that we collected such data for two settings: (Q_{en}, C_{bn}) and (Q_{en}, C_{sw}), asking bilingual speakers native in Bengali and Swahili to translate questions in English, which we then transcribed using publicly available ASR systems, while also hand-creating gold transcriptions for Bengali.[9]

In this real world scenario, the results are more mixed. As before, we find that XLM-R generally performs better than mBERT, and that task-tuning with the synthetically augmented data helps significantly. For the passage selection task, interestingly, the alignment-finetuned models lag behind the best baseline for all settings. For the minimal answer task, the alignment-based fine-tuning does lead to additional improvements, increasing the obtained F-score by around 2 percentage points over the best baseline. In these cases, the best performing model is the one where we used data from 111 languages for alignment – in such noisy settings, as in the case of the two automatic transcriptions, using only the TyDi-QA languages is inferior. Of importance, also, is the general drop in performance when comparing the gold Bengali question transcriptions to the automatic ones, denoting that future work is required to make QA models robust to ASR noise, as Ravichander et al. (2021) and Faisal et al. (2021) have noted.

Last, we compare the above scenario with the scenario where the speakers asked the same questions

[9] One of the authors is a native Bengali speaker.

Model	Tr. Data	Q_{en}, C_{ar}	Q_{en}, C_{bn}	Q_{en}, C_{sw}	Q_{en}, C_{ko}	avg	Q_{ar}, C_{en}	Q_{bn}, C_{en}	Q_{sw}, C_{en}	Q_{ko}, C_{en}	avg
Passage selection:											
+TYDI-S		80.9	51.7	61.8	**50.7**	**61.3**	57.0	**56.5**	55.4	54.8	55.9
+TYDI-M	+aug	81.0	**51.7**	61.1	50.4	61.0	57.6	54.9	53.7	56.3	55.6
+TYDI-L		**81.0**	50.5	**62.2**	50.2	61.0	**57.7**	55.7	**55.9**	**56.5**	**56.5**
Minimal answer:											
+TYDI-S		**71.2**	44.6	55.1	37.7	52.2	42.8	38.7	40.0	41.5	40.8
+TYDI-M	+aug	71.1	**46.5**	54.1	36.8	52.1	42.8	40.7	39.0	41.1	40.9
+TYDI-L		70.4	45.6	**55.2**	**38.4**	**52.4**	**43.3**	**41.0**	**42.2**	**42.3**	**42.2**

Table 4: Primary Task Results (XLM-R) varying training size for alignment.

in their native language. The results for this monolingual setting are at the bottom row of Table 5, and are comparable to the results in the rest of the Table (column-wise), as they are over the exact same test set. Notably, the monolingual scenario yields more than 10 percentage points improvements for passage selection in Bengali (and 2 points for the minimal answer task), but it is much worse, by more than 15 percentage points for both tasks in Swahili. This is due to the poor quality of the ASR transcription for Swahili, as Faisal et al. (2021) discuss. This means that a Swahili speaker who also speaks English would receive almost 60% more utility out of our systems if they also speak and can ask their question in English. This highlights the need for advancing both the monolingual *and* cross-lingual capabilities of QA systems, as well as the need for making these systems robust to noise and other variations. Furthermore, we emphasize the need for realistic datasets that reflect the users usage of QA systems across more of the world's languages and language varieties.

We further analyze the cross-lingual results in Table 6, where we compare the correct-incorrect frequency of minimal answers for Bengali and Swahili in two settings: asking questions in the context language or in the English translations (human-recorded, asr transcriptions). Here we only report comparison on the answers which are either fully correct or incorrect leaving the partially correct ones. Overall, our models get less instances completely wrong. Interestingly, we observe that in a number of cases, alignment based fine-tuning helps in predicting correct answers in cross lingual setting which were incorrectly predicted in a monolingual setting: for example, in XLM-R for Swahili, 101 instances were originally wrong regardless of the language of the question (English or Swahili). Our version of XLM-R, though, gets less examples completely wrong (93 vs 101) and gets the answer correct in at least one of the settings. This categorization of the dev/test instances could perhaps further help classify examples into easy or hard for multilingual models and be of further use in further studies of multilingual fairness and robustness.

6 Related Work

A significant amount of work is devoted to studying and improving the cross-lingual capabilities of QA models. TyDi-QA (Clark et al., 2020) is a notable recent dataset focusing on the inclusion of 11 typologically diverse languages. XOR-QA (Asai et al., 2021) builds on top of TyDi-QA, exploring open domain QA systems, where the search for an answer to a question unanswerable in the original language integrates translated resources from relevant English Wikipedia pages, in a task reflective of our setting. We view our work as orthogonal to XOR-QA, as Asai et al. (2021) put more emphasis on the retrieval of relevant passages rather than the cross-lingual capabilities of the QA ("reader") model per se.

There exist a number of multilingual QA benchmarks, including MLQA (Lewis et al., 2020), MKQA (Longpre et al., 2020) and XQuAD (Artetxe et al., 2020). MLQA translates original English questions to 7 other languages to train a multilingual QA model. MKQA comprises of questions from 26 diverse languages. XQuAD uses translated questions from SQuAD (Rajpurkar et al., 2016) (originally in English) to prepare a widely used and easily adaptable multilingual benchmark of SQuAD baseline. In SD-QA (Faisal et al., 2021) from which our work is inspired, the authors prepare a naturally spoken version of TyDi-QA over 5 languages. In this work, we further expand the scope to study the cross-lingual abilities of QA systems for these 5 languages.

Using cross-lingual objectives that leverage parallel language data is a promising direction towards improving the cross-lingual abilities of lan-

Model	Tr. Data	Passage Selection Q_{en}, C_{bn} (Gold Transc.)	Q_{en}, C_{bn} (ASR)	Q_{en}, C_{sw} (ASR)	Minimal Answer Q_{en}, C_{bn} (Gold Transc.)	Q_{en}, C_{bn} (ASR)	Q_{en}, C_{sw} (ASR)
Baselines:							
mBERT	mono	41.1	37.2	53.4	32.0	26.5	43.1
mBERT	+aug	46.6	45.9	54.1	38.8	36.4	45.0
XLM-R	mono	41.0	37.0	52.6	28.7	25.1	42.1
XLM-R	+aug	**55.2**	**52.4**	**59.0**	43.8	41.6	47.4
mBERT +Alignment FT:							
+CAO-HIGH		48.4 (✗)	40.7 (✗)	53.2 (✗)	38.0 (✗)	31.5 (✗)	42.6 (✗)
+ZHAO-LOW		47.4 (✓)	42.1 (✓)	51.6 (✗)	38.6 (✓)	32.4 (✓)	42.3 (✗)
+TYDI-L	+aug	45.9 (✓)	39.6 (✓)	54.0 (✓)	39.1 (✓)	33.7 (✓)	44.2 (✓)
+111-S		51.0 (✓)	45.1 (✓)	51.4 (✓)	38.6 (✓)	34.0 (✓)	41.7 (✓)
+111-L		47.5 (✓)	43.5 (✓)	52.3 (✓)	37.7 (✓)	36.1 (✓)	41.8 (✓)
XLM-R +Alignment FT:							
+ZHAO-(LOW+HIGH)		52.5 (✓)	50.8 (✓)	56.9 (✗)	43.4 (✓)	39.8 (✓)	47.1 (✗)
+TYDI-L	+aug	49.3 (✓)	47.5 (✓)	57.0 (✓)	40.5 (✓)	38.7 (✓)	48.2 (✓)
+111-S		52.8 (✓)	50.8 (✓)	58.6 (✓)	**45.6** (✓)	**43.4** (✓)	48.2 (✓)
+111-L		49.6 (✓)	48.9 (✓)	57.1 (✓)	41.7 (✓)	41.0 (✓)	**49.2** (✓)
Monolingual Setting: (no translation)		Q_{bn}, C_{bn} 61.9	Q_{bn}, C_{bn} 60.3	Q_{sw}, C_{sw} 43.8	Q_{bn}, C_{bn} 47.9	Q_{bn}, C_{bn} 47.2	Q_{sw}, C_{sw} 31.4

Table 5: Primary tasks result for the real-world scenario (human-translated and ASR-transcribed English questions) over foreign contexts (test set).

		Baselines mBERT		XLM-R		mBERT+Align. FT 111-S		XLM-R+Align. FT 111-S	
		Q_{en}, C_{bn} Correct	Wrong	Q_{en}, C_{bn} Correct	Wrong	Q_{en}, C_{bn} Correct	Wrong	Q_{en}, C_{bn} Correct	Wrong
Q_{bn}, C_{bn}	Correct	34	14	**43**	12	32	14	42	**8**
	Wrong	6	41	2	**33**	3	42	**6**	34
		Q_{en}, C_{sw} Correct	Wrong	Q_{en}, C_{sw} Correct	Wrong	Q_{en}, C_{sw} Correct	Wrong	Q_{en}, C_{sw} Correct	Wrong
Q_{sw}, C_{sw}	Correct	222	27	**229**	20	228	32	221	**18**
	Wrong	10	108	8	101	12	115	**15**	**93**

Table 6: Frequency comparison of correct/incorrect min-F1 using original and translated questions. The baseline ones are trained on augmented data and evaluated on ASR outputs of human translations.

guage models (Conneau and Lample, 2019). Cao et al. (2020) fine-tuned mBERT on a parallel corpus (taken from Europarl) using word-level alignments obtained with fast-align (Dyer et al., 2013). This model aims to decrease the representation distance between words with similar meanings across languages. Zhao et al. (2021) used the fine-tuning process defined by Cao et al. (2020) and further tuned it for low resource languages. After the alignment fine-tuning stage, the authors also perform last-layer embedding normalization and language specific word-word coordination to further improve on downstream tasks. These contextual representation alignment works are evaluated on tasks designed for cross-lingual and zero-shot transfer like XNLI (Conneau et al., 2018) or RFEVAL (Zhao et al., 2020). Our work is the first to evaluate these methods on the QA task, but also the first to expand the alignment-based fine-tuning to include almost all languages used in the pre-trained models, as opposed to only using the languages on which evaluation is performed.

7 Conclusion and Future Work

In this work, we have studied the cross-lingual extractive QA setting where the question and context-to-search are in different languages. Through experiments on synthetic and newly collected data in 4 languages, we have shown that data augmentation along with alignment-based fine-tuning can lead to big improvements in downstream performance. In future work, we plan to collect a larger dataset covering more languages for such cross-lingual settings. We also aim to extend this study using even more parallel data whenever available, as well as to investigate the feasibility of using language-specific tools in parts of the system's pipelines (e.g. in segmentation or tokenization).

Acknowledgments

This work is generously supported by NSF Awards IIS-2040926 and IIS-2125466. The dataset creation was supported though a Google Award for Inclusion Research. We also want to thank Jacob Eisenstein, Manaal Faruqui, and Jon Clark for helpful discussions on question answering and data collection. The authors are grateful to Kathleen Siminyu for her help with collecting Kiswahili and Kenyan English speech samples.

References

Chris Alberti, Kenton Lee, and Michael Collins. 2019. A BERT baseline for the natural questions.

Antonios Anastasopoulos and Graham Neubig. 2020. Should all cross-lingual embeddings speak english? In *Proceedings of the 58th Annual Meeting of the Association for Computational Linguistics*, pages 8658–8679, Online. Association for Computational Linguistics.

Mikel Artetxe, Sebastian Ruder, and Dani Yogatama. 2020. On the cross-lingual transferability of monolingual representations. In *Proceedings of the 58th Annual Meeting of the Association for Computational Linguistics*, pages 4623–4637, Online. Association for Computational Linguistics.

Akari Asai, Jungo Kasai, Jonathan Clark, Kenton Lee, Eunsol Choi, and Hannaneh Hajishirzi. 2021. XOR QA: Cross-lingual open-retrieval question answering. In *Proceedings of the 2021 Conference of the North American Chapter of the Association for Computational Linguistics: Human Language Technologies*, pages 547–564, Online. Association for Computational Linguistics.

Steven Cao, Nikita Kitaev, and Dan Klein. 2020. Multilingual alignment of contextual word representations. In *International Conference on Learning Representations*.

Jonathan H Clark, Eunsol Choi, Michael Collins, Dan Garrette, Tom Kwiatkowski, Vitaly Nikolaev, and Jennimaria Palomaki. 2020. TyDi QA: A benchmark for information-seeking question answering in typologically diverse languages. *Transactions of the Association for Computational Linguistics*, 8:454–470.

Alexis Conneau, Kartikay Khandelwal, Naman Goyal, Vishrav Chaudhary, Guillaume Wenzek, Francisco Guzmán, Edouard Grave, Myle Ott, Luke Zettlemoyer, and Veselin Stoyanov. 2020. Unsupervised cross-lingual representation learning at scale. In *Proceedings of the 58th Annual Meeting of the Association for Computational Linguistics*, pages 8440–8451, Online. Association for Computational Linguistics.

Alexis Conneau and Guillaume Lample. 2019. Cross-lingual language model pretraining. *Advances in Neural Information Processing Systems*, 32:7059–7069.

Alexis Conneau, Ruty Rinott, Guillaume Lample, Adina Williams, Samuel R. Bowman, Holger Schwenk, and Veselin Stoyanov. 2018. Xnli: Evaluating cross-lingual sentence representations. In *Proceedings of the 2018 Conference on Empirical Methods in Natural Language Processing*. Association for Computational Linguistics.

Arnab Debnath, Navid Rajabi, Fardina Fathmiul Alam, and Antonios Anastasopoulos. 2021. Towards more equitable question answering systems: How much more data do you need? In *Proceedings of the 59th Annual Meeting of the Association for Computational Linguistics and the 11th International Joint Conference on Natural Language Processing (ACL-IJCNLP)*. Association for Computational Linguistics.

Jacob Devlin, Ming-Wei Chang, Kenton Lee, and Kristina Toutanova. 2019. Bert: Pre-training of deep bidirectional transformers for language understanding. In *Proceedings of the 2019 Conference of the North American Chapter of the Association for Computational Linguistics: Human Language Technologies, Volume 1 (Long and Short Papers)*, pages 4171–4186.

Zi-Yi Dou and Graham Neubig. 2021. Word alignment by fine-tuning embeddings on parallel corpora. In *Conference of the European Chapter of the Association for Computational Linguistics (EACL)*.

Chris Dyer, Victor Chahuneau, and Noah A. Smith. 2013. A simple, fast, and effective reparameterization of IBM model 2. In *Proceedings of the 2013 Conference of the North American Chapter of the Association for Computational Linguistics: Human Language Technologies*, pages 644–648, Atlanta, Georgia. Association for Computational Linguistics.

Ahmed El-Kishky, Vishrav Chaudhary, Francisco Guzmán, and Philipp Koehn. 2020. CCAligned: A massive collection of cross-lingual web-document pairs. In *Proceedings of the 2020 Conference on Empirical Methods in Natural Language Processing (EMNLP)*, pages 5960–5969, Online. Association for Computational Linguistics.

Fahim Faisal, Sharlina Keshava, Md Mahfuz ibn Alam, and Antonios Anastasopoulos. 2021. SD-QA: Spoken Dialectal Question Answering for the Real World. In *Findings of the 2021 Conference on Empirical Methods in Natural Language Processing (EMNLP Findings)*. Association for Computational Linguistics.

Manaal Faruqui, Jesse Dodge, Sujay Kumar Jauhar, Chris Dyer, Eduard Hovy, and Noah A. Smith. 2015. Retrofitting word vectors to semantic lexicons. In *Proceedings of the 2015 Conference of the North American Chapter of the Association for Computational Linguistics: Human Language Technologies*, pages 1606–1615, Denver, Colorado. Association for Computational Linguistics.

Robert M. French. 1999. Catastrophic forgetting in connectionist networks. *Trends in Cognitive Sciences*, 3(4):128–135.

Jianfeng Gao, Michel Galley, and Lihong Li. 2018. Neural approaches to conversational ai. *The 41st International ACM SIGIR Conference on Research & Development in Information Retrieval.*

Kuan-Hao Huang, Wasi Uddin Ahmad, Nanyun Peng, and Kai-Wei Chang. 2021. Improving zero-shot cross-lingual transfer learning via robust training.

Zhengbao Jiang, Antonios Anastasopoulos, Jun Araki, Haibo Ding, and Graham Neubig. 2020. X-factr: Multilingual factual knowledge retrieval from pretrained language models. In *Proceedings of the 2020 Conference on Empirical Methods in Natural Language Processing (EMNLP)*, pages 5943–5959, Online. Association for Computational Linguistics.

Philipp Koehn. 2004. Statistical significance tests for machine translation evaluation. In *Proceedings of the 2004 Conference on Empirical Methods in Natural Language Processing*, pages 388–395, Barcelona, Spain. Association for Computational Linguistics.

Saurabh Kulshreshtha, Jose Luis Redondo Garcia, and Ching Yun Chang. 2020. Cross-lingual alignment methods for multilingual bert: A comparative study. In *Proceedings of the 2020 Conference on Empirical Methods in Natural Language Processing: Findings*, pages 933–942.

Tom Kwiatkowski, Jennimaria Palomaki, Olivia Redfield, Michael Collins, Ankur Parikh, Chris Alberti, Danielle Epstein, Illia Polosukhin, Matthew Kelcey, Jacob Devlin, Kenton Lee, Kristina N. Toutanova, Llion Jones, Ming-Wei Chang, Andrew Dai, Jakob Uszkoreit, Quoc Le, and Slav Petrov. 2019. Natural questions: a benchmark for question answering research. *Transactions of the Association of Computational Linguistics.*

Patrick Lewis, Barlas Oguz, Ruty Rinott, Sebastian Riedel, and Holger Schwenk. 2020. Mlqa: Evaluating cross-lingual extractive question answering. In *Proceedings of the 58th Annual Meeting of the Association for Computational Linguistics*, pages 7315–7330.

Yinhan Liu, Myle Ott, Naman Goyal, Jingfei Du, Mandar Joshi, Danqi Chen, Omer Levy, Mike Lewis, Luke Zettlemoyer, and Veselin Stoyanov. 2019. Roberta: A robustly optimized bert pretraining approach. arXiv:1907.11692.

Shayne Longpre, Yi Lu, and Joachim Daiber. 2020. MKQA: A linguistically diverse benchmark for multilingual open domain question answering.

Michael McCloskey and Neal J. Cohen. 1989. Catastrophic interference in connectionist networks: The sequential learning problem. volume 24 of *Psychology of Learning and Motivation*, pages 109–165. Academic Press.

Benjamin Muller, Antonios Anastasopoulos, Benoît Sagot, and Djamé Seddah. 2020. When being unseen from mBERT is just the beginning: Handling new languages with multilingual LMs. In *Proceedings of the 2021 Conference of the North American Chapter of the Association for Computational Linguistics: Human Language Technologies*, Online. Association for Computational Linguistics.

Pranav Rajpurkar, Jian Zhang, Konstantin Lopyrev, and Percy Liang. 2016. SQuAD: 100,000+ questions for machine comprehension of text. In *Proceedings of the 2016 Conference on Empirical Methods in Natural Language Processing*, pages 2383–2392, Austin, Texas. Association for Computational Linguistics.

Roger Ratcliff. 1990. Connectionist models of recognition memory: Constraints imposed by learning and forgetting functions. *Psychological Review*, 97(2):285–308.

Abhilasha Ravichander, Siddharth Dalmia, Maria Ryskina, Florian Metze, Eduard Hovy, and Alan W Black. 2021. NoiseQA: Challenge set evaluation for user-centric question answering. In *Proceedings of the 16th Conference of the European Chapter of the Association for Computational Linguistics: Main Volume*, pages 2976–2992, Online. Association for Computational Linguistics.

Anna Rogers, Matt Gardner, and Isabelle Augenstein. 2021. Qa dataset explosion: A taxonomy of nlp resources for question answering and reading comprehension. arXiv:2107.12708.

Holger Schwenk, Vishrav Chaudhary, Shuo Sun, Hongyu Gong, and Francisco Guzmán. 2021. WikiMatrix: Mining 135M parallel sentences in 1620 language pairs from Wikipedia. In *Proceedings of the 16th Conference of the European Chapter of the Association for Computational Linguistics: Main Volume*, pages 1351–1361, Online. Association for Computational Linguistics.

Aditya Siddhant, Melvin Johnson, Henry Tsai, Naveen Ari, Jason Riesa, Ankur Bapna, Orhan Firat, and Karthik Raman. 2020. Evaluating the cross-lingual effectiveness of massively multilingual neural machine translation. In *Proceedings of the AAAI Conference on Artificial Intelligence*, volume 34, pages 8854–8861.

Jörg Tiedemann. 2012. Parallel data, tools and interfaces in OPUS. In *Proceedings of the Eight International Conference on Language Resources and Evaluation (LREC'12)*, Istanbul, Turkey. European Language Resources Association (ELRA).

Zirui Wang, Zachary C. Lipton, and Yulia Tsvetkov. 2020. On negative interference in multilingual models: Findings and a meta-learning treatment. In *Proceedings of the 2020 Conference on Empirical Methods in Natural Language Processing (EMNLP)*, pages 4438–4450, Online. Association for Computational Linguistics.

Yi Yang, Wen-tau Yih, and Christopher Meek. 2015. WikiQA: A challenge dataset for open-domain question answering. In *Proceedings of the 2015 Conference on Empirical Methods in Natural Language Processing*, pages 2013–2018, Lisbon, Portugal. Association for Computational Linguistics.

Wei Zhao, Steffen Eger, Johannes Bjerva, and Isabelle Augenstein. 2021. Inducing language-agnostic multilingual representations. In *Proceedings of *SEM 2021: The Tenth Joint Conference on Lexical and Computational Semantics*, pages 229–240, Online. Association for Computational Linguistics.

Wei Zhao, Goran Glavaš, Maxime Peyrard, Yang Gao, Robert West, and Steffen Eger. 2020. On the limitations of cross-lingual encoders as exposed by reference-free machine translation evaluation. In *Proceedings of the 58th Annual Meeting of the Association for Computational Linguistics*, pages 1656–1671, Online. Association for Computational Linguistics.

A Evaluation on custom development set

In this section, we report the experimental result on TyDi-QA custom development set. See Table 7 for passage selection and Table 8 for minimal answer results

B Parallel corpus selection

In Table 9, we present the parallel language statistics used in our multilingual alignment fine-tuning for the 111-S and 111-L models. We used in total 111 X-English parallel language datasets. Among these languages, 86 were used to pre-train mBERT and 87 were used during XLM-R pre-training. For training model 111-S, the maximum number of sentences per language pair was set to 1000, whereas we set the threshold to 5000 for model 111-L. We used parallel data from OPUS-100 (Tiedemann, 2012), WikiMatrix (Schwenk et al., 2021) and CCAligned (El-Kishky et al., 2020).

Model	Tr. Data	Q_{en}, C_{ar}	Q_{en}, C_{bn}	Q_{en}, C_{sw}	Q_{en}, C_{ko}	avg
Best Baselines:						
mBERT	mono	60.2	41.9	61.8	36.5	50.1
mBERT	+aug	65.6	51.9	68.6	37.3	55.8
XLM-R	mono	58.7	29.7	62.5	25.4	44.1
XLM-R	+aug	65.1	51.9	69.0	41.7	56.9
mBERT +Alignment FT:						
+CAO-HIGH		63.9 (✗)	45.3 (✗)	66.2 (✗)	34.3 (✗)	52.4
+ZHAO-LOW		67.2 (✗)	46.4 (✓)	67.2 (✗)	45.1 (✗)	56.5
+TYDI-L	+aug	64.7 (✓)	48.1 (✓)	**69.9** (✓)	43.8 (✓)	56.6
+111-S		66.0 (✓)	47.3 (✓)	68.6 (✓)	**44.1** (✓)	56.5
+111-L		**66.8** (✓)	44.4 (✓)	68.3 (✓)	41.1 (✓)	55.1
XLM-R +Alignment FT:						
+ZHAO-(LOW+HIGH)		64.3 (✗)	48.1 (✓)	69.2 (✗)	32.3 (✗)	53.5
+TYDI-L	+aug	64.3 (✓)	**52.5** (✓)	69.4 (✓)	39.5 (✓)	56.4
+111-S		64.4 (✓)	49.4 (✓)	68.8 (✓)	39.0 (✓)	55.4
+111-L		64.7 (✓)	50.0 (✓)	68.2 (✓)	39.4 (✓)	55.6

Model	Tr. Data	Q_{ar}, C_{en}	Q_{bn}, C_{en}	Q_{sw}, C_{en}	Q_{ko}, C_{en}	avg
Best Baselines:						
mBERT	mono	49.2	41.0	43.1	47.2	45.1
mBERT	+aug	50.0	46.3	48.2	48.2	48.2
XLM-R	mono	45.8	43.3	37.3	47.6	43.5
XLM-R	+aug	51.0	50.9	50.6	50.8	50.8
mBERT +Alignment FT:						
+CAO-HIGH		47.8 (✗)	47.6 (✗)	46.9 (✗)	48.6 (✗)	47.7
+ZHAO-LOW		48.6 (✗)	46.7 (✓)	46.1 (✗)	47.9 (✗)	47.3
+TYDI-L	+aug	48.9 (✓)	46.4 (✓)	47.1 (✓)	47.0 (✓)	47.4
+111-S		50.2 (✓)	49.0 (✓)	48.7 (✓)	49.2 (✓)	49.3
+111-L		48.3 (✓)	47.0 (✓)	46.2 (✓)	48.3 (✓)	47.5
XLM-R +Alignment FT:						
+ZHAO-(LOW+HIGH)		52.1 (✗)	50.6 (✓)	50.2 (✗)	50.5 (✗)	50.9
+TYDI-L	+aug	**53.4** (✓)	**53.5** (✓)	**52.3** (✓)	**53.2** (✓)	53.1
+111-S		52.8 (✓)	52.6 (✓)	50.9 (✓)	51.9 (✓)	52.1
+111-L		51.4 (✓)	51.2 (✓)	49.1 (✓)	51.6 (✓)	50.8

Table 7: Passage Selection Results for Foreign questions over english contexts (dev set).✓/✗: the language is/isn't included in the finetuning mix.

Model	Tr. Data	Q_{en}, C_{ar}	Q_{en}, C_{bn}	Q_{en}, C_{sw}	Q_{en}, C_{ko}	avg
Best Baselines:						
mBERT	mono	43.4	30.4	50.9	31.3	39.0
mBERT	+aug	50.4	43.5	55.9	29.7	44.9
XLM-R	mono	46.1	23.0	50.6	22.6	35.6
XLM-R	+aug	51.7	42.5	56.7	36.4	46.8
mBERT +Alignment FT:						
+CAO-HIGH	+aug	48.6 (✗)	36.0 (✗)	54.4 (✗)	23.0 (✗)	40.5
+ZHAO-LOW	+aug	51.7 (✗)	36.0 (✓)	55.3 (✗)	35.7 (✗)	44.7
+TYDI-L	+aug	50.7 (✓)	36.0 (✓)	**57.9** (✓)	**37.2** (✓)	45.5
+111-S	+aug	**52.2** (✓)	35.9 (✓)	56.6 (✓)	32.9 (✓)	44.4
+111-L	+aug	51.6 (✓)	35.9 (✓)	55.7 (✓)	29.9 (✓)	43.3
XLM-R +Alignment FT:						
+ZHAO-(LOW+HIGH)	+aug	50.3 (✗)	38.1 (✓)	56.3 (✗)	26.5 (✗)	42.8
+TYDI-L	+aug	50.6 (✓)	**44.1** (✓)	57.8 (✓)	29.8 (✓)	45.6
+111-S	+aug	49.2 (✓)	37.4 (✓)	56.7 (✓)	29.5 (✓)	43.2
+111-L	+aug	50.7 (✓)	41.6 (✓)	57.1 (✓)	33.6 (✓)	45.8
Model	Tr. Data	Q_{ar}, C_{en}	Q_{bn}, C_{en}	Q_{sw}, C_{en}	Q_{ko}, C_{en}	avg
Best Baselines:						
mBERT	mono	33.2	17.9	22.5	29.2	25.7
mBERT	+aug	31.0	28.4	29.5	32.2	30.3
XLM-R	mono	26.1	22.6	14.7	29.3	23.2
XLM-R	+aug	34.4	34.4	35.1	34.5	34.6
mBERT +Alignment FT:						
+CAO-HIGH	+aug	31.1 (✗)	29.2 (✗)	27.5 (✗)	30.6 (✗)	29.6
+ZHAO-LOW	+aug	32.0 (✗)	28.4 (✓)	29.1 (✗)	30.9 (✗)	30.1
+TYDI-L	+aug	29.8 (✓)	28.8 (✓)	28.2 (✓)	31.3 (✓)	29.5
+111-S	+aug	32.8 (✓)	30.3 (✓)	29.4 (✓)	32.3 (✓)	31.2
+111-L	+aug	29.6 (✓)	28.1 (✓)	28.0 (✓)	29.4 (✓)	28.8
XLM-R +Alignment FT:						
+ZHAO-(LOW+HIGH)	+aug	34.8 (✗)	33.3 (✓)	33.8 (✗)	34.8 (✗)	34.2
+TYDI-L	+aug	36.4 (✓)	34.8 (✓)	**35.4** (✓)	36.6 (✓)	35.8
+111-S	+aug	35.6 (✓)	35.4 (✓)	33.1 (✓)	37.0 (✓)	35.3
+111-L	+aug	37.7 (✓)	**36.2** (✓)	35.2 (✓)	**37.9** (✓)	36.8

Table 8: Minimal Answer Results for Foreign questions over english contexts (dev set).✓/✗: the language is/isn't included in the finetuning mix.

Index	Language	Parallel Lang. code	In training of mBERT	XLM-R	Sentence count
1	afrikaans	af-en			1507
2	amharic	am-en	✗		4446
3	aragonese	an-en		✗	463
4	arabic	ar-en			4174
5	assamese	as-en	✗		5192
6	azerbaijani	az-en			1860
7	bashkir	ba-en		✗	5753
8	belarusian	be-en			2556
9	bulgarian	bg-en			4131
10	bengali	bn-en			6873
11	breton	br-en			754
12	bosnian	bs-en			2017
13	catalan	ca-en			1563
14	czech	cs-en			2276
15	chuvash	cv-en		✗	6299
16	welsh	cy-en			1513
17	danish	da-en			1858
18	german	de-en			1567
19	dzongkha	dz-en	✗	✗	215
20	greek	el-en			4514
21	esperanto	eo-en	✗		1707
22	spanish	es-en			2405
23	estonian	et-en			2349
24	basque	eu-en			2299
25	persian (farsi)	fa-en			3907
26	finnish	fi-en			2544
27	french	fr-en			2197
28	western frisian	fy-en	✗		1305
29	irish	ga-en			2360
30	scots	gd-en			1010
31	galician	gl-en			1177
32	gujarati	gu-en			5588
33	hausa	ha-en	✗		3163
34	hebrew	he-en			3109
35	hindi	hi-en			4953
36	croatian	hr-en			1728
37	haitian	ht-en		✗	675
38	hungarian	hu-en			1786
39	armenian	hy-en			1733
40	indonesian	id-en			1526
41	igbo	ig-en	✗	✗	1386
42	ido	io-en		✗	3440
43	icelandic	is-en			1897
44	italian	it-en			2582
45	japanese	ja-en			8386
46	javanese	jv-en			3351
47	georgian	ka-en			4983
48	kazakh	kk-en			3213
49	central khmer	km-en	✗		2662
50	kannada	kn-en			2238
51	korean	ko-en			2691
52	kurdish	ku-en	✗		4001
53	kirghiz	ky-en			1052
54	latin	la-en			2515
55	luxembourgish	lb-en		✗	1588
56	limburgan; limburger; limburgish	li-en	✗	✗	1836
57	lithuanian	lt-en			2911
58	latvian	lv-en			3340
59	malagasy	mg-en			3990
60	macedonian	mk-en			3607
61	malayalam	ml-en			5658
62	mongolian	mn-en	✗		291
63	marathi	mr-en			4487
64	malay	ms-en			1632
65	maltese	mt-en	✗	✗	2162
66	burmese	my-en			5897

67	bokmål, norwegian; norwegian bokmål	nb-en	✗	✗	1665
68	nepali	ne-en			5587
69	dutch	nl-en			1961
70	norwegian (nynorsk)	nn-en		✗	1689
71	norwegian (bokmal)	no-en			1345
72	occitan	oc-en		✗	203
73	oriya	or-en	✗		2070
74	punjabi	pa-en			3893
75	polish	pl-en			2205
76	pushto; pashto	ps-en	✗		2302
77	portuguese	pt-en			1987
78	romanian	ro-en			1593
79	russian	ru-en			3902
80	kinyarwanda	rw-en	✗	✗	791
81	northern sami	se-en	✗	✗	336
82	sinhala; sinhalese	si-en	✗		5546
83	slovak	sk-en			2322
84	slovenian	sl-en			2051
85	albanian	sq-en			1881
86	serbian	sr-en			1717
87	sundanese	su-en			572
88	swedish	sv-en			1939
89	swahili	sw-en			4234
90	tamil	ta-en			5065
91	telugu	te-en			5514
92	tajik	tg-en		✗	4434
93	thai	th-en	✗		5853
94	turkmen	tk-en	✗	✗	576
95	tagalog	tl-en			2885
96	turkish	tr-en			1945
97	tatar	tt-en		✗	5107
98	uighur; uyghur	ug-en	✗		4529
99	ukrainian	uk-en			3544
100	urdu	ur-en			4295
101	uzbek	uz-en			4675
102	vietnamese	vi-en			2260
103	walloon	wa-en	✗	✗	1181
104	xhosa	xh-en	✗		2597
105	yiddish	yi-en	✗		1856
106	yoruba	yo-en		✗	1082
107	chinese (simplified)	zh-en			3302
108	zulu	zu-en	✗	✗	1801
109	serbo-croatian	sh-en		✗	3423
110	asturian	ast-en		✗	895
111	cebuano	ceb-en		✗	1575

Table 9: Parallel language data used in multilingual alignment finetuning.

Semantic Answer Similarity for Evaluating Question Answering Models

Julian Risch* and **Timo Möller*** and **Julian Gutsch** and **Malte Pietsch**
deepset
{julian.risch, timo.moeller, julian.gutsch, malte.pietsch}@deepset.ai

Abstract

The evaluation of question answering models compares ground-truth annotations with model predictions. However, as of today, this comparison is mostly lexical-based and therefore misses out on answers that have no lexical overlap but are still semantically similar, thus treating correct answers as false. This underestimation of the true performance of models hinders user acceptance in applications and complicates a fair comparison of different models. Therefore, there is a need for an evaluation metric that is based on semantics instead of pure string similarity. In this short paper, we present SAS, a cross-encoder-based metric for the estimation of semantic answer similarity, and compare it to seven existing metrics. To this end, we create an English and a German three-way annotated evaluation dataset containing pairs of answers along with human judgment of their semantic similarity, which we release along with an implementation of the SAS metric and the experiments. We find that semantic similarity metrics based on recent transformer models correlate much better with human judgment than traditional lexical similarity metrics on our two newly created datasets and one dataset from related work.

1 Introduction

The evaluation of question answering (QA) models relies on human-annotated datasets of question-answer pairs. Given a question, the ground-truth answer is compared to the answer predicted by a model with regard to different similarity metrics. Currently, the most prominent metrics for the evaluation of QA models are exact match (EM), F1-score, and top-n-accuracy. All these three metrics rely on string-based comparison. EM is a binary metric that checks whether the predicted answer string matches exactly the ground-truth answer. While this metric works well for short factual answers, such as names of persons or locations, it has some obvious flaws when it comes to comparing slightly differing short answers or longer, more elaborate answers. Even a prediction that differs from the ground truth in only one character in the answer string is evaluated as completely wrong. To mitigate this problem and have a continuous score ranging between 0 and 1, the F1-score can be used. In this case, precision is calculated based on the relative number of tokens in the prediction that are also in the ground-truth answer and recall is calculated based on the relative number of tokens in the ground-truth answer that are also in the prediction. An extension of this metric runs stop word removal and lowercasing before the comparison, for example, to disregard prepositions. As an F1-score is not as simple to interpret as accuracy, there is a third common metric for the evaluation of QA models. Top-n-accuracy evaluates the first n model predictions as a group and considers the predictions correct if there is any *positional* overlap between the ground-truth answer and one of the first n model predictions — otherwise, they are considered incorrect. The answer string itself is not compared for top-n-accuracy but the start and end index of the answer within the text document from where the answer is extracted, called context.

If a dataset contains multi-way annotations, there can be multiple different ground-truth answers for the same question. The maximum similarity score of a prediction over all ground-truth answers is used in that case, which works with all the metrics above. However, a problem is that sometimes only one correct answer is annotated when in fact there are multiple correct answers in a document. If the multiple correct answers are semantically but not lexically the same, existing metrics require all correct answers within a document to be annotated and cannot be used reliably otherwise. Figure 1 gives an example of a context, a question, multiple ground-truth answers, a prediction and different similarity

*Both authors contributed equally to this research.

Proceedings of the 3rd Workshop on Machine Reading for Question Answering, pages 149–157
Nov 10th, 2021 ©2021 Association for Computational Linguistics

Question: How many plant species are estimated to be in the Amazon region?
Context: The region is home to about 2.5 million insect species, tens of thousands of plants, and some 2,000 birds and mammals. To date, at least 40,000 plant species [...]
Ground-Truth Answer: "40,000"
Predicted Answer: "tens of thousands"
Exact Match: 0.00
F1-Score: 0.00
Top-1-Accuracy: 0.00
SAS: 0.55
Human Judgment: 0.50

Figure 1: Exact match, F1-score, and top-1-accuracy are no good metrics to evaluate QA models. They do not take into account semantic similarity of predictions and ground-truth answers but only their lexical similarity. SAS is close to human judgment of similarity.

scores. Besides EM, F1-score, and top-1-accuracy, we also list human judgment. The example shows that the existing metrics cannot capture the semantic similarity of the prediction and the ground-truth answers but are limited to lexical similarity.

Extractive QA is not the only QA task that requires evaluation metrics that go beyond string-based matching. Abstractive QA requires generative models to synthesize an answer and they need to be evaluated differently, too. As of today, the evaluation of this task reuses metrics from the research field of natural language generation (NLG) but they are mostly string-based and not tailored to QA. Given the shortcomings of the existing metrics, a novel metric for QA is needed and we address this challenge by presenting SAS, a cross-encoder-based semantic answer similarity metric, and compare it with traditional lexical metrics and two recently proposed metrics for the more general task of semantic textual similarity (STS). To encourage and support research in this area, we release the annotated dataset[1] and the trained model[2] under the Creative Commons Attribution-ShareAlike 4.0 International License (CC BY-SA 4.0).

The remainder of this paper is structured as follows: Section 2 describes related work on metrics used for the evaluation of QA and similar tasks. In Section 3, we present our new metric SAS along with two existing STS metrics. Three datasets, two newly created, three-way annotated datasets and one existing dataset from related work, are the basis of the experiments presented in Section 4, which compare four lexical and three semantic similarity metrics. We conclude in Section 5 with directions for future work.

2 Related Work

The related work discussed in this section goes beyond evaluation metrics explicitly meant for QA. The task can be generalized to estimating the semantic similarity of a pair of text inputs, which is often referred to as semantic textual similarity (STS). While there is a benchmark dataset for STS estimation (Cer et al., 2017), to the best of our knowledge, not even a single dataset has been created for the subtask of estimating semantic answer similarity. STS is closely related to paraphrasing, which, strictly speaking, refers to semantic equivalence. As a consequence of this strict definition, Bhagat and Hovy (2013) introduce the concept of *approximate* paraphrases as conveying a similar meaning. Measuring to what extent a text is an approximate paraphrase of another text has been addressed in several subfields of research on natural language processing and we list different approaches in the following.

A recent tutorial summarizes evaluation metrics used in NLG, including but not limited to the QA task (Khapra and Sai, 2021). The challenge of evaluating NLG has also been recently addressed by Gehrmann et al. (2021), who introduce the GEM benchmark comprising eleven datasets. Besides traditional, lexical similarity metrics, such as BLEU (Papineni et al., 2002), ROUGE (Lin and Hovy, 2003), and METEOR (Banerjee and Lavie, 2005), the benchmark also includes the two semantic similarity metrics BERTScore (Zhang et al., 2020) and BLEURT (Sellam et al., 2020). Both BERTScore and BLEURT are BERT-based (Devlin et al., 2019) metrics tailored to evaluating NLG.

BLEU (BiLingual Evaluation Understudy) (Papineni et al., 2002) is a metric used to evaluate the quality of machine translations by measuring the n-gram overlap of prediction and ground truth. Similarly, there is ROUGE (Recall-Oriented Understudy for Gisting Evaluation), which comes in different variations, such as using n-gram overlap (ROUGE-N) (Lin and Hovy, 2003) or the

[1] https://semantic-answer-similarity.s3.amazonaws.com/data.zip

[2] https://huggingface.co/deepset/gbert-large-sts

longest common subsequence (ROUGE-L) (Lin and Och, 2004) of prediction and ground truth. METEOR (Banerjee and Lavie, 2005) addresses the same task but aims to improve on BLEU, for example, by using a weighted harmonic mean of precision and recall of uni-gram overlap. It relies on WordNet (Miller, 1995) and, for this reason, can only be used for English. There are also slightly modified versions of BLEU and Rouge for yes-no answers and entity answers that introduce a bonus term that gives more weight to correct answers of that type Yang et al. (2018). Still, these modified versions rely on the standard implementations of BLEU and ROUGE, thus inheriting their shortcomings with regard to lexical vs. semantic similarity.

BERTScore (Zhang et al., 2020) is similar to F1-score in that it performs stop word removal and lowercasing before the comparison. TF-IDF is used to lower the influence of stop words on the score. In our work, we argue that stopword removal should not be an extra step of the metric. Instead, the metrics should be based on models that have been trained to recognize what words and phrases are more or less important when comparing the meaning of two answers. The main advantage of BERTScore over traditional metrics is that it compares contextual embeddings of tokens in the prediction and the ground truth instead of the actual tokens. As future work, Zhang et al. (2020) mention that BERTScore could be adapted for the evaluation of different tasks and in this paper, we discuss whether BERTScore is superior to other metrics for the evaluation of QA tasks. Chen et al. (2019) apply BERTScore as an evaluation metric for QA and find that METEOR has a stronger correlation with human judgment.

While evaluating the correctness of predicted answers is the by far the most popular QA evaluation task, there are also approaches to evaluate the consistency of the predicted answers (Ribeiro et al., 2019) or other desirable properties of open-domain QA models, such as efficiency, context awareness, fine granularity of answers, end-to-end trainability or ability to generalize to different input data (Ahmad et al., 2019). Perturbations can serve as a means to evaluate the latter (Shah et al., 2020) and, in the same way, perturbations of the training data allow training models that are more robust (Khashabi et al., 2020). The correctness of answers can be estimated with methods from natural language inference: Chen et al. (2021) convert answers to declarative statements and check whether the statement can be inferred from the relevant document (context). Nema and Khapra (2018) consider the task of evaluating the answerability of generated questions. They find that existing string-based evaluation metrics do not correlate well with human judgment and propose modifications of these metrics, which give more weight to relevant content words, named entities, etc. With the metrics and the underlying models presented in this paper, we present end-to-end deep learning approaches, which learn these features automatically if they increase the correlation between the automated metric and human judgment.

Semantic similarity metrics might also mitigate the influence of an annotator bias on the evaluation, which has been reported to be learned by models and is currently not recognized if the same annotators create both the training and test dataset (Geva et al., 2019; Ko et al., 2020). That bias could be, for example, the position of the answer within a document always being in the first few sentences or a specific style of phrasing the questions. With the help of semantic similarity metrics the position of the annotated answer within the context would not make a difference for the evaluation.

In line with the evaluation of QA models, the automated evaluation of models for question *generation* also relies on BLEU, ROUGE, and METEOR, while human evaluation is limited to small datasets (Du et al., 2017). For the evaluation of conversational QA, Siblini et al. (2021) address the problems that arise from teacher forcing, which refers to earlier ground-truth answers being available to a model at each step in the conversation. The authors discuss ideas to mitigate this problem, such as using the model's own predicted answers instead of the ground-truth answers. However, this approach only considers the ground-truth user reaction to the ground-truth answer but not the predicted answer as other reactions are not available in offline training and evaluation. Last but not least, there is research on error analyses of QA models, which defines guidelines (Wu et al., 2019) or identifies challenges and promising directions for future work (Rondeau and Hazen, 2018; Wadhwa et al., 2018; Pugaliya et al., 2019). These publications present anecdotal evidence of predictions that are evaluated as wrong due to the limitations of lexical similarity metrics but are in fact correct.

3 Approach

We consider four different approaches to estimate the semantic similarity of pairs of answers: a bi-encoder approach, a cross-encoder approach, a vanilla version of BERTScore, and a trained version of BERTScore. This section describes each of these four approaches and the pre-trained language models they are based on.

Bi-Encoder The bi-encoder approach is based on the sentence transformers architecture (Reimers and Gurevych, 2019), which is a siamese neural network architecture comprising two language models that encode the two text inputs and cosine similarity to calculate a similarity score of the two encoded texts. The model that we use is based on xlm-roberta-base, where the training has been continued on an unreleased multi-lingual paraphrase dataset. The resulting model, called paraphrase-xlm-r-multilingual-v1, has then been fine-tuned on the English-language STS benchmark dataset (Cer et al., 2017) and a machine-translated German-language version[3] of the same data. The final model is called T-Systems-onsite/cross-en-de-roberta-sentence-transformer and is available on the huggingface model hub. As the model has been trained on English- and German-language data, we use the exact same model for all three datasets in our experiments. An advantage of the bi-encoder architecture is that the embeddings of the two text inputs are calculated separately. As a consequence, the embeddings of the ground-truth answers can be pre-computed and reused when comparing with the predictions of several different models. This pre-computation can almost halve the time needed to run the evaluation.

SAS Our new approach called SAS differs from the bi-encoder in that it does not calculate separate embeddings for the input texts. Instead, we use a cross-encoder architecture, where the two texts are concatenated with a special separator token in between. The underlying language model is called cross-encoder/stsb-roberta-large and has been trained on the STS benchmark dataset (Cer et al., 2017). Unfortunately, there are only English cross-encoder models for STS estimation available. Therefore, we train a German cross-encoder model for STS estimation, which we release online. This model is based on deepset/gbert-base and we train it for four epochs with a batch size of 16 and the Adam optimizer on the machine-translated version of the STS benchmark that has previously been used to train a bi-encoder STS model for German. For the warm-up phase of the training, we use 10% of the training data and linearly increase the learning rate to 2e-5. While pre-computation is not possible with the cross-encoder architecture, its advantage over bi-encoders is that it takes into account both text inputs at the same time when applying the language model in a monolithic way rather than calculating encodings separately and comparing them afterward.

BERTScore vanilla or trained The BERTScore vanilla approach uses the task-agnostic, pre-trained language models bert-base-uncased for the English-language datasets and deepset/gelectra-base for the German-language dataset. In line with the approach by Zhang et al. (2020), we use the language models to generate contextual embeddings, match the embeddings of the tokens in the ground-truth answer and in the prediction and take the maximum cosine similarity of the matched tokens as the similarity score of the two answers. The optional step of importance weighting of tokens based on inverse document frequency scores is not applied. For the vanilla version, we extract embeddings from the second layer and for the trained version from the last layer. In contrast to the vanilla model, the BERTScore trained model uses a task-specific model tailored to STS estimation. It is the same multi-lingual model that is used by the bi-encoder approach, called T-Systems-onsite/cross-en-de-roberta-sentence-transformer.

4 Experiments

To evaluate the ability of the different approaches to estimate semantic answer similarity, we measure their correlation with human judgment of similarity on three datasets. This section describes the dataset creation, experiment setup, and the final results.

4.1 Datasets

The evaluation uses subsets of three existing datasets: SQuAD, GermanQuAD, and NQ-open. We process and hand-annotate the datasets as described in the following so that each of the processed subsets contains pairs of answers and a class label that indicates their semantic similarity. There

[3] https://github.com/t-systems-on-site-services-gmbh/german-STSbenchmark

0	The two answers are completely dissimilar. "power steering" $\neq$ "air conditioning"
1	The two answers have a similar meaning but one of them is less detailed and could be derived from the more elaborate answer. "Joseph Priestley" $\approx$ "Priestley"
2	The two answers have the same meaning. "UV" = "ultraviolet"

Table 1: Similarity scores with descriptions and example pairs of answers.

are three similarity classes: dissimilar answers, approximately similar answers, and equivalent answers, which are all described in Table 1.

SQuAD We annotate the semantic similarity of pairs of answers in a subset of the English-language SQuAD test dataset (Rajpurkar et al., 2018). The original dataset contains multi-way annotated questions, which means there are on average 4.8 answers per question. Answers to the same question by different annotators often are the same but in some cases they have only a small overlap or no overlap at all. We consider a subset where 566 pairs of ground-truth answers have an F1-score of 0 (no lexical overlap of the answers) and 376 pairs have an F1-score larger than 0 (some lexical overlap of the answers). As we use the majority vote as the ground-truth label of semantic similarity in our experiments, we let two of the authors label each pair of answers while a third author acts as a tie-breaker labeling only those samples, where the first two labels disagree. The resulting dataset comprises 942 pairs of answers each with a majority vote indicating either dissimilar answers, approximately similar answers, or equivalent answers.

GermanQuAD To show that the presented approaches also work on non-English datasets, we consider the German-language GermanQuAD dataset (Möller et al., 2021). It contains a three-way annotated test set, which means there are three correct answers given for each question. After removing questions where all answers are the same, there are 137 pairs of ground-truth answers that have an F1-score of 0 and 288 pairs of answers have an F1-score larger than 0. We label these 425 pairs in the same way as the SQuAD subset resulting in 425 pairs of answers each with a majority vote indicating their semantic similarity.

NQ-open The original Natural Questions dataset (NQ) (Kwiatkowski et al., 2019) was meant for reading comprehension but Lee et al. (2019) adapted the dataset for open-domain QA and it has been released under the name NQ-open. We use the test dataset of NQ-open as it contains not only questions and ground-truth answers but also model predictions and annotations how similar these predictions are to the ground-truth answer. There are three classes of definitely incorrect predictions, possibly correct predictions, and definitely correct predictions. Min et al. (2021) report in more detail on how these additional annotations were created. They resemble the three similarity classes we defined in Table 1. After filtering for only those questions that have exactly one ground-truth answer, we create pairs of ground-truth answers and model predictions accompanied with the label indicating the correctness of the prediction, which also corresponds to the similarity of the ground-truth answer and the predicted answer. There are 3,658 pairs of answers of which 3118 have an F1-score of 0 and 540 pairs that have an F1-score larger than 0.

4.2 Results

Table 2 lists the correlation between different automated evaluation metrics and human judgment using Spearman's rho and Kendall's tau-b rank correlation coefficients on labeled subsets of SQuAD, GermanQuAD, and NQ-open datasets. The traditional metrics ROUGE-L and METEOR have very weak correlation with human judgement if there is no lexical overlap between the pair of answers, in which case the F1-score and BLEU are 0. If there is some lexical overlap, the correlation is stronger for all these metrics but BLEU lags far behind the others. METEOR is outperformed by ROUGE-L and F1-score, which achieve almost equal correlation. All four semantic answer similarity approaches outperform the traditional metrics and among them, the cross-encoder model is consistently achieving the strongest correlation with human judgment except for slightly underperforming the trained BERTScore metric with regard to τ on English-language pairs of answers with no lexical overlap. This result shows that semantic similarity metrics are needed in addition to lexical-based metrics for automated evaluation of QA models. The former correlate much better with human judgment and thus, are a better estimation of a model's performance in real-world applications.

Metrics	SQuAD				GermanQuAD				NQ-open			
	$F1 = 0$		$F1 \neq 0$		$F1 = 0$		$F1 \neq 0$		$F1 = 0$		$F1 \neq 0$	
	ρ	τ	ρ	τ	ρ	τ	ρ	τ	ρ	τ	ρ	τ
Human	0.61	0.48	0.68	0.64	0.64	0.57	0.57	0.54	-	-	-	-
BLEU	00.0	00.0	0.18	0.16	00.0	00.0	0.13	0.05	00.0	00.0	0.08	0.08
ROUGE-L	0.10	0.04	0.56	0.46	0.16	0.02	0.54	0.43	0.14	0.12	0.40	0.33
METEOR	0.38	0.19	0.45	0.37	-	-	-	-	0.21	0.16	0.30	0.25
F1-score	00.0	00.0	0.60	0.50	00.0	00.0	0.55	0.44	00.0	00.0	0.37	0.31
Bi-Encoder	0.48	0.30	0.69	0.57	0.39	0.27	0.56	0.47	0.23	0.15	0.38	0.30
BERTScore vanilla	0.27	0.15	0.61	0.48	0.21	0.01	0.52	0.41	0.14	0.13	0.16	0.11
BERTScore trained	0.52	**0.32**	0.70	0.57	0.41	0.28	0.57	0.47	0.25	**0.16**	0.38	0.30
SAS (ours)	**0.56**	0.29	**0.75**	**0.61**	**0.49**	**0.33**	**0.68**	**0.55**	**0.31**	0.13	**0.54**	**0.42**

Table 2: Correlation between human judgment and automated metrics using Spearman's rho (ρ) and Kendall's tau-b (τ) rank correlation coefficients on subsets of SQuAD, GermanQuAD, and NQ-open. Human baseline correlations on SQuAD and GermanQUAD were measured between first and second annotator. METEOR is not available for German and scores of individual annotators have not been reported on NQ-open (indicated as "-" in the table).

Embedding Extraction for BERTScore BERTScore can be used with different language models to generate contextual embeddings of text inputs. While the embeddings are typically extracted from the last layer of the model, they can be extracted from any of its layers and related work has shown that for some tasks the last layer is not the best (Liu et al., 2019). The experiment visualized in Figure 2 evaluates the correlation between human judgment of semantic answer similarity and a vanilla and a trained BERTScore model. Comparing the extraction of embeddings from the different layers, we find that the last layer drastically outperforms all other models for the trained model. For the vanilla BERTScore model, the choice of the layer has a much smaller influence on the performance, with the first two layers resulting in the strongest correlation with human judgment. For comparison, Figure 2 also includes the results of a cross-encoder model, which does not have the option to choose different layers due to its architecture.

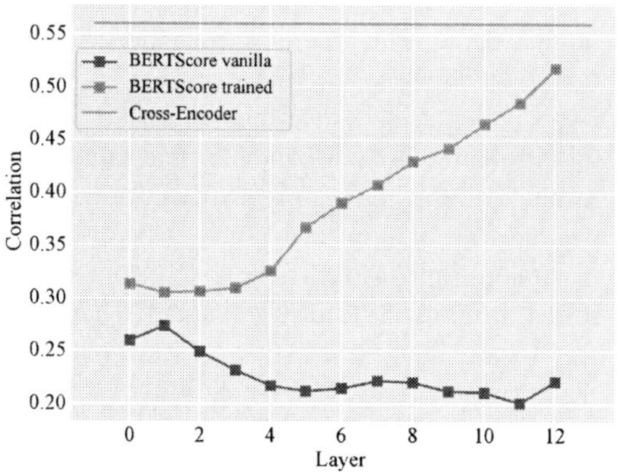

Figure 2: Pearson correlation between BERTScore (computed across different layers) and human judgement of similarity of answer pairs on SQuAD dev set. BERTScore vanilla is pretrained only on Wikipedia, whereas BERTScore trained is fine-tuned on the STS benchmark dataset (Cer et al., 2017).

5 Conclusion and Future Work

Current evaluation metrics for QA models are limited in that they check for lexical or positional overlap of ground-truth answers and predictions but do not take into account semantic similarity. In this paper, we present SAS, a semantic answer similarity metric that overcomes this limitation. It leverages a cross-encoder architecture and transformer-based language models, which are pre-trained on STS datasets that have not been used in the context of QA so far. Experiments on three datasets demonstrate that SAS outperforms four lexical-based and three semantics-based similarity metrics regarding the correlation between the automated metrics and human judgment of the semantic similarity of pairs of answers. A promising path for future work is to analyze pairs of answers where SAS differs from human judgment and find types of common errors. Based on these findings, a dataset tailored to training models for estimating semantic answer similarity could be created.

References

Amin Ahmad, Noah Constant, Yinfei Yang, and Daniel Cer. 2019. Reqa: An evaluation for end-to-end answer retrieval models. In *Proceedings of the Workshop on Machine Reading for Question Answering (MRQA@EMNLP-IJCNLP)*, pages 137–146. Association for Computational Linguistics.

Satanjeev Banerjee and Alon Lavie. 2005. Meteor: An automatic metric for mt evaluation with improved correlation with human judgments. In *Proceedings of the ACL Workshop on Intrinsic and Extrinsic Evaluation Measures for Machine Translation and/or Summarization*, pages 65–72. Association for Computational Linguistics.

Rahul Bhagat and Eduard Hovy. 2013. Squibs: What is a paraphrase? *Computational Linguistics*, 39(3):463–472.

Daniel Cer, Mona Diab, Eneko Agirre, Inigo Lopez-Gazpio, and Lucia Specia. 2017. Semeval-2017 task 1: Semantic textual similarity-multilingual and cross-lingual focused evaluation. In *Proceedings of the International Workshop on Semantic Evaluations (SemEval@ACL*, pages 1–14. Association for Computational Linguistics.

Anthony Chen, Gabriel Stanovsky, Sameer Singh, and Matt Gardner. 2019. Evaluating question answering evaluation. In *Proceedings of the Workshop on Machine Reading for Question Answering (MRQA@EMNLP-IJCNLP)*, pages 119–124. Association for Computational Linguistics.

Jifan Chen, Eunsol Choi, and Greg Durrett. 2021. Can NLI models verify QA systems' predictions? *arXiv preprint arXiv:2104.08731*.

Jacob Devlin, Ming-Wei Chang, Kenton Lee, and Kristina Toutanova. 2019. BERT: Pre-training of deep bidirectional transformers for language understanding. In *Proceedings of the Conference of the North American Chapter of the Association for Computational Linguistics: Human Language Technologies (NAACL-HLT)*, pages 4171–4186. Association for Computational Linguistics.

Xinya Du, Junru Shao, and Claire Cardie. 2017. Learning to ask: Neural question generation for reading comprehension. In *Proceedings of the Annual Meeting of the Association for Computational Linguistics (ACL)*, pages 1342–1352. Association for Computational Linguistics.

Sebastian Gehrmann, Tosin Adewumi, Karmanya Aggarwal, Pawan Sasanka Ammanamanchi, Anuoluwapo Aremu, Antoine Bosselut, Khyathi Raghavi Chandu, Miruna-Adriana Clinciu, Dipanjan Das, Kaustubh Dhole, Wanyu Du, Esin Durmus, Ondřej Dušek, Chris Chinenye Emezue, Varun Gangal, Cristina Garbacea, Tatsunori Hashimoto, Yufang Hou, Yacine Jernite, Harsh Jhamtani, Yangfeng Ji, Shailza Jolly, Mihir Kale, Dhruv Kumar, Faisal Ladhak, Aman Madaan, Mounica Maddela, Khyati Mahajan, Saad Mahamood, Bodhisattwa Prasad Majumder, Pedro Henrique Martins, Angelina McMillan-Major, Simon Mille, Emiel van Miltenburg, Moin Nadeem, Shashi Narayan, Vitaly Nikolaev, Andre Niyongabo Rubungo, Salomey Osei, Ankur Parikh, Laura Perez-Beltrachini, Niranjan Ramesh Rao, Vikas Raunak, Juan Diego Rodriguez, Sashank Santhanam, João Sedoc, Thibault Sellam, Samira Shaikh, Anastasia Shimorina, Marco Antonio Sobrevilla Cabezudo, Hendrik Strobelt, Nishant Subramani, Wei Xu, Diyi Yang, Akhila Yerukola, and Jiawei Zhou. 2021. The GEM benchmark: Natural language generation, its evaluation and metrics. In *Proceedings of the Workshop on Natural Language Generation, Evaluation, and Metrics (GEM@ACL-IJCNLP)*, pages 96–120. Association for Computational Linguistics.

Mor Geva, Yoav Goldberg, and Jonathan Berant. 2019. Are we modeling the task or the annotator? an investigation of annotator bias in natural language understanding datasets. In *Proceedings of the Conference on Empirical Methods in Natural Language Processing and the International Joint Conference on Natural Language Processing (EMNLP-IJCNLP)*, pages 1161–1166. Association for Computational Linguistics.

Mitesh M. Khapra and Ananya B. Sai. 2021. A tutorial on evaluation metrics used in natural language generation. In *Proceedings of the Conference of the North American Chapter of the Association for Computational Linguistics: Human Language Technologies (NAACL-HLT)*, pages 15–19. Association for Computational Linguistics.

Daniel Khashabi, Tushar Khot, and Ashish Sabharwal. 2020. More bang for your buck: Natural perturbation for robust question answering. In *Proceedings of the Conference on Empirical Methods in Natural Language Processing (EMNLP)*, pages 163–170. Association for Computational Linguistics.

Miyoung Ko, Jinhyuk Lee, Hyunjae Kim, Gangwoo Kim, and Jaewoo Kang. 2020. Look at the first sentence: Position bias in question answering. In *Proceedings of the Conference on Empirical Methods in Natural Language Processing (EMNLP)*, pages 1109–1121. Association for Computational Linguistics.

Tom Kwiatkowski, Jennimaria Palomaki, Olivia Redfield, Michael Collins, Ankur Parikh, Chris Alberti, Danielle Epstein, Illia Polosukhin, Jacob Devlin, Kenton Lee, Kristina Toutanova, Llion Jones, Matthew Kelcey, Ming-Wei Chang, Andrew M. Dai, Jakob Uszkoreit, Quoc Le, and Slav Petrov. 2019. Natural questions: A benchmark for question answering research. *Transactions of the Association for Computational Linguistics (TACL)*, 7:452–466.

Kenton Lee, Ming-Wei Chang, and Kristina Toutanova. 2019. Latent retrieval for weakly supervised open domain question answering. In *Proceedings of the*

Annual Meeting of the Association for Computational Linguistics (ACL), pages 6086–6096. Association for Computational Linguistics.

Chin-Yew Lin and Eduard Hovy. 2003. Automatic evaluation of summaries using n-gram cooccurrence statistics. In *Proceedings of the Human Language Technology Conference of the North American Chapter of the Association for Computational Linguistics (NAACL-HLT)*, pages 150–157.

Chin-Yew Lin and Franz Josef Och. 2004. Automatic evaluation of machine translation quality using longest common subsequence and skip-bigram statistics. In *Proceedings of the Annual Meeting of the Association for Computational Linguistics (ACL)*, pages 605–612.

Nelson F. Liu, Matt Gardner, Yonatan Belinkov, Matthew E. Peters, and Noah A. Smith. 2019. Linguistic knowledge and transferability of contextual representations. In *Proceedings of the Conference of the North American Chapter of the Association for Computational Linguistics: Human Language Technologies (NAACL-HLT)*, pages 1073–1094. Association for Computational Linguistics.

George A Miller. 1995. Wordnet: a lexical database for english. *Communications of the ACM*, 38(11):39–41.

Sewon Min, Jordan Boyd-Graber, Chris Alberti, Danqi Chen, Eunsol Choi, Michael Collins, Kelvin Guu, Hannaneh Hajishirzi, Kenton Lee, Jennimaria Palomaki, Colin Raffel, Adam Roberts, Tom Kwiatkowski, Patrick Lewis, Yuxiang Wu, Heinrich Küttler, Linqing Liu, Pasquale Minervini, Pontus Stenetorp, Sebastian Riedel, Sohee Yang, Minjoon Seo, Gautier Izacard, Fabio Petroni, Lucas Hosseini, Nicola De Cao, Edouard Grave, Ikuya Yamada, Sonse Shimaoka, Masatoshi Suzuki, Shumpei Miyawaki, Shun Sato, Ryo Takahashi, Jun Suzuki, Martin Fajcik, Martin Docekal, Karel Ondrej, Pavel Smrz, Hao Cheng, Yelong Shen, Xiaodong Liu, Pengcheng He, Weizhu Chen, Jianfeng Gao, Barlas Oguz, Xilun Chen, Vladimir Karpukhin, Stan Peshterliev, Dmytro Okhonko, Michael Schlichtkrull, Sonal Gupta, Yashar Mehdad, and Wen tau Yih. 2021. NeurIPS 2020 EfficientQA competition: Systems, analyses and lessons learned. *arXiv preprint arXiv:2101.00133*.

Timo Möller, Julian Risch, and Malte Pietsch. 2021. GermanQuAD and GermanDPR: Improving nonenglish question answering and passage retrieval. *arXiv preprint arXiv:2104.12741*.

Preksha Nema and Mitesh M. Khapra. 2018. Towards a better metric for evaluating question generation systems. In *Proceedings of the Conference on Empirical Methods in Natural Language Processing (EMNLP)*, pages 3950–3959. Association for Computational Linguistics.

Kishore Papineni, Salim Roukos, Todd Ward, and Wei-Jing Zhu. 2002. Bleu: a method for automatic evaluation of machine translation. In *Proceedings of the Annual Meeting of the Association for Computational Linguistics (ACL)*, pages 311–318. Association for Computational Linguistics.

Hemant Pugaliya, James Route, Kaixin Ma, Yixuan Geng, and Eric Nyberg. 2019. Bend but don't break? multi-challenge stress test for qa models. In *Proceedings of the Workshop on Machine Reading for Question Answering (MRQA@EMNLP-IJCNLP)*, pages 125–136. Association for Computational Linguistics.

Pranav Rajpurkar, Robin Jia, and Percy Liang. 2018. Know what you don't know: Unanswerable questions for SQuAD. In *Proceedings of the Annual Meeting of the Association for Computational Linguistics (ACL)*, pages 784–789. Association for Computational Linguistics.

Nils Reimers and Iryna Gurevych. 2019. Sentence-BERT: Sentence embeddings using Siamese BERT-networks. In *Proceedings of the Conference on Empirical Methods in Natural Language Processing and the 9th International Joint Conference on Natural Language Processing (EMNLP-IJCNLP)*, pages 3982–3992. Association for Computational Linguistics.

Marco Tulio Ribeiro, Carlos Guestrin, and Sameer Singh. 2019. Are red roses red? evaluating consistency of question-answering models. In *Proceedings of the Annual Meeting of the Association for Computational Linguistics (ACL)*, pages 6174–6184. Association for Computational Linguistics.

Marc-Antoine Rondeau and T. J. Hazen. 2018. Systematic error analysis of the Stanford question answering dataset. In *Proceedings of the Workshop on Machine Reading for Question Answering (MRQA@ACL)*, pages 12–20. Association for Computational Linguistics.

Thibault Sellam, Dipanjan Das, and Ankur Parikh. 2020. BLEURT: Learning robust metrics for text generation. In *Proceedings of the Annual Meeting of the Association for Computational Linguistics (ACL)*, pages 7881–7892. Association for Computational Linguistics.

Krunal Shah, Nitish Gupta, and Dan Roth. 2020. What do we expect from multiple-choice QA systems? In *Findings of the Association for Computational Linguistics: EMNLP*, pages 3547–3553. Association for Computational Linguistics.

Wissam Siblini, Baris Sayil, and Yacine Kessaci. 2021. Towards a more robust evaluation for conversational question answering. In *Proceedings of the Annual Meeting of the Association for Computational Linguistics and the International Joint Conference on Natural Language Processing (ACL-IJCNLP)*, pages 1028–1034. Association for Computational Linguistics.

Soumya Wadhwa, Khyathi Chandu, and Eric Nyberg. 2018. Comparative analysis of neural QA models on SQuAD. In *Proceedings of the Workshop on Machine Reading for Question Answering (MRQA@ACL)*, pages 89–97. Association for Computational Linguistics.

Tongshuang Wu, Marco Tulio Ribeiro, Jeffrey Heer, and Daniel S Weld. 2019. Errudite: Scalable, reproducible, and testable error analysis. In *Proceedings of the Annual Meeting of the Association for Computational Linguistics (ACL)*, pages 747–763. Association for Computational Linguistics.

An Yang, Kai Liu, Jing Liu, Yajuan Lyu, and Sujian Li. 2018. Adaptations of ROUGE and BLEU to better evaluate machine reading comprehension task. In *Proceedings of the Workshop on Machine Reading for Question Answering (MRQA@ACL)*, pages 98–104. Association for Computational Linguistics.

Tianyi Zhang, Varsha Kishore, Felix Wu, Kilian Q. Weinberger, and Yoav Artzi. 2020. BERTScore: Evaluating text generation with bert. In *International Conference on Learning Representations (ICLR)*.

Simple and Efficient ways to Improve REALM

Vidhisha Balachandran[1] **Ashish Vaswani**[2] **Yulia Tsvetkov**[3] **Niki Parmar**[2]
[1] Language Technologies Institute, Carnegie Mellon University
[2] Google Research
[3] Paul G. Allen School of Computer Science & Engineering, University of Washington
vbalacha@cs.cmu.edu
yuliats@cs.washington.edu
{avaswani, nikip}@google.com

Abstract

Dense retrieval has been shown to be effective for Open Domain Question Answering, surpassing sparse retrieval methods like BM25. One such model, REALM, (Guu et al., 2020) is an end-to-end dense retrieval system that uses MLM based pretraining for improved downstream QA performance. However, the current REALM setup uses limited resources and is not comparable in scale to more recent systems, contributing to its lower performance. Additionally, it relies on noisy supervision for retrieval during fine-tuning. We propose REALM++, where we improve upon the training and inference setups and introduce better supervision signal for improving performance, without any architectural changes. REALM++ achieves ~5.5% absolute accuracy gains over the baseline while being faster to train. It also matches the performance of large models which have 3x more parameters demonstrating the efficiency of our setup.

1 Introduction

Open-domain question answering (ODQA) (Voorhees et al., 1999) is a task that aims to answer questions directly using a large set of documents without being given a specific document. These systems generally employ a "retriever-reader" based approach where a *document retriever* first retrieves a subset of evidence documents and a *document reader* processes the documents to identify the correct answer (Chen et al., 2017). Recently, dense retrieval methods (Seo et al., 2018, 2019; Das et al., 2019; Karpukhin et al., 2020) have improved over sparse retrievers like BM25 (Robertson and Zaragoza, 2009) and made training these systems end-to-end by leveraging approximate MIPS search (Shrivastava and Li, 2014). REALM is an end-to-end model, pre-trained on masked language modeling, that can be finetuned for QA tasks without relying on external sources like BM25 for supervision like DPR (Karpukhin et al., 2020). Hence, it is simple and easier to train but is not competitive to pipeline alternatives like DPR. When finetuning, it uses a single GPU making it not directly comparable in scale to DPR which uses more resources for better optimization. Due to limited resources it is inefficient, taking more than a day to train. Additionally, it uses distant supervision for the retriever in the form of passages containing the target answer leading to ambiguous supervision for training.

In this paper, we present a study of REALM aimed at understanding and improving its limitations. We find that REALM is significantly under-optimized and improve the training by scaling the system through (i) using exact MIPS search, (ii) introducing larger batch training, and (iii) scaling the reader to process more documents. We further address the noisy distant retrieval supervision by augmenting the training sets with human-annotated evidence passages. Since such human annotations are not available for every dataset and is expensive to obtain, we show that models trained with strong supervision transfer well to other datasets where such annotations are not available, indicating the benefits beyond a single annotated dataset.

Incorporating our best findings, we show that an improved version of REALM, which we call REALM++ achieves ~5.5% absolute accuracy improvements over the baseline on multiple ODQA benchmarks while processing 4x more examples/sec and outperforms all prior methods of similar parameter regime. Further, it shows comparable performance to models with 3x more parameters. Our results demonstrate that scale and supervision play an important role in ODQA systems highlighting the need for careful comparisons across systems in ODQA and for taking scale and efficiency into account in addition to performance when reporting results.

Proceedings of the 3rd Workshop on Machine Reading for Question Answering , pages 158–164

Experiments	Test EM	Dev EM	Dev R@10
REALM (Guu et al., 2020)	40.4	38.2	-
REALM (Ours)	39.4	35.6	68.8
+Scale	42.8	37.9	69.5
+Scale+PS (10 docs inf)	43.2	38.6	69.9
+Scale+PS (100 docs inf)	44.8	38.6	69.9
+Scale+Rerank	42.3	37.4	67.5

Table 1: Answer Span EM Accuracy and Answer Recall@10. **Improving training setup improves Test EM Acc.** Test = test set, Dev = development set

Model	R@10	DevEM
REALM	68.8	35.6
ScaledR (FixedRet)	59.6	33.1
ScaledR+Rerank (FixedRet)	67.9	35.8
ScaledR+Rerank+PS (FixedRet)	67.5	37.1
ScaledR (TrainedRet)	**69.5**	**37.9**
ScaledR+Rerank (TrainedRet)	67.5	37.4

Table 2: Answer Recall and Span EM for fixed v/s finetuned retriever. ScaledR = Scaled REALM, PS = Passage Supervision. **Reranking is useful when retriever is fixed** but is not effective when the retriever is trained.

2 Exploring Limits of REALM

Open Domain QA is typically modeled as a Machine Reading Comprehension (MRC) model which answers a question using a large corpus of text documents/passages by employing a "retriever-reader" approach. REALM specifically uses dense retrieval to identify c ($c = 5000$) relevant passages and a BERT based reader to process a smaller set of top-k ($k = 5$) passages and find answer spans. When finetuning[1], the retriever is trained using distant supervision with passages containing the target answer as positive and the reader is supervised using human annotated short answer spans (Lee et al., 2019). We follow the same design and optimization setup of finetuning REALM on QA.

We explore the limits of various experiment choices by introducing simple changes to the training and inference setup. Table 1 compares results from our replicated experiments of REALM to prior published results and shows that our experiments produce similar results on the Natural Questions (NQ) (Kwiatkowski et al., 2019) dataset. Detailed analysis across other metrics is in in A.2.

2.1 Scaling the Training Setup

REALM performs an approximate MIPS for retrieving the top c relevant documents based on a retrieval score, $S_{retr}(p_i, q) = h_q^\top h_{p_i}$ where h_q and h_{p_i} are question and passage representations respectively. The system is finetuned in practice on a single machine with a 12GB GPU with batch size 1. While this is modest use of resources, we show that this results in suboptimal training. We begin by scaling the REALM system during training. We perform *exact* MIPS search by leveraging the efficiency of large matrix multiplications of TPUs (Wang et al., 2019) to compute the retrieval score, S_{retr}, for $\sim$13M passages of corpus and extract c passages having the highest scores. We further increase the training batch size to 16 by leveraging 8 TPUv3 cores on Google Cloud for distributed training. Finally, we increase the number of documents passed to the reader to $k = 10$ during training.

Scaling training setup improves QA results: From Table 1 we observe that simple experiment choices like larger batch training and exact MIPS search significantly improve the Exact-Match Accuracy by 3.4% without introducing any model design changes. This shows that the original REALM setup was under-optimized and has much better performance than previously reported.

2.2 Introducing Strong Passage Supervision

To finetune the retriever, REALM relies on distant supervision in the form of passages containing the target answer. However, such a signal can lead to noisy and unrelated documents to be given a positive signal (Lin et al., 2018) as examples in Table 5 of Appendix A show. We address this by introducing supervision from human annotations similar to Yang et al. (2015); Nguyen et al. (2016), to train the retriever by updating the retrieval scores by optimizing their marginal log-likelihood.

$$P(p_i|Q) = \frac{\exp(S_{retr}(p_i, Q))}{\sum_{p_j \in \{p_i\}_{1:c}} \exp(S_{retr}(p_j, Q))}$$

$$L(Q, LA) = -\log \sum_{p_j \in \{p_i\}_{1:c}, p_i \in LA} P(p_i|Q)$$

where LA is a list of human annotated evidence passages (e.g. Long Answers in Natural Questions), $L(Q, LA)$ denotes the passage supervision loss that is augmented to the existing retriever distant supervision and span prediction loss, and $p_i \in LA$ indicates whether the passage was in the annotated passages. Here, we assume that the passages in corpus and the annotated evidence passages in the dataset are from the same source (e.g.

[1]REALM is pretrained using MLM on CC-News corpus

Wikipedia). Since corpus passages and annotated passages in the dataset can differ (e.g. due to different Wikipedia versions), we consider any passage in the retrieved set that has 50%[2] word overlap[3] with the target passages as a positive match.

Supervision through evidence passage annotations improves performance: From Table 1 we see an improvement of 0.5% over the scaled REALM model leading to 3.8% improvement over the prior baseline REALM model, showing the benefit of providing better supervision. In §A.3 we present qualitative examples where the improved passage supervision leads to answer spans being extracted from the most relevant document to the question. While noisy distant supervision has been shown as effective for dense retrieval, our work experimentally shows that it can be limiting and simply introducing better supervision through gold evidence passages is beneficial.

2.3 Reranking

Table 4 in A.2 shows that though the retrieved 5000 documents has high answer recall ($\sim$ 95%), the recall significantly drops ($\sim$ 77%) in the top 10 documents processed by the reader. Readers are computationally intensive and memory limits makes scaling them to process more documents difficult. We explore an approach to rerank the retrieved documents to improve recall@10 and end accuracy.

Our Document Reranker has L layers of cross-document and query-document interactions to learn rich document representations. For each layer, the output passage representations from the previous layer, $\{u^{l-1}\}_{1:c}$ are first passed through a Transformer block (T) with multi-headed self-attention (Vaswani et al., 2017) which allows for interaction between the passage representations and produces cross-document aware representations u_i^l.

$$u_i^l = \mathrm{T}(Q{=}u_i^{l-1}, K{=}\{u^{l-1}\}_{1:c}, V{=}\{u^{l-1}\}_{1:c})$$

where Q, K, V represent the query, key and value respectively in the transformer attention module. To model interaction between passages and query, the attended passage representation u^l and query representations from the previous layer v^{l-1} are passed through a multi-head cross-attention Transformer to produce query aware representations v_i^l.

$$v_q^l{=}\mathrm{T}(Q{=}v_q^{l-1}, K{=}\{u^l\}_{1:c}, V{=}\{u^l\}_{1:c})$$

For the first layer we consider the dense retriever's query and document representations as the input u^0 and v^0 to the reranker. The rich document and query representations from the final layer ($\{u^L\}_{1:c}$,v_q^L) are used to compute the retriever score, $S_{retr}(p_i, q)$ to find the top-k documents for the reader.

Document Reranking does not significant gains when retriever is jointly trained but is highly effective when retriever is fixed: In Table 1 We observe that the accuracy of the system drops by 0.5% and the recall@10 drops by 0.2% when augmenting the reranker. We further study the role of the reranker in a fixed retriever setting where the top 5000 documents are retrieved once and kept constant during training. While, such a setting is a more efficient since documents are not retrieved at every training step, the retriever's zero-shot performance can be quite low, potentially hurting end accuracy. From Table 2, we see that the scaled REALM model with a fixed-retriever has very low recall@Top-10 and EM. Here, augmenting the model with the Document Reranker significantly improves recall and EM performance, where recall@Top-10 improves by 8.3% and EM by 2.7%. Further introducing passage supervision during training improves performance by increasing the end accuracy by $\sim$ 1.3% making the fixed retriever setting very competitive in performance to a jointly trained retriever-reader setting.

2.4 Scaling the Reader at Inference

Due to memory constraints the reader cannot be scaled to process more documents during training without architectural changes. Such constraints do not apply during inference, since optimization based weights and parameters are not saved, the memory usage of the model reduces, allowing for the reader to process more documents. We experiment with scaling the reader to process more documents only during inference.

Scaling the reader during inference significantly boosts performance: In Table 1 we see that the reader processing $k = 100$ documents significantly improves accuracy, achieving 44.8% on NQ which surpasses the baseline REALM by 4.4%. This shows that such systems can leverage a small number of documents ($k = 10$) for faster training and gain the benefits of scaling the reader ($k = 100$) at inference. Further from Figure 1 we

[2]We experimented with thresholds=(0.3, 0.5, 0.75) and used threshold with best performance based on validation set

[3]We also experimented with ngram overlap which was similar in performance but computationally expensive.

Model	Size	NQ (79k/4k)	WQ (3k/2k)	CT (1k/1k)
ORQA (Lee et al., 2019)	Base	33.3	36.4	30.1
PathRetriever (Asai et al., 2020)	Base	32.6	-	-
$REALM_{News}$ (Guu et al., 2020)	Base	40.4	40.7	42.9
DPR (Karpukhin et al., 2020)	Base	41.5	42.4	49.4
$ReConsider_{Base}$ (Iyer et al., 2020)	Base	43.1	44.4	49.3
REALM++ (10 docs)	Base	43.2	44.5*	47.2*
REALM++ (100 docs)	Base	**44.8**	**45.6***	**49.7***
$DPR\text{-}BERT_{Large}$ (Iyer et al., 2020)	Large	44.6	44.8	53.5
RAG_{Large} (Lewis et al., 2020b)	Large	44.5	45.5	52.2
$ReConsider^{\dagger}_{Large}$ (Iyer et al., 2020)	Large	**45.5**	**45.9**	**55.3**

Table 3: Test QA (Exact Match) Accuracy on Open-QA benchmarks showing **REALM++ improving over prior methods of similar size.** The number of train/test examples are shown in parentheses next to each benchmark. *indicates models finetuned on trained NQ model, as proposed in (Karpukhin et al., 2020). †Though $ReConsider_{large}$ has higher accuracy, their approach of using answer span focused reranking model is orthogonal can be directly applied to our output.

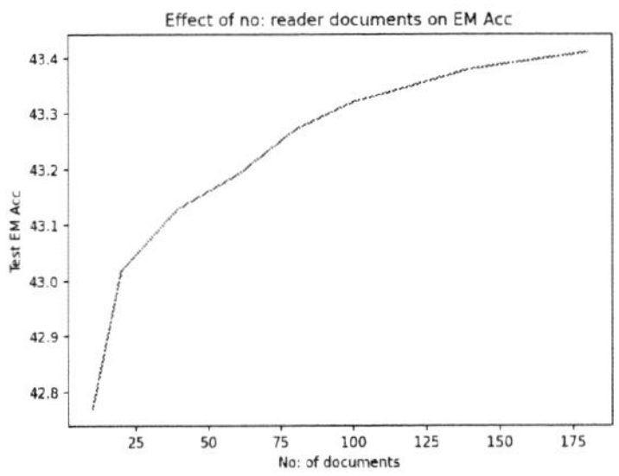

Figure 1: Test QA EM Acc v/s No: Reader Documents on NQ. **QA Span EM increases when more documents are processed by the reader during inference.**

see that the gains increase with increasing number documents with a slight saturation beyond 120 documents. This is potentially due to increased answer recall in documents[4].

3 REALM ++

Based on the findings in §2, we incorporate the best working components: (i) scaling at training §2.1 (ii) better passage supervision §2.2 and (iii) scaling reader during inference §2.4 to establish an improved REALM model, which we call REALM++. We study the effect of REALM++ on three datasets NQ, Web Questions (WQ) (Berant et al., 2013), and Curated Trec (CT) (Baudiš and Šedivý, 2015). As WQ and CT do not have evidence passage annotations, we use them to study the transfer capabilities of the passage supervised NQ model.

REALM++ outperforms models of similar size and is comparable to large models: Table 3 shows that REALM++ outperforms prior methods of similar size (models based on $BERT_{base}$) with no modifications to the model design. When transferred to WQ and CT which do not have human annotation for evidence passages, REALM++ shows an improvement of 3.8% on WQ and 4.3% on CT over base REALM showing benefit beyond a single dataset. REALM++ produces state-of-art results on extractive ODQA among models of similar size in all three datasets using a single end-to-end model. Additionally REALM++, which uses $BERT_{base}$ ($\sim$ 110M params), performs comparable to large models based on $BERT_{large}$ and $BART_{large}$ (Lewis et al., 2020a) ($\sim$ 340M params) with 3x lesser params.

Discussion of speed and memory usage: By using 8 TPUv3 cores and increased batch size for training our REALM++ model, we can process 4x more examples/sec as compared to REALM and reduce training time from 2 days to 12hrs. REALM++ maintains the same number of parameters as the base REALM model and the entire model fits within 12GB memory which is the equivalent of an Nvidia Titan X. This demonstrates that our REALM++ model is efficient and can improve training time by leveraging distributed training.

4 Conclusion

In this work, we present a study of a dense-retrieval QA system, REALM, and identify key limitations in its experimental setup. We find that REALM is significantly undertrained and we improve REALM by introducing simple changes to its training, supervision, and inference setup. We

[4]For the rest of the experiments in Table 3, we use 100 documents for fair comparison to other methods

propose REALM++ which incorporates our best findings and show that it can achieve significant improvement over prior methods and perform comparably with models with 3x more parameters.

References

Akari Asai, Kazuma Hashimoto, Hannaneh Hajishirzi, Richard Socher, and Caiming Xiong. 2020. Learning to retrieve reasoning paths over Wikipedia graph for question answering. In *ICLR*.

Petr Baudiš and Jan Šedivý. 2015. Modeling of the question answering task in the yodaqa system. In *International Conference of the Cross-Language Evaluation Forum for European Languages*.

Jonathan Berant, Andrew Chou, Roy Frostig, and Percy Liang. 2013. Semantic parsing on Freebase from question-answer pairs. In *EMNLP*.

Danqi Chen, Adam Fisch, Jason Weston, and Antoine Bordes. 2017. Reading Wikipedia to answer open-domain questions. In *ACL*.

Rajarshi Das, S. Dhuliawala, M. Zaheer, and A. McCallum. 2019. Multi-step retriever-reader interaction for scalable open-domain question answering. *ICLR*.

Kelvin Guu, Kenton Lee, Zora Tung, Panupong Pasupat, and Ming-Wei Chang. 2020. REALM: Retrieval-augmented language model pre-training. In *ICML*.

Srinivasan Iyer, Sewon Min, Yashar Mehdad, and Wen-tau Yih. 2020. Reconsider: Re-ranking using span-focused cross-attention for open domain question answering. *arXiv preprint arXiv:2010.10757*.

Vladimir Karpukhin, Barlas Oğuz, Sewon Min, Patrick Lewis, Ledell Wu, Sergey Edunov, Danqi Chen, and Wen-tau Yih. 2020. Dense passage retrieval for open-domain question answering. In *EMNLP*.

Tom Kwiatkowski, Jennimaria Palomaki, Olivia Redfield, Michael Collins, Ankur Parikh, Chris Alberti, Danielle Epstein, Illia Polosukhin, Matthew Kelcey, Jacob Devlin, Kenton Lee, Kristina N. Toutanova, Llion Jones, Ming-Wei Chang, Andrew Dai, Jakob Uszkoreit, Quoc Le, and Slav Petrov. 2019. Natural questions: a benchmark for question answering research. *TACL*.

Kenton Lee, Ming-Wei Chang, and Kristina Toutanova. 2019. Latent retrieval for weakly supervised open domain question answering. In *ACL*.

Mike Lewis, Yinhan Liu, Naman Goyal, Marjan Ghazvininejad, Abdelrahman Mohamed, Omer Levy, Veselin Stoyanov, and Luke Zettlemoyer. 2020a. BART: Denoising sequence-to-sequence pre-training for natural language generation, translation, and comprehension. In *Proceedings of the 58th Annual Meeting of the Association for Computational Linguistics*, pages 7871–7880, Online. Association for Computational Linguistics.

Patrick Lewis, Ethan Perez, Aleksandara Piktus, Fabio Petroni, Vladimir Karpukhin, Naman Goyal, Heinrich Küttler, Mike Lewis, Wen tau Yih, Tim Rocktäschel, Sebastian Riedel, and Douwe Kiela. 2020b. Retrieval-augmented generation for knowledge-intensive nlp tasks. In *neurips*.

Yankai Lin, Haozhe Ji, Zhiyuan Liu, and Maosong Sun. 2018. Denoising distantly supervised open-domain question answering. In *Proceedings of the 56th Annual Meeting of the Association for Computational Linguistics (Volume 1: Long Papers)*, pages 1736–1745.

Tri Nguyen, Mir Rosenberg, Xia Song, Jianfeng Gao, Saurabh Tiwary, Rangan Majumder, and Li Deng. 2016. Ms marco: A human-generated machine reading comprehension dataset.

S. Robertson and H. Zaragoza. 2009. The probabilistic relevance framework: Bm25 and beyond. *Found. Trends Inf. Retr.*, 3:333–389.

Minjoon Seo, T. Kwiatkowski, Ankur P. Parikh, Ali Farhadi, and Hannaneh Hajishirzi. 2018. Phrase-indexed question answering: A new challenge for scalable document comprehension. In *EMNLP*.

Minjoon Seo, Jinhyuk Lee, Tom Kwiatkowski, Ankur Parikh, Ali Farhadi, and Hannaneh Hajishirzi. 2019. Real-time open-domain question answering with dense-sparse phrase index. In *ACL*.

Anshumali Shrivastava and P. Li. 2014. Asymmetric lsh (alsh) for sublinear time maximum inner product search (mips). In *NIPS*.

Ashish Vaswani, Noam Shazeer, Niki Parmar, Jakob Uszkoreit, Llion Jones, Aidan N Gomez, Lukasz Kaiser, and Illia Polosukhin. 2017. Attention is all you need. In *NIPS*.

Ellen M Voorhees et al. 1999. The TREC-8 question answering track report. In *TREC*.

Yu Emma Wang, Gu-Yeon Wei, and David Brooks. 2019. Benchmarking tpu, gpu, and cpu platforms for deep learning. *arXiv preprint arXiv:1907.10701*.

Yi Yang, Wen-tau Yih, and Christopher Meek. 2015. WikiQA: A challenge dataset for open-domain question answering. In *Proceedings of the 2015 Conference on Empirical Methods in Natural Language Processing*, pages 2013–2018, Lisbon, Portugal. Association for Computational Linguistics.

A Example Appendix

A.1 Datasets

For our study, we use three open-domain QA datasets following Guu et al. (2020):
Natural Questions (NQ) (Kwiatkowski et al., 2019) contains real user queries from Google Search. We consider questions with short answers (<=5 tokens) and the long answers for passage supervision.
WebQuestions (WQ) (Berant et al., 2013) is a collection of questions collected from Google Suggest API, with Freebase entity answers whose string forms are the target short answers.
CuratedTREC (CT) (Baudiš and Šedivý, 2015) contains curated questions from TREC QA track with real user questions and answer as regular expression matching all acceptable answers.

A.2 REALM baseline analysis

Experiments fairly reproduce results: Table 4 reports the results from our experiments and compares them to published results from REALM (Guu et al., 2020). We find that our experiments produce similar results on NQ and WQ with slightly lower results on CT on the test set. We believe that this could be due to varying checkpoints due to early stopping. For fair evaluation, we use results from our experiments as a comparison for the remainder of the study.

Answer recall drops significantly with reducing documents: We additionally present a breakdown of REALM's retriever and reader performances on the development set across the three datasets. While REALM retrieves $c = 5000$ documents for distantly supervising the retriever, only the top $k = 5$ documents are processed by the reader for finding the right answer. Comparing the recall of answers in the retrieved documents at different subsets of documents we observe very high ($> 90\%$) recall@5000 for all three datasets but the recall@5 effectively drops to $\sim$70%, showing that the document that contains the answer is not necessarily present in the top-5 highlighting limitations in the retriever.

Wide margins exist for improving reader performance: Comparing the Exact Match accuracy of the system with the upper bound (the system is right if the passage contains the answer) shows wide gaps in the performance of the reader. While $\sim$63% of the questions from NQ have the answer in the top retrieved documents, REALM is only able to get the exact span of the answer for $\sim$36% of them showing the limitations of the reader in identifying the exact answer span in the document.

Metric	NQ	WQ	CT
Test EM (Guu et al., 2020)	40.4	40.7	42.9
Test EM	39.4	40.8	39.3
Dev EM	35.6	45.4	42.9
Dev EM Upper Bound	63.3	75.9	70.8
R@5	63.9	78.5	70.0
R@10	69.4	85.7	76.4
R@100	80.7	94.0	85.6
R@1000	86.8	97.7	91.7
R@5000	91.1	99.2	93.3

Table 4: **Experiments reproduce results of REALM on NQ dataset**. First section compares Test EM from our experiments with previous published results from (Guu et al., 2020). The bottom section compares Dev EM with Upper Bound performance of the Reader.

A.3 Qualitative Analysis

In §2.2, we introduced strong passage supervision from annotated evidence passages to enable the model to distinguish misleading passages that might contain the target answer. Table 6 shows examples of questions where using passage supervision helps retrieve correct passages for the QA task. For Questions 1 and 3, the baseline model incorrectly retrieves a wrong passage of a similar genre or topic as the question, while for Question 2 the baseline model retrieves a completely incorrect, irrelevant passage. The model trained with passage supervision identifies the right context for answering the question, which aligns with the human annotation for each question.

Question	Incorrect Passage	Correct Passage from Human Annotations
Where did the idea of a unicorn come from?	Unicorn is a privately held startup company whose name was coined in 2013 by venture capitalist Aileen Lee.	Unicorns are not found in Greek mythology, but rather in the accounts of natural history, for Greek writers of natural history were convinced of the reality of unicorns.
What type of reproduction do whiptail lizards use?	MLB Whiparound is an American baseball television show on Fox Sports 1 hosted by Chris Myers and Kevin Burkhardt.	The New Mexico whiptail lizard is a crossbreed of a western whiptail and the little striped whiptail. The lizard is a female-only species that reproduces asexually by producing an egg through parthenogenesis.
Which president supported the creation of the Environmental Protection Agency(EPA)?	Some historians say that President Richard Nixon's southern strategy turned the southern United States into a republican stronghold, while others deem economic factors more important in the change.	The Environmental Protection Agency (EPA) is an agency of the federal government of the United States created for the purpose of protecting human health and the environment. President Richard Nixon proposed the establishment of EPA and it began operation on December 2, 1970, after Nixon signed an executive order.

Table 5: Examples of Questions from Natural Questions with incorrect retrieved passages from Guu et al. (2020) with the correct human annotated relevant passages showing the necessity for human annotation based supervision.

Question	Incorrect Ret Passage	Correct REALM++ Ret Passage
Where did the Battle of Issus take place?	The Battle of Alexander at Issus is a 1529 oil painting by the German artist Albrecht Altdorfer, a pioneer of landscape art and a founding member of the Danube School .	The Battle of Issus occurred in southern Anatolia, on November 5, 333 BC between the Hellenic League led by Alexander the Great and the Achaemenid Empire, led by Darius III.
Who played bubba in the Heat of the Night?	A late Stevan Ridley touchdown run set up by a 23 - yard Deangelo Peterson run on a fourth - down play gave LSU the upset victory and effectively ended the opportunity for an Alabama repeat of the national championship.	Carlos Alan Autry Jr. is an American actor, politician, and former National Football League player. He played the role of Captain Bubba Skinner on the NBC television series, "In the Heat of the Night", starring Carroll O'Connor.
Actress who plays penelope garcia on criminal minds?	How to get away with Murder is an American television series created by Peter Nowalk and produced by Shonda Rhimes and ABC Studios.	Kirsten Simone Vangsness is an American actress, currently staring as FBI Analyst Penelope Garcia on the CBS series "Criminal Minds".

Table 6: Qualitative Analysis of questions from NQ showing questions where baseline REALM retrieved incorrect passages and **training with passage supervision helped retrieve the right passage.**

Association for Computational Linguistics
209 N. Eighth Street
Stroudsburg, Pennsylvania 18360

ISBN 978-1-7138-9179-6

CURRAN ASSOCIATES INC.
proceedings.com